HOLLYWOOD
50
Great Years

JACK LODGE • JOHN RUSSELL TAYLOR • ADRIAN TURNER
DOUGLAS JARVIS • DAVID CASTELL

HOLLYWOOD 50 *Great Years*

Colour Library Books

CLB 2802
This edition published 1991 by Colour Library Books Ltd.,
    Godalming, Surrey

Devised and produced by Multimedia Books Ltd
Copyright © 1989 Multimedia Books Ltd

Printed and bound in Italy by New Interlitho

ISBN 0 86283 924 6

Contents

1950s
Adrian Turner

1960s
Douglas Jarvis

1970s
David Castell

Jack Lodge

Hollywood 1930s

Marlene Dietrich

The Hollywood Studios

Chapter 1

Hollywood movies of the thirties came in all styles and sizes, but the best of them – and some of the worst – share a common quality. They are filled with confidence, and a confidence that at times borders on audacity. There are two very different reasons for this paradox. The world that these movies were made in, and for, was a world much lacking in confidence, a world that was slowly recovering from the Depression at the beginning of the period, and was to move at its end into the threat of war and, although not yet in America, into war itself. The second reason lies in the nature of the medium. The sound film was only three years old in 1930, and it was not merely a silent film with spoken words replacing intertitles; it was a radically different art. By all the rules of art the movies of the early thirties should have been immature, tentative things, not the brash and arrogant delights that, in fact, they were.

The films were like this because the film-makers themselves lived in an enclosed society cut off from surrounding social problems. Also, most of them had learned their craft in the studio system of the twenties where the technical excellence of the Hollywood film had reached a triumphant peak by around 1927. The studio system flourished for a further two decades and its virtues, outweighing its faults, gave the movies of the period their distinctive look and feel.

The magnificent seven

In the thirties there were seven leading studios, known as the "majors". Three of them were giants: Metro-Goldwyn-Mayer, Paramount and Warner Brothers, to be joined in 1935 by a fourth, when the two-year-old firm of Twentieth Century merged with the twenty-year-old Fox company to form Twentieth Century-Fox. A little below the giants in prestige and glamour, but often rivaling, and from time to time surpassing them in quality, were Universal, RKO Radio, and Columbia. In a sense there was an eighth major – United Artists – but this company was now primarily a releasing outfit, with its most important films made by the independent studio of Samuel Goldwyn.

Since the major studios owned their own chains of theaters, they had to produce the right quality and quantity of films to keep their theaters profitably filled. That meant producing almost one film a week; a year's output of fifty. And because the double feature was, by the thirties, a fact of theater-going, around half those fifty films were what are now referred to as B-movies, cheaply and quickly made, designed to entertain until the "big" picture started, but enjoying practically the very same technical facilities as more expensive productions.

*Jean Harlow and Wallace Beery in MGM's star-packed **Dinner at Eight** (1933). As they prepare to dine, Beery has his mind on a big deal; Harlow has hers on lover Edmund Lowe, and Beery knows it all too well.*

Main picture: *Nils Asther and Barbara Stanwyck in Frank Capra's* **The Bitter Tea of General Yen** *(1933).*
Far top right: *Gary Cooper at Helen Hayes' deathbed in Frank Borzage's* **A Farewell to Arms** *(1932). A great stage actress, Hayes made a handful of films in the early thirties, also appearing so successfully on the stage that she became known as the "First Lady of the American Theatre".*

Far bottom right: *Marlene Dietrich in* **Morocco.** *The lighting, the glitter, the costume and décor are the hallmarks of director Josef von Sternberg and Paramount at this period.*

Writers, directors, cameramen, editors and others learned their trade on these B-movies. However, because these company-owned theaters provided a guaranteed release, and because the income was largely dependent on the numbers each main film attracted, the major studios felt no need to play it safe with their Bs, and exercised slightly less tight control over them. Although many of these small films were run off the "production line", many others were unexpected off-beat delights. And nearly all the Bs were economical and fast. Pared down to 55-65 minutes, they had to be.

Supporting cast

One of the great strengths of thirties Hollywood was the quality of acting in big and small films alike. There were great stars, as great as in any period, but also rosters of supporting players, colorful character actors for the most part, whom the major studios had under contract. These actors might be in thirty or forty films in any given year. Audiences welcomed the familiar faces; film buffs could put names to them. You could watch a thirties movie and recognize every credited player, and usually another half dozen who weren't even credited. When the studio system withered and contract players were no longer hired, this kind of continuity became impossible. It would be hard to name five or six small-part actors today. Thirties fans could name two hundred. No film was so bad that it did not contain half a dozen perfectly executed cameos. If stars, or script, or direction let you down there was always Allen Jenkins or Herman Bing, Ward Bond or Irving Bacon, to put things right. And a thirties Hollywood movie without George Chandler was a rare event.

That certain style

Most of the big studios developed a distinctive style. MGM spent the most money, and it showed in their richly furnished sets and elaborate spectacles. They were rich, too, in star quality, with Greta Garbo and Clark Gable, William Powell and Myrna Loy, Jean Harlow, Norma Shearer and Robert Montgomery among them, and by the end of the period the young Judy Garland, too. Some of their great successes have not aged kindly – *Smilin' Through* (1932) and *Mutiny on the Bounty* (1935), for example – but their polished comedies, their comedy-thrillers and their musicals stand up as fresh as ever. MGM made few of the period's masterpieces – apart from Clarence Brown they lacked a great director – because there was a prevalent blandness and unwillingness to take chances, but no MGM film was ever careless or tatty, and those stars could always carry the day. They made some of the finest Bs, too, but with their substantial resources these films had a finish that compared with that of some of the other studios' As.

Paramount was the most sophisticated of the majors. Originally known as Famous Players-Lasky (Paramount itself was once a distribution company), it went back almost to the earliest days of West Coast production, and throughout the twenties led the field. In the thirties the Paramount "look" became famous. Dazzling, often fantastic sets, camerawork that seemed to have a peculiarly luminous quality and acting with a casual elegance all contributed to a string of visual successes. The main contributor was Paramount's art director Hans Dreier, who came to Paramount from German films in the twenties and had an enormous share in making films like *Trouble in Paradise, Love Me Tonight* (both 1932) and *The Devil Is a Woman* (1935). In its directors, too, Paramount was unequalled, with Ernst Lubitsch, Rouben Mamoulian, Josef von Sternberg and Mitchell Leisen all working mainly for that studio during the period.

Bottom left: *Henry Fonda and Bette Davis in William Wyler's* **Jezebel** *(1938). For her performance as a headstrong Southern beauty Davis won her second Academy Award as Best Actress: her first had been three years earlier, for* **Dangerous.** *In 1938 Fonda was still making his way. One year on he appeared in* **Young Mr Lincoln** *with John Ford, his stepping stone to stardom.*

Main picture: *Will Rogers in Henry King's* **State Fair** *(1933). King and John Ford between them brought the best out of Rogers, underlining his quiet sensitivity, and turning a homespun philosopher into a notable actor.*

13

Crime pays at Warners

The average Warner Brothers product hardly seemed to come from the same world. Warners concentrated on contemporary, often low-life material. They made the best crime and gangster films; for a short but glorious period around 1933 they produced the best musicals (still unrivaled), and they had a nice sideline in the macabre. They, too, had a great art director in Anton Grot, who could give the flavor of a German silent to a horror film as easily as he could create the shimmering magic of *A Midsummer Night's Dream* (1935). The volatile and enormously versatile Hungarian Michael Curtiz was the studio's leading director in the period, flitting from genre to genre and always giving his movies pace and a gutsy flavor, while the German William Dieterle could make a routine studio chore like *Fog Over Frisco* (1934) into an astounding display of calculated eccentricity.

Twentieth Century-Fox never quite reached the level of those three (they had started rather later, after all). That they are best remembered now, as far as the thirties go, for their Charlie Chan series of B-movie detection – admirable as the best of the Chans are – does not say a great deal for the overall quality of the studio's major movies. They made a lot of very creditable, very enjoyable pictures, but somehow the indefinable spark that might have transformed a good studio into a great one never quite ignited. There were some

average musicals – made to seem better than they were by the charming Alice Faye – and there was Shirley Temple to bring in the cash. Late in the decade the great director Fritz Lang arrived, but for most of the thirties John Ford, who worked frequently at the studio throughout the period, was the only major talent of which the company could boast.

At the beginning of the thirties Columbia was scarcely rated as a major. Columbia's studios were in Gower Street – in the heart of Hollywood – a thoroughfare associated with the numerous minor and short-lived companies that worked there. Columbia took time to shake off these 'Poverty Row' connections, but with *It Happened One Night* in 1934 the studio managed it, and that picture gave them unarguable major status. The talent of director Frank Capra and the drive of studio chief Harry Cohn ensured that they kept it.

Far left: Peter Lorre as Raskolnikov in Josef von Sternberg's **Crime and Punishment** (1935). This was Lorre's second Hollywood film, and a prestige production reinforcing Columbia's claim to major status.

Left: John Boles and Margaret Sullavan in John M. Stahl's **Only Yesterday** (1933). This was Sullavan's first film, to which she brought a unique mixture of resolution and vulnerability.

Perfect horrors

Universal made many pretty dire movies, their B-Westerns and B-musicals among them, but they also made the superb horror films that began with *Dracula* and *Frankenstein* (both 1931); they had one director in James Whale who for a few years could seemingly do no wrong, whether in horror movies, romantic comedies or sophisticated thrillers, and they could from time to time come up with something as shattering as the anti-war epic *All Quiet on the Western Front* (1930). You could forgive many a Universal disaster for the sake of that one extraordinary achievement.

And finally, RKO. This was the most totally unpredictable of the studios. RKO made so many offbeat and quirky movies that oddness sometimes seemed to be the studio's norm. Fortunately most of the oddness was entirely enjoyable, and a studio that from time to time came out with such widely different masterpieces as *King Kong* (1933), *The Informer* (1935), *Winterset* (1936), *Stage Door* (1937) and *Bringing up Baby* (1938) could easily be forgiven any lapses. There were also their Astaire-Rogers musicals and a fair quota of attractive Bs, although in that field RKO's golden days would come a little later with the Val Lewton unit. In short, RKO was the connoisseur's studio, and fifty years on it still looks just like that.

Outside the majors, there was Walt Disney, who ventured into feature-length movies with *Snow White and the Seven Dwarfs* (1938); from 1935 on there was Republic, making mainly action-filled Bs but destined for higher things in the forties; and a number of small and often short-lived outfits that were still capable of surprising everyone, as Tiffany did with James Whale's *Journey's End* in 1930, based on the play by R.C. Sheriff.

These then were the sources of our thirties pleasures. When the films are seen again today, remarkably few of them fail the test of time. The age looks an age of endless richness, an age when a great popular art engaged people with an intensity difficult to imagine now. For today there is art-house cinema on the one side, youth-orientated spectaculars on the other, and the great middle ground of movies for everyone lies almost empty. In the thirties it was full. There were no bad years in that decade, and two of the years, 1933 and 1939, seem beyond argument the sound cinema's greatest heights.

Right: *Miriam Hopkins surrounded by admirers in Rouben Mamoulian's* **Becky Sharp** *(1935). This was the first feature film to be made in the new three-color Technicolor process, and this particular scene was a dazzling success.*

Below: *Richard Carlson, Janet Gaynor and Minnie Dupree in* **The Young in Heart** *(1938). Gaynor plays one of a charming family of confidence tricksters who, under Dupree's benign influence, see the error of their ways. The film was a pleasant trifle; after it, Gaynor, who 10 years earlier had won the first ever Best Actress Oscar, retired.*

Crime and Punishment

Chapter 2

With the thirties the crime film became, for the first time, a major genre. It was there, of course, in the early days of cinema, but then, in films like D.W. Griffith's *The Musketeers of Pig Alley* (1912) and Thomas Ince's *The Gangsters and the Girl* (1914), crime had been seen more as a working-class aberration, engendered by poverty, than as the glamorous pursuit it later became. The romantic twenties, at least in their major films, preferred to leave crime on one side, although the gangster cycle had one distinguished forerunner in Josef von Sternberg's *Underworld* (1927), and the macabre creations through which Tod Browning guided Lon Chaney prefigured much that was to recur in crime and horror films when sound came.

Big-city blues

An outstanding year for the crime movie was 1931, when William A. Wellman made *The Public Enemy*, propelling James Cagney to stardom. This film, like the early silents, points its finger at the sadness and deprivation of the big city as the cause of crime. The mood is drab and low-key. Cagney, in only his second year in films, and cast originally as the hero's friend, made so dynamic an impression that Warner Brothers tried switching his role with that of Edward Woods, and Cagney seized his chance. That rapid delivery, pugnacious strut and penetrating glare carried the actor through thirty years of stardom.

In this film he plays a tough youngster tempted into petty crime, attaching himself to the local bigshots, and enjoying a brief year or two of luxury (during which he pushes the celebrated grapefruit into Mae Clarke's face) before, in one of cinema's most jolting scenes, he is kidnapped from a hospital bed and delivered, trussed up and swathed in bandages, at his mother's front door. Indeed, the film set a new standard of ruthlessness: when the gangster who is Cagney's boss dies from a fall from his horse, Cagney and his sidekick go to the stable with revolvers to execute the offending animal.

Warners had two other great successes in the crime field in 1931, both directed by Mervyn LeRoy. *Little Caesar* did for Edward G. Robinson what *Public Enemy* did for Cagney. Cagney at his most vicious had a sympathetic side (his mother loved and admired him throughout *Public Enemy*), but Robinson's Rico in *Little Caesar* is coarse, vain, flashy and utterly repellent. The film is quintessential thirties Warners – gray and unlovely, rancid and corrupt. There is no trace of sentiment or glamour. Robinson's gang boss has his days of power and wealth, then sinks to the flop-house and finally to a wretched and dismal death in a deserted street.

*A shocked Phillips Holmes reads of the discovery of Sylvia Sidney's body in Sternberg's **An American Tragedy** (1931). This was to have been directed by the great Russian director Sergei Eisenstein, but Paramount rejected his treatment of Dreiser's novel, and consequently withdrew their offer to him.*

Below: *James Cagney, Joan Blondell and Edward Woods in William A. Wellman's* **The Public Enemy** *(1931). The positions on the stairway are prophetic. The film sent Cagney to the top; Blondell flowered as a perky comedienne, but remained a star of middle rank; Woods was little heard of after this.*

Right: *Edward G. Robinson radiates a gloating defiance in* **Little Caesar** *(also 1931).*

In LeRoy's *Five Star Final* Robinson's image is softer than his later one. Here he is an unscrupulous newspaper editor who in the pursuit of increased sales decides to dig up an ancient scandal, and in so doing drives a decent man and wife to suicide. This time there is a final cop-out, with Robinson allowed to repent and change his ways, but until then it is harsh, unsparing drama, with some fine supporting playing, notably from Aline MacMahon as Robinson's adoring secretary and Boris Karloff (with *Frankenstein* and his own stardom a few months ahead) as an unctuous ex-clergyman chasing the dirt.

Killer's code

Still in 1931, Karloff is just as impressive in Howard Hawks' *The Criminal Code*, one of the first of the prison movies that became so popular in the first years of sound. Perhaps Hawks (who was to prove, alongside John Ford, the finest of thirties directors) had not quite come to terms with sound, for there is a certain tentativeness about the film, and a lack of Hawks' characteristic warmth and easy openness.

Nonetheless the film has its fine moments, most memorably in the scene in which Karloff, as a prisoner who is the warden's barber, uses the tool of his trade to despatch a squealer who has violated the code of the title.

21

Rouben Mamoulian's *City Streets* (1931) is a gangster film with a difference. It is a love story beautifully played by Sylvia Sidney and the young Gary Cooper, interwoven with bootlegging and murder. In his early movies Mamoulian was so in love with the medium and its innovatory possibilities that in this film, as in his next, the entrancing musical *Love Me Tonight* (1932), he uses a whole battery of technical experiments. *City Streets* has bravura camerawork, expressionist lighting, distorted sound, the odd touch of symbolism, but none of it is permitted to get in the way of an exciting story lucidly told. Mamoulian was also one of Broadway's most distinguished stage directors.

Rowland Brown's *Quick Millions* (1931) was the first of only three films that this talented director made. Brown did not take easily to the studio system which denied the director's right to the ultimate decision, and his directorial career allegedly ended when he punched a supervisor. (Thereafter he became a scriptwriter.) *Quick Millions*, made for Fox before the merger with Twentieth Century, shows what a talent was lost. The film stars Spencer Tracy, who back in the early thirties was far from the benign and friendly father-figure of his

Inset far left: *Edward G. Robinson with, on the receiving end, Douglas Fairbanks Jr (second from left), in* **Little Caesar** *(1931). Note the cat on the counter, framing the composition.*

Left: *Spencer Tracy and Marguerite Churchill in* **Quick Millions** *(1931). In this shot there seems to be a trace of the later, kindly Tracy, but it is very misleading. Early thirties Tracy was every bit as rough and tough as they come.*

Below: *Phillips Holmes and Walter Huston in Howard Hawks'* **The Criminal Code** *(1931).*

famous days. The younger Tracy often played a snarling tough, and in Brown's movie he is a truck-driver who rises to become a powerful racketeer. This is another fast and savage film, and its world accepts the murder of people as a casual fact of life.

One director, however, ended his career in 1931. Roland West had been directing on and off since 1918, and his best work had shown a flair for eerie atmospheres and a somewhat grisly humor. His 1925 Lon Chaney silent, *The Monster*, is a good example, being set in a sanatorium presided over by an insane doctor intent on resuscitating the dead. West's last two films (both 1931) were *The Bat Whispers*, a beguiling mixture of detective thriller and old-dark-house horror comedy, and *Corsair*, a more straightforward, vigorous thriller about rumrunners during Prohibition (which ended with Roosevelt's election the following year). West, a somewhat shadowy and mysterious character, never directed again, for reasons still unknown. Certainly those last films, especially *The Bat Whispers*, with its striking sets and restlessly prowling camera, show no lessening of his talents.

Shame of a nation

Next year, 1932, brought two of the greatest crime movies. One was Howard Hawks' *Scarface – Shame of a Nation*. Hawks had found himself with a vengeance. *Scarface* is as devoid of pity as any of those 1931 films, but it also brings to the gangster film a sardonic, biting humor that no other similar movie possesses. Essentially the same story as *Little Caesar*, the rise and fall of a gang boss, and based this time on the career of Al Capone, *Scarface* is an exuberant, bouncing film about a character whose larger-than-life vigor almost bursts out of the screen. Paul Muni is excellent as Tony Camonte, who revels in his power and his apparent immunity from the law.

This was just before the Breen code set sharply defined limits to what a film could say or show, and even in 1932 *Scarface* contains one interpolated scene in which a group of good citizens is shown making up their minds to do something about such lawlessness. But that is the only moment that rings false. Hawks used the moving

Left: *Issuing prison clothes to Spencer Tracy proves somewhat difficult. The film is* **Twenty Thousand Years in Sing Sing** *(1933), based on the memoirs of prison guard Lewis E. Lawes, and remade by Warners in 1940 as* **Castle on the Hudson/Years Without Days,** *with John Garfield in the Tracy role.*

Below and bottom: *Paul Muni as Tony Camonte and Ann Dvorak as his sister Cesca in Howard Hawks'* **Scarface** *(1932). Tony, jealous of any man's attentions to Cesca, has dragged her away from a dance, and a violent quarrel ensues.*

Top right: *Donald Woods, Margaret Lindsay, Bette Davis and Lyle Talbot in* **Fog Over Frisco** *(1934).*
Top left: *The perfect marriage: William Powell and Myrna Loy in* **After the Thin Man** *(1936).*
Above *Paul Muni in* **I am a Fugitive from a Chain Gang** *(1932). This was such an effective movie that it was one of the few films to promote social reform, giving voice to and shaping the public's antagonism toward chain gangs.*

camera sparingly, but always to telling effect, and never more so than in the marvelous opening passage of *Scarface*, with the camera gliding through deserted rooms littered with the débris of a wild party, and the killer (Muni) stalking his victim. Memorable, too, is the killing of another rival (Karloff yet again), despatched in a bowling alley just after he has released his ball, with the camera following it into the pins, and the last pin tottering to fall with a sickening finality.

No hiding place

I am a Fugitive from a Chain Gang, directed in 1932 by Mervyn LeRoy, is a harrowing experience, based on the true story of Robert E. Burns, who was condemned to a Georgia chain gang for a small, unwitting part in a minor crime, escaped, made good, returned on a promise of parole, and was finally betrayed. The film follows its protagonist (Muni again) with an unflinching realism through to the hopeless end. Muni escapes a second time, and meets, for a moment, the girl who loves him (Helen Vinson). She asks how he lives. "I steal," he answers, quietly, and fades into the dark. LeRoy was a superb director of hard-hitting, socially aware movies, both in his handling of actors and in his creative use of sound, particularly in this film in the scenes on the chain gang.

The best crime movie of 1933 was another prison drama, Michael Curtiz's *Twenty Thousand Years in Sing Sing*, with Spencer Tracy, again in his tough guy persona, released on parole and going back of his own accord to confess to a crime committed by his girl. There is no escape here – Tracy goes to the chair. The girl is played with a fragile, nervous intensity by Bette Davis, who quarrelled a year or two later with the studio, Warner Brothers, because she was being cast in so many crime films and other undignified affairs. Time has played a wicked irony here, for the early Davis films like this one, *Three on a Match* (1932), *Bureau of Missing Persons* (1933), and *Fog Over Frisco* (1934), and her performances in them, look far better now than some of the lavish costume pictures and highly regarded sob stories of her later days.

The film historian William K. Everson called *Fog Over Frisco*, directed by William Dieterle, the fastest film ever made, and that verdict still stands. Dieterle races his characters upstairs and downstairs, in and out of cars and ships, into nightclubs and out in a couple of minutes, and manages to wrap up an intrigue of bewildering complexity in barely an hour. Davis is the bad girl, Margaret Lindsay (Warners' ever-charming girl-next-door) the good one, and nothing about the movie is normal. The star (Davis) is the victim, murdered half way through, Douglas Dumbrille for once is *not* the killer and the good girl's name is Val, which isn't short for Valerie but believe it or not Valkyr!

Opposite page: William Powell as Nick Charles, amateur detective, seeking inspiration from a fictional colleague. This is a scene from **The Thin Man Goes Home** *(1944). The series lasted into the forties.*

Right: *This was a vital letter, until terrier Asta got to work – from the first* **Thin Man** *(1934). Unlike some movie dogs, Asta never played leads, but this engaging hound deserved to. He triumphed again in* **Bringing Up Baby** *(1938).*

Below: *Spencer Tracy and the stray which has attached itself to him in jail in Fritz Lang's* **Fury** *(1936).*

Enter the Thin Man

In 1934 the comedy murder mystery cycle began with MGM's *The Thin Man*. This film has everything going for it: a superb plot (courtesy of Dashiell Hammett), whiplash direction from 'One-take Woody' Van Dyke, the first appearance of the terrier Asta (the best canine actor since the great Rin-Tin-Tin), lots of MGM gloss, and above all the pairing of William Powell and Myrna Loy as amateur sleuth Nick Charles and his wife Nora. Loy, after years playing dubious oriental ladies and the like, blossomed as an enchanting comedienne, and teamed beautifully with the dry and quizzical Powell. They fill the screen with the easy badinage of a happy marriage.

There were to be five more "Thin Man" films, all with Powell and Loy (the last in 1947), and if they did tail off a little towards the end, they added up to one of the period's most reliable pleasures. Murder-cum-comedy, usually with husband-and-wife teams, caught on. RKO's *The Ex-Mrs Bradford* (1936) had Powell opposite the delectable Jean Arthur, and was virtually another "Thin Man" film, and MGM themselves brought out three nice little programmers (not quite As and not quite Bs) in the "Fast Company" series, with a married couple doing the detecting in the pleasantly original surroundings of the rare book business. Universal, too, joined in the act with *Remember Last Night?* (1934), with director James Whale showing himself as much at home with a rapid-fire mystery in a heavy-drinking socialite milieu as he had been in the World War I trenches or the austere castle of Victor Frankenstein.

War on crime

By 1935 the Breen code was in full operation, and the impact on the gangster film was noteworthy. There were two important gangster films that year, and each of them in its different way showed that the moral climate had changed. Cagney could no longer play a killer and still carry the audience's sympathy: in Warners' *G-Men*, directed by William Keighley, a friend's death results in his joining the FBI – the war against crime is conducted with a heavy emphasis on law and order. *G-Men* had its exciting moments, and Cagney was never a dull actor, but some of the pre-Breen flavor had gone.

John Ford's *The Whole Town's Talking* (also 1935) adopts different tactics. Edward G. Robinson still plays a vicious thug, but to make it abundantly clear that he is no longer the hero, he also plays the role of the thug's double, an innocuous clerk who is constantly mistaken for him. This was much the better picture of the two. Jean Arthur as the clerk's girlfriend joyously seizes her chance to pose as a gun-moll; one of the great character actors, bald, bewildered Donald Meek, has one of his richest parts as a little man desperately trying to get the reward for spotting the killer. Although it tends to be forgotten, Ford in his middle period handled comedy with splendid panache (as in *Steamboat Round the Bend* the same year). *The Whole Town's Talking* may have the thinnest of plots, but for those players and that director it was quite enough.

Exiled from Nazi Germany, the great director Fritz Lang went to MGM for his first American film, *Fury* (1936). At first the studio thought little of the film, but it became an enormous critical success, and Lang's American career, which was to be as remarkable as his previous one in silent and sound films in Germany, was assured. The hero of *Fury* (Spencer Tracy, here playing an ordinary nice guy) is a man wrongfully accused of kidnapping, and narrowly escapes being lynched by a small-town mob. Believed dead, he hides out while a zealous DA prosecutes his attackers for murder until conscience sends him back to town. Lang gave the film a throbbing urgency, moving from the tenderness of the opening scenes between Tracy and his girl (Sylvia Sidney) to the appalling frenzy of the attack upon the prison in which Tracy is detained, and then to a superb court-room scene in which newsreel film of the attack is played to confound the defendants' well-planned alibis.

Bogart in town

Archie Mayo's *The Petrified Forest* (1936) brought Humphrey Bogart back to the screen. Bogart had made a few unimpressive appearances (usually in minor films) a few years before, and had returned to the stage. There he played a killer on the run, Duke Mantee, in Robert E. Sherwood's *The Petrified Forest*, and he repeated the role when Warners filmed the play. Highly praised at the time, the film now seems overstrained and whimsical, with Leslie Howard and Bette Davis struggling with unconvincing parts as poet and waitress meeting in a gas-station in Arizona, but there is no mistaking Bogart's power. The sympathetic edge that he later gave to all his characters, however deplorable they were, is not yet here; his Mantee is little more than a savage animal, yet in him, somewhere, are the faintly discernible outlines of the later presence.

That presence is clearly recognizable in *Black Legion* (1937), also directed by Mayo. This is one of the most courageous, and most unjustly forgotten, films of the period. An overtly political movie, a rare event in thirties Hollywood, it casts Bogart as a factory worker who is passed over for a coveted foremanship in favor of a foreigner. Embittered by this, he joins a right-wing, "America first" organization, closely modeled on the Ku Klux Klan. Eventually, when he sees the iniquity of his new friends it is too late – his life is already destroyed. He is too deeply implicated in crime. There are few believable working-man heroes in Hollywood movies of the time. Bogart's portrayal here, rough, well-meaning, hopelessly confused, is one that demands belief. But the film has other merits, particularly in its closing courtroom scenes, which carry a powerful denunciation of the Klan and other similarly oppressive and wicked societies.

A miscarriage of justice

Where *The Petrified Forest* strives in vain for poetry, *Winterset*, directed by Alfred Santell in 1936 from Maxwell Anderson's verse play, achieves it effortlessly. This magnificent film takes as its starting point the Sacco/Vanzetti case, and imagines that years later the son of an unjustly executed man comes to New York in search of the men really guilty of the killing. A marvelous screenplay by Anthony Veiller replaced Anderson's verse, or most of it, with finely wrought poetic prose, and substituted a happy ending for the original's bleak tragedy, yet miraculously sustained the spirit of the piece, and even suggested that this was the more logical and more moving resolution.

The action of *Winterset* takes place in a huddle of tenements by the East River, a perfectly achieved studio design, and contains probably the greatest set of performances of the whole period. RKO wisely used most of the Broadway cast, which ensured that the lines would be spoken as they deserved to be, and of this group of actors, most relatively new to cinema, Burgess Meredith as the hero Mio, Margo as the girl he meets on his quest, and Eduardo Ciannelli as the real killer Trock Estrella, went on to new careers in films.

Margo, who couldn't be blamed for shortening her name, which was Marie Marguerita Guadalupe Teresa Estela Bolado Castilla y O'Donnell, had in fact made a film or two before *Winterset*. She had attracted attention as the girl murdered by Claude Rains in Ben Hecht and Charles MacArthur's imaginatively eccentric *Crime Without*

Far left: *Henry Fonda in Fritz Lang's* **You Only Live Once** *(1937). Hollywood hated to waste good footage so the brilliant bank robbery sequence from this movie turned up again in* **Dillinger** *(1945)!*

Left: *Joel McCrea and Humphrey Bogart in William Wyler's* **Dead End** *(also 1937). This shot conveys the solidity and detail of Richard Day's magnificent studio set, infinitely more effective than any location shooting could ever be. Bogart made seven films in 1937. In* **Dead End** *he played a vicious hoodlum. In* **Marked Woman (below),** *made earlier the same year, he was an idealistic District Attorney, here seen trying to persuade Bette Davis to help him nail the vice ring run by Eduardo Ciannelli. Davis' sister, played by Jane Bryan, is killed by the ring, so Davis talks, but not before she has been badly scarred by the gang.*

Below: *Bogart, in **Dead End** (1937), visiting his mother, superbly played by Marjorie Main. This was her first important film part at the comparatively late age of 47; she went on to specialize in comedy.*

Inset below: *Cagney and Bogart, this time in **Angels With Dirty Faces** (1938). The film ingeniously combines a social conscience with the crackling vitality of the gangster genre.*

Below right: *Cagney, in a scene from the same film, visited in jail by Bogart playing the crooked lawyer whom Cagney eventually kills.*

Passion (1934), and later on played effectively in Frank Capra's *Lost Horizon* (1937). Meredith was a fine, sensitive actor whose rare thirties appearances were eagerly awaited. They include a piece of zestful comedy in another forgotten movie, S. Sylvan Simon's *Spring Madness* (1938), and an impressive part as the pacifist in Clarence Brown's *Idiot's Delight* (1939), in which the plot cruelly removed him after a couple of reels and left one with a hopelessly miscast Clark Gable and Norma Shearer for the rest of the long trek.

Ciannelli had no equal at depicting a quiet, sleek and lethal Latin, and he was again to feature in *Marked Woman* (1937). This was Bette Davis' last crime movie for Warners. It came after her quarrel with the studio, and represented something of a compromise. It was another crime melodrama. She plays a night-club hostess (it was impossible at that time to use a more accurate term) working under racketeers who scar her face savagely when she acts against their wishes. She gives the part her particular blend of bitterness and jaunty courage. The film, directed by Lloyd Bacon, was lavish, and admirably terse and pointed in its attack on corruption.

Criminal independents

In spite of the success of *Fury*, Fritz Lang and MGM parted after that film. Lang's second American effort, as uncompromising as the first, was *You Only Live Once*, which he made in 1937 for the independent producer Walter Wanger. Henry Fonda, just two years into his long career, plays a petty criminal whose ill luck and weakness lead to murder, a prison break and death. Cloaked in rain and mist, and heavy with the sense of destiny that had permeated Lang's German films, *You Only Live Once* has fittingly atmospheric photography from Leon Shamroy. It also has three fine performances: from Fonda himself; Sylvia Sidney, once again bravely ministering to a man in dire trouble; and, as the prison chaplain whom Fonda kills in his breakout, William Gargan, an underrated actor who was seldom as well served as here.

Another outstanding independent production of the time was *Dead End* (1937), directed by William Wyler for Samuel Goldwyn, and derived from Sidney Kingsley's hit Broadway play. Bogart plays a gangster returning to his old home in the riverside tenements of New York, with Joel McCrea and Sylvia Sidney as the architect and his girl caught up in the intrigue. In a film of superlative acting there are also the Dead End Kids – half a dozen streetwise youngsters who later appeared in *Angels With Dirty Faces* (1938).

Dead End's other fine performances came from Marjorie Main as Bogart's sad, harsh mother, and, best of all, Claire Trevor, one of the thirties' unsung talents, as the gangster's former sweetheart, now on the streets and ravaged by illness. The five minutes she was allowed contain the most memorable close-ups of the entire decade. The art director Richard Day also made a huge contribution to the movie, building an amazing cityscape of slum houses, waterfront, and rich men's towers which recalled the architectural splendors of the German silents. Day won seven Academy Awards, but curiously missed out with this, his finest work.

The rich year of 1937 also contained Mervyn LeRoy's *They Won't Forget*, perhaps the best of all Warners' crusading movies, and one of the thirties' finest in any genre. The film describes how a Southern court convicts, on the flimsiest of evidence, a Northern teacher of the murder of a schoolgirl (a very young Lana Turner), and how a Southern mob proceeds to lynch him. LeRoy's handling of the dangerous North-South hostility uses some striking visual coups,

Far left: *Former hoofer James Cagney's familiar glower, perfectly captured in this portrait by Hollywood photographer Scotty Welbourne, and his machine-gun delivery were turned to marvelous effect time after time by Warner Brothers during the thirties. Although Cagney was more accustomed to grappling with the likes of all-purpose Warners heavy Barton Maclane (**left**), in Lloyd Bacon's* **Frisco Kid** *(1935), he grappled, too, with molls like Jean Harlow (**above**), in William Wellman's* **Public Enemy** *(1931), the gangster film which shot him to immediate stardom.*

such as the moment when the lynching is conveyed by a shot of a speeding train snatching a mailbag from its container by the track. Claude Rains is superb as the self-seeking Southern lawyer, winning his case because he is a man of the people, which his Northern opponent, the smooth and cultivated Otto Kruger, so manifestly isn't. Allyn Joslyn as a cynical reporter, Clinton Rosemond as a terrified janitor who is going to be framed until a more profitable victim appears and Gloria Dickson as the teacher's wife all make *They Won't Forget* into one of the most fierce indictments of irrational emotional behavior. What one realizes only afterwards, when for a while the movie relinquishes its grip, is that the teacher might have been guilty after all. The script never reveals the guilty party.

Wild angels

Angels With Dirty Faces, directed by Michael Curtiz, shows Hollywood evading the demands of the Production Code in a highly ingenious way, but the duplicity was pardonable in view of the film's excitement and energy. Two slum kids dabble in juvenile crime. One of them (Pat O'Brien, settling down to a life of dependability after the flamboyant skulduggery of *The Front Page*, 1931) becomes the neighborhood priest, the other (James Cagney) becomes a cocky gangster idolized by the local youth (the Dead End Kids). When at the end Cagney is led to the chair, O'Brien, still his friend, persuades him to take the last walk as a babbling coward to break his influence over the local kids. Acceptable morality kept the Breen Office happy; audiences too were happy, because the Cagney of *G-Men* had given way to the old, devil-may-care Cagney of *The Public Enemy*.

These were the best of the crime movies of the thirties, but there were many others, including detective series, with such sleuths as Hildegarde Withers (engaging comedy with ZaSu Pitts or Helen

Broderick); Mr Moto (where poor plots and indifferent support tended to waste Peter Lorre); Perry Mason (better plots, and the forceful Warren William in the lead); and above all Charlie Chan.

From 1931 until 1938, when he died, the Swedish actor Warner Oland was the perfect incarnation of the aphoristic and ever-perceptive Chinese detective, with Keye Luke, who really was Chinese, as the brash and pushy "Number One Son". At least two of the Chans were really first-rate movies: in *Charlie Chan at the Opera* (1936) Karloff as an opera singer escaped from an asylum gives Oland a real rival to play against, while *Charlie Chan on Broadway* (1937), the best of all, has a diabolically clever plot raced through, in true thirties style, at breakneck speed and with perfect clarity.

Petty crime?

Finally, a few not-quite-greats, but films which, long unseen, stay in the mind as particular joys. *Death on the Diamond* (1934) is a baseball mystery directed, strangely, by comedy specialist Edward Sedgwick. There is a marvelously macabre 1937 MGM piece called *Under Cover of Night*, which has that master of sardonic lordliness, Henry Daniell, cast as a crazed professor who knocks off half the faculty before they catch up with him; this was directed by George B. Seitz, a great master of the small movie, also responsible for such good little MGM thrillers as *Absolute Quiet* (1936), *The Thirteenth Chair* (1937) and *Kind Lady* (1935). Sadly, the studio never let Seitz loose on their prestige productions, some of which really needed livening up. Other joys include *Night Must Fall* (1937), with the excellent Rosalind Russell, but suave Robert Montgomery hardly convincing as a homicidal Welsh pageboy, and *The Doorway to Hell* (1930), with gentle, idealistic Lew Ayres just as oddly cast as a hoodlum, but getting away with it.

The Berkeley Touch

Chapter 3

As soon as sound came in the studios leapt at the opportunity to create something entirely new – the musical. The first offerings were very simple. Studios used most of their stars – often regardless of their singing or dancing skills – and sometimes a whole bevy of directors to mount a lavish revue. A storyline was replaced by a series of star turns. Such were Warners' *The Show of Shows* (1929), MGM's *The Hollywood Revue of 1929*, and *Paramount on Parade* (1930). But in 1929 there were two entirely successful attempts at better things. *The Broadway Melody*, directed by Harry Beaumont, contain good numbers, a strong story, and a heart-rending performance from Bessie Love, while Ernst Lubitsch's *The Love Parade* had the pairing of Maurice Chevalier and Jeanette MacDonald, and enough sparkle to suggest that Lubitsch would soon make musicals as engaging as his silent comedies.

The delights of Lubitsch

With *Monte Carlo* (1930) the promise was fulfilled. MacDonald sang "Beyond the Blue Horizon" aboard a speeding train – the wheels whirred, the rails danced, and happy workers in the passing fields joined in the chorus; the cinematic musical was born. In her Paramount days MacDonald was an enchanting comedienne with a wicked twinkle in her eye; she needed a director like Lubitsch or Mamoulian to keep the twinkle there, and when she later went on to MGM, who saw her as a ladylike partner for stolid Nelson Eddy, a thirties treasure was lost.

In 1931 came *The Smiling Lieutenant*: Lubitsch again, the elegant swagger of the Paramount look, and one delicious number that had bubbling Claudette Colbert urging the staid princess of Miriam Hopkins to "Jazz up Your Lingerie". Lubitsch's next musical, *One Hour with You* (1932), an unnecessary remake of his finest silent comedy, *The Marriage Circle* (1924), was curiously lifeless; perhaps it suffered from the stresses that had led to the removal of the original director, George Cukor, after two weeks' shooting, but for whatever reason, the movie tried too hard and too consciously for gaiety, and fell with a thud.

However, Lubitsch's fifth musical, but this time at MGM, *The Merry Widow* (1934), was a triumph all the way, though it didn't find immediate popularity with audiences – by now conditioned to the totally different Warners musical style – and was compared unfavorably by critics with Stroheim's silent version. Lubitsch had Chevalier and MacDonald again, joined by two superlative comedians in Edward Everett Horton and Una Merkel, and the marvelous Léhar score coming from the screen (not, as it had for Stroheim, from the

Right: *Tap-dancing queen Eleanor Powell serenaded by the American navy in Roy Del Ruth's lavish 1936 musical* **Born to Dance,** *made at MGM. Miss Powell was supported in this innocent froth by James Stewart, Virginia Bruce and Una Merkel.*

orchestra pit). Wisely, he didn't aim for the underlying gravity of the Stroheim film, but was content to mix Ruritanian court with Parisian restaurant, ironic comedy with lyrical romance, and make the whole an irresistibly heady delight.

On 42nd Street...

In the early months of 1933 there was turmoil at the Burbank studios of Warner Brothers. The Depression had hit the studio so hard that it inflicted a 50 per cent salary cut on all employees. In March 1933, amid the rancor, disaffection and talk of court action this caused, the studio released a movie of boundless energy and devastating wit, a movie that looks and sounds as though made by a studio without a care in the world – the immortal *42nd Street*. The film loosed on the world the intricate exuberance of Busby Berkeley's choreography – something entirely new and daring and, at its best, a perfect blending of cinema and dance.

Nowadays people talk, and write, as though *42nd Street* were a Berkeley film alone, but that is to miss much of its glory. There were Berkeley numbers, some of them even better than *42nd Street*'s, in a dozen other films of the period, yet none of those films is as inexhaustibly rewarding as this one. *42nd Street* is a Berkeley triumph in which he directed the numbers; the remaining three-quarters of the film was the work of Lloyd Bacon who directed a strong story and dialogue with tang and bite and a cast of superb straight actors (with the exception of Ruby Keeler, who made up for it with her charm). That was the essence of the trick, and while Warners brought it off to some degree in other movies, it never worked as well as here.

Far left: *Jeanette MacDonald and Maurice Chevalier in* **The Merry Widow** *(1934). For this film director Ernst Lubitsch left Paramount for MGM, but he took his stars with him, with all their sparkle and lightness. In the film Maurice Chevalier* **(right)** *plays the part of Danilo. Here, the ladies of Maxim's establishment decide that he deserves their closest attentions.*

Above: *The Goldwyn Girls performing a Busby Berkeley number on their way to the bath in* **The Kid From Spain** *(1932). The Kid was Eddie Cantor, whose strident vaudeville style didn't always work on film.*

Consider that cast: Warner Baxter as the hard driving producer; Bebe Daniels, a great silent star, as the elegant if aging lead; Ginger Rogers and Una Merkel as two chorines on the make, one a transparently fake grande dame, the other pure Brooklyn, with an acid tongue; chirpy little George E. Stone as the dance director, earthy Allen Jenkins stage managing, and a host more. *42nd Street* could even afford to toss in a talented player of hoodlums like Jack LaRue for a half-minute appearance, while in the original cut there was a cameo of an old actor played by none other than Henry B. Walthall, the Little Colonel of *The Birth of a Nation* (1915). Unhappily, Walthall's part vanished from the release prints, save for one unexplained glimpse of him by the stage door.

Busy hands and Busby Berkeley

The pre-code dialogue is still a great delight, some of it so fast and casual that you pick up fresh lines at almost every viewing. "You've got the busiest hands," exclaims Merkel as she is swung back and forwards by a chorus boy. And in the same scene there is this — rather risqué — exchange: "Where you sitting, dearie, where you sitting?" asks the boy. "On a flagpole — on a flagpole", she replies as she sits on his lap. "Afraid I've gotta run", says a chorine as she lifts her skirt for the producer, and "First door on the left," cracks her neighbor. Cynicism pervades. "Okay those three on the left, Mr Marsh," says Stone, meaning Rogers, Merkel and Keeler. "If I were you I'd keep 'em." "I suppose if I don't, you'll have to," Baxter fires back, keeping them.

Busby Berkeley had been a Broadway dance director before Samuel Goldwyn called him to Hollywood to choreograph *Whoopee*

Far left: *Lyda Roberti and Eddie Cantor in* **The Kid From Spain** *(1932). Roberti, a vivacious blonde from Poland, enlivened a number of Hollywood musicals before suffering a fatal heart attack in 1938.* **The Kid From Spain,** *zestfully directed by comedy expert Leo McCarey, was easily Cantor's best sound film.*

Main picture: *Producer Warner Baxter lectures novice chorine Ruby Keeler in* **42nd Street** *(1933). In spite of this unpromising start, Keeler keeps her job, and ends up making the classic transition from chorus-girl to star.*

Above: *George Stone and the chorus line in the same film. Another carefully posed still for cinema use, with Keeler, just another girl at this stage of the film, conveniently at the head of the line.*

(1930) and other musicals for Eddie Cantor. He contributed attractive, routine chorus-line scenes for these films. With his move to Warners Berkeley was transformed. He moved his camera with a fine abandon along and over and under his innumerable girls; he shot them from above as the complex patterns of his kaleidoscope revolved; he played tricks with waterfalls and sleeping-cars, moving pianos, and violins glowing in the dark.

Berkeley also told stories in the best of his numbers, stories that played on every kind of emotion, sometimes most unexpected ones. In *Footlight Parade* (1933) Cagney prowls through sleazy Chinese dives "looking for his Shanghai Lil"; Wini Shaw falls to her death from a high window in *Gold Diggers of 1935* (1935), playing a doomed night club girl who sings her "Lullaby of Broadway"; and there is a sharp, savage killing in the climactic ballet of *42nd Street*. In another mood, in Mervyn LeRoy's *Gold Diggers of 1933* (1933), Berkeley's camera glides past the beaten faces of a Depression breadline, while the figure of Joan Blondell and the voice of Etta Moten evoke pity for "My Forgotten Man".

Berkeley's comic sense could be alarming at times. One of his trademarks was the introduction into a musical number of a lecherous toddler, gleefully played by Billy Barty, who licked his lips at the goings-on he should never have been allowed to see. Barty's best moment came in the "Pettin' in the Park" number from *Gold Diggers of 1933*. Berkeley encased his chorines in tight-fitting metal sheaths for this one. Dick Powell finds that this frustrates his designs on Keeler, whereupon Barty sidles up and presents him with a can-opener.

Berkeley duly became a full director. He was in charge of the whole of *Gold Diggers of 1935*, and later moved to MGM and Twentieth Century-Fox, but his work there seldom had the sheer cinematic flair of the early thirties days.

Left: *Chorus-girls and boys in the "Pettin' in the Park" number from* **Gold Diggers of 1933.** *A musical born of the Depression,* **Gold Diggers** *was directed by Mervyn LeRoy, Warners' specialist in movies with a social comment.*

Below: *The Goldwyn Girls who starred in* **Whoopee!** *(1930),* **Palmy Days** *(1932) and* **Roman Scandals** *(1933), as well as* **The Kid From Spain** *(1932).*

43

The musical takes wings

MGM turned seriously to musicals in the mid-thirties with *Broadway Melody of 1936* (1935), *Born to Dance* (1936) and *Rosalie* (1937). The great strength of these was the astonishing tap-dancing of Eleanor Powell. There are some memorable songs ("Broadway Rhythm" from the first, "I've Got You Under My Skin" from the second), ingenious sets and no expense spared. Far from masterpieces, these films are extremely happy diversions, as are the teenage musicals with Mickey Rooney and Judy Garland which appeared at the end of the decade.

The studio's most famous musical is *The Great Ziegfeld* (1936); the musical interludes were grandiose but not particularly memorable, and the movie didn't actually need them. It had other things to offer: William Powell as the great man himself, Luise Rainer and Myrna Loy as Anna Held and Billie Burke, and one of the rare film appearances of the Broadway comedienne Fanny Brice, the "Funny Girl" herself.

RKO contributed richly to the thirties musical with their Fred Astaire and Ginger Rogers series. In all, the pair danced in 10 films beginning with supporting roles in *Flying Down to Rio* (1933). The movie is best remembered for the final aerial ballet, with dance director Dave Gould's chorus gyrating on the wings of airplanes in flight. Earlier in this film Fred and Ginger danced the "Carioca", and a chapter in film history began.

Fred Astaire had been a Broadway star since 1917, but had made just one film, *Dancing Lady* (1933). Rogers had been in movies rather longer, with her sharp comedy in *42nd Street* the culmination of four years playing leads in small pictures and supporting roles in larger ones. She found Astaire, the chemistry between them worked, and a new kind of musical was born.

Astaire and Rogers didn't really rely too much on the eye-catching gimmickry of their occasional all-over-the-furniture routines. Other dancers could do those just as well. Their finest numbers were those in which a romantic elegance had full play, and fluid movement and a depth of affection extraordinary in a musical made the screen throb with delight. This happened in numbers like Cole Porter's "Night and Day" from *The Gay Divorcee* (1934), Jerome Kern's "Lovely to Look At" from *Roberta* (1935) and his "The Way You Look Tonight" from *Swing Time* (1936). Perhaps the most entrancing of them all is Irving Berlin's "Let's Face the Music and Dance" from *Follow the Fleet* (1936). Fred and Ginger were lucky in their composers (the four movies cited had the three best), in their directors (especially the gifted Mark Sandrich), in their art director (RKO's Van Nest Polgase, a great hand at the shining black and white surfaces that set the pair off to perfection), and in their regular supporting casts (proud, pained Eric Blore; waspish continental Erik Rhodes; and down-to-earth Helen Broderick). Their films are star movies if ever any were. Not only in their dancing did they suit one another perfectly – their personalities matched as well, with Ginger's gritty common sense anchoring Fred's more wayward flights. It was noticeable, too, that when Fred's tendency to cocksureness got the better of him, as with his gum-chewing sailor in *Follow the Fleet*, the warmth that was expected from him was absent.

Main picture: *The extraordinary "Remember My Forgotten Man" number from* **Gold Diggers of 1933.** *The musical shocked many because it spelled out that war brought poverty and degradation – some reviewers even suggested that the song should be eliminated. Joan Blondell, seen here, mimed – Etta Moten provided the voice.*

Top right: *Busby Berkeley's kaleidoscope at work in the title number of* **Dames** *(1934), directed by Ray Enright. The last of Berkeley's great quartet,* **Dames** *had an extremely funny script, with Hugh Herbert and ZaSu Pitts as Purity Leaguers gunning for Broadway.*

Showboat sails again

In 1936 Universal made one of the period's finest musicals, the second of the cinema's three versions of *Showboat*. The 1929 version, coming at the transition between silence and sound, had done its best, preceding an essentially silent film with a sound prologue featuring singers from the stage production. These included Helen Morgan who, in the 1936 film, played the tragic half-caste Julie, the last film but one of a career that in real life was as sad as that of the unhappy, fallen women she played so movingly.

The 1936 version was directed by James Whale, unused to musicals but the only top-notch director at Universal and an inspired choice. Whale had Irene Dunne for his lead, a sweet singer and a considerable actress, both in romantic drama and in the screwball comedy that was to be so popular in the late thirties; he had Paul Robeson singing "Ol' Man River", where the camerawork was as striking as the song; genial old Charles Winninger as the show boat's skipper; and that formidable lady Helen Westley as his wife. Dunne, Robeson and Morgan, with Allan Jones as the handsome scapegrace who comes back to Dunne after the years, do full justice to Jerome Kern's superlative score, the emotion is nicely managed without becoming over-powering, and the film shows that stage musical comedy, given a director with Whale's eye for composition, works as well, if not better, on the screen.

Universal's Deanna Durbin musicals, starting with *Three Smart Girls* (1937), rescued the studio from financial crisis. She was 14 when the first film was made, and instantly became immensely popular. She sang with patent enjoyment, acted with no trace of child-star affectation or winsomeness, and could make the crustiest spectator give in. In Deanna's day, the great W.C. Fields was also a denizen of Universal; the studio never teamed them, and wisely so, for Deanna would have broken down even that great child-hater's defences, and done irreparable harm to his image. For the rest of the thirties Universal found her fresh and lively vehicles, with *Mad about Music* (1938) just about the best of them. Later they did become a great deal thinner, and it took a brave venture into *film noir* with Robert Siodmak's *Christmas Holiday* (1944) to give Deanna a success to rank with those early ones.

Twentieth Century-Fox's prestige musical of the decade was Henry King's *Alexander's Ragtime Band* that was released in 1938. Since then the film has been so beset by copyright problems that it has never been revived. It was a stylish, tastefully mounted production, too slight emotionally to engage the director fully (in King's best films feeling ran deep) but giving Alice Faye and her husky contralto far more scope than Fox's routine musicals had ever done. But Alice's gently winning ways — no one ever wrinkled a nose as fetchingly as Faye — make most Fox musicals enjoyable, and her eventual replacement as the studio's top musical star by the brassy Betty Grable was a symptom of the rougher days that lay ahead.

Good and bad notes

This chapter ends where it began, with Paramount. For Paramount's musical history contained rather more than the work of Ernst Lubitsch. For instance, the studio made a lot of really dreadful comedies with music starring Bing Crosby, who, though a fine singer and a cosy personality, simply couldn't carry the terrible stories and lifeless direction he was lumbered with. As examples of how dire a thirties musical could be, look at two characteristic Paramount efforts, *We're Not Dressing* (1934) and *Doctor Rhythm* (1938). The first of these creaking horrors had a superb comedienne in Carole Lombard, the second the uniquely witty Beatrice Lillie, but all to no avail. Paramount thought Crosby's numbers would do, but they didn't. However, the studio made money without really trying. When they did try, as with the Lubitsch films, the results could be spectacular, and they include two musicals from Rouben Mamoulian that far outweigh all the misbegotten ventures.

Left and right: *Ilona Massey in MGM's* **Rosalie** *(1937). The studio's musical style was not really formed until the forties, but the thirties did provide occasional pleasures.* **Rosalie** *was the first of Hungarian Ilona Massey's few American films.*
Top: *More Berkeley ingenuity. In* **Dames** *(1934) cut outs of Ruby Keeler's face formed themselves into fantastic patterns at a twitch of the maestro's wand.*

Mamoulian made his first five films for Paramount between 1929 and 1933. His debut film, *Applause*, though not primarily a musical, had Helen Morgan songs; the fourth, *Love Me Tonight* (1932), could well be the finest of all thirties musicals. It looks like a Lubitsch film, with the same stars, Chevalier and MacDonald, the same sophisticated art direction from Hans Dreier, the same Ruritanian setting, although this time it is nominally Paris and the country around. But Mamoulian outdid the master with this perfect jewel of a film. The whole movie is a piece of music, from the opening in the city with its soundtrack filled with the noises of Paris coming to life, recalling, but effortlessly surpassing, René Clair's *Sous les Toits de Paris/Under the Roofs of Paris* (1930), into the first song, the intoxicating "Isn't It Romantic?" sung by Chevalier as a hard-up tailor, and carried on enthusiastically by taxi-drivers, musicians, soldiers and gypsies, through an hour and a half of enchantment.

The film contains such startling pleasures as dignified old C. Aubrey Smith actually joining in a song ("The son of a gun's a tailor"), moving on to a climax that parodies early movies yet creates its own delirious charm as MacDonald races to stand defiantly across a railroad track to stop the train that is carrying Chevalier away. That stance encapsulates all the undaunted wit and pride that Lubitsch and Mamoulian, and no one else, managed to uncover in this delectable actress.

Below: *Paul Robeson sings "Ol' Man River" in one of the most famous scenes from James Whale's **Showboat** (1936). The Second of three versions, this featured a superb score by Jerome Kern.*

Left: *Ginger Rogers and Fred Astaire in* **Shall We Dance?** *(1937), directed by Mark Sandrich, and with a score by George and Ira Gershwin. Note the look which Astaire casts towards Rogers. A posed shot it may well be, but that look sums up the sympathy that was there between the two.*

There was more, too, in *Love Me Tonight*: Charles Butterworth, ineffable silly-ass of thirties comedies, tumbling off a ladder as he woos MacDonald and "falling flat on his flute"; the trio of elderly aunts who provide a pessimistic commentary on the action; even the odd shift into verse dialogue when the movie gets so airborne that prose won't do. And there is Myrna Loy, still the unregenerate Myrna of the days before she "married" Powell, but a thoroughly nice girl too, strictly brought up by her uncle Aubrey Smith. Thoroughly nice, but just a little overfond of men. She is sitting alone when Charles Ruggles bursts in. "Can you go for a doctor?" says a worried Ruggles. "Certainly," Loy whips back. "Send him right in!"

Mamoulian came back to Paramount in 1937 for one more musical, *High, Wide and Handsome*, an offbeat movie with marvelous moments. It had a Jerome Kern score, Irene Dunne in spirited form to sing it, and a story that only Mamoulian could have lifted up so easily into the artifices of the musical without sacrificing a lot of its dramatic force. It is a very good story – a sort of Western, though set in Pennsylvania, about oil-prospectors and the wicked railroad tycoons who are threatening their land. It had good Western type he-men too – Randolph Scott, Charles Bickford, Alan Hale – and it would have made a nice John Ford movie. Instead it had Mamoulian – and as a result it took off.

Below left: Ethel Merman in **Alexander's Ragtime Band** *(1938).
One of the greatest musical stars of the American theater, Merman
made relatively few films, mostly ephemeral. In another scene from
the same film,* **below,** *Alice Faye and Tyrone Power are on the verge
of wonderful things.*

Fantasy Thirties Style

Chapter 4

What the thirties called horror films are not really that at all. They do all kinds of things, but they do not horrify. The thirties films send an occasional pleasurable shiver down the spine; they can amaze, but not alarm, divert, but not discomfort. If there are exceptions to this, they are films like Tod Browning's *Freaks* (1932), which set out from the beginning to do something more than shock. Thirties horror is more properly fantasy, and as fantasy it roams far and wide, from islands inhabited by prehistoric creatures, islands where men hunted men or turned beasts into men, to hilltop castles in Eastern Europe, gloomy laboratories in Paris or New York, and decaying, rainswept old mansions in remote parts of Wales.

Return of the vampire

Universal set the pace and kept up the fashion longest. In 1931 they released Tod Browning's version of *Dracula*. Bram Stoker's classic novel had been filmed before, by F.W. Murnau in Germany, as *Nosferatu* (1922). Murnau's feeling for space, and the silent cinema's unique ability to lull its audiences into dream, made *Nosferatu* into a masterpiece; Browning's film was less ambitious, but powerful enough on its own terms. Garrett Fort's screenplay was derived from a stage version rather than the original novel, which meant that the latter half in particular, after the traveling to and from the castle in Transylvania, was overburdened with talk about which Browning could do little. But the casting of the title role made the film. Lon Chaney had been the first choice, and inevitably so, for Browning had directed many of Chaney's silent films with enormous success. But Chaney died before production started, and the part passed to the Hungarian actor Bela Lugosi, who had previously played Dracula on Broadway back in 1927.

For the rest of his life, Lugosi's career was haunted by memories of this one part. He fitted it to perfection. The lilting, slightly accented voice, the piercing eyes, the proud stance, the measured walk, all made Lugosi's Count so devilishly effective that the unsatisfactory script ceased to matter. Lugosi's voice made lines like the opening "I am – Dracula" and the invocation of the wolves in "Listen to them – children of the night – what music they make!" burn in the mind. Visually, too, there were splendid moments, like the awakening of Dracula's brides, gliding gauzily about their dark tomb, and the crossing to England in a ship of the dead. And Lugosi did not lack support. Helen Chandler was the fragile and lovely heroine who disappeared from the screen all too soon – her wistful beauty would have made her a great star in silent days; Edward Van Sloan was the vampire hunter Van Helsing and, as the crazed, insect-eating Renfield, there was Dwight Frye. The last two players reveled in eccentric characterizations, the stranger the better.

*King Kong fights off a huge prehistoric bird which is attacking Fay Wray in Merian C. Cooper's famous production of **King Kong** (1933).*

Made for Karloff

Frye was around again, this time as the Baron's dwarfish assistant, in *Frankenstein*, which at the end of the year was Universal's second, and even greater, success. Again there were one or two last-minute changes of plan. Lugosi turned down the role of the Monster, fearing, it is said, that his face would be unrecognizable behind make-up, with the result that Boris Karloff, hitherto a character heavy, became a star; and for reasons unclear the direction was taken from the Frenchman Robert Florey (who was offered *The Murders in the Rue Morgue* as a consolation prize in 1932) and given to James Whale, then a newcomer with only *Journey's End* and one other film behind him. *Frankenstein* would lift Whale above Browning as the thirties master of fantasy.

As before, the lead actor dominated the film. Unhampered by the make-up – an elaborate job by Universal's master of the craft, Jack Pierce, which took hours each day to apply – Karloff managed to make the Monster an uncanny mingling of the tender and the grotesque, never playing overtly for sympathy yet obtaining a great deal. Everyone remembers the scene by the lakeside with the little girl, shot by Whale with a moving reticence; no less striking was a scene in total contrast, when the Monster was brought to life. Universal's art director, Charles D. Hall, excelled himself in the magnificent scene with the platform bearing the Monster rising up into the stormy sky from the cavernous workshop with all its outlandish equipment. Whale and Karloff made the creature's subsequent first bemused moments into something touching and wonderful.

Left: *Boris Karloff as the Monster in James Whale's* **Frankenstein** *(1931). When the film came out, Bioscope's reviewer found it "a rather crudely constructed blood curdler", deplored the artificial sets, and even spotted creases in the backcloth at one point. But the years have made it an undisputed classic, creases and all.*

Right: *Bela Lugosi threatens the sleeping Frances Dade in Tod Browning's* **Dracula** *(1931). Lugosi had appeared in films in his native Hungary, in Germany and (since 1923) in America. This one film transformed him from a character player into a star.*

Making the most of their good fortune, Universal turned out three more "horror" films in 1932. In *The Mummy* Karloff is swathed in bandages but of a different kind, and plays a deadly ancient Egyptian at large in modern Cairo. A little tamer than its predecessors, it has a notable moment when the Mummy first stirs from its long sleep, and the later plot developments, with Karloff now incarnated as an elderly priest, give the actor a chance to change key to the silkily sinister.

Murders in the Rue Morgue has little in common with the Edgar Allan Poe story it claims to tell (none of the variants played on *The Black Cat* had much to do with him either), but the stylized sets could have graced a German silent, and Robert Florey, an accomplished director whose talents the studios shamefully misused, handled the whole thing with an engaging lightness of touch. Lugosi plays Doctor Mirakle, one of the first of the "mad doctors" so numerous in the thirties fantasy cycle, who was seeking a human bride for the gorilla he exhibited as a fairground attraction. He unfortunately insisted on injecting the poor girls with ape blood to see if they were suitable – a precaution that seldom turned out well. Nonsense it was, but it was good fun nonetheless.

Left: *Gloria Stuart in James Whale's* **The Old Dark House** *(1932). The arm belongs to Boris Karloff as the dumb butler, Morgan. Stuart and a young Melvyn Douglas were a couple marooned in the strange house, and Charles Laughton played a self-made business man.*

Above: *Bela Lugosi as Dr Mirakle, having trouble with his ape in* **Murders in the Rue Morgue** *(1932). Universal retained little of Edgar Allan Poe's story beyond having the heroine's mother's body pushed up a chimney!*

57

Ghouls and ghosts

James Whale followed *Frankenstein* with *The Old Dark House* (1932), transforming J. B. Priestley's novel *Benighted* into something its creator would hardly have recognized. Derived more essentially from such twenties movies as *The Cat and the Canary* (1927), the film transports half a dozen characters marooned by floods to a curious house in the Welsh mountains inhabited by a dumb and malevolent butler (Karloff), a centenarian baronet (played by an elderly woman, Elspeth Dudgeon, although John Dudgeon is the name on the credits) and a mad arsonist; Ernest Thesiger as the master of the house presides, and Thesiger's usual line, that of a sweetly demented academic, makes him seem a model of normality in comparison.

The visitors include a young Melvyn Douglas, and a Charles Laughton still making his way as a screen actor and in rich form here as a self-made Lancashire businessman. Legal difficulties kept the film off the screen for many years. On its recent reappearance it looked better than ever – shot through with ironic comedy and an ingenuous delight in the grotesque.

Other studios were quick to follow Universal's lead: 1932 was also the year of Paramount's version of *Dr Jekyll and Mr Hyde*, of MGM's *Freaks* and *The Mask of Fu Manchu*, and of RKO's *The Most Dangerous Game*, all of them fantasies in their widely differing ways. This *Dr Jekyll and Mr Hyde*, directed by Rouben Mamoulian, is much the best of the surviving versions of the story and, unless some miracle brings back Murnau's 1920 film, is likely to remain so. As always with Mamoulian, the film looks magnificent – a totally convincing panorama of Victorian London, marvelously shot by the great cameraman Karl Struss. It has Fredric March in the dual role, displaying as Hyde a ferocity that owes far more to the actor than to the make-up (and is worlds away from the serenity that was the actor's normal stock in trade); it includes a splendid slut played by Miriam Hopkins as the girl Hyde kills; and it displays Mamoulian's novel approach, beginning with a subjective camera sequence, with the audience as Jekyll's eyes, that had many imitators.

The Mask of Fu Manchu is a rather stiffly directed film (credited to

Below left: *Fredric March and Miriam Hopkins in Rouben Mamoulian's version of **Dr Jekyll and Mr Hyde** (1932). A staple of popular cinema ever since the Selig Polyscope company made the first version back in 1908, the story provided great roles for Conrad Veidt, John Barrymore, Fredric March and Spencer Tracy. March's performance won him a share in the Best Actor Award that year, with Wallace Beery equally honored for **The Champ.***

Right: *March drains the potion to convince the sceptical Lanyon (Holmes Herbert), out of shot, that Jekyll and Hyde are the same. (When Hollywood wanted sturdy common sense, Herbert, an English actor who had been a romantic lead in the silents, was usually there to answer the call.)*

Inset below: *A tense moment for Boris Karloff and Gloria Stuart in **The Old Dark House** released in 1932.*

Charles Brabin, but in fact partly the work of Charles Vidor), but has a performance of gloating relish from Karloff as the megalomaniac Chinaman, and one to match it from Myrna Loy as Fu Manchu's daughter, enthusiastically devoted to love and torture alike. This is a film of joyful wickedness, owing almost everything to the actors, and lucky to slip through in those final years of lax censorship.

Beauties, beasts and freaks

Freaks is the most bizarre of all Tod Browning's creations – and his masterpiece. It is the story of a group of fairground freaks, played in the main by real freaks, who wear their deformity with a touching pride. The film tells the story of a heartless jest played upon a midget (Harry Earles) by a callous trapeze artiste (former silent star Olga Baclanova) and her strong-man lover. In a terrible climax the whole company of freaks creeps and slithers across the dark fairground to take a macabre vengeance; Baclanova is by some unholy alchemy translated to a freak herself – half-woman, half-chicken.

Beside this, *The Most Dangerous Game* is a piece of healthy outdoor exercise, with a crazed hunter (Leslie Banks) pursuing his human quarry (Joel McCrea) through the *King Kong* jungle. The two films were made back-to-back on the RKO lot, with Ernest B. Schoedsack, co-director of *Kong*, in charge of the lesser movie too, and Robert Armstrong bravely acting away in both with co-star Fay Wray, never one to be daunted by man or beast.

The glory of Schoedsack and Merian C. Cooper's *King Kong* (1933) remains undimmed by the years. The screen's most familiar story needs no retelling. The film is the kind of triumph that only the studio system, with its technical resources and its array of attendant experts, could produce – the stop-motion animation of the old master Willis O'Brien, ingenious process photography, Murray Spivack's astonishing sound effects and Max Steiner's lively score. In addition, *Kong* is a marvelously structured film. There is a quiet

Top: *Claude Rains in James Whale's* **The Invisible Man** *(1933). A stage actor in his mid-forties at the time of this, his film debut, Rains was perhaps the best actor never to win an Academy Award.*
Main picture: *The spikes are nasty enough, but the walls that hold them slide inwards as well. Jean Hersholt is the victim in* **The Mask of Fu Manchu** *(1932).*
Inset right: *Myrna Loy, who started out portraying Oriental villainesses, Charles Starrett and Boris Karloff in a scene from the same film.*

beginning in the city and on the ship, drawn out almost, but not quite, to the point of impatience; then the arrival at the lost island and Kong's appearance, before the pace really quickens with a return to New York. There are just a few moments to gather one's shaken nerves, before being plunged into the effrontery of the final scenes on the Elevated Railroad and the Empire State Building. *King Kong* is thirties film-making at its swaggering best – self-assured and self-sufficient, inviting admiration and commanding belief.

Universal's *The Invisible Man*, directed by James Whale in 1933, would have led the field in most other years. Once again a leading role changed hands at the last minute. Rightly, Boris Karloff thought his voice unsuited to a part that would stand or fall by that, and gave way to Claude Rains, an English stage actor making his first film. Rains' voice has just the right suggestion of edgy nerves and barely controlled threat. John P. Fulton's special effects are smoothly executed without distracting the viewer from the human tragedy; and if the English villagers and their picture-book village are not particularly convincing, it is after all not a movie where reality matters very much. Claude Rains became one of the great character actors.

Tod Browning retired at the end of the thirties, but two of his last films kept his reputation high to the last. *The Mark of the Vampire* (1935) plays a gentle joke on *Dracula*, with Lugosi back in the vampire's cloak, and accompanied by a dark beauty (Carol Borland)

clearly as nefarious as her friend. Browning gives their sequences a gliding, almost balletic poetry that turns out to be entirely suitable, for the pair are eventually revealed as actors, hired to put the fear of God into some poor wretch.

Browning followed up with something better still – *The Devil Doll* (1936). Lionel Barrymore emerges from a long, unjust imprisonment, stumbles upon deranged Henry B. Walthall, the inventor of tiny dolls that carry out orders, and uses the dolls to destroy the men who framed him. Disguised in what looks very like Lon Chaney's old lady outfit from *The Unholy Three* (1925), Barrymore steers the dolls on their deadly missions with ill-concealed glee, while out-sized furniture is ingeniously used to create the necessary illusion.

Above: *Rafaela Ottiano and Lionel Barrymore in Tod Browning's* **The Devil Doll** *(1936). These toys are innocent enough: the lethal ones were actors skilfully photographed against huge props and furniture, the technique used later in* **The Incredible Shrinking Man** *(1957). Browning managed the trick beautifully, and the dolls carried a genuine threat.*

Right: *Bela Lugosi in another Browning classic,* **The Mark of the Vampire** *(1935).*

Bride for a monster

Whale's *The Bride of Frankenstein* (1935) achieves the near impossible – a sequel that is even better than a good original. Karloff's monster gains in pathos as he learns more of the hostile world that surrounds him, and he has an immensely moving scene with O.P. Heggie as a blind hermit who welcomes and entertains him. Elsa Lanchester is Karloff's bride (not Frankenstein's, in spite of the title), and Ernest Thesiger as a sacked university professor (and another creator of living dolls, this time kept safely in glass jars) shows that the gentlemanly way to treat Karloff is the right one, offering him a cigar ("my only weakness") with true old-world courtesy.

There were simply so many films released in the thirties that some of the best slipped by unnoticed, shown as the bottom half of a double bill. One such movie was Edgar G. Ulmer's *The Black Cat* (1934). Much later, Ulmer, a one-time assistant of Murnau who made films in half a dozen countries and languages, including some engaging thirties movies shot in New York in Yiddish, acquired such a considerable reputation as a cult director that *The Black Cat* and other of his early films were properly looked at for the first time.

The Black Cat proved a discovery indeed, and one of the most startlingly original of all thirties films. Set in a castle in Austria, standing over the carnage of a world war battlefield – an inspired invention that lent a feeling of surrounding death to the whole movie – the film brought Karloff and Lugosi together, with Lugosi in a rare sympathe-tic role as a scientist seeking out the man who has stolen his wife and ruined him. Karloff has, in fact, done rather worse than that, and the two play out a deadly contest (with time out for a little Satanism and necrophilia) that has an apocalyptic end, with the flaying of Karloff and the eruption of all the explosives that still mine the foundations of the house. Perhaps this one alone was, genuinely, a horror film. Certainly Ulmer and his cinematographer, John Mescall, who had also shot *The Invisible Man*, gave it a sustained atmosphere of menace that makes it disturbing watching even today.

MGM's *Mad Love*, directed by Karl Freund in 1935, introduced Peter Lorre to the American cinema, and gave him the role of a surgeon who grafts the hands of an executed murderer to the arms of a pianist injured in a train wreck, with results not entirely therapeutic. It was all rather second-hand, being the remake of a 1925 Austrian film that had combined the talents of Robert Wiene, director of *Das Kabinett des Dr Caligari/The Cabinet of Dr Caligari* (1919), and of two great actors, Werner Krauss as the surgeon and Conrad Veidt as the pianist, but few of its thirties audiences had seen the original – *Orlacs Hände/The Hands of Orlac* (1924) – and Freund's version had many merits. He had worked as photographer on many German films of the great years, and here as director made such striking use of distorted shadows and extravagant architecture that his return to photography (he never directed again) seems a curious decision.

Peter Lorre **(above)** makes his Hollywood debut as an extremely sinister surgeon in Karl Freund's **Mad Love** (1935), while **(left)** Frances Drake is put to the torture. Freund's photographic credits included **The Last Laugh** and **Variety** in Germany, **Dracula** and **The Good Earth** in America. Between 1932 and 1935 he directed eight films, but only this one and **The Mummy** fully exploited his visual sense.

Right: Colin Clive, Elsa Lanchester, and Boris Karloff in **The Bride of Frankenstein** (1935).

Few films of the kind were made in the later thirties. By around 1936 the impetus of *Dracula* and the rest seemed exhausted, but still the occasional pleasure came to light. Warners were never considered as one of the main fantasy film studios, but they had had their moments with films like *Doctor X* (1932) and *The Mystery of the Wax Museum* (1933), both directed by Michael Curtiz. The latter was shot in the early two-strip Technicolor that was so successful in creating a threatening ambience.

Now, at the end of the cycle, Curtiz made one of the most impressive of Karloff's films, *The Walking Dead* (1936). As yet another innocent man seeking revenge, Karloff differed from others of the kind in that he actually had been electrocuted and restored to life by the wizardry of scientist Edmund Gwenn. One by one the guilty men die, always with Karloff around, using some sixth sense to ease them gently to their doom. In spite of the many deaths it encompasses, *The Walking Dead* is a quiet and understated film, and none the worse for that.

Outward bound course

Films of pure fantasy, without a touch of horror, are rare in the thirties. *Outward Bound* (1930) is a version of a stage play by Sutton Vane, set on a ship taking the recently dead to an appointment with the Examiner who will decide their destination. There is far too much dialogue just two short years into sound (stage plays were dangerous material in this respect) and a shamefully contrived happy end, but two pieces of good casting help to suspend disbelief. Leslie Howard in his first sound film (his last silent had been in 1920) plays a scapegoat son, now happily reunited with his adoring old mother, with the muted charm that would become famous, while Helen Chandler is a suicide as poignant as could be without a trace of morbid self-pity.

Finally, Paramount and Mitchell Leisen's *Death Takes a Holiday* (1934) provides a lesson in how a stage play should be transferred to the screen. The play, an adaptation from the Spanish by Maxwell Anderson of *Winterset* (1936), was further adapted by Anderson. It has a marvelous subject. Death comes to earth to find out why men fear him so greatly, and what there is in this world that they so much prefer. While Death is thus on holiday, no one can die, whatever illness or accident befalls him. A lesser film would have made a great deal of that. Leisen's skimmed over it lightly; his concerns are with the character of Death and his struggle for understanding, and with the love between Death and a girl who comes to discover who he is.

Fredric March and Evelyn Venable (who never had so rich a part again) played the strange lovers with an overwhelming sincerity; Leisen devised some breathtaking camera movements; the special effects used for March's various appearances were tactfully unsensational; and the whole delicate structure, which one false step could have wrecked, survives harmonious and intact. *Death Takes a Holiday* is forgotten now, but of all thirties films, this is the one that most demands revival.

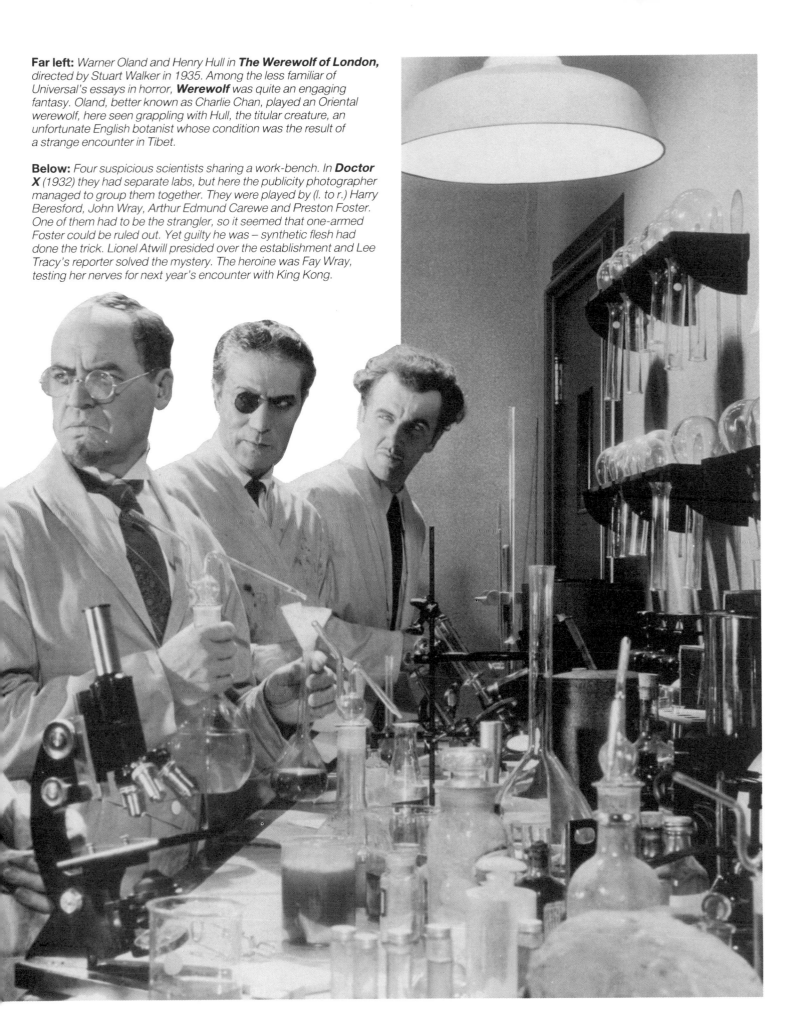

Far left: *Warner Oland and Henry Hull in* **The Werewolf of London,** *directed by Stuart Walker in 1935. Among the less familiar of Universal's essays in horror,* **Werewolf** *was quite an engaging fantasy. Oland, better known as Charlie Chan, played an Oriental werewolf, here seen grappling with Hull, the titular creature, an unfortunate English botanist whose condition was the result of a strange encounter in Tibet.*

Below: *Four suspicious scientists sharing a work-bench. In* **Doctor X** *(1932) they had separate labs, but here the publicity photographer managed to group them together. They were played by (l. to r.) Harry Beresford, John Wray, Arthur Edmund Carewe and Preston Foster. One of them had to be the strangler, so it seemed that one-armed Foster could be ruled out. Yet guilty he was – synthetic flesh had done the trick. Lionel Atwill presided over the establishment and Lee Tracy's reporter solved the mystery. The heroine was Fay Wray, testing her nerves for next year's encounter with King Kong.*

The Great Comedians

Chapter 5

Comedy as the twenties had known it was rudely shaken by the arrival of sound. The three great comedians, Charles Chaplin, Buster Keaton and Harold Lloyd, went down different paths. Chaplin, reluctant to compromise, released two films only in this period, *City Lights* (1931) and *Modern Times* (1936). *City Lights* is a silent film with score and sound effects and is Chaplin's richest work; not so much a comedy as a gentle romance with supremely funny comic interludes, it matches him, for perhaps the only time, with an actress who in her own right could have carried a film, the lovely and gentle Virginia Cherrill (whom Chaplin at one point dropped from the film, before realizing the enormity of his error), and it shows that the silent film could have lived on happily, side by side with sound, if only others too had had the courage to persist.

Modern Times, still speechless apart from announcements and a nonsense song, marks the last appearance of Chaplin's little tramp, and closes a distinguished chapter of history. Inventive as its best passages are, there is a kind of tiredness about the film, a feeling that the moment has arrived when it is time to move on. In the forties Chaplin tackled new, exciting and surprising tasks.

Re-scaling the heights

Harold Lloyd did not hesitate to use the spoken word, but his voice proved flat and solemn, and the "regular fellow" of his great silents lost most of his sparkle as he grew older. Lloyd worked on, with five thirties features to his name, but his character was firmly rooted in the twenties scene, and only when he went back to the purely visual comedy of the climbing sequence in *Feet First* (1930) or the adventure of the moving tent in *Professor Beware* (1938) did something of the old zest come through.

Buster Keaton in the thirties was the saddest of figures. He had already lost his battle with MGM to retain complete control of his films; now personal problems hastened his decline. Until 1933 the studio still starred him in features, but good slapstick stuff though they were, anyone could have done them as well as Keaton did, and he sank to two-reel shorts and cameo appearances. The only genuine Keaton film of the thirties, *Le Roi des Champs-Elysées* (1934), was made in France. Far ahead, however, lay recovery, and a fuller recognition of Keaton's genius than the twenties had known.

The one silent comedian to relish and gain immeasurably by the coming of sound was W.C. Fields. That unmelodious, grating drawl added the last perfect touch to Fields's character – the rancorous, self-centered and self-deluding loner at odds with family, society and the world. Fields's thirties comedies never missed. In one year alone, 1934, he had three of his greatest successes: *The Old Fashioned Way*, a delicious period piece in the course of which Fields gleefully booted the obnoxious Baby LeRoy out of the room; *Mrs Wiggs of the*

*Cary Grant and Irene Dunne in Leo McCarey's **The Awful Truth** (1937). McCarey won the Best Director Oscar for the film.*

Below: *Harpo Marx and friend in* **Animal Crackers** *(1930). This was the Brothers' second film, made cheaply – and somewhat shoddily – at Paramount's Eastern studio at Astoria, Long Island. It was really just an appetizing hint of glories to come.*

Main picture: *Charles Chaplin and Virginia Cherrill in* **City Lights** *(1931). Chaplin spent three years and two months on this, his masterpiece. The scene shown here, the Tramp's first meeting with the blind flower girl, proved the hardest of all to complete, takes and retakes going on for months. The result was ample reward.*

Far right: *Chico and Groucho Marx in some devious skulduggery in* **Monkey Business** *(1931), the team's first Hollywood film.*

Cabbage Patch, when he appeared for the last half hour to enjoy the cooking of ZaSu Pitts ("More meat," he demands, with the air of a man just glimpsing paradise); and his masterpiece, *It's a Gift.* There have been few darker comedies than this. Fields's tribulations are even more painful than usual (the opening sequence as he vainly seeks sleep on his balcony is almost sadistic), and his relations with his dreadful family more fraught; the final escape to the orange grove in California seems merely to promise a temporary release. In *It's a Gift* a great clown touched the edge of tragedy.

Brothers in anarchy

The Marx Brothers at their best contrived a perfect blending of silent and sound techniques. Their first five films, from *The Cocoanuts* (1929) to *Duck Soup* (1933) were made for Paramount. That these films were their best was once accepted as an article of faith. Certainly Groucho's outrageous dialogue is at its most uninhibited here, and Harpo's visual punning and disordered logic attain a surreal intensity, but, and especially at the beginning, the production values were shoddy, Chico's function as an almost sane bridge between Groucho and Harpo is not fully developed and there is always poor Zeppo trying to justify his existence with a bland song or some half-hearted love-making. *Duck Soup* is far better than the other Paramount movies for it has a first-rate comedy director, Leo McCarey, and a less ramshackle plot.

The Brothers' move to MGM may not have promised well, but it came off splendidly. *A Night at the Opera* (1935) and *A Day at the Races* (1937), both directed by Sam Wood, are filled to the brim with joyous invention. Production is lavish, plots strong; Chico has some of the finest moments, and rises to them, and Allan Jones acts and sings a great deal better than Zeppo. Most of the cherished Marx memories come from these two films. *Opera* has the crowded cabin, the discussion over the contract, and the football game across the opera house, with the orchestra conned into a spirited rendering of "Take Me Out to the Ball Game". *Races* has Chico selling Groucho the form books and the breeding guides, Chico and Harpo and their ice-cream stall, and Groucho dumping his watch in the water ("Better rusty than missing"). It was all downhill after that, but the boys had done enough.

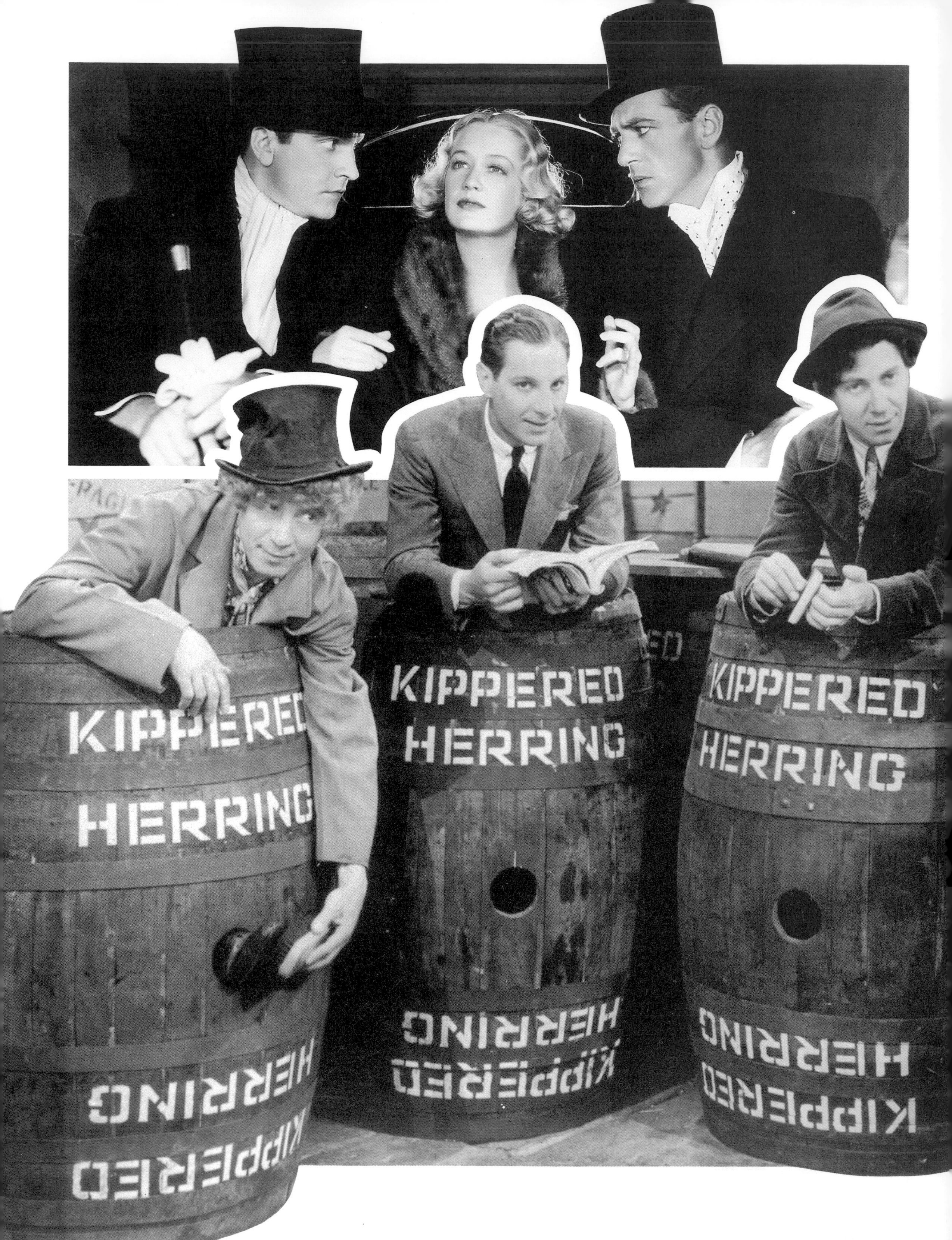
KIPPERED
HERRING
KIPPERED
HERRING
KIPPERED
HERRING

Main picture: *The stowaways and their hiding place. Harpo, Zeppo, Chico and Groucho in* **Monkey Business** *(1931).*

Left: *Fredric March, Miriam Hopkins and Gary Cooper in Ernst Lubitsch's* **Design for Living** *(1933).*

Below: *ZaSu Pitts, Jimmy Butler and W. C. Fields in* **Mrs Wiggs of the Cabbage Patch** *(1934). Fields is doomed to disappointment. He thinks Pitts is a magnificent cook, and marries her, little realizing that his meals arrive via a grinning Jimmy Butler.*

Memories of the comedies that Joe E. Brown made for Warners are much fainter – not Brown's fault, for these movies have rarely been revived. One at least should come back, the baseball farce *Alibi Ike* (1935). This has a story by Ring Lardner and a frenzied energy. Brown was a master of mugging and of comic timing, and it is sad that he should now be known simply for his occasional ventures, brilliant as they were, into prestige productions in supporting roles. The amorous millionaire of *Some Like It Hot* (1959) had been a star in his own right once.

These were the comedians, but there were other kinds of thirties comedy in which the comedians did not appear. In the polished, sophisticated comedy of manners the thirties excelled. They had much to build on, for the twenties had seen Chaplin (in *A Woman of Paris,* 1923), Lubitsch (in *The Marriage Circle* and *Lady Windermere's Fan,* 1925) and others raise the form to a delicate precision that the harsh intrusion of sound may have seemed to threaten. But Lubitsch himself, with *Trouble in Paradise* (1932), was there to show the way, and this delectable, entirely amoral comedy of two charming jewel thieves (Herbert Marshall and Miriam Hopkins) and their equally charming victim (Kay Francis) was an unflawed joy.

Marshall was cast too often as a stiffly respectable type, but here he showed an engaging lightness of touch; Hopkins was always twice the actress with this director than with anyone else, and the supremely ladylike Francis brought an ironic edge to all her poised elegance. This was a comedy of deceptive appearances, and Lubitsch makes the point succinctly in his opening shot. A Venetian gondolier sings romantically, and the camera cuts away to show that his gondola is a garbage scow. A lovely running gag makes the same point, with Edward Everett Horton, who has glimpsed Marshall at work, meeting him again and again, each time making desperate attempts to recall where he saw him before. *Design for Living* (1933) also paired Hopkins and Horton, but Noel Coward's play was intractable material, and although scenarist Ben Hecht claimed that one line only of Coward's survived, even Lubitsch couldn't turn it into cinema, despite a cast including Gary Cooper and Fredric March.

"Capra-corn"

Frank Capra gave the romantic comedy a different outlook. Lubitsch's characters would have caught the eye anywhere; Capra's could have lived next door, except that some of them were rather rich. His first thirties hit, *Platinum Blonde* (1931), is a familiar tale of an honest reporter dazzled for a while by a rich girl but coming back in the end to fellow-journalist Loretta Young. The rich girl is played by a young and uncertain Jean Harlow; the reporter by Robert Williams, a gifted leading man who died tragically young. Capra showed that he had learned to undercut the flippancy with a feeling for genuine emotion that was never forced or sentimental.

The ending of *Platinum Blonde* is essential Capra. Williams is consoling Young, who had thought she had lost him: "There, there, Gallagher," he says, "there, there." A trite enough line, but the way it is delivered makes you remember it for ever.

Capra's *It Happened One Night* (1934) is more famous and more familiar. Reporter and rich girl again, with ebullient Claudette Colbert, Clark Gable perfect as the tough, sceptical reporter, and one of the thirties' sublime character players, the querulous, choleric Walter Connolly, as Colbert's much abused father. The wayward adventure fairly bounced along, with the people encountered on the way an unfailing delight. Roscoe Karns was at his most hollowly ingratiating as a traveling man trying his charm on Colbert, with Ward Bond as a hot-tempered bus-driver coming a close second. The film swept up numerous Oscars.

In *You Can't Take It with You* (1938) Capra's eccentrics leave the margins to fill the screen. This is a fairytale of a feckless household with Lionel Barrymore at its head and accumulating a lifetime of unpaid tax demands. Spring Byington churns out unactable plays, Ann Miller practises ballet under the tuition of Mischa Auer, Donald Meek meets Barrymore by chance and moves in to make toys, and the ultra-dignified Halliwell Hobbes makes fireworks in the basement. And Jean Arthur is the one sane member, captivating the audience every bit as much as rich James Stewart.

Master of screwball

Preston Sturges directed some of the forties' most sparkling comedies, but in the thirties he was a scriptwriter, and in *Easy Living* (1937) provides director Mitchell Leisen with the material for one of those movies that in such days of wealth seemed like just one of countless carefree pleasures; on re-viewing now it amazes with its pace, control and featherlight daintiness of touch. Tycoon Edward

Left: *Jean Harlow in one of her first starring roles in Frank Capra's* **Platinum Blonde** *(1931).*

Two contrasting shots from **You Can't Take it With You** *(1938).* **Inset far left** *Ann Miller displays her balletic skills, rich visitor James Stewart is amused and sister Jean Arthur beams with pride. Meanwhile,* **below,** *Scottish character actor Donald Meek poses for a publicity shot. Somewhere along the line the ape bit the dust; there is no trace of him in the finished film. Nervous little Meek contributed richly to many a thirties film;* **Stagecoach** *(1939) and* **Young Mr Lincoln** *(1939) perhaps contained the finest Meek cameos.*

This page: *Alice Brady as hostess and Mischa Auer as simian guest, in Universal's* **My Man Godfrey** *(1936). After a brilliant stage career and some silent films, Alice Brady in the thirties was a versatile character player. She won an Oscar for* **In Old Chicago** *in 1938, and in her last film,* **Young Mr Lincoln** *in 1939, was outstanding as the accused boy's mother.*

Far right: *Carole Lombard, Roscoe Karns (above), John Barrymore and Walter Connolly in Howard Hawks'* **Twentieth Century** *(1934). Thinking that Barrymore is dying, Lombard at last signs a theatrical contract. Connolly and Karns, driven to distraction by the temperamental duo, envisage peace at last*

Arnold hurls a fur coat from a high window. It falls on working girl Jean Arthur – how many of the great comedies revolved round that fair head, wide eyes and husky voice? – setting up a delightfully complicated chain of events. At one point Arthur is shown into, and presented with, a luxury hotel suite. She looks at all the opulence without a word. Left alone, she sinks down and breathes "Golly!"

Comedies like *Easy Living* began as comedies of character, but often shaded off into the kind of zany farce that was called "crazy" or "screwball" comedy at the time. Gregory La Cava was a notable practitioner in this line, with *The Half Naked Truth* (1932) and *My Man Godfrey* (1936). The first of these, a ribald and unashamed riot set in Manhattan theaterland, has Lee Tracy in his non-stop-talking act as a press agent, flustered Frank Morgan as an impresario blackmailed by Tracy – who arranges for compromising photographs of Morgan and the luscious Lupe Velez to crop up in all kinds of surprising places – and the morose and massive Eugene Pallette as Tracy's assistant,

who, in a running gag worthy of Lubitsch, everyone in the movie comes to believe is a eunuch. *My Man Godfrey* sends scatterbrained rich girl Carole Lombard on a treasure hunt. Her treasure is William Powell, a gentleman down-and-out whom Lombard finds sleeping rough and introduces to her household as a butler. The debonair Powell straightens the family out in no time – what with a manic Mischa Auer prone to sit on the mantelpiece imitating an ape, it needed doing.

Carole Lombard had already shown that she was a great comic actress in Howard Hawks's *Twentieth Century* (1934). This astonishing film, which bewildered its first audiences by the sheer extravagance of its invention, is an abiding masterpiece. John Barrymore plays Oscar Jaffe, theater producer and egomaniac, who grooms Lombard to stardom, has her run out on him for Hollywood, finds her again in Chicago, and in the course of the journey back to New York on the Twentieth Century express, traps her into a return. Hawks let loose wispy little Etienne Girardot as a gentle lunatic plastering the train with religious stickers, spluttering Herman Bing as a fugitive from the Oberammergau Passion Play, Karns and Connolly as Barrymore's tormented entourage. Barrymore makes his penniless getaway from Chicago disguised as a Southern colonel, seizes on the Passion Play idea to offer Lombard the role of Mary Magdalen – she is not impressed – and has her back in the end, slavishly treading the chalk lines he draws on the stage floor, a puppet on the master's strings.

Grant and Hepburn

Hawks's other great thirties comedy, *Bringing Up Baby* (1938), presents a different kind of clash of temperament. Cary Grant is sane, if that is the word for a palaeontologist spending years reconstituting a brontosaurus; Katharine Hepburn the sweet madcap who changes his life. The comedy is serious enough at heart – what happens to Grant's ordered existence is frightening if you stand back to think – but the decorations are an irresistible distraction. Hepburn was at her peak at that time, and Grant approaching his. The way that they struck sparks off one another was something that actors managed with Hawks better than with anyone else. All Hawks's films were really about companionship. Sheer happiness sounds dull; Hawks saw things differently.

Nothing Sacred, directed by William A. Wellman in 1937, was the most mordant comedy of the period. Beautifully shot in the new three-strip Technicolor – which at that time was much brighter and sharper-edged than the subdued naturalism of later color – it has Lombard, wonderfully fey and vulnerable as a girl from Vermont who is believed (mistakenly) to be dying of radium poisoning, Fredric March as the reporter who takes her to town for a last fling and milks the story for every drop of fake emotion, and Charles Winninger as the country doctor whose wrong diagnosis causes all the trouble. Winninger is a man with a low opinion of journalists. "The hand of God," he fumes, "reaching down into the mire, couldn't elevate one of them to the depths of degradation." The film was a savage onslaught that should have made audiences ashamed to read a tabloid again.

But the age had its quieter comedies. Leo McCarey's *Ruggles of Red Gap* (1935) was among the best of them. Charles Laughton was perfectly cast as the suave English butler marooned in the mid-West as the result of a bet his master has made with roughneck Charles Ruggles. Roland Young, master of underplaying and the ideal foil to Laughton, is the master in question, ZaSu Pitts and Mary Boland flutter happily around, and the film comes to a splendid climax, using Laughton's superb delivery to marvelous effect, when the actor quietens and conquers the locals with his recital of Lincoln's Gettysburg Address. It took all the thirties' arrogance to believe they could get away with that. And of course they did.

*A master must always live up to his butler's standards. In **Ruggles of Red Gap** (1935), Charles Laughton (left) indicates the need for further drastic measures, while Charles Ruggles makes the best of it. Laughton gave perhaps his finest screen performance in this film, the third of four versions of a perennial American favorite.*

Above: *Clark Gable and Claudette Colbert urgently in need of a lift in* **It Happened One Night** *(1934). Colbert manages it, in one of the thirties' most fondly remembered scenes. The film collected all four major Oscars: Best Film, Best Director, Best Actor and Best Actress, a feat not matched until 1975.*

Below: *Cary Grant and Katharine Hepburn in the restaurant scene from* **Bringing Up Baby** *(1938). Hepburn's spectacular dress has suffered a revealing rip; Grant's embarrassment, and his efforts to cope, are a delight to watch.*

Main picture: *Will Rogers as steamboat captain and Berton Churchill as river-bank prophet in John Ford's* **Steamboat Round the Bend** *(1935).*
Below: *Humphrey Bogart is a one-man picket-line (aided by the dog) in* **Stand-in** *(1937). In a rare appearance in comedy, Bogart played Douglas Quintain, a producer driven to drink by his studio's troubles.*

Far right: **Ruggles of Red Gap,** *with the impeccable Charles Laughton a little under the influence. In the thirties players like Arthur Treacher and Robert Greig could make a living playing butlers: Laughton did it this once, and outshone them all. That fine comedian Edward Everett Horton had played Ruggles in the 1923 version, directed by James Cruze.*

Crackerbarrel philosopher

Will Rogers, vaudeville star, wry philosopher, and incarnation of the common man, died in an air crash in 1935. Rogers had had limited success in silent films, but like Fields he was one to gain enormously from sound. He needed the soft burr of his voice, the anecdotes, the easy, unmalicious wit. The last three years of his life were the years of his finest films. Henry King's *State Fair* (1933) was by far the best of the three versions Fox made of the story, and one of the all-time charmers. King was a master of Americana, quietly recording the small pleasures and the passing sadness of a way of life that was passing too. This story of a country family's visit, prize pig in tow, to the fair was beautifully cast (Rogers and Louise Dresser as the parents, Janet Gaynor and Norman Foster as their children, Lew Ayres as Gaynor's suitor) and superbly shot by Hal Mohr.

After this Rogers made three films for another director who loved the feel of the small American town – John Ford. *Dr Bull* (1933) was not strictly comedy – it was the story of a local doctor in Connecticut and his fight against an epidemic – but still revolved round Rogers' character, and his shrewd humors kept breaking through. *Judge Priest* (1934) had him down in Kentucky playing the little judge Billy Priest in a film that Ford would later remake, with much the same themes and characters, as *The Sun Shines Bright* (1953). Star and director showed an uncanny affinity, and in 1935 their last film together, *Steamboat Round the Bend*, was in its own right a

masterpiece. Rogers sells his medicine show to buy an old Mississippi steamboat, installs a wax museum, shelters a swamp girl touchingly played by Anne Shirley, and finally, in a sustained comedy sequence involving burning waxworks and patent medicines alike to squeeze out the last ounce of steam, discovers the missing witness, a vagrant prophet, who can save his nephew from a hanging. While *Steamboat* was being shot, Fox merged with Twentieth Century, and Ford claimed that the new management, eager to make an impression, cut out most of his comedy. But directors are not always the best guides to their own work, and one may well feel that the film's balance of comedy, drama and peaceful contemplation is just about right.

And there were others. Alfred E. Green's *The Dark Horse* (1932) was only a B-movie that rolled off the Warners production line, but it was that rarity, a political comedy. Publicist Warren William's attempts to promote an honest but entirely stupid Guy Kibbee for Governor ("Every time he opens his mouth he subtracts from the total sum of human knowledge") provided an hour of devious skulduggery and biting wit. Green also made *Baby Face* (1934), in which Barbara Stanwyck goes from rags to riches by offering her favors, rising floor by floor, to what seemed half the personnel of an enormous bank. Viewed seriously, this was a trashy melodrama; taken as a very dark comedy, which Green's camera rising gently up the bank's façade suggested it should be, it was a malevolent joy.

Below: *Irene Dunne and Melvyn Douglas in Richard Boleslawski's* **Theodora Goes Wild** *(1936). This was one of the first of the screwball comedies which were immensely popular in the later thirties.* **Bottom:** *Jean Harlow is unimpressed by Lee Tracy's latest piece of artwork in* **Bombshell** *(1933). Victor Fleming directed with enormous verve.* **Right:** *Constance Bennett and Roland Young in* **Topper** *(1937). Bennett and Cary Grant played ghosts who can only reach Heaven if they can point to a good deed; the deed is teaching Young, as Topper, how to enjoy life.* **Far right:** *Spencer Tracy in* **Libeled Lady,** *directed by Jack Conway in 1936. An heiress sued a newspaper for five million dollars; MGM deserved to make as much with this brilliant comedy.*

That's showbiz

The show-business comedy was usually musical, but it could be straight, when it liked to draw its fun from temperamental stars. Two such were Leslie Howard and Bette Davis in Archie L. Mayo's *It's Love I'm After* (1937). They played a quarrelling stage team, long engaged but frightened of the plunge, who took their feelings onstage with them, peppering their rendering of *Romeo and Juliet* with sotto – and not so sotto – voce insults. With Eric Blore always in attendance to stoke up the fires, this one was a brilliantly sustained comic tour de force, and Howard must have enjoyed it a great deal more than he had the year before, when he played Romeo in earnest in MGM's staid middle-aged romance.

In *Stand In* (1937) the movie business poked fun at itself. Leslie Howard's vein of studious puzzlement was just right for the role of Atterbury Dodd, a New York efficiency expert sent to examine the workings of an ailing studio. Aided by Joan Blondell as a stand-in who becomes his secretary, Howard routs the crooked tycoons, rescues producer Humphrey Bogart from the bottle, and puts the studio on its feet, with Bogart ensuring the success of its latest opus by cutting glamor girl Marla Shelton out of the movie and restructuring it round a gorilla. Blondell was her perky, delightful self, but Shelton had the film's great moment, helplessly drunk and sliding so, so slowly under the table during a vital discussion.

But the classic film of Hollywood self-mockery was *Bombshell* (1933). Jean Harlow, two years on from *Platinum Blonde* and now a polished performer, plays a star who has to endure the full blast of the studio's publicity machine, Lee Tracy runs that machine with a ruthless fury, and the movie never loses a chance to bite the hand that feeds it. In a beautiful piece of plotting, a group of aristocrats with whom Harlow is involved turn out to be hard-up actors hired by Tracy, and the most aristocratic of them all, dear old C. Aubrey Smith, is caught lamenting that back at the studio Lewis Stone gets all the good old man parts.

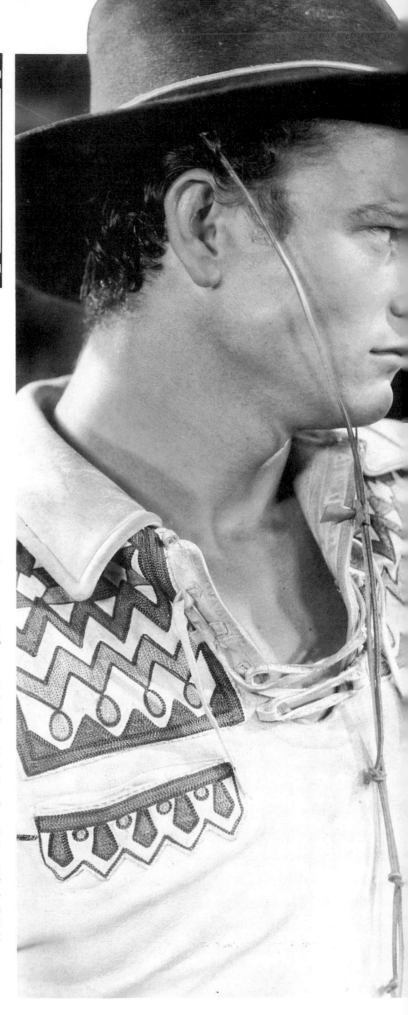

The Rough Side of Life

Chapter 6

One of the cinema's great staples, the Western, was hardly prominent in the thirties. At the beginning, perhaps, that was not surprising. Difficulties of sound recording in the open took time to surmount; studios wanted to exploit the spoken word, and the cowboy was seldom a loquacious man. But as early as 1930 two directors, Raoul Walsh with *The Big Trail* and King Vidor with *Billy the Kid*, showed that it could be done. Walsh's film was in *The Covered Wagon* tradition, an episodic, spectacular production about the pioneers on the Oregon trail. It starred a very young, very raw John Wayne, who went on to a long apprenticeship in B-Westerns before his career took off with *Stagecoach* in 1939. Vidor's film, too, if not among his best, was a workmanlike job, steadily unsentimental, but a shade hampered by the uncharismatic John Mack Brown and Wallace Beery (and incidentally, one of the first films to be shown, in suitable theaters, in 70mm wide format, an innovation too expensive at that time to follow up).

But curiously, that was virtually that. Although minor Westerns were made in abundance, there was only one considered to be of any real importance, Cecil B. De Mille's *The Plainsman* (1936), between the beginning and the end of the decade.

A pacifist masterpiece

The war film was also infrequent in the thirties, but those that did emerge were uncommonly good. Lewis Milestone's *All Quiet on the Western Front* (1930) seemed to be one of the great ones in its time, and the years have taken nothing from it. For all the horror of its setting, *All Quiet* was a film of restraint, its most moving moments isolated from the mindless turmoil around. The idyllic pause with the French girls, the scenes of Lew Ayres's leave with his mother in Berlin, the off-duty scenes of the soldiers unsentimentally talking of war and peace, Ayres with the dying French soldier in the shellhole, the butterfly and the quiet, unnoticed death, all these and more went to make a film of intense humanity and understanding. *All Quiet* was a film that dared to see a war from the enemy's point of view, and a film that said, uncompromisingly, that all war was hideous and wrong.

No thirties film saw war as heroic. *The Dawn Patrol* was made twice, by Howard Hawks in 1930 and by Edmund Goulding in 1938. *Hell's Angels*, directed by Howard Hughes, had taken the headlines and the public's fancy in 1930, but Hawks's far less spectacular film was infinitely better. It concentrated on the officers of one squadron, with Neil Hamilton as the commanding officer who has to sit and watch his flyers die. It was a film about professionalism, always one of Hawks's concerns, but also a film about the misery of waste, as gray and undramatic as the theme demanded. Goulding's version fell little short. Basil Rathbone was excellent in the Hamilton role, but Errol Flynn's stock portrayal of a jaunty devil-may-care was a little distant from the mood of the rest.

*John Wayne and Tyrone Power, Snr, in **The Big Trail** (1930). Wayne had played a few bit parts only when director Raoul Walsh gave him this first real chance.*

Left: *Jean Arthur as Calamity Jane in* **The Plainsman** *(1936). This was one of the decade's most curious pieces of casting, and in this publicity still Arthur doesn't look too happy about it. But her sheer professionalism won through.*

Main picture: *Wallace Beery and John Mack Brown in* **Billy The Kid.**

Right: *Richard Barthelmess helps David Manners from their wrecked aircraft in **The Last Flight** (1931). Audiences expecting, from the title and stills like this, an action drama found themselves facing something very different. The film soon vanished. Only in the seventies did it reappear, and its impact was astonishing. A masterpiece came into its own.*

Not a war film but a film on the consequences of war was *The Last Flight* (1931). Another film that had to wait years for full recognition, this was the story of four flyers so damaged mentally and physically by the war that they cannot return home, staying in Paris and drifting from woman to woman, bar to bar. Not all survive. This was a film that spoke for a lost generation, a film that shunned pity as wholly as it did censure, preferring to watch and understand.

Zoo time

Crime, fantasy, musicals, comedy, Westerns, war films – these fit into their compartments easily enough. But one of the most striking aspects of the thirties was the sheer variety of the movies. The rest of this chapter is a random list of films that defy classification, but are an essential part of the decade's cinema history. Was there ever another movie, for instance, like Rowland V. Lee's *Zoo in Budapest* (1933)? The story takes place in one day, featuring a romance between zoo-keeper Gene Raymond and orphanage girl Loretta Young, ravishing photography from Lee Garmes, and a climax in the zoo at night with Young and Raymond, each a fugitive from an oppressive authority, being hunted down, and a frenzy of escaping animals pointing the moral that we are all prisoners until we break our bonds.

Another unique film was *The Power and the Glory* (1933). This consists of a series of intricate flashbacks with a probing commentary about the secret truths behind the life story of a great railroad magnate (Spencer Tracy). The film leaps back and forth across the years, the dead of one sequence are young again in the next, the narrator – the magnate's friend – sets moment against moment to build the whole sad mosaic of a life. Perhaps, after all, there was another movie like that. They made it eight years later, and called it *Citizen Kane*.

Every man's home...

The thirties had time, too, for the people at the bottom of the heap. The director Frank Borzage carried the unabashed lyricism of his silents across into the new medium in *A Man's Castle* (1933), where Spencer Tracy and Loretta Young are living through the Depression in a ruined shack on waste ground in New York, and *Little Man, What Now?* (1934) a love story set in depressed post-war Germany. There was no finer director of actresses than Borzage, and actresses like Janet Gaynor and Margaret Sullavan, who played some of their first and finest roles for him, carried over the loving serenity they had learned from him to their films for other directors. Sullavan was heart-breaking in *Little Man, What Now?* and no less so in Borzage's *Three Comrades* (1938), where his lovers are caught in the storms of rising Nazism in Germany. In *No Greater Glory* (1934) Borzage uses the battles of two gangs of street kids to make his anti-war moral; this was so powerful an indictment that some European countries, busily re-arming, took fright and banned it outright.

Another director, King Vidor, who had always shown sympathy with the small people of the world, made one of the most unexpected of Hollywood movies in *Our Daily Bread* (1934), the story of an agricultural co-operative in the New Deal's early days, and a film that brought to its climax – the irrigation of the hard-won land – an urgent and passionate joy. In these films Hollywood was far indeed from the dream factory of legend.

Borzage and Vidor were film-makers carried by the sheer force of their commitment. At another pole stood William Wyler, a craftsman who strained his players' patience with take after take until he had the result he wanted, but a craftsman of taste and intelligence, too. His *Dead End* has been discussed already. That was a filmed play, beautifully opened up for cinema, and the filmed play was Wyler's specialty. He turned Elmer Rice's *Counsellor-at-Law* (1933), the story of a high-powered attorney who comes to the verge of disbarment and suicide, into a compact and energetic film, with a towering performance from John Barrymore and a touching one from Bebe Daniels. In *These Three* (1936), a version of Lillian Hellman's play *The Children's Hour*, Wyler scored a notable victory over the censors and their code. The play had dealt with a supposed lesbian relationship between two teachers, as did the second film version in 1962, also directed by Wyler. In 1936, this had to go. Substituting a heterosexual triangle, Wyler left the play's charge – the destructive effects of scandal-mongering – intact, drew a portrait of a malevolent child (Bonita Granville) that had a lethal intensity, and gave Miriam Hopkins, the thirties' most underrated actress, the part of her career as the odd-girl-out of the triangle.

For *Dodsworth* (1936) Wyler turned to a novel by Sinclair Lewis. It was a film of quiet character-building, marvelously played by Walter Huston as the retired motor-manufacturer whose trip to Europe changes his life, by Ruth Chatterton, startlingly honest as the selfish and unfaithful wife, and by Mary Astor as the tranquil woman to whom Dodsworth turns. The last passage of the film, with Huston coming back across the bay to an Astor who thinks she has lost him, had a sudden surge of emotion that caught one by the throat, especially as it came from a director normally so unassertive.

Far left: *Wallace Beery, as Pat Garrett, confronts John Mack Brown in* **Billy The Kid** *(1930).*

Below: *Lew Ayres in* **All Quiet on the Western Front** *(1930). Perhaps in part through his involvement in this pacifist masterpiece, Ayres himself became a conscientious objector in World War II. Here he prepares to defend his shelter. A moment later he stabs a French soldier, and through the night has to watch him die. The Frenchman was played by silent comedian Raymond Griffith.*

Main picture: *Loretta Young in **Zoo in Budapest** (1933). The shot gives an idea of the visual splendor of this astonishing film.*

Left: *Helen Chandler, Walter Byron and Richard Barthelmess in **The Last Flight** (1931). This film, apart from a few German-language versions of other men's work, was the American début of German director William Dieterle, the man who, along with Michael Curtiz, set the pattern for Warners in the thirties.*

Right: *David Niven, Michael Brooke and Errol Flynn in the 1938 remake of **The Dawn Patrol**. This was a rare light-hearted moment in a film that, like the Hawks' original, looked at the war in the air with pity and pain.*

Headline material

Other thirties films of distinction stemmed from the stage. Lewis Milestone's *The Front Page* (1931) was from a play by Ben Hecht and Charles MacArthur, refilmed later by both Howard Hawks and Billy Wilder. Hawks and Wilder refashioned the piece to suit their own concerns, and gloriously so. Milestone left it relatively undisturbed, while doing justice to its savage cynicism and cut-throat wit. This was a newspaper film that made *Five Star Final* look benevolent.

Stage Door (1937) was from a play by Edna Ferber and George S. Kaufman, but arrived on the screen much rewritten, and almost certainly improved, by Morrie Ryskind, Anthony Veiller of *Winterset* and director Gregory LaCava. It tells the story of a group of actresses in a theatrical boarding house, has scathing dialogue (the sharpest darts delivered by Ginger Rogers and Eve Arden), a glowing performance from Katharine Hepburn as a society girl fighting for stage success, with a final speech, when she gets there, whose every intonation still echoes in the mind ("the calla lilies are in bloom again – such a strange flower..."), and a small part of a young, failed actress played by a newcomer, Andrea Leeds, with a dreaming, rapt intensity. Unhappily, Miss Leeds stayed in films for a short four years, had no other part that mattered, and retired to marry a millionaire.

Stage Door was the best film ever made about the theater. William A. Wellman's *A Star Is Born* (1937) did as much for the movies. This story had already been filmed by George Cukor in 1932 (as *What Price Hollywood?*), and Cukor would do it again in 1954 with Judy Garland, but Wellman's version was incomparably the best. With Janet Gaynor as the rising star, Fredric March as the setting one, Lionel Stander in his most venomous form as a brutal publicity man, and Adolphe Menjou all perplexed elegance as the studio chief, this was another superbly acted film, alive with memorable scenes – Gaynor's first meeting with March at the Hollywood Bowl, Stander's callous attack on March at the race-track, and the heartbreaking closing scene when, with March dead, Gaynor faces the crowds at her premiere ("This is Mrs Norman Maine...").

Giants at Fox

The Informer (1935) was also a remake, this time of Arthur Robison's neglected and excellent film of the same title, made in Britain in 1929. Robison was a German director, and Ford's film had a Germanic look about it, too, with its misty streets and flickering lamps, distorted camera angles and acting that verged on the Expressionistic. It had a tremendous central performance from Victor MacLaglen as the dull giant of a man who for a few pounds betrays his comrades (the film comes from Liam O'Flaherty's novel of the Civil War in Ireland), and a script from Dudley Nichols, who wrote *Stagecoach* and other films for Ford, that tinged the squalor and waste with a melancholy poetry.

This side of Ford, which it is now unfashionable to enjoy, had been there in late silents like *Four Sons* and *Hangman's House* (both 1928), and may have owed much to the fact that Ford was working then at Fox alongside the German master F.W. Murnau (*Four Sons*, in fact, uses sets from Murnau's triumphant *Sunrise*, made the year

Two scenes from **Dodsworth** (1936). **Far left:** Ruth Chatterton, who had been a stage star for many years before beginning her short film career in the late twenties. **Dodsworth** was her last American film. She made two more in Britain, and then returned to the stage.

Right: Walter Huston and David Niven (right). Niven played one of Fran Dodsworth's numerous admirers; Ruth Chatterton's brilliant performance made the woman fascinating and appalling at once.

Main picture: Douglass Montgomery and Margaret Sullavan in **Little Man, What Now?** (1934).

Above: *Edward G. Robinson and Boris Karloff in* **Five Star Final** *(1931). Editor Robinson is sending failed clergyman Karloff to dig out more dirt about a murder. The result was two suicides, a family ruined, and a chastened Robinson quitting the tabloids. Crusading films could put an end to a social evil, but this one was here to stay.*

Far right: *Ginger Rogers, Adolphe Menjou and Katharine Hepburn in Gregory La Cava's* **Stage Door** *(1937). A marvelous example of ensemble playing, the film was a perfect demonstration of the strength of the studio system. There were at least a dozen superb parts in this film, and as many more rewarding small ones. The actors were there, all RKO had to do was fit them in. Note the elegant contrasts of the décor, the work of Van Nest Polgase.*

before). Murnau died in a motor accident in 1931, but he had made two films that just fall into the thirties, and showed his powers intact. *City Girl* (1930) was a lyrical romance set in the Oregon wheatfields. Conceived and made by Murnau as a silent film, it suffered indignities at the hands of a studio prepared to make any sacrifice on the altar of sound. *City Girl* was recut, reshot, had comedy added, dialogue superimposed, all by other hands, and after all that, was little shown. The film lay in the vaults for forty years, reappeared in the seventies, with some intrusions removed, and was a revelation. Murnau's feel for wide open spaces, the gentle radiance of his lighting, his way of making a small, private drama into something as timeless as myth: these remained.

Murnau left Fox, set up a partnership with Robert Flaherty, and sailed for the South Seas to make his last film, *Tabu* (1931). Nominally a collaboration, the film is far more Murnau than Flaherty, the documentarist submerged beneath the poet. Still in 1931 a silent film, save for some natural sound and a voice raised here and there in song, *Tabu* was a dance of light and shadow, sunshine and bright water and quiet nights. The actors were natives who had never appeared before a camera, and the story was a simple, sad one, of two lovers parted by the curse of "tabu", of renunciation and a tragic end. Murnau had no time for cinema's eternal South Seas theme of happy islanders corrupted by the white man and his ways. His islanders played their story in their own world and on their own terms. *Tabu* was a thirties masterpiece – and the last, proud defiance of the silent film.

Starburst

Chapter 7

No one, back in the thirties, had yet coined the word "megastar", but the phenomenon was there just the same. MGM, of course, led the way with their slogan "More stars than there are in heaven", and those stars included Greta Garbo and Clark Gable, William Powell and Myrna Loy, Joan Crawford, Norma Shearer, Robert Montgomery and a host of others now among the all-time greats.

The divine Garbo

Effortlessly, Garbo dominated them all. She was not only the finest actress of her time; she was one of the most fortunate. Through all of her American career she made no film away from MGM, and the reward of that loyalty was that she had the best the studio could offer – the best in sets and costumes, a variety of serviceable stories, the camerawork of William Daniels, the direction of Clarence Brown, who made five of her thirties films, and of such fine stylists as Edmund Goulding, George Fitzmaurice, and Rouben Mamoulian. Garbo was always herself, serene, secret, lit from within, but screen acting has always been about being oneself. The camera is a merciless critic of mere impersonation; the great screen actor offers a series of variations on the self, and manages to inhabit those variations with an unshaken belief.

Garbo made 13 films in the decade; they were part of a continuing autobiography. In *Anna Christie* (1930) she speaks for the first time, giving Eugene O'Neill's sad waif her own dignity and pride. *As You Desire Me* (1932) sees her essaying Pirandello, matching his mysteries with her own, and granted a worthy partner in Erich von Stroheim. For *Queen Christina* (1933) she insisted that her old partner John Gilbert, now facing a ruined career, play opposite her. Gilbert justified her faith; the old gaiety returned, a new maturity with it, and he seemed set to re-establish himself. Unhappily Gilbert's personal troubles persisted, and he made only one more film before his death in 1936. With *Anna Karenina* (1935), *Camille* (1936), and *Conquest* (1937), Garbo had three triumphs in a row. Of three very good films the last was perhaps the best, a beautifully mounted and really convincing historical film. She was marvelous as Marie Walewska, Napoleon's Polish love; Charles Boyer was an energetic and extremely human Napoleon; and Maria Ouspenskaya was in terrific form as an old lady who will stand no nonsense from this upstart Frenchman. He has to play cards with her, like a good boy.

The magic of Marlene

Over at Paramount, Marlene Dietrich reigned. Of her first seven American films, six were directed by Josef von Sternberg, whose film *Der Blaue Engel* (*The Blue Angel*, 1930), made in Germany, had

Greta Garbo and Ramon Novarro in George Fitzmaurice's **Mata Hari** *(1932). This was their only film together, and in it Garbo as the glamorous spy performed what* Variety *magazine described as "a polite cooch to Oriental music". But she performed it with pride.*

transformed Dietrich from an actress little known outside her own country into an international star. Seldom have the careers of a star and a director been so closely interwoven. Sternberg's genius was for the pictorial; a master of lighting, as well as of design, he filled his movies with one harmonious, richly decorated composition after another, with the focal point always his star. A lesser actress might have become part of Sternberg's set, as lovely and as lavishly adorned as the rest, living but null. But with Dietrich it was not so. Her personality, mocking, arrogant and sensual, needed to be tamed by Sternberg's delicate artifice, just as his eternal perfectionism cried out for the warmth of his star.

Of their films together, two are masterpieces. *Shanghai Express* (1932) is one of those films where the sheer mastery of the opening sequence (in this case the train weaving its slow way through the crowded chaos of a Chinese town) makes one certain that everything will go well. Quoted and caricatured a hundred times, Dietrich's Shanghai Lily is still a fantastic creation, striking fire from the buttoned-up Englishness of Clive Brook, and making exotic Anna May Wong seem in comparison a mundane little thing. Yet *The Scarlet Empress* (1934), where Dietrich plays Catherine the Great, is even better, with the star marvelously extending her range to embrace the shy girl of the beginning, the passionate empress of the central love affair, and the triumphant Amazon of the climax, riding her white horse up the palace stairway as music, camera and set seem to blend and dissolve into one exultant whirl of delight.

What Katy did next

This was too heady a brew for its first audiences, and the film made very little money. Neither did many of the movies that another great star, Katharine Hepburn, made for RKO. Hepburn at that time just did not fit the popular image of a film star. Strikingly beautiful she was, but her voice was high-pitched, cultured and sharp, her eyes agleam with intelligence. This one was too much her own woman to capture her audiences' affection. In the end, of course, she did, but not until the forties, the move to MGM, and the partnership with Spencer Tracy. Yet to those who did warm to her, the young Hepburn's thirties films were a succession of surprising pleasures. At another studio she might have been groomed into a semblance of convention. At RKO, the studio's weakness for the wayward, and even bizarre, was the very thing needed to engage her formidable talent.

Hepburn's range was astonishing. In *Morning Glory* (1933) she was herself, an ambitious young actress aquiver with high ideals; in *Spitfire* (1934) she became a hoydenish mountain girl; in *Alice Adams* (1935) she was a small town girl with intellectual pretensions; while in *Sylvia Scarlett* (1934) she became a fairground nomad, most of the time disguised as a boy: four different women, yet once again, four variations on a single theme. There was *Stage Door*, too, and *Bringing up Baby*, *Mary of Scotland* (1936), a romanticized account lent conviction by Hepburn's radiant queen, and, on loan to Columbia, *Holiday* (1938). Here she rejoins Cary Grant to play the eccentric daughter of a stuffy family, taking refuge in her room and the company of her two low friends, caustic Jean Dixon and Edward Everett Horton at his bumbling best. It adds up to a wonderful decade for Hepburn, despite the poor box-office, and she entered the forties with one of her best films, *The Philadelphia Story* (1940).

Right: *All that director von Sternberg and Paramount had made of the incomparable Marlene Dietrich went by the board when she crossed to MGM for the musical* **Kismet** *(1944), once described as "a musical looking for a score". Dietrich not only had to endure this outrageous costume; her name was billed below the title for the first time in her Hollywood career.*

Far right: *Katharine Hepburn in* **Christopher Strong** *(1933), directed by Dorothy Arzner. A superior soap-opera, this movie had Hepburn as an aviatrix who deliberately crashes her plane and kills herself because she loves a married man who cannot bear to leave his wife. Arzner was a talented director, but only* **Nana** *(1934) and* **Craig's Wife** *(1936) gave her real chances.*

Ladies in waiting

Garbo, Dietrich, Hepburn – these three had the star quality, the presence, that is as unmistakable as it is impossible to define. But others shone brightly too, if not as intensely, and sometimes not as long. Darkly beautiful and elegant, the patrician Kay Francis was immensely popular in the early thirties, proving that audiences didn't mind your being a lady so long as you weren't intellectual with it. Before Dietrich established herself, Francis was Paramount's leading star, and lucky in her films, with *Ladies' Man* (1931), *Cynara* (1932) and *Trouble in Paradise*, and when she moved to Warners in 1932 she gave her finest performance, in *One Way Passage* (1932). The story of a shipboard romance between a dying woman and a man returning to be executed for murder (William Powell), this should have been mawkish rubbish, but the quality of the playing, the tactful script, and director Tay Garnett's cool refusal to linger on sentiment, make it a triumph. And the movie said it all in just 69 minutes – it was a different world.

Another elegant lady was Norma Shearer, who in 1927 had married Irving Thalberg, MGM's wonder boy and supervisor of production until his death in 1936. This was no unmixed blessing for Shearer. In silent days she had been a charming and witty soubrette; now, with Thalberg behind her, she could pick her parts, and too often picked them in the studio's most prestigious, and dullest, efforts. But she was perfectly cast as Elizabeth Barrett in *The Barretts of Wimpole Street* (1934), acted with a touching restraint, and convinced one that she might have written the poetry (as Fredric March's boisterous Browning singularly did not).

Also at MGM was Joan Crawford, whose urgent portrayals of ambitious working girls were worthy of rather better films. For Crawford, the directors and stories she needed lay ahead. In the thirties, only the occasional *Grand Hotel* (1932) or *The Women* (1939) rose above the routine affairs to which the studio consigned her.

The stars whose forte was sophisticated comedy fared much better, for here the thirties could do no wrong. Claudette Colbert was not everyone's Cleopatra (in the 1934 version), but her effervescence and her irresistible smile carried her happily through almost everything else. Carole Lombard, once Paramount realized her gift for comedy, was fey, scatter-brained and adorable, and after *Twentieth Century* never looked back, while Jean Arthur had the same warmth and sense of fun as Lombard, and a full measure of shrewd realism as well. And by the time the thirties ended, other reputations were being made. Rosalind Russell was developing from the ultra-refinement of her early roles into a comedienne with poise, a way with a line and a ferocious attack; the young Judy Garland was making her way; Ginger Rogers was striking out, without Astaire, as a comedy star in her own right; and Bette Davis at last had the dramatic roles for which she had fought so long. The forties would bring yet more.

Right: *Kay Francis and William Powell in **One Way Passage** (1932). They were a popular team, with seven films together in the early thirties. They matched each other in elegance, sophistication and for quality acting.*

Below: *Rosalind Russell, Joan Fontaine and Norma Shearer in George Cukor's **The Women** (1939). Russell stole the film with an all-out display of predatory, self-centered bitchiness.*

Left: *Ronald Colman and Madeleine Carroll in* **The Prisoner of Zenda** *(1937). The high adventure and high romance of Anthony Hope's much filmed tale were perfectly suited to Colman, but director John Cromwell fared less well. The film was made for independent producer David Selznick, who had additional scenes shot by WS Van Dyke and George Cukor without even consulting Cromwell, fine as Cromwell's work on the film had been. It had to be to keep up with his predecessors; Edwin S. Porter, George Loane Tucker and the great Rex Ingram had made the three previous versions.* **Above:** *Douglas Fairbanks Junior, and Colman in the same film. Fairbanks was Rupert of Hentzau, a part which made Novarro a star in 1922.*

The perfect gentleman

In the twenties Rudolph Valentino, Ramon Novarro and Ronald Colman had been the greatest stars. Now the sex balance was shifting. Valentino was dead, Novarro and Gilbert in decline, and no man's popularity rivalled that of Garbo or Dietrich. Yet Ronald Colman was a survivor. The romantic hero supreme of silents like *Stella Dallas* (1925) and *Beau Geste* (1926), Colman continued playing leads for another twenty years, his mellifluous voice making him even more effective with sound. Sometimes, with Colman, time seemed to stand still. *The Prisoner of Zenda* (1937) was the remake of a silent film, and had the same uncomplicated morality, the same unassuming charm. Colman was adept at suggesting a kind of raffish nobility. His Sydney Carton in *A Tale of Two Cities* (1935) and his François Villon in *If I Were King* (1938) were perfect examples of this, but his occasional forays into the modern world, as in John Ford's *Arrowsmith* (1931), gave the impression that he had seen it all so many times before, and the result was not so convincing.

King Gable

Through the thirties, Clark Gable was the king of MGM. In his first years at the studio there was a touch of the heavy about Gable, and in retrospect these films seem to be his best. His first great hit was in *A Free Soul* (1931), where as a gangster he came near to taking the film away from Shearer and Leslie Howard. He played opposite Garbo in *Susan Lenox: Her Fall and Rise* (1931), and was at his tough and swaggering best with Jean Harlow in the steamy jungle passions of *Red Dust* (1932). As Gable's popularity grew, the studio made his parts more sympathetic, and he lost something of his fire; sometimes, too, he was sadly miscast, in *Idiot's Delight*, for example, and *Parnell* (1937). A little ahead, however, lurked *Gone with the Wind*.

John Barrymore in the thirties was not the star he had been. Now in his fifties, his health broken by alcoholism, he was often dependent upon a cue-board for his lines. Yet Barrymore was the supreme professional, and none of his troubles, save perhaps at the very end, was visible upon the screen. The list of his thirties performances is as impressive as that of his glory days in the silent films; to the old panache he added a sad sense of fatality that fairly wrenched one's sympathies. In one scene from *Grand Hotel* he outacts Garbo (the first, and the only, time); in *A Bill of Divorcement* (1932) he plays father to the young Hepburn, a father just back in the world after years in an asylum, and gave her her first glimpse of what great screen acting could be; and in *Romeo and Juliet* (1936) his Mercutio, though

inevitably far too old, blazes gloriously, and for a while makes that misjudged venture take on a semblance of life.

Barrymore emerged late in his career as a great comedian. First there was *Twentieth Century*; then *True Confession* (1937), where he was with Lombard again, playing a character who was sometimes agreeably eccentric, sometimes unnervingly deranged; he ran away with the film, leaving you wondering whether perhaps it wasn't comedy at all. His last triumph was in *Midnight* (1939). Here he plays a French count, serenely unflappable, concerned only to save his wife (Mary Astor) from the consequences of a foolish affair, who at one point (in one of the thirties' sublime moments) finds himself compelled, in his bedroom in Paris, to give a devastating impersonation, by telephone, of an ailing baby in Budapest. That was how far thirties comedy could go.

Above: *Carole Lombard and Gable starred in Paramount's **No Man of Her Own** in 1932. Here they are seen off duty during the filming. Gable and Lombard married in 1939. Three years later came the tragic air disaster in which she died.*

Left: *Clark Gable and Jean Harlow in **Red Dust** (1932). Mary Astor was the third member of this triangle drama set in the Malayan jungle. Twenty-one years later, the movie was remade as **Mogambo.***

Below: *Margaret Sullavan and Robert Taylor in Frank Borzage's* **Three Comrades** *(1938). Taylor, Franchot Tone (outstanding) and Robert Young played the three friends caught up in the social and political turmoil of post-war Germany; Sullavan was the girl who married Taylor and died of consumption. The script, with its romantic insistence that friendship and love could lightly conquer death, provided a rare screen credit for Scott Fitzgerald, who adapted Erich Maria Remarque's novel.*

Right: *Clark Gable and Spencer Tracy in* **San Francisco***, one of the biggest hits of 1936. The climax, with the earthquake and fire of 1906, was a stunning sequence, with superb special effects by Arnold Gillespie. It ended with Jeanette MacDonald leading the survivors back from the hills into the now quiet city as the title song welled up. Nonsense, but wonderful.*

The MGM men

The personality of Spencer Tracy underwent an odd change in mid-career. Fox had seen him in the early thirties as a rough and rugged type. As soon as he moved to MGM in 1935 the image changed and the gentle, reliable, almost patriarchal Tracy was born. In *San Francisco* (1936) and *Boys' Town* (1938) he played priests, still ready to use his fists if necessary, true, but that total integrity was not as interesting as the old, flawed hero. He went on, inevitably, to great men of history, in *Edison the Man* (1940) and *Northwest Passage* (1940), but the forties saved him. The characters he played opposite Hepburn fused the two Tracys. The roughness came back, counter-pointing her elegance, and the honesty remained.

The climate of the later thirties worked a similar change in the character of James Cagney, and as the decade went on, it became apparent that smoothness, even suavity, was the quality a male star must have. There had always been a cultured poise about Herbert Marshall, William Powell and Adolphe Menjou, but now, and particularly at MGM, there came the day of the man about town. That studio alone had Powell, Robert Montgomery, Franchot Tone, Robert Taylor, Robert Young and Melvyn Douglas. The quality of their material varied, but these, too, were professionals, and their work made the tritest story watchable. And they could all rise to a better opportunity, as did Tone and Young in *Three Comrades*, Douglas in *Tell No Tales* (1939), Taylor with Garbo in *Camille*, Powell in the Thin Man series and *My Man Godfrey* (1936). Montgomery would not have a real chance until later on, with *They Were Expendable* (1945).

More than mere charm

Finally, a reputation that would steadily grow through the thirties and beyond – that of Cary Grant. Grant began at Paramount in 1932, soon appeared opposite Dietrich in *Blonde Venus* (1932), and twice with Mae West, in *She Done Him Wrong* (1933) and *I'm No Angel* (1933). That was competition indeed. Ramshackle affairs though her movies were, Mae West swept through them like a force of nature, joyously mocking her own sexuality, and Grant perforce, as he had done with Dietrich, stayed quietly on the sidelines. But these films led to better things for him. He went on to RKO and Columbia, specializing at first in crazy comedy, and one of cinema's great actors made his presence felt. Superficially, Grant belonged to the man-about-town brigade, but behind the casual charm and the easy confidence a much more complex character was barely hidden. *Bringing up Baby* (1938) is as moving as it is, for all the comic trappings, precisely because it is so clear that Grant's work matters very much and that he cannot lightly surrender to the Hepburn world. Later still, that side of Grant could take on a darker tinge, and he became the perfect ambivalent hero for Alfred Hitchcock. And it is in his thirties films – *Bringing up Baby*, *Holiday*, and above all *Only Angels Have Wings* (1939) – that the outlines of his Hitchcock heroes can be traced.

Above: *Cary Grant and Irene Dunne, with Ralph Bellamy (**right**), in Leo McCarey's **The Awful Truth**, made at Columbia in 1937. One of the biggest box-office hits of the year, it was a sophisticated screwball comedy which had Grant and Dunne as a young couple who divorce and contest access right to their dog. They get together at the end of the film, of course – the remarriage theme being fairly common to the genre (see also **His Girl Friday**, 1940; **The Philadelphia Story**, 1940; **Woman of the Year**, 1942; **Adam's Rib**, 1949), but enacted only after the couple has gone through a period of learning. The dog? He was played by Asta, William Powell and Myrna Loy's wire-hair terrier co-star in the 'Thin Man' films.*

1939
The End of an Era

Chapter 8

The thirties had begun with the Depression. They ended with war in Europe, but they ended in cinema with such an outpouring of riches, in that one year of 1939, as had not been seen before – nor would ever be again. This was not an American phenomenon alone. In the Soviet Union, Alexander Dovzhenko made *Shors*; in Britain, there was the young Carol Reed's *The Stars Look Down*; in France two complete masterpieces in Marcel Carné's *Le Jour Se Lève* and Jean Renoir's *La Règle du Jeu*. As for America, there had been one miraculous year before, 1927, the year of Murnau's *Sunrise*, Vidor's *The Crowd*, Borzage's *Seventh Heaven*, Sternberg's *Underworld* and Paul Leni's *The Cat and the Canary*. But even 1927 could not boast the sheer number and variety of great films made in 1939.

Ford out West

Even since 1917, John Ford had produced great works from time to time, and in between had done his best as a studio pro, but now Ford made three films in the year; two of them were magnificent, and the third not far behind. Ford's contribution to 1939 was *Stagecoach, Young Mr Lincoln*, and *Drums along the Mohawk*. (Next year he added *The Grapes of Wrath* and *The Long Voyage Home* – no director ever made five films of such stature in so short a time.) *Stagecoach* rescued the Western from obscurity, and John Wayne from the B-movie grind. Ford went to Monument Valley, to become with the years his personal preserve, and brought back a movie perfectly shaped and timed, a movie that progressed, with not one dead or irrelevant frame, from the quiet intimations of trouble in the opening scenes to the shattering double climax of the Indian attack and the shoot-out at Lordsburg, and had still up its sleeve the most delicate and joyful of codas. And it was a film of great character performances too, with Thomas Mitchell, Donald Meek, Andy Devine, all of them down to Chris-Pin Martin's frightened little Mexican, supporting the central duo of Wayne and the marvelous Claire Trevor with their varied, idiosyncratic, unassertive skills.

With *Young Mr Lincoln* Ford was returning to a subject he had treated in *The Prisoner of Shark Island* (1936). That film had begun by rivalling D.W. Griffith with a masterly handling of Lincoln's assassination, had followed this with a harrowing sequence of the execution of the conspirators, and then tailed off somewhat as it traced the story of Dr Mudd, the man who tended John Wilkes Booth. Now there was no faltering. Taking its hero only as far as his election to Congress, *Young Mr Lincoln* was at once an affectionate picture of small-town

Claudette Colbert arrives in Paris in the opening scene of **Midnight** *(1939). One group of cameramen shot exteriors and background at the real Gare de l'Est; Paramount duplicated the carriage interior back at the studio, with hard wooden seats contrasting beautifully with the gold lamé gown.*

life and a reflection on greatness in the making, and it drew from Henry Fonda, in the first of his seven films with Ford, the definitive portrait of utter integrity. Fonda had been in films for four years, always competent, never quite imposing himself. Now the Fonda character was molded, and would endure for forty years.

Drums along the Mohawk, set in the Revolutionary War period, was Ford's first film in color, and if not the equal of its two predecessors, was still a film with a great deal to admire. There was Claudette Colbert, spirited as ever as a young bride coming to live in the Mohawk Valley, and only briefly disconcerted by finding Chief Big Tree standing silently in her kitchen; Edna May Oliver defying the world from her great bed; the melancholy return of a defeated army; and a marvellous final scene, with Fonda pursued by Indians across fields and forest, in which Ford used shades of color superbly to convey an emerging and brooding mystery.

Garbo laughs!

Ernst Lubitsch went to MGM to make his only film with Garbo. The result was one of the decade's finest comedies, *Ninotchka*. Garbo was the Soviet envoy captivated by Paris, a pretty hat and capitalist idler Melvyn Douglas – by the Lubitsch world, in fact – and the shrewd comic sense she revealed did not lessen the warmth of feeling that was hers alone. There were nicely varied characters in the three officials whom she is sent to check on, explosive Sig Rumann, wistful Felix Bressart, and dour Alexander Granach; a touching cameo from old Richard Carle as Douglas's servant whom Garbo wants to free from serfdom ("Go to bed, little father"); that memorable scene in the workmen's cafe when Garbo fails to see the cream-in-your-coffee joke before being convulsed by a simple pratfall; and so much more. Lubitsch gave the whole film a happy glow, scoring points off East and West alike, and in his response to Garbo finding a deeper humanity than he had shown before.

Mr Smith Goes to Washington, Frank Capra's contribution to 1939, was naive enough as a political tract, and its story of a country boy triumphing over the hard hearts and cynical moralities of Washington invited a total disbelief. But it was Capra's privilege to see the world in those terms if he chose, and his skill with actors was never more evident. This time he had Claude Rains (as a silkily devious senator) and Thomas Mitchell, Edward Arnold and Eugene Pallette, and with Jean Arthur doing her best to help the country boy prevail, and James Stewart as the shy idealist hero, there was a built-in guarantee.

John Ford's three triumphs of 1939.
Far left: *Jessie Ralph, Ward Bond, Henry Fonda and Claudette Colbert in* **Drums Along the Mohawk.** *One of Ford's great strengths was his use of the same actors in film after film; the rock-solid yet sensitive Bond was a vital member of that stock company.* **Top:** *Henry Fonda in* **Young Mr Lincoln.** *The young lawyer broods on the future, and on the world far away from Springfield.* **Above:** *John Carradine, Louise Platt and John Wayne in* **Stagecoach.** *Carradine, another Ford regular, played a courtly Southern gambler; Platt was the wife on her way to join her cavalry officer husband, and bearing her child en route: Wayne as the Ringo Kid is out for revenge.*

Left: *James Stewart makes his marathon speech to the Senate in* **Mr Smith Goes to Washington** *(1939). The book is the Standing Rules of the Senate. Jean Arthur has just signaled from the gallery that he should turn to Rule 5, Section 3. On doing so he recalls all Senators who have walked out on him, so outsmarting the professionals.*

Below: *Marlene Dietrich in* **Destry Rides Again** *(1939). Her condition is the result of that famous fight with Una Merkel.*

Right: *James Stewart and Dietrich in the same film. Neither had appeared in a Western before. Stewart would go on to many more, Dietrich to only one. That is Fritz Lang's* **Rancho Notorious** *(1952), where her femme fatale was a typical Dietrich role.*

Stewart's career ran parallel to Fonda's in many ways. They began in the same year, 1935, reached the top at the same time, projected the same image of unassuming decency – and each did some of his best work for John Ford. Stewart's roles were varied in his first years – and he was even the murderer in *After the Thin Man* (1936). The Stewart character could be distraught, tentative or ill at ease, but perseverance was the keynote, pleasantness the weapon that disarmed. Though he made many Westerns later, it was a surprise to find him in one in 1939, and an even greater surprise to find Marlene Dietrich leaving her silks and satins to join him there. The movie was George Marshall's *Destry Rides Again*, an old Tom Mix vehicle dusted off and given lashings of comedy (Mischa Auer was a lugubrious Russian out West), catchy ballads, a hero who disapproved of gunplay and, to make up for that, a scratching, kicking, hair-pulling battle between Dietrich and Una Merkel. Those who had found Sternberg too rarefied warmed to Dietrich in this one.

In George Cukor's *The Women* battling ladies were the whole film. A ruthless parade of sharp-clawed scandalmongering, *The Women* gave glorious chances to Rosalind Russell as the most lethal-tongued of them all, to Joan Crawford as a home-breaking, hard-as-nails shopgirl, and to Norma Shearer as the nice woman who is the victim of it all. And Paulette Goddard, away from her work with Chaplin, scored as a spunky chorine.

Angels with Dirty Faces, the year before, had brought back the gangster film, and now Warners followed up with Raoul Walsh's *The Roaring Twenties*. A leading director since 1915, with a notable record in the twenties, Walsh had faded of late, but with this one he was right back on form. Again the film found an ingenious way of retaining the gangster as hero. An authentic-seeming prohibition period piece, it presented James Cagney as a basically decent man who comes back from the war, loses his job, and drifts into the rackets, but redeems himself by a noble self-sacrifice. The really evil character, played by Humphrey Bogart, still a supporting actor, is killed by Cagney. There was a documentary air about parts of the film, an interesting look ahead to the forties thrillers like *Boomerang* and *The Naked City* with their location shooting and realism.

Good Queen Bette

By 1939 Bette Davis was the unchallenged queen of Warners. She made four films for the studio that year. *The Private Lives of Elizabeth and Essex* has striking sets, and Michael Curtiz to whip it into life, but Errol Flynn, splendid as Robin Hood the year before, was a lightweight Essex, and Davis had to battle on alone. In Edmund Goulding's *The Old Maid*, a tactfully managed tearjerker, she has the strongest of competition from Miriam Hopkins, and profits by it, and in William Dieterle's *Juarez* plays the unbalanced Empress Carlotta, making a relatively small part, if a showy one, really crackle with energy. By far the best of the four films, however, was Goulding's *Dark Victory*. Davis plays a selfish society girl who learns that she is suffering from a brain tumor, and within months will go blind, then die. She was perfectly cast, the petulance and tantrums of the early scenes slowly yielding to a serenity that was something entirely new in her work.

John Barrymore's tour de force in *Midnight* has been noted, but it was not the only delight in director Mitchell Leisen's finest film. Claudette Colbert is a dancer stranded in Paris, posing as a countess to enjoy the luxury of Barrymore's house for a few days; Don Ameche plays the cab-driver who loyally supports her (by far the best thing Ameche ever did); and the dazzling script is by Billy Wilder and his writing partner Charles Brackett. Although he had directed one film in France, Hollywood did not give Wilder the chance to direct until 1942. In 1939 he was flourishing as a writer. He and Brackett had (along with Walter Reisch) written *Ninotchka*, and *Midnight*, an oddly tender film behind airy badinage was a fit companion piece.

Far left: Bette Davis, who begun her illustrious film career in 1931 and by the end of the decade was recognized as one of Hollywood's greatest actresses; this studio portrait actually dates from 1943. **Left:** Davis as cockney waitress Mildred in John Cromwell's **Of Human Bondage** (1934). She made this film on loan from Warner Brothers to RKO, and it gave her one of her first important roles as a scheming woman. Her co-star, Leslie Howard, would reappear with her back at Warners in two films directed by Archie L. Mayo, **The Petrified Forest** (1936) and **It's Love I'm After** (1937). **Above:** Claudette Colbert and Don Ameche in Mitchell Leisen's **Midnight** (1939), an elegant, cynical screwball comedy that could have only come from one studio — Paramount.

Above: *Ray Bolger (Scarecrow), Judy Garland (Dorothy, carrying Toto) and Jack Haley (Tin Man) in* **The Wizard of Oz** *(1939). Bolger's film appearances were sporadic, and often in poorish films, but he was an unfailing pleasure. Haley's other films were unrewarding, but his gentle humor was perfect for this, his richest part.* **Far right:** *Vivien Leigh and Clark Gable in* **Gone With the Wind** *(1939). Gable's performance as Rhett Butler was the high point of his career. Effortlessly dominating every scene in which he appeared, he gave his parts of the film a force and directness, and a humanity, that were often lacking elsewhere. Vivien Leigh* **right:** *in the same film, wanders through crowds of Confederate wounded. This sequence, with its famous crane-shot, was the work of the gifted designer Cameron Menzies. Selznick wanted 2500 extras for the scene. 1500 were available: 1000 dummies made up.*

Over the rainbow

Some of the finest thirties films are seldom seen. Others, luckier, have had unending revivals, in repertory cinemas, on TV and video. MGM made one such in 1939 – *The Wizard of Oz*. No film is better known, or better loved, and *Wizard* deserves all its acclaim. It gives full scope to the rich and little used talents of Ray Bolger, Bert Lahr and Jack Haley as Dorothy's three companions, has the enchanting freshness of Judy Garland, some of the screen's best songs, and an overwhelming air of happiness. You feel that, once again, as they said it had been in the pioneer days, movie-making was fun. And *Wizard* teaches one lesson that a student of the thirties needs, that you don't have to believe the credits. The director of record is Victor Fleming, who did indeed make most of the film, and finely too, but the opening, sepia-toned sequences in Kansas and Garland's song of the Yellow Brick Road were the work of King Vidor.

Victor Fleming is credited, too, as the sole director of *Gone With the Wind*, the most famous film of 1939 – and of the whole decade. Again the credits lie. George Cukor directed a few scenes, Sam Wood and the art director William Cameron Menzies several more. The sheer scale of the film commands respect. Menzies' designs are outstanding, Margaret Mitchell might have written Rhett Butler for Gable (and probably did), Leslie Howard and Olivia de Havilland are perfectly cast, too, but a nagging doubt remains. Without the years of assiduous publicity, the worldwide search for Scarlett, would the film have made the impact it undeniably did? For *Gone With the Wind* is hollow at the core, partly because of producer David O. Selznick's numbing conviction that this trashy best-seller was a great novel, partly because Vivien Leigh's Scarlett is a posturing doll. The part cried out for Bette Davis; failing that, Carole Lombard could have schemed and charmed her way through, and mocked all the pretensions as she went.

Flying out in style

As *Gone with the Wind* went on its garlanded way, a simple action melodrama crept almost unnoticed through the cinemas. Made by Howard Hawks, it stars Cary Grant and Jean Arthur, Richard Barthelmess and Rita Hayworth, and is called *Only Angels Have Wings*. *Only Angels* is set in a South American port called Barranca, headquarters of a tiny airline whose pilots fly mail across the Andes. Grant is the chief pilot; Barthelmess a disgraced flier ending up in this God-forsaken place to escape, and work again; Hayworth his wife (and an old flame of Grant); Arthur an entertainer marooned there; Thomas Mitchell Grant's right-hand. A fine cast, and a routine story, it seems. But that is to forget Hawks. Hawks had made great comedies, but not yet a dramatic masterpiece, though in *Scarface* he had come near.

The great triumph of *Only Angels Have Wings* could not have been planned. It is far too easy and spontaneous for that. In every foot of the film there is a breathtaking sympathy between director and players. The tone is laconic, casual; two people die in the film, two people whom the audience has come to admire, yet still the mood is joyous and carefree. In *Love's Labour's Lost* there is the line to "move wild laughter in the throat of death", and that is precisely what *Only Angels* does. Joe (Noah Beery) dies, and Grant eats the steak that Beery has ordered. "Who's dead? Who's Joe?", he says to an uncomprehending Arthur, and before the film ends Arthur will understand in her turn. The Kid (Mitchell) is dying. He asks Grant what has happened. "Your neck's broken, Kid," says Grant, and Mitchell, taking a last puff at Grant's cigarette, understands too, not just the fact, but the weight of love behind the words.

The flying scenes in the film are thrilling enough, but many directors could have made them. In *Only Angels* it is the people that matter, and in that run-down building that is airport, hotel, restaurant and bar all in one, Hawks's characters learn, and teach each other, how to face the world outside, and survive. And in this hard-won optimism is the magic of the film. *Only Angels Have Wings* was the bravest of endings to the decade, and perhaps the greatest of American sound films.

So the thirties ended, and with them a world. The cinema would go on, but while thirties audiences still lived, the cinema as they had known it, a universal, popular art, was nearing an end. Yet how the thirties movies, the best of them, and at odd moments the worst of them, had soared. In the last analysis Howard Hawks was wrong. Not only angels had wings.

John Russell Taylor

Hollywood 1940s

Marilyn Monroe and Groucho Marx

The Business of War 1940-1

Chapter 9

The time-honored tradition of dividing trends and movements in the cinema into decades is essentially a matter of convenience. In the forties, all aspects of life were dictated by the decade's momentous political events – rather than the arbitrary notion of a contained timespan existing between 1940 and 1950 – and cinema was no exception.

As far as Hollywood goes, the period we regard as the thirties really starts in 1927 with the coming of sound, contains the greatest era of the studio system, and ends in December 1941 when America became involved in World War II. The forties, for all intents and purposes, begin there – and the film traditions that were established during and after the conflict would dominate until the early fifties, when the McCarthy witch-hunts and the emergence of television changed the shape and flavor of American cinema.

Music and murder

An idea of the forties still persists, but it is too nebulous a tag. The two great screen movements that grew up during the era in Hollywood were the great MGM musical and the dark murder thriller that came to be known as *film noir*. The former really starts with the arrival of producer Arthur Freed at Louis B. Mayer's studio in 1939 and lingers on until the later fifties – a period bookended by Freed's productions of **Babes in Arms** (1939) and **Gigi** (1958). *Film noir* emerged from the shadows of **Citizen Kane** (1941) – the first film directed by Orson Welles, who was the single most important figure to arrive on the film scene since talkies began – and **The Maltese Falcon** (1941), still going in 1953, though its resonances could be felt on into the seventies.

All the same, the forties may have more than accidental significance in the history of Hollywood. The decade's beginning, even before America was forced to declare war on Japan, was marked by an alarming slump in cinema attendance that put an end, forever, to the extravagance that had characterized film-making in the previous ten years. By the year 1950, Hollywood was again in a chastened frame of mind, with the menace of the small screen already apparent, along with the break-up of the old studio empires of production, distribution and exhibition through the strict application of the anti-trust laws.

That makes the forties sound like a pretty miserable decade – and there was another alarming slump in the number of cinema-goers about half way through. By 1946 the studios were obliged to feel their way towards a new definition of audiences and their tastes – which

Right: *The tough private-eye Sam Spade (Humphrey Bogart – left) and the effeminate crook Joel Cairo (Peter Lorre) having second thoughts about smooth-talking Brigid O'Shaughnessy (Mary Astor) in John Huston's* **The Maltese Falcon** *(1941).*

necessarily reflected the emotional impact of the war. In fact, the salient characteristic of Hollywood at this particular time was its extraordinary buoyancy.

There had always been a swiftness in adjusting to new market pressures in Hollywood, but the beginning of the forties required a greater adaptability than had ever been needed before. Although the war that had started in Europe on 3 September 1939 must have seemed remote from Hollywood concerns, the European market still mattered very much. In the late thirties, Hitler's invasion of Austria and Czechoslovakia had caused a significant drop in the revenues for Hollywood films from those countries. The outbreak of war made the whole commercial scene in Europe more impenetrable still. The

contraction of the home market – with profits for 1940 almost a third less than those of 1939 (when **Gone With the Wind** was the chief attraction) also needed to be curtailed.

Alone at last

The first victims of this period of transition were two of the gems in MGM's crown. Greta Garbo, Hollywood's supreme "love goddess", had been appreciated more enthusiastically in Europe than in America for the previous few years. Arriving in Hollywood from Sweden with her mentor the director Mauritz Stiller, in 1925, Garbo had moved through the silent era and the first ten years of talkies as a gloomy, tempest-tossed woman made radiantly divine by cameraman William Daniels in such films as Clarence Brown's **Flesh and the Devil** (1926), **Anna Christie** (1930) and **Anna Karenina** (1935), Edmund Goulding's **Love** (1927) and **Grand Hotel** (1932), and George Cukor's **Camille** (1936). But to stay at the top she had to lose her remoteness – the very thing that made her a star – and her grand airs, and be remade closer to the hearts of middle America. She was still glacial, but less so, in Ernst Lubitsch's **Ninotchka** (1939), "the film that made Garbo laugh", and then MGM came up with Cukor's **Two-Faced Woman** (1941), which turned her into a

Left: *Sam Spade (Humphrey Bogart) about to hand over murderess Brigid O'Shaughnessy to the law in* **The Maltese Falcon** *(1941). Bebe Daniels (1931) and Bette Davis (1936) had previously played Brigid.*

Below: *Karin Blake (Greta Garbo) recovers from an evening of playing her own imaginary glamorous twin sister Katrin in* **Two-Faced Woman** *(1941). Ruth Ellis (Ruth Gordon) tends to her.*

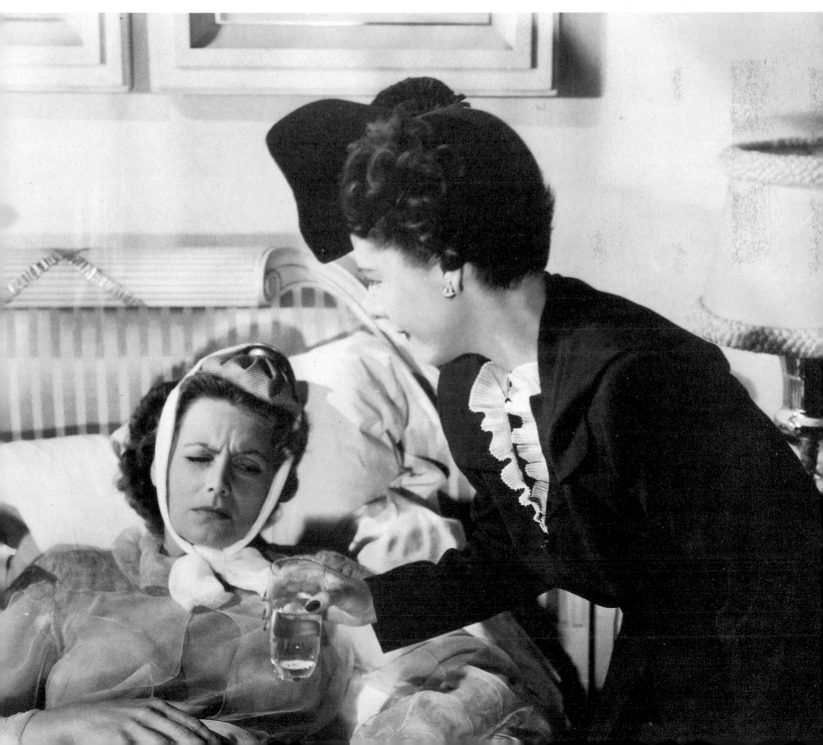

neglected American wife bent on getting even with her philandering husband by posing as her own more glamorous double. She wore a swimsuit and introduced a dance novelty called the Choka-Chika – all to no avail. Voluntarily she retired from movies, and never came back – a move that preserved her stardom forever.

It is significant that Garbo's great rival through the thirties, Marlene Dietrich, would leave behind her the mists and shadows that her director Josef von Sternberg had wreathed around her on Paramount's sound stages in six masterpieces of eroticism – including **Morocco** (1930), **Shanghai Express** (1932) and **The Devil Is a Woman** (1935) – and, from the late thirties, find herself in the more accessible world of Westerns, including **Destry Rides Again** (1939) and **The Spoilers** (1942), and lighter romances, dramas or comedies. Other than that, she was a tireless entertainer of the troops overseas.

MGM's other major casualty at this time was the light-operatic duo of Nelson Eddy and Jeannette MacDonald, the stars of such saccharine vehicles as **Naughty Marietta** (1935) and **The Girl of the Golden West** (1938). As with Garbo, a newer American look was required for the fashion-conscious forties and so they graduated to a Rodgers and Hart score with **I Married an Angel** (1942). And that was the end of another long and successful run.

Tried and tested

These were the most dramatic of a series of similar quick and perhaps precipitate decisions to try and alter the stars' profiles. Though war and the loss of European markets had affected Garbo's and MacDonald and Eddy's popularity, it is very likely that changing tastes would have diminished the box-office receipts from their films anyway. On the whole, thirties-style movies and stars still dominated the scene at the beginning of the forties. Well-upholstered biopics, swashbuckling costume epics, screwball comedies, highly wrought melodramas for important female stars – all these were still around and very popular with moviegoers.

Right: *Queen Elizabeth I (Flora Robson) is won over by Captain Geoffrey Thorpe (Errol Flynn), who is scheming to plunder the galleons of the Spanish Main in **The Sea Hawk** (1940). Flora Robson had previously played this royal role in **Fire Over England** (1937), with Laurence Olivier and Vivien Leigh among her subjects.*

Left: *Vivien Leigh playing Emma Hamilton to Laurence Olivier's Lord Nelson in Alexander Korda's patriotic* **That Hamilton Woman** *(1941).*
Bottom: *The glamorous Bette Davis playing Regina Giddens in William Wyler's production of* **The Little Foxes** *(1941).*

Below: *A performance of Hamlet in Warsaw being interrupted by the approach of the German invasion in* **To Be or Not to Be** *(1942). Manager Charles Halton is alarmed, but not as much as the actor Joseph Tura (Jack Benny), wondering whether his unfaithful wife Maria (Carole Lombard) can explain away her latest admirer.*

After their success with such socially concerned biographical pictures as **The Story of Louis Pasteur** (1935) and **The Life of Emile Zola** (1937), both directed by William Dieterle and starring Paul Muni, Warner Brothers continued in a similar vein in 1940. That year, Dieterle directed Edward G. Robinson in **The Story of Dr Ehrlich's Magic Bullet** and **A Dispatch From Reuters**. In the first Robinson played the discoverer of a cure for syphilis, a curiously daring choice of subject sanctioned by the Hays Office (the official arbiter of morality and censorship in American films) for its superior taste and message. In the second he played the founder of the famous press agency working his way up in the communications world from humble beginnings with carrier pigeons.

Also at Warners, Errol Flynn, the star of **Captain Blood** (1935) and **The Adventures of Robin Hood** (1938), completed his trio of spectacular swashbucklers for Michael Curtiz with **The Sea Hawk** (1940), made with all the luxurious back-up the studio could muster – sweeping music by Erich Wolfgang Korngold, lavish sets by Anton Grot. A rousing tale of privateers, it was also an ingenious propaganda piece with a strong anti-Nazi message, mainly delivered by Flora Robson as Queen Elizabeth I. Since Hollywood was still bound by an act ensuring the preservation in word and deed of America's neutrality, it was both a bold and cunning film. But otherwise it was the last of its kind; after a couple of Westerns the uneasy Curtiz-Flynn partnership ended and Flynn went into more Westerns and war films for Raoul Walsh, also at Warner Brothers.

Names to conjure with

Meanwhile the other studios essayed Warner-style biopics and social dramas at their peril. By 1940-1 the former was so well established as a successful genre that everyone seemed to be getting in on the act. At MGM it took two films, **Young Tom Edison** and **Edison, the Man** (both 1940), to cover the life of America's all-purpose inventor, who grew up from Mickey Rooney to Spencer Tracy somewhere in between the two movies.

Fox for its part discovered a new swashbuckling star in Tyrone Power, whom Rouben Mamoulian directed with dash and verve in **The Mark of Zorro** (1940) and **Blood and Sand** (1941).

Among all these films made prior to America's entering the war, the strongest propaganda statement was made in Alexander Korda's **That Hamilton Woman** (1941), with Laurence Olivier as Lord Nelson and Vivien Leigh in the title role. It was a brasher, more pro-British, anti-Nazi piece than **The Sea Hawk** – Korda was known to be a close friend of Winston Churchill and it was suspected that he had been sent to Hollywood to carry Britain's fight into American hearts and minds.

The thirties-style melodrama remained in vogue at the beginning of the forties and the reigning female stars were to be found in weepies and women's pictures. Joan Crawford played a hideously scarred, mentally deranged criminal who becomes a new woman after plastic surgery in **A Woman's Face** (1941); Bette Davis played a murderess in **The Letter** and was passionately malicious in **The Little Foxes** (1941); and Vivien Leigh was a ballerina who turns to prostitution in a

Below: *Wealthy Tracy Lord (Katharine Hepburn) in* **The Philadelphia Story** *(1940) having a brief fling with James Stewart before deciding to remarry her first husband, Cary Grant* **right**.

Above: *Comedy-film director (Joel McCrea) sets out to discover real life but finally gets too much of it in* **Sullivan's Travels** *(1941).*

Right: *Charlie Chaplin, who brilliantly plays both the fascist leader Adenoid Hynkel and the Jewish barber who impersonates him to speak to the world of peace and brotherhood in* **The Great Dictator** *(1940).*

remake of **Waterloo Bridge** (1940). But Norma Shearer was on her way out, with her stock falling fast in such ill-suited vehicles as the anti-fascist **Escape** (1940) and the stand-by romantic comedy **Her Cardboard Lover** (1942).

Comedy with class

Of the great funny ladies, Carole Lombard, undisputed queen of screwball comedy, appeared in Hitchcock's **Mr and Mrs Smith** (1941) and Ernst Lubitsch's **To Be or Not to Be** (1942) before she was tragically killed in an air crash while on tour selling war bonds. **To Be or Not to Be**, starring Jack Benny as an actor playing Hamlet in occupied Poland and Lombard as his adulterous wife scheming with him against the Germans, is now regarded as a classic of black comedy and an acerbic anti-Nazi piece. Lubitsch, Hollywood's master of sophisticated wit and frothy comedy, had earlier abandoned his usual Ruritanian setting for **The Shop Around the Corner** (1940), a gentle and touching romantic comedy set in an imaginary Budapest department store and matching the comic gifts of the usually tearful Margaret Sullavan with those of James Stewart to charming effect.

Much more in tune with the forties, however, was a film that put Stewart in the fast-talking and bitchy high society of Cary Grant and Katharine Hepburn. It was George Cukor's **The Philadelphia Story** (1940), a comedy of manners sharper and more polished than most Hollywood products of the time.

Screwball comedies were still in vogue. Howard Hawks, who in the forties as in the thirties, tackled most genres with characteristic skill and ease, contributed two excellent entries in **His Girl Friday** (1940), a remake of **The Front Page** (1931) with Cary Grant and Rosalind Russell battling for the headlines, and **Ball of Fire** (1941), with Gary Cooper as one of seven professors surrounding Barbara Stanwyck's stripper Sugarpuss O'Shea. But there was nothing in either of these films to suggest the forties had ushered in any new trends.

The new comic genius on the horizon was Preston Sturges, a highly successful writer of cynical comedies, who finally bludgeoned Paramount into letting him direct his own scripts. The first results of this, **The Great McGinty** and **Christmas in July** (both 1940), were trial runs, comedies that took a few easy digs at political corruption and the money-ethos without seriously challenging audience expectations. But with **The Lady Eve** (1941), Sturges abandoned social comment in favor of sexual warfare, pitching a wily lady gambler (Barbara Stanwyck) against a moralistic biologist (Henry Fonda) who is more at home with snakes. Sturges' fourth film, **Sullivan's Travels** (1941), about a crusading film-maker who learns the hard way that entertainment means more than messages, was perhaps the funniest film of 1941.

Chaplin speaks out

Even in this uneasy period before Hollywood really took stock of the war, it was possible for film-makers to use comedy to comment on the European situation. **To Be or Not to Be** was one mordant example, but the most famous was Charles Chaplin's **The Great Dictator** (1940), his first talkie.

Chaplin was a reluctant convert to sound. He had made only two films in the thirties, **City Lights** (1931) and **Modern Times** (1936). Both were brilliant, but both evaded the new medium. **City Lights** uses sound effects and a musical score but is wordless; **Modern Times**, which saw the last appearance of the little Tramp, is, in fact, a rejection of the new technological age, another silent whose only concession to dialogue is a scene in which Chaplin speaks gibberish.

Below: *Three members of the Joad family, on their way from Oklahoma to California in* **The Grapes of Wrath** *(1940): pregnant Rosasharn (Dorris Bowdon), Ma (Jane Darwell) and Tom (Henry Fonda), just out of prison for homicide. The others* **bottom right** *(from left to right) are Rosasharn's husband Connie (Eddie Quillan), Pa (Russell Simpson), Uncle John (Frank Darien), Al (O. Z. Whitehead) and the itinerant ex-preacher Jim Casy (John Carradine).*

Right: *Joel McCrea, pictured here with Barbara Pepper and Robert Benchley, stars as an American journalist caught up with the Nazis in the Alfred Hitchcock thriller* **Foreign Correspondent** *(1940).*

Prolific during the silent era, Chaplin now spaced his films out by years – there would be only one more from him in the forties, **Monsieur Verdoux** (1947), the story of a Bluebeard murderer. With marital problems and a political smear campaign against him to contend with, it was a difficult decade for Chaplin.

The Great Dictator had him in the dual role of Adenoid Hynkel, Dictator of Tomania, and his double, a little Jewish barber. Fierce in his attack on European fascism, Chaplin satirized not only Hitler, but Goebbels (Henry Daniell as Garbitsch), Goering (Billy Gilbert as Marshall Herring) and Mussolini (Jack Oakie as Benzino Napaloni,

Dictator of Bacteria). The film made Chaplin's political position very clear and earned him a great deal of criticism. His independence from the studios enabled him to speak freely, but he in particular suffered from the loss of the European intellectual audience his silent comedy had built up. And since he was, though a long time back, an emigré from Britain and had not troubled to hide, either privately or in his films, his left-wing sympathies, he was viewed with suspicion by the Senate committee investigating possible infringements of the Neutrality Act by "inciting to war".

Hitch under suspicion

Alfred Hitchcock was, too. Hitchcock had arrived in Hollywood in 1939 – his greatest years still in front of him. He had quickly mastered the silent film in Britain and had directed one or two films a year through the thirties, building up his familiar world of espionage, murder and suspense in such films as **The Man Who Knew Too Much** (1934), **The Thirty-Nine Steps** (1935) and **The Lady Vanishes** (1938). In America he started with **Rebecca** (1940), a classic of female psychology adapted from Daphne du Maurier's best-selling novel and set in Cornwall, England, and followed it with **Foreign Correspondent** (1940), set in Europe, and (after the matrimonial comedy **Mr and Mrs Smith**) **Suspicion** (1941). It was originally intended that the murder-suspect hero (Cary Grant) of **Suspicion**, a masterful Hitchcock suspense thriller, should go off to redeem himself in the Battle of Britain, but good sense prevailed.

However, Hitchcock was clearly not pleasing the isolationists in America – the real culprit, in their eyes, was **Foreign Correspondent**. Under the guise of another suspense film, this was about spies who might be from anywhere, and showed the political education of one American journalist whose ignorance about Europe gives way to a strongly pro-British and anti-Nazi position. The final scene is an

Right: *The publisher of the scurrilous "New York Inquirer", Charles Foster Kane (Orson Welles) and his drama critic (Joseph Cotten) in* **Citizen Kane** *(1941). Kane's bid to become Governor* **far right** *is ruined by precisely the kind of scandal he printed in his own paper.*

impassioned radio appeal to America not to turn its head away but to get involved in the soon-to-be universal fight for freedom.

In the main, though, if such liberal sentiments found serious expression at all in the years 1940-1, they were firmly anchored in the past. No doubt it was still quite bold in 1940 to make a major film out of **The Grapes of Wrath**, John Steinbeck's grim novel of the Depression in rural America. The dustbowl years were, after all, not that far back – but with the full force of Darryl F. Zanuck's production facilities at 20th Century-Fox behind it, the poetic eye of John Ford guiding the camera and Henry Fonda leading an excellent cast, it was bound to be at least a formidable critical success. This quiet epic stirred audiences throughout the country while turning its back resolutely on anything that might be happening anywhere in the world other than America.

Darker visions

The two films of the period that would prove most important for the future of Hollywood movies, Orson Welles' **Citizen Kane** and John Huston's **The Maltese Falcon**, were equally oblivious of the outside world. And yet both films offered an index to the real tone of the times. Both were directorial debuts by Hollywood whiz-kids. Welles had been imported from the New York stage at the age of 26 with an unprecedented contract from RKO giving him a completely free hand to produce, write and direct his own films for his own unit. Huston, at 34, was already an experienced screenwriter who had worked on several major Warner Brothers films, including **Jezebel** (1938) and **High Sierra** (1941). And both films shared a darkness of viewpoint, a cool cynicism in their assessment of human nature, which became a vital factor in the Hollywood films of the late forties.

Citizen Kane was to have the most immediate effect. The story of a newspaper tycoon, based largely on the life of William Randolph Hearst and with Welles himself in the title role, it was put together like a jigsaw in a daringly fragmented structure. **Kane** put all Welles' ideas about cinema and life into the shop-window at once. Consequently it highlighted more technical innovations than any single film for decades, and other film-makers, even those who professed to despise Welles as an arty flash-in-the-pan, leapt with delight at the idea of deep-focus photography and low-angled shots. The former

served to keep foreground and background clearly visible at the same time, enabling elaborate and eloquent use of composition; the latter, a particular passion of Welles', enabled elements in the film frame to be emphasized (or diminished) in relation to their surroundings for a specific emotional effect.

It is unlikely that any of the technical "innovations" in the film were entirely new to movies, but the dash and vigor with which Welles used them, and his undoubted flair for publicity, made them seem so, and dramatized the art of film for moviegoers as never before. **Kane** had the reputation of being a financial disaster but, in fact, it wasn't. It had a longer shelf-life than most movies and soon recovered its negative cost. That did not make life any easier for the ambitious and temperamental Welles, and his subsequent films nearly all ran into financial difficulties and executive interference. But if there was a major Hollywood film to start the forties, it was undoubtedly the unforgettable film **Citizen Kane**.

In comparison, **The Maltese Falcon** looks at first sight like a modest and fairly conventional studio success – another private-eye thriller based on a Dashiell Hammett novel that had already been filmed twice before. But John Huston's film finally defined the very specific qualities of tough disenchantment (and possible soft center) that made Humphrey Bogart not only a star and a legend, but an icon for the decade. **The Maltese Falcon** lines up the duplicitous Brigid O'Shaughnessy (Mary Astor) against the gross Gutman (Sydney Greenstreet) and the effeminate Joel Cairo (Peter Lorre) in their search for the mysterious jewelled antique, and calls on private-eye Sam Spade (Bogart) to sort them out. Astor was the first of the forties breed of beautiful *femmes fatales*; Lorre and Greenstreet (aided by little Elisha Cook Jr in one of many small-fry gunmen roles he would play) were paired as unlikely partners-in-crime for the first time.

But, crucially, **The Maltese Falcon**, with its web of lies and deceit, its shadowy world of greed, ambiguity and murder, and above all the cynicism of Bogart, brought together many of the elements that would make up *film noir*. In other words, Huston flipped the cool, sophisticated *Thin Man* kind of thirties thriller straight into the dark and troubled world of the forties, creating a model for the kind of cruel, sceptical movie that was to dominate Hollywood later in the war after the first thrill of flag-waving patriotism had worn off.

Movie Mobilization 1942-3

Chapter 10

O n 7 December 1941 the Japanese attacked the American naval base at Pearl Harbor and war was declared. At first there was a faint possibility that this conflict could be confined to the Pacific, but all such hopes were shattered when, four days later, Germany and Italy also declared war on the United States. The result in the film world was no more than a few seconds' stunned silence before the mad rush to be first on the new topical bandwagon of patriotic war movies began.

In the immediate pre-war period the American cinema had been going through an escapist phase, characterized best, perhaps, by **The Wizard of Oz** (1939) and **The Thief of Bagdad** (1940), both seen mainly in 1940. Even now, with hostilities declared, not everything became real, earnest and immediate. It might be said that many new films were styled to create a rose-tinted and far from realistic view of the war-torn world. A prime example of this was the Oscar-winning **Mrs Miniver** (1942), directed by William Wyler and starring Greer Garson in the title role of the plucky, resourceful, ever cheerful wife and mother withstanding the Blitz and Dunkirk and winning the war on the British home front. In general, however, there was a clear polarization between the films that one way or another took account of the war and films that clearly recognized an audience need for escapist entertainment in this time of strife.

First things first, of course. Poverty Row rushed into action immediately, and in no time at all Republic had managed to get on to American screens **Remember Pearl Harbor** (1942), so quickly and cheaply made that the attack itself had to take place off-screen, while the irresponsible American soldier hero was vainly struggling to get a message of warning to headquarters in time. He made up for this by achieving almost single-handed, and with optimistic speed, a victory in the Philippines.

Meanwhile the major studios, after a flurry of rapidly announced plans for topical war subjects, decided to hold off, as the speed of developments in the war quickly rendered many likely subjects outdated before they could even be made. Completion of Paramount's **Wake Island** (1942) for example, was held up for a few weeks in May 1942 awaiting the result of the military action in progress at that time – though the outcome proved to be less than cheering when it finally emerged. The main problem, in fact, for most of these immediate responses to the Pacific war was that they would have to dramatize defeat, since in the first four months of the war Japan was largely victorious. Therefore relatively realistic depictions such as **Bataan** (1943) had to stand on their heads to make a defeat

Right: *Defeat posing as moral victory in the East. In Tay Garnett's* **Bataan** *(1943), 13 American soldiers, including George Murphy (center left), Robert Taylor (center) and Lloyd Nolan (center right), are killed off one at a time by the ruthless Japanese.*

look like a victory, and only Paramount's **So Proudly We Hail** (1943) succeeded by being essentially a woman's picture in uniform.

Initially, Pacific war stories were difficult to depict as well as of doubtful appeal, and so studios started to pull back from their first premature enthusiasm. But the war in Europe was simpler to portray: lots of spies and secret service, suave and sinister Nazis and brave Europeans fighting them. In rapid succession moviegoers encountered French patriots in Jean Renoir's **This Land is Mine** (1943), with Charles Laughton, and **The Cross of Lorraine** (1943); an invaded Russian village in **North Star** (1943); Norwegian resistance in **The Moon is Down** and **Edge of Darkness** (both 1943); heroic Czechs in **Hitler's Madman** (1942) and the impressive **Hangmen Also Die!** (1943).

Few of these films had much distinction – Fritz Lang's **Hangmen Also Die!**, at least, was notable as the only Hollywood script by then resident Bertolt Brecht to reach the screen reasonably intact – but at least they provided starring roles for Paul Muni, Errol Flynn, Ann Sheridan, and even Gene Kelly, and proved quite popular for a while.

Right: *A beleaguered American unit holding on to a bridge at all costs in* **Bataan** *(1943). Although Bataan was a peninsula in the Philippines, near Manila, the film's plot much more closely resembles that of John Ford's* **The Lost Patrol** *(1934), set in the far-away Mesopotamian desert.*

Below: *Donald Barry (left) was more at home on the Western ranges of Republic serials and B movies than in the Philippines jungle of* **Remember Pearl Harbor** *(1942); but he was ably supported by Alan Curtis (right), now best remembered as the murder suspect desperately looking for an alibi in* **Phantom Lady** *(1944).*

Below: *Dr Franz Svoboda (Brian Donlevy) kills the top Nazi in Prague, Reinhard Heydrich, and escapes with the help of Mascha Novotny (Anna Lee) in Fritz Lang's* **Hangmen Also Die!** *(1943). Although the script was largely written by playwright Bertolt Brecht, his role was played down and the screenplay was credited to John Wexley.*

You must remember this...

None of them were quite so popular, or for that matter quite so star-studded, as the model example of the genre, **Casablanca** (1943). Towards the end of her life Ingrid Bergman used to say that she had progressed from being delighted when anyone actually remembered **Casablanca** to being irritated that no one seemed to remember anything else. And it is true that the film's ascent to its present legendary status was quite gradual. But at the same time it is perfectly understandable, since all the elements come together with peculiar force and conviction.

The star power of the emotional triangle – Rick (Humphrey Bogart), Ilsa (Ingrid Bergman), Victor Laszlo (Paul Henreid) – is sufficient to keep audiences interested in the romance at the center of the story: will Ilsa make it up with Rick, with whom she previously had an affair and a misunderstanding, and stay with him, or will she do the noble thing and go away with her dedicated anti-Nazi husband? And with Conrad Veidt as the suave and supercilious Nazi Strasser, Claude Rains as the cynical but sympathetic Captain Renault, Dooley Wilson as Sam playing "As Time Goes By" and Peter Lorre and Sydney

Above: *Although timid French schoolmaster Albert Mory (Charles Laughton) is unable to declare his love for his colleague, Louise Martin (Maureen O'Hara), he takes the blame for her brother's Resistance activities and dies a hero in* **This Land is Mine** *(1943).*

Right: *Lovers Rick Blaine (Humphrey Bogart) and Ilsa Lund (Ingrid Bergman) sharing passion and champagne in pre-war Paris, before being parted by war, misunderstanding and her husband in* **Casablanca** *(1943), an evergreen classic of nostalgia.*

Greenstreet as disreputable inhabitants of Vichy North Africa, it is hardly surprising that after forty years the film still seems fresh.

The real secret of its success, then as now, is that its devisers, writer Howard Koch and director Michael Curtiz, knew uncannily well how to separate the topical issues of war, patriotism, honor and democracy, from the real concern – romance and the choices it involves. The fundamental things apply as time goes by...

Back home

Much safer, obviously, than frontline dispatches in fictional form or such romanticized or stiff-upper-lip tributes to the British home or society as **Mrs Miniver**, **Random Harvest** (1942), **Forever and a Day** (1943) and **The White Cliffs of Dover** (1944) were tributes to the American home. It was in **Since You Went Away** (1944) that Claudette Colbert provided America's answer to Mrs Miniver. She played a wife whose husband has been drafted, and she is left to defend the domestic fortress along with her two daughters, played by

Left: Resistance leader Victor Laszlo (Paul Henreid), wife Ilsa and cafe owner Rick Blaine exchanging glances in the night in **Casablanca**; Sam (Dooley Wilson, **above**) is about to receive a request he just can't refuse; and Captain Renault (Claude Rains), collaborationist prefect of police **top** recruits Rick to help Laszlo and Ilsa escape from the Nazis. After condoning the murder of a Gestapo captain, Renault's final act is to drop an empty bottle of Vichy water (symbol of the puppet French government based in that spa town) into a wastepaper basket. So the story's end is the beginning of "a beautiful friendship" between the two men.

Jennifer Jones and the teenage Shirley Temple, and with Hattie McDaniel as the black maid who is paid off in the interests of wartime economy. She also takes in a boarder (Charles Coburn), much as Jean Arthur had done in **The More the Merrier** (1943) to help combat a wartime accommodation shortage in Washington. About halfway through **Since You Went Away** a cable arrives to report the husband missing in action, but at the end another comes to say that he is all right and coming home. It is all too easy, at this distance in time, to make fun of such a confection, with its glossy unreality disguised as unsparing realism, but writer/producer David O. Selznick and director John Cromwell's film is still a persuasive vision of the American home "at war".

Such films did, after all, remind audiences of real problems in the real world at war. There were many other films being made in Hollywood at this time that took a quite opposite course, by turning their back completely on the war, and there were some, comedies and musicals especially, that aimed somewhere between the two. In **You'll Never Get Rich** (1941), Fred Astaire starts as a dance director sparring romantically with showgirl Rita Hayworth, and is then called up for military service and, by a series of convenient

Left: *Anne Hilton (Claudette Colbert) receiving the wrong kind of cable giving news that her husband is missing in* **Since You Went Away** *(1944).*

coincidences, is able to carry on both his career and his romance, while also achieving patriotic credit. But in the subsequent Astaire/Hayworth vehicle of the period, **You Were Never Lovelier** (1942) the war plays only an indirect role – the South American milieu of the story seems to be used mainly to show off Roosevelt's Good Neighbor policy towards Central and South America. Pan-American friendship was no doubt an important factor in a number of other, even lighter-weight movies of this time. Though it may seem to be forcing a point to analyze films starring Latin spitfires Carmen Miranda or Lupe Velez in political terms, undoubtedly they and the exotic settings of such films as **Down Argentine Way** (1940), **A Weekend in Havana** and **That Night in Rio** (both 1941) chimed so well with government policy that one wonders if they were entirely coincidental or the result of gentle persuasion.

Mobilizing the movies

A number of other films made before the United States actually entered the war played their part in preparing Americans to think of themselves again as a military nation. These include two of the biggest comedy hits of 1941, **Caught in the Draft**, a Bob Hope vehicle with a self-explanatory title, and **Buck Privates**, in which the newly popular comedy duo of Bud Abbott and Lou Costello were precipitated unwillingly into the Service. Here Bud and Lou go through all kinds of familiar slapstick situations and in the end emerge with a new respect for themselves, each other (they start out as spoilt heir and chauffeur but learn a lesson in democracy) and all the patriotic values of army and country. As the Andrews Sisters sing joyfully during the movie, "Red, white and blue/Are colors that look good on you".

Right above and below: *Bob Hope in **Caught in the Draft** (1941) in which he tries to avoid the draft but enlists by mistake — watched, **above**, by a none-too-impressed Dorothy Lamour.*

Below: *Rita Hayworth, as the aloof daughter of an Argentinian hotel owner, being swept off her feet by Fred Astaire, a New York dancer over-fond of the racetrack, in **You Were Never Lovelier** (1942). Although Hayworth's voice was dubbed over by singer Nan Wynn's for the "Dearly Beloved" number, she did all her own footwork in the dance routines. The film was enlivened by Jerome Kern's and Johnny Mercer's music and lyrics, and Xavier Cugat's Orchestra which added a Latin-American touch to the soundtrack.*

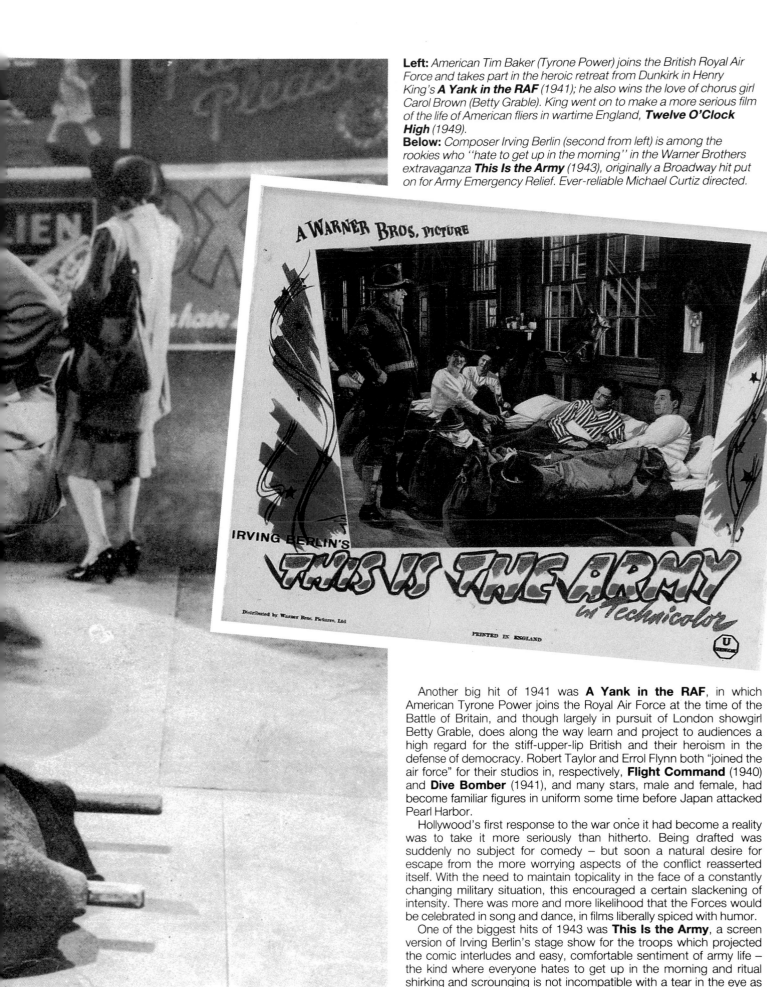

Left: *American Tim Baker (Tyrone Power) joins the British Royal Air Force and takes part in the heroic retreat from Dunkirk in Henry King's* **A Yank in the RAF** *(1941); he also wins the love of chorus girl Carol Brown (Betty Grable). King went on to make a more serious film of the life of American fliers in wartime England,* **Twelve O'Clock High** *(1949).*

Below: *Composer Irving Berlin (second from left) is among the rookies who "hate to get up in the morning" in the Warner Brothers extravaganza* **This Is the Army** *(1943), originally a Broadway hit put on for Army Emergency Relief. Ever-reliable Michael Curtiz directed.*

A WARNER BROS. PICTURE

IRVING BERLIN'S

THIS IS THE ARMY

in Technicolor

Distributed by Warner Bros. Pictures, Ltd

PRINTED IN ENGLAND

Another big hit of 1941 was **A Yank in the RAF**, in which American Tyrone Power joins the Royal Air Force at the time of the Battle of Britain, and though largely in pursuit of London showgirl Betty Grable, does along the way learn and project to audiences a high regard for the stiff-upper-lip British and their heroism in the defense of democracy. Robert Taylor and Errol Flynn both "joined the air force" for their studios in, respectively, **Flight Command** (1940) and **Dive Bomber** (1941), and many stars, male and female, had become familiar figures in uniform some time before Japan attacked Pearl Harbor.

Hollywood's first response to the war once it had become a reality was to take it more seriously than hitherto. Being drafted was suddenly no subject for comedy – but soon a natural desire for escape from the more worrying aspects of the conflict reasserted itself. With the need to maintain topicality in the face of a constantly changing military situation, this encouraged a certain slackening of intensity. There was more and more likelihood that the Forces would be celebrated in song and dance, in films liberally spiced with humor.

One of the biggest hits of 1943 was **This Is the Army**, a screen version of Irving Berlin's stage show for the troops which projected the comic interludes and easy, comfortable sentiment of army life – the kind where everyone hates to get up in the morning and ritual shirking and scrounging is not incompatible with a tear in the eye as one salutes the flag or thinks of lost comrades.

151

Paramount's **Star Spangled Rhythm** and Warner Brothers' **Thank Your Lucky Stars** (both 1943) had an even vaguer connection with wartime realities: the entertaining of a few suitably glamorized servicemen on leave was an excuse for all-star studio revues in which the house specialities were paraded or good-naturedly parodied. The atmosphere created by such films was deliberately informal – everyone pulling together for the war effort, whether by selling bonds, dancing with soldiers at the Hollywood Canteen, singing patriotic songs, or raising a laugh through the incongruity of Bette Davis growling about the men left at home, "They're Either Too Young or Too Old", or Paulette Goddard, Dorothy Lamour and Veronica Lake, reigning queens of Paramount, drawing humorous attention to their prime attributes in "A Sweater, a Sarong and a Peekaboo Bang".

There were, of course, even less direct expressions of American patriotism and solidarity with the war effort; a film like Warners' biography of George M. Cohan, **Yankee Doodle Dandy** (1942), being a celebration of a major show-business personality with a role tailor-made for James Cagney, might in principle have been made at any time, but in 1942 it gave more emphasis to the patriotism of the great Broadway man who wrote "Over There" and was quite shameless about hitting audiences over the head with its jingoistic message.

Such films counted as "serious"; Cagney even got an Oscar for his impersonation of Cohan. Sentimentality was definitely in, but audiences could not stomach ruthless or satirical approaches to the war. Ernst Lubitsch's **To Be or Not to Be** (1942) was a prime example. A

Left and right: *The ebullient George M. Cohan (James Cagney) is riding high in* **Yankee Doodle Dandy** *(1942), one of several showbiz pictures directed by the indefatigable Michael Curtiz, who (according to Peter Ustinov) had a long career in Hollywood despite the handicap that he "forgot his native Hungarian without taking the precaution of learning any other language".*

Cagney, who started as a song-and-dance man, won an Oscar for his portrayal of Cohan. Orson Welles has said of him that his performances are "always unreal and always true".

comedy about Polish actors caught up in the invasion of their country, it expressly makes the point that actors are actors first, and political beings way afterwards. Legend has it that at the main preview everything went smoothly until it got to the line, delivered by Sig Ruman as an idiotic Gestapo officer, in which Jack Benny's Hamlet is commented on, thus: "Believe me, what he did to Shakespeare we are now doing to Poland." From this point, witnesses insist, laughter died and the film was castigated as, at best, unfeeling and in bad taste, at worst a vicious attempt by the "Berlin-born" (though Jewish) Lubitsch to play Goebbels's game and support the Nazi cause.

Lubitsch and his co-producer, the Hungarian-born British film mogul Alexander Korda, were left mystified: did a war mean that all sense of humor had to go by the board, that the eccentricities of one's allies could not be the occasion of a little teasing? The answer, for the moment, was a resounding "yes".

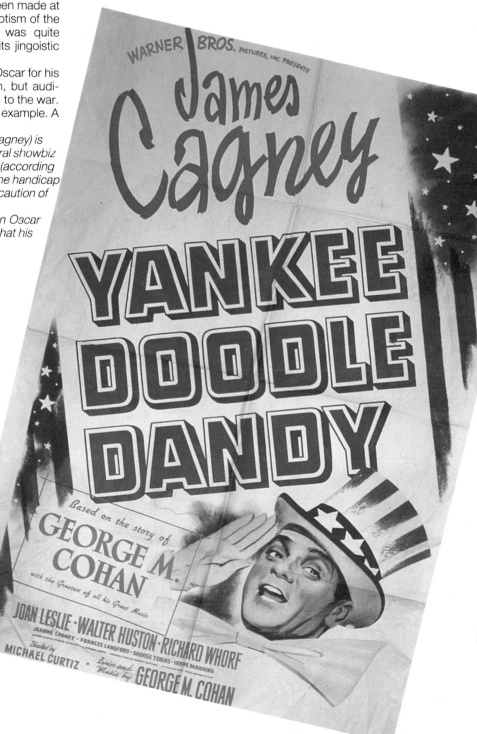

Disney's war

But what was Hollywood doing when it was not concerning itself in any appreciable way with the war? Certainly at the forefront of escapist cinema in the dark days of 1942-3 were Walt Disney's films. Though the Disney animation studio did its bit for the war effort with directly instructional films like **Victory Through Air Power** (1943) and tactful tributes to the Good Neighbor policy like **Saludos Amigos** (1943) and **The Three Caballeros** (1945), its central concern was still magical entertainment for the whole family, whether with a self-consciously cultural slant – as in **Fantasia**, which

Left and below: *Fantasia* (1940; general release by RKO, 1942) put animated pictures to a series of popular orchestral pieces, played by the Philadelphia Orchestra, conducted by Leopold Stokowski. One of adviser Deems Taylor's more adventurous choices was Stravinsky's "The Rite of Spring" (1913), originally composed as a ballet score for Diaghilev's company. Its dissonances and jagged rhythms suggested to the Disney team the creation and evolution of a savage world in which dinosaurs struggle for survival and destroy each other in a process of Darwinian selection.

"The Concert Feature" section originated with the idea of starring Mickey Mouse in a short feature, backed by music from "The Sorcerer's Apprentice" (1897) by Dukas. This finally became one of the most popular sections of the completed film, now endlessly reshown on television.

Mickey is a trainee magician who knows how to start a spell to help him with the household chores but cannot control it. He is quickly overwhelmed by multiplying brooms (eventually 16 of them) and cascading buckets of water.

Pinocchio (1940) carried to new heights the experiments with the multi-plane Technicolor begun in **Fantasia.** But the process was too elaborate and expensive, so that **Pinocchio** remains technically supreme and unique among Disney's creations. Based on Carlo Collodi's story, it describes how a boy puppet is made by the old puppet-maker Geppetto, who longs for a son **left**. Brought to life by the Blue Fairy (below) to the accompaniment of "When You Wish Upon a Star", Pinocchio soon begins to be confusedly aware of human desires and temptations **bottom**, later symbolized by a monstrous nose and then by even more grotesque attributes.

Left and below left: *Pinocchio*'s conscience is Jiminy Cricket, given a marvellously moralistic voice by Cliff Edwards (Pinocchio's voice was Dickie Jones). Other new friends are Figaro the cat and Cleo the confident goldfish.

Below: In *Dumbo* (1941) a baby elephant with giant ears is given a flying lesson by some at first not very friendly crows – who sing disbelievingly, "When I See an Elephant Fly", to the much-mocked infant pachyderm.

Bottom: *Bambi* (1942) relates the adventures of a young fawn and his forest friends, such as Thumper the rabbit and Flower the skunk. But the real star of the film is the beautifully animated forest itself.

illustrated a whole program of classical music in easily comprehensible terms – or the fairy-tale approach of **Pinocchio** (1940), **Dumbo** (1941) and **Bambi** (1942).

It was surely an important part of these films' appeal that nothing could be further removed from the reality of war. And in this heyday of the animated feature there was even room for others, notably Max Fleischer's **Gulliver's Travels** (1939) and his parable of insects heading for a rooftop paradise, **Mr Bug Goes to Town** (1941).

Babes in Hollywood

Meanwhile the musicals of the early forties willingly emphasized those elements that removed them from real life. They might be set in an MGM never-never land of wholesome teenagers perpetually putting on a show; from **Babes in Arms** (1939) to **Babes on Broadway** (1941), Judy Garland and Mickey Rooney seldom seemed to do anything else.

At 20th Century-Fox their leading ladies – Betty Grable, Alice Faye, Carmen Miranda, Sonja Henie – appeared in a number of unlikely locations, entirely re-created on the studio backlot, in which Rio and Havana were virtually indistinguishable from the Rockies in springtime or Miami with a moon over it. In their films there was never more than a whiff of war. At most one of the male characters might be drafted, so that his beloved could dream musically of him or comical

Below: *Cabin in the Sky* (1943), the first all-black musical since *Hallelujah!* (1929), was also Vincente Minnelli's directorial debut. The hero, played by radio star Eddie ''Rochester'' Anderson, is torn between his virtuous wife (Ethel Waters) and the enticing Georgia Brown (Lena Horne). Here Georgia takes time off from seduction while ''Shine'' is performed by Willie Best (at piano) and the talented singer/dancer John W. ''Bubbles'' Bublett.

Below right: *Babes in Arms* (1939), directed by ex-Warners choreographer Busby Berkeley for MGM, was the original ''kids putting on a show'' musical. The ''show'' featured two blackface numbers, ''The Darktown Strutters' Ball'' and ''My Daddy Was a Minstrel Man''. Here Mickey Rooney (left) is being upstaged by the ''white'' star, Douglas McPhail, with Betty Jaynes. His regular co-star in MGM musicals, Judy Garland, is offstage in this scene.

misunderstandings could arise when he came home on furlough. The classic example of all this is **The Gang's All Here** (1943), a Busby Berkeley extravaganza that permits Alice Faye to sing one of the key songs of the war years, "No Love, No Nothing (Until My Baby Comes Home)", while her soldier-hero extricates himself from a romance with someone else. Also here the "Lady in the Tutti-Frutti Hat" number was the apotheosis of Carmen Miranda's career, and the film climaxes with one of those surrealistic Berkeley numbers that had made him the greatest dance director of the thirties, when the innocent-sounding "Polka-Dot Polka" turns into a bizarre fantasy and the grand finale merges into "A Journey to a Star" with all the mad imagery that implies. The whole intention of this dazzlingly achieved movie was to make its audience forget the war and enter the magic world that was created by Hollywood alone.

Heaven's gate?

There were other types of screen fantasies being made at this time. In **Cabin in the Sky** (1943), for instance, Vincente Minnelli, an important directorial recruit from the Broadway stage, created a beguiling all-black heaven and hell, with angels and devils fighting musically for the souls of mortals. Heavenly (or hellish) intervention in human affairs was, in fact, very popular in early forties films. Entries include William Dieterle's stylish period piece **All That Money Can Buy**, Alexander Hall's **Here Comes Mr Jordan** (both 1941), and Lubitsch's **Heaven Can Wait** (1943). Lubitsch's contribution to the cycle is probably the best – it features a great performance from suave Don Ameche as the average man given a chance to look over the faults of his life and, if he can, make amends. This film saw probably the last flourish of the famed "Lubitsch touch", especially in its visual depiction of the geography of hell. Yet another piece of

supernatural hokum was René Clair's **I Married a Witch** (1942), starring Veronica Lake as a Salem witch returning from the dead to fall in love with one of her persecutor's descendants (Fredric March).

These films took a fairly sunny view of the supernatural. But there was little or no actual magic in the series of vaguely Arabian Nights entertainments that poured out of Universal in the wake of Korda's **The Thief of Bagdad** (1940). In such films as **Arabian Nights** (1942) and **White Savage** (1943) the atmosphere remained happily fantastical – perhaps because it was difficult to take the resident temptress Maria Montez, with her heavy Latin accent and impassive acting style, too seriously in anything. Probably the best of these films, which also starred muscular Jon Hall and Turkish Turhan Bey, was **Ali Baba and the Forty Thieves** (1943), co-starring Sabu. However, the genre retained its slightly tatty charms through many variations like **Gypsy Wildcat** (1944), which updated the fantasy to an eighteenth century setting; **Sudan** (1945), with Bey as a slave prince; and, perhaps best and most bizarre of all, Robert Siodmak's **Cobra Woman** (1944), in which Jon Hall was a modern mariner wrecked on a forgotten Pacific paradise ruled by evil Maria Montez – ever busy sending all the available women up to bathe fatally in the "fire of eternal life" while her good twin waits in the wings wringing her hands until the inevitable volcanic eruption ends it all.

Above: *Double value for fans of Maria Montez in* **Cobra Woman** *(1944). She plays two parts – an evil South Seas priestess who is obsessed with snakes, and her virtuous sister. Here she is the cobra woman, with Lon Chaney Jr and Indian boy Sabu.*
Right: *The famous staircase quarrel, from* **The Magnificent Ambersons** *(1942), between spoiled George Amberson Minafter (Tim Holt) and his hysterical maiden Aunt Fanny (Agnes Moorehead).*

After Kane

Not all reflections on the supernatural were quite so cheerful, and it was at RKO that an horrific new trend grew up in the early forties. Before we look at Val Lewton's macabre movies, however, another, non-supernatural, masterpiece from RKO must be considered. This is 1942's **The Magnificent Ambersons**, a grim story of family decline with some of the most exquisite, sensitive and penetrating film-making ever done by Orson Welles, whose follow-up to **Citizen Kane** this was. It contained nothing even peripherally connected with the war; sadly, it was tampered with, though not made more popular, while Welles was away in South America making a tribute to the Good Neighbor policy, the unfinished **It's All True**, at the direct instigation of Washington.

But the most influential RKO film at this time was far less costly and prestigious than the beautiful **Ambersons**. It was a zero-budget horror film called **Cat People** (1942), made by Lewton, who was a new graduate to production. It gave a first chance at directing to Welles' editor, Robert Wise, and chose (largely of economic necessity) to create its effects by absence, darkness, suggestion, recognizing that the horror our own minds can create, stalking undefined in the shadows, is bound to be infinitely more frightening than any extra in an ill-fitting cat-suit. The film was one of the great "sleepers" of its time, achieving such unexpected success that it led to a succession of Lewton productions in the same mould – **I Walked With a Zombie**, **The Seventh Victim**, **Leopard Man** (all 1943) and **Curse of the Cat People** (1944).

The popularity of the Lewton cycle can be attributed to audiences looking for distraction from the very real menace outside by seeking out psychologically manageable horrors. It was a good trick as long as it could be pulled off. But by 1944 the lurker in the shadows was less a supernatural cat than a very contemporary con man, killer or broad on the make. It was the time of *film noir*, that most characteristic of wartime Hollywood genres, and neurosis could no longer be confined to an alternative world, a nightmare that would evaporate as soon as one ceased to suspend one's disbelief.

Left: *Alice Moore (Jane Randolph) in* **Cat People** *(1942), moments after having bumped into a clawed creature in the swimming pool. Here she shows her ripped robe to Blondie (Mary Halsey).*

Below: *"Can you tell me how to get to . . . ?" Jessica Holland (Christine Gordon) and friend Betsy (Frances Dee) being stopped on the way to the local voodoo ceremony in* **I Walked With a Zombie** *(1943).*

Escape to the Shadows 1944-5

Chapter 11

John Cromwell's film **Since You Went Away**, that hymn to the American home in 1943, did not come out until 1944, and by then it was strangely anachronistic. Most of the married American men who were going off to war had already gone – including such movie stars as Henry Fonda, James Stewart, Robert Taylor and the recently widowed Clark Gable (his wife, the star Carole Lombard, had been killed in a plane crash while on tour selling war bonds) – and the women they left behind had got used to it.

Since You Went Away was indeed made with the idea of enshrining the recent past rather than reflecting the immediate present. But, oddly enough, it was out of touch in its psychological rather than its physical presentation: it offered up a sanitized world where all worries could be dealt with by good will and fortitude; the war, though troublesome and painful for many, was still kept safely in an airtight compartment, somewhere over there. But by 1944 neither film-makers nor audiences saw it quite that way anymore.

It was not that the war in the Pacific and in Europe had moved centerscreen either, for most of the dark Hollywood dramas and thrillers that dominated the period do not specify very clearly when they are taking place, though generally it is in a world that is clearly not at war. In that respect, at least, *film noir* – a term later coined for the movement by appreciative French critics – could be regarded as escapist. But these films cannot be explained so easily as the Val Lewton horror cycle of the mid forties and its offshoots, for example. This time the horror is interior, something you cannot run away from.

Black souls

Superficially, "horror" might seem an overstatement of what *film noir* actually presented. Certainly some of the classics of the genre, such as **Gaslight** or **The Lodger** (both 1944), are on the verge of the psychological horror movie. But **Laura** (1944), the film that more than any other started it all off, is not a horror film, nor are **Phantom Lady, The Woman in the Window, Double Indemnity** (all 1944) or **Mildred Pierce** (1945), to cite a handful of the more obvious examples. They definitely open up a dark world of powerful and perverse passions for us, but that is not quite the same thing, and not so easy to shrug off. The "black" of *film noir* is literally the blackness of night and metaphorically the blackness of the soul of at least one major character.

Fear, greed and lust for power are at the root of much of the *film noir*'s action, and insanity or obsession frequently provides the paradoxical rationale. The locale is usually Los Angeles or some other

Right: *In George Cukor's splendid version of **Gaslight** (1944), sadistic Gregory Anton (Charles Boyer) tries to drive his wife Paula (Ingrid Bergman) mad while unearthing the family jewels. She gains her revenge after he's caught – she pretends that she really is mad and capable of anything . . .*

unnamed American urban hell, but it may be somewhere slightly offbeat, at a period somewhat removed in time – **The Lodger**'s London in the nineties, say, or the American West of **Pursued** (1947) – but the links with everyday life must remain strong.

An American nightmare

It has been usual to credit the group of German and Austrian emigrés who came to prominence in Hollywood at this time for the appearance of *film noir*, and to link it with the *Angst*-ridden German Expressionist cinema of the silent era. But that is a drastic over-simplification. It is true that **Laura**, normally regarded as the first fully fledged Hollywood *film noir*, was directed by the Viennese Otto Preminger after the first director, Rouben Mamoulian, had been fired,

but the origins of the project and its materials were entirely American.

Robert Siodmak, the director of **Phantom Lady**, a small-budget surprise success, was born in Memphis but raised in Leipzig and had become a notable film-maker in Germany, but worked in the opposite camp to Expressionism. His **Menschen am Sonntag** (1929), co-directed by a genuine maker of Gothic horror films, Edgar G. Ulmer, and with the assistance of the young Billy Wilder and Fred Zinnemann, was a working-class comedy that pioneered location realism. Wilder himself was primarily known as a writer and director of comedy when he made **Double Indemnity**, and the *film noir* genre was well established in Hollywood before Fritz Lang, a more convincing example of an Expressionist director, turned to it with **The Woman in the Window** and **Scarlet Street** (1945).

Left: *Jack the Ripper (Laird Cregar) is about to find another victim in **The Lodger** (1944). The movie was a remake of Alfred Hitchcock's 1926 film by John Brahm, who appropriately began his film career in London.*

Above: *In **Laura** (1944), a decadent columnist (Clifton Webb), a self-indulgent playboy (Vincent Price), his ex-mistress (Judith Anderson), an obsessed detective (Dana Andrews) – and a portrait of Laura (Gene Tierney) provide a complex network of jealousy and murder.*

Before night fell…

In any case, the audiences to whom these dark dramas proved so instantly attractive were almost entirely American. If we suppose that the European emigrés had some kind of intuitive knowledge of how to cater to the taste for such a dark world, the presence and nature of the need has still to be explained. Earlier in the forties there had been one or two films that anticipated *film noir*. In 1941 Josef von Sternberg came up with his last bizarre masterpiece, an opulent version of the old stage shocker **The Shanghai Gesture**. Its brothel location was not exactly emphasized, but the film is still full of perfumed perversity and the kind of twisted eroticism that became crucial to the new form.

In 1943 Alfred Hitchcock made his first truly American film, **Shadow of a Doubt**, about the going into hiding of a murderer (Joseph Cotten) with his small-town family and his final exposure, at least in the eyes of his doting niece (Teresa Wright). Though the film was noted at the time for its innovatory use of real locations (in the West Coast town of Santa Rosa), and most of the menace lies hidden under the implacable glare of the Californian sun, the plot material, the suggestions of decay, and the heroine's almost fatal brush with evil and obsession, at once link it with the *film noir* proper of only a year or so later. Although Sternberg was another Viennese and Hitchcock a Londoner, these were clearly *Hollywood* films, as were the pivotal works in *film noir*'s studio origins, **Citizen Kane** and **The Maltese Falcon** (both 1941).

Left: *The Shanghai Gesture* (1941) was Josef von Sternberg's only feature movie of the forties, an unrestrained fantasy of oriental decadence set in a gambling den where chance and destiny conspire to destroy doomed, unhappy lives.

Above: *The Shanghai Gesture* is a monument to the doomed. Mother Gin-Sling (Ona Munson) controls the wretched lives of the gamblers who patronize her establishment, hiding all emotions behind a masklike countenance. Her vulnerable, drug-addicted Eurasian daughter Poppy is played by Gene Tierney.
Below: In Alfred Hitchcock's **Shadow of a Doubt** (1943), Uncle Charlie (Joseph Cotten), the "Merry Widow" murderer, seeks refuge in a small Californian town. Unluckily for him he's front page news, and his attempts to remove the story in front of his niece while pretending that he's performing a trick only increase her suspicions.

Left: *"A tragic and eternal work of art"* was how critic James Agee described William Wellman's **The Story of GI Joe** (1945). It was based on the reminiscences of Pulitzer Prize-winning war correspondent Ernie Pyle (Burgess Meredith, center), who goes through the Italian campaign with Captain Walker (Robert Mitchum, left) and his men, sharing their hazards and mourning their losses. The film ends with the death of Walker in an attack on a monastery near Rome. The real-life Ernie Pyle later went to the Pacific front where (like many of the soldier actors) he was killed in action.

Below: Also about the Italian campaign, Lewis Milestone's **A Walk in the Sun** (1945) concentrated on a single morning during the Salerno landings, south of Naples, in 1943 and the attempt of an American battalion to capture a German emplacement.
Dana Andrews is the sergeant (front left) conferring with John Ireland (center) and Lloyd Bridges (front right). The fatalistic screenplay, from Harry Brown's novel, was by Robert Rossen, who went on to direct **Body and Soul** (1947), **All the King's Men** (1949) and, much later, **The Hustler** (1961).

Dark corners

When the fully conceived *film noir* arrived on the scene, it arrived with a vengeance. Suddenly, in 1944 it seemed that every film in sight had dramatic low-key lighting, was full of mysterious pursuits through rainwashed streets and otherwise took place in small basement bars or overstuffed "artistic" apartments. No situation depicted was without its *femme fatale*, its secretly demented artist, its effete and sexually obsessed wit, its murder and mayhem as a part of normal expectation, and its innocents, male and female, caught in the toils of a strange life they cannot understand. And sometimes the innocent are as doomed as the guilty – perhaps more so, since they lack the perception to defend themselves. It was, indeed, a depressing landscape that was under scrutiny at this less than cheering point in world history. It was even odder still, perhaps, since the prospect of Allied defeat in the war had faded and been replaced by a rapid and fairly confident victory following the opening of a Western front in Europe on 6 June 1944.

The road to glory?

We can only speculate why a taste for picturesque gloom and studies of the trapped, helpless and hopeless should have dominated American cinema at this time of outward advance and hope. A key to it might be provided if we look at the war and the films that depicted it. During the three-and-a-half years America was directly involved in World War II precisely this happened: the heroic expectations of the American public and the American cinema in 1942-3 had gradually worn out, to be replaced by an anti-heroic view of war as a painful necessity with precious little glory. A characteristic war film of the period was William Wellman's **The Story of GI Joe** (1945). Here, war correspondent Ernie Pyle (portrayed by Burgess Meredith in the film), who wrote the source book **Here Is the War**, insisted in his contract that there should be no extraneous heroics, and the picture was accordingly gritty, downbeat and sympathetic to the plight of the wretched soldiers.

Lewis Milestone contributed **The Purple Heart** (1944), in which a group of captured American flyers are tortured by the Japanese with no eventual reprieve (despite some appalling jingoism), and **A Walk in the Sun** (1945), a similarly fatalistic picture of the slow grind of war and the virtual inevitability of death for the majority. None of this could be described as outright pacifism, but these films generally eschewed war glory in favor of one which saw the dreadful conflict as an unwanted necessity.

Trouble on the home front

In the circumstances, it is not surprising that the "civilian" cinema should have been so preoccupied with neurosis. Frequently, though not always, *film noir*'s nasty goings-on involve the privileged classes: old money tries to protect itself in any imaginable way, artists and intellectuals hide murderous frenzy behind a suave and debonair façade, the family has endless horrors committed in its name. That pattern is applied to most of the famous firsts of the genre.

In **Phantom Lady** the fundamentally decent characters are entangled in a dark, night-time world of madness, represented by the opposite poles of the cool artist killer and the lady in the hat, the only person who could establish the hero's innocence of his wife's murder if she had not gone irrevocably mad from the pangs of love. In **Laura** virtually everybody around the mysterious vanished figure of Laura herself (Gene Tierney) is vicious and corrupt, peddling flesh or harboring obsessive jealousy and possessiveness behind a mask of cynical wit; Clifton Webb here played one of *film noir*'s most compelling villains in the acid Waldo Lydekker. In **Christmas Holiday** (1944) nice Deanna Durbin marries charming New Orleans playboy Gene Kelly only to find that he is a gambler, an embezzler and ultimately a murderer, aided and abetted by his classy mother, with whom he is linked in suspicious closeness. In **Dark Waters** (1944), rich but vulnerable Merle Oberon is almost driven mad by evil supposed friends and relatives after her property. In **Gaslight** rich Ingrid Bergman is driven almost mad by avaricious husband Charles Boyer, searching for an inheritance she does not even know she has.

The suffocating nineties setting of **Gaslight** recurs also in **Hangover Square** (1944), a curious but brilliantly atmospheric reworking of another Patrick Hamilton work, which transfers it from the uneasy Munich atmosphere of 1938 to a Victorian world where the composer hero undergoes a Jekyll-and-Hyde transformation (supposedly schizophrenic) to become a sex murderer by night. The same idea of the artist/intellectual as unbalanced and potentially evil had occurred in the 1941 version of **Dr Jekyll and Mr Hyde** itself, with Spencer Tracy as the schizophrenic hero flaying Ingrid Bergman and Lana Turner. And the theme was repeated in Albert Lewin's culture-littered **The Picture of Dorian Gray** (1945), starring Hurd Hatfield. Meanwhile, John Brahm, who had directed Laird Cregar in **Hangover Square**, made **The Lodger**, a fictionalization of Jack the Ripper, also starring Cregar.

Left: Brian Cameron (Joseph Cotten) in **Gaslight** (1944) plays the Scotland Yard detective who is falling in love with Paula Anton (Ingrid Bergman), sharing her suspicions that husband Gregory (played by Charles Boyer) is trying to drive her mad. Bergman won an Oscar and Boyer was nominated; more remarkably, seventeen-year-old Angela Lansbury, a refugee from the London blitz, was nominated for the best supporting actress award in her first role — a cockney maid.

Above: John Brahm's second – and last – good film was **Hangover Square** (1945), based on the novel by Patrick Hamilton. The cast seemed to have been cursed. Laird Cregar (left) slimmed so drastically for his part as a demented pianist-composer who murders beautiful women that he died, aged just 28. Linda Darnell seen here as a typically sluttish femme fatale, survived for another twenty years but was burned to death in a house fire in Chicago.

A touch of Germanic dread

All of these films, amazingly, emerged in 1944-5. But they do not exhaust the list. There are *films noirs*, also, that take place in much more basic suburban society or take their characters down to depths of social and sexual degradation all the more alarming because they do not have, like **The Lodger**, the saving and distancing grace of period picturesqueness. No doubt the greatest degradation suffered by any "hero" at this time was that meted out to Edward G. Robinson in Fritz Lang's **The Woman in the Window** and **Scarlet Street**.

In his native Germany Lang had accustomed himself to the fact that the world was a dark and dangerous place in **Dr Mabuse der Spieler** (1922) and other early films, and there are, of course, great moments of bleakness in his **Die Nibelungen** saga of 1924 and futuristic epic **Metropolis** (1927). But it is **M** (1931), in which Peter Lorre plays a child-murderer, that most powerfully foreshadows the tortured, guilty passions of Lang's *noir* period in Hollywood. Arriving in America in 1934, Lang took time to learn about American society before delivering such caustic comments on it as **Fury** (1936) and **You Only Live Once** (1937). His Edward G. Robinson/Joan Bennett films then perfectly caught the mood of the times.

Left: *Complications set in in Otto Preminger's **Fallen Angel** (1945). Stella the waitress is nothing but trouble for her admirer Eric Stanton (center), who decides to marry Alice Faye for her money. With this, he hopes to pacify and win over Stella. Alas, on his wedding night longed-for Stella is murdered by another lover, who then sets about finding Eric to add to his kill. As luck would have it, Eric chose well in Alice Faye who shields him from the worst and proves her love, enabling the film to resolve itself happily for audience and participants alike.*

Above: *The Woman in the Window* (1944). Professor Richard Wanley (Edward G. Robinson) admires a portrait of Alice Reed (Joan Bennett) in a store window, but soon regrets meeting its original subject, who ensnares him in a nightmare of murder and blackmail.

In **The Woman in the Window** Robinson plays a mild and innocent professor who gets entangled with a beautiful but dangerous kept woman and so inevitably with blackmail and murder. In **Scarlet Street** he is a timid clerk who is also a gifted Sunday painter, held hopelessly in thrall by trashy Joan Bennett even to the extent of letting her pass off his paintings as hers while she kicks him around and insults him; in one classic sado-masochistic moment she makes him varnish her toenails with the laconic order, "Here. You're a painter. Paint these."

Otto Preminger's **Fallen Angel** (1945) dissects small-town life with admirable irony: a man marries for money (but not very much) just so that he can keep his place in the affections of the town slut, desired by all. If this was small-time duplicity, **Double Indemnity** was big-time. Here, Barbara Stanwyck's evil wife, with her eyes set on adultery and her husband's insurance, and with her vulgar blonde bangs and suggestive ankle-bracelet, is one of the definitive *femmes fatales* of the forties. She easily seduces the compliant insurance agent, played by Fred MacMurray, into helping her murder her husband for his money, and the intrigue this pair is involved in, set in shuttered Spanish-Colonial rooms, and bleak, anonymous supermarkets, is unforgettably sour and unappetizing.

In one sense all these films are escapist: they not only avoid almost all mention of the war, even though the setting of most of them is clearly contemporary, but they also reach areas of life – and death – that must have been far from the everyday concerns of the average audience. For example, they probed the still "exotic" worlds of psychiatry and psychoanalysis, which became fashionable in films like Hitchcock's **Spellbound** (1945), where Ingrid Bergman resolves Gregory Peck's amnesia with the help of a dream sequence by Salvador Dali; William Dieterle's **Love Letters** (1945), where Joseph

Below and left: *In Alfred Hitchcock's **Spellbound** (1945) Dr Constance Peterson (Ingrid Bergman) is in for a shock as she discovers that the new head of the clinic where she works, ''Dr Edwardes'' (Gregory Peck), is an impostor. He is really John Ballantine, suffering loss of memory and under the illusion that he may have murdered the real Edwardes. But with the help of her trusty old psychiatry professor (played by Michael Chekhov, the playwright's nephew) she establishes her lover's innocence and exposes the real killer.*

Cotten resolves Jennifer Jones' trauma over the death of her first husband; and Billy Wilder's **The Lost Weekend** (1945), where Jane Wyman works valiantly to retrieve Ray Milland from alcoholism on the assumption that explaining his weakness – a writer's block – will explain it away. In America at the time few filmgoers would have been personally acquainted with a psychiatrist, or knew more about psychiatry than might be gleaned from *Readers' Digest*; these films offered fresh insights.

Mother's ruin

Only one of the really important *films noirs* of the period touched on the real lives of those in the audience, or at least on their dreams, ambitions and fears. This was **Mildred Pierce**, based on a novel by James M. Cain, which returned Joan Crawford to major stardom after some years in the doldrums. The film is a very interesting combination of old and new elements. In many of her thirties films at MGM Crawford had played a character clawing her way up the social

Far left: *Joan Crawford is in for a rough time in and as* **Mildred Pierce** *(1945). She plays a successful business woman who unwisely takes up with wealthy playboy Monty Berrigan (Zachary Scott), marries him, and finds herself under police suspicion when he is murdered.*

Below: *Ray Milland as alcoholic Don Birnam in Billy Wilder's* **The Lost Weekend** *(1945). Critic James Agee commented: ''I undershtand that liquor interesh: innerish: intereshtsh are rather worried about thish film. Thash tough.''*

and financial ladder, to represent a version of the basic American success story – though there was almost always a message suggesting material success could not itself bring happiness.

Crawford as Mildred Pierce bakes pies to become a restaurant tycoon, all for the sake of her daughter, who grows up into a spoiled and snobbish little minx ready to reject her mother for her "commonness" and steal her mother's man in the bargain. She also kills him and expects mother to take the blame. Michael Curtiz's direction presents a mixture of *film noir* fatalism, successful career-ism, the decadence of the rich and idle, and the psychological implications of obsessive mother-love. No wonder the film, aided by

the moody, low-key art direction of Anton Grot and photography of Ernest Haller, was a runaway success that launched a whole series of pictures in which Crawford suffered in the greatest luxury, a revolver tucked away in the pocket of every mink.

Down these mean streets

Another trend was indicated by **Double Indemnity**, in that it was based on a James M. Cain story and scripted by the most distinguished practitioner of that particular kind of disenchanted American thriller novel, Raymond Chandler. Several of Chandler's own novels were to find their way onto the screen in the next two or

Love trouble in **Double Indemnity** (1944). Insurance investigator Barton Keyes (Edward G. Robinson, **left**) reluctantly comes to realize that his younger colleague, salesman Walter Neff, is involved with scheming Phyllis Dietrichson **below** in a plot to kill her husband and collect the insurance money. However, the murderous duo soon come to distrust each other, which – in a typical James M. Cain finale – leads to their violent end. Cain's story is supposed to have been based on the notorious Ruth Snyder case of 1927.

three years, starting with **Murder, My Sweet** in 1945, and followed by **The Big Sleep, The Brasher Doubloon** and **The Blue Dahlia** (a screen original) in 1946, and **The Lady in the Lake** in 1947. In 1946 Cain's most famous book, **The Postman Always Rings Twice**, was also filmed for the first time in America (it had already been filmed without authorization in France and Italy).

These films make a coherent group because they all share a certain sour romanticism and a bleak California location. Both Cain and Chandler claim to be tough and disillusioned, but in fact they both hide a soft, idealistic center beneath the deadpan cynicism. Chandler in particular tends to make of his private eye Philip Marlowe a sort of contemporary knight on a quest for lost innocence. The character, variously embodied by Dick Powell (**Murder, My Sweet**), George Montgomery (**The Brasher Doubloon**), Robert Montgomery (virtually unseen in the subjective camerawork of **The Lady in the Lake**) and, magisterially, by Humphrey Bogart (**The Big Sleep**), always retains the heroic lineaments beyond the outwardly gruff and spiky exterior.

Bogart was the greatest Marlowe, perhaps because he was like him in real life. Certainly man and myth have now become one in the popular imagination. Emerging out of the shadows of the war and *film noir*, Bogart became the greatest cinematic icon of the period because his Marlowe, his Sam Spade and his Rick in **Casablanca** were each, in Chandler's words, a man "who is not himself mean, who is neither tarnished nor afraid", for all that he has been bruised by experience. The Bogart hero, pug-ugly, rasping, trench-coated and smoking, caught exactly that forties mood of disenchantment but never bowed to sentiment or cruelty. Beginning with hoodlums in the mid thirties, Bogart had gone on to more complex gangsters in films like **High Sierra** (1941), and by the time of **The Maltese Falcon** was a major star. If we remember him best as Rick, it is his two films for

Left: *Raymond Chandler's only screen original,* **The Blue Dahlia** *(1946), is a too predictable tale of a war veteran (Alan Ladd) whose unfaithful wife is murdered by his unstable best friend. He is suspected, but fortunately a young blonde passer-by (Veronica Lake) helps him to prove his innocence.*

Above: *Private-eye Philip Marlowe (Humphrey Bogart) prepares to defend himself against vicious gambler Eddie Mars and his thugs, ably supported by wealthy client Vivian Rutledge (Lauren Bacall) in* **The Big Sleep** *(1946). This was easily the best Chandler adaptation before Robert Altman's* **The Long Goodbye** *(1973).*

Below and right: The Postman Always Rings Twice (1946) was based on James Cain's 1934 novel of murder, jealousy and betrayal set in the small towns and suburbs of Southern California. Cora Smith (Lana Turner), bored by her elderly, kindly husband and his lonely roadside café develops a taste for excitement at the sight of handsome drifter Frank Chambers who happens by and decides to stay on as handyman.

Howard Hawks, **The Big Sleep** and **To Have and Have Not** (1945), that brought him his finest moments, as well as Lauren Bacall.

When Bogart is Marlowe we are left in no doubt that the streets he traverses are very mean indeed, while the occasional brushes with riches – as in his employer's household in **The Big Sleep** – show something as decadent and corrupt as one could imagine, at any rate within the bounds of the Production Code at that time.

The Code was circumvented another way in Tay Garnett's simmering version of **The Postman Always Rings Twice**. Despite the much-vaunted freedom that permitted a sexually explicit version with Jack Nicholson and Jessica Lange in 1981, the erotic effect of the 1946 version is much more powerful because the animal chemistry between John Garfield and Lana Turner is palpable even though they are fully clothed and nothing is visibly going on that the censor could possibly object to.

Left: *Alice Maybery (Judy Garland), a New York girl, accidentally encounters Corporal Joe Allen (Robert Walker), an out-of-town soldier on 48 hours' leave, at Pennsylvania Station. She shows him the sights of the city, they part but miraculously meet again and impulsively decide to get married.* **The Clock** *(1945) was entirely a Hollywood studio movie, despite its New York atmosphere. Director Vincente Minnelli promptly married Judy Garland on its completion.*

Below: *Small-town boy Woodrow (Eddie Bracken), rejected by the army because of his non-stop sneezing, manages to return home to loud applause in* **Hail the Conquering Hero** *(1944), snappily directed by Preston Sturges, the decade's top comedy director.*

A lighter touch

Obviously not everything in the last two years of the war was entirely gloomy and negative – not even everything related to the war. There were still occasional comedies with some kind of war background, most notably Preston Sturges' **Hail the Conquering Hero** (1944), which uses the return to his home town of a totally undistinguished marine – invalided out of the service because he sneezes endlessly – as catalyst for a mordant picture of American small-town life. He is accepted as a hero, and the various reactions to his return and elevation to star status in the local community are sharply etched.

There was even room for a bittersweet romantic comedy like Vincente Minnelli's **The Clock** (1945), with Judy Garland and Robert Walker as war-crossed lovers who meet, marry, separate and eventually reunite in New York while he is waiting to be shipped abroad. The other images of GIs on furlough or invalided out were hardly more reassuring. In **I'll Be Seeing You** (1944) shell-shocked Joseph Cotten is encouraged to believe in himself again by the confidence of Ginger Rogers, only to be shattered when he finds that she is actually a jailbird let out briefly for good conduct. In **The Enchanted Cottage** (1945) a badly scarred veteran marries a very plain girl who has loved him all along, and to one another they become beautiful, though they learn the hard way that the miracle is for their eyes only. Both stories end happily, of course: the hero of **I'll Be Seeing You** manages finally to accept the heroine's plight and wait for her; the couple in **The Enchanted Cottage** manage to be content with their own view of life, without expecting insensitive outsiders to share it. This was fine in the movies, but suggested a widespread unwillingness on Hollywood's part to deal with the uncomfortable realities of war and its aftermath.

187

Road to laughter?

Indeed, escapism was in general the watchword, and not necessarily always the perverse escapism of *film noir* either: it might be into the cheery fantasy of the "Road" films, or the innocuous world of the MGM musical, or the nostalgia craze that had many studios rummaging through their old properties and creating new ones to take audiences back to the happy days before the Depression or even World War I.

It was never a classic period for comedy. Even the generally expert Frank Capra succumbed to the general frenzy in his version of the famous comedy of murders, **Arsenic and Old Lace** (made in 1942 but not released till 1944), directing even such an old and sure hand as Cary Grant to mug up a storm. However, the "Road" films, with the

Below and right: *Frank Capra's excellent **Arsenic and Old Lace** (1944) is a comedy of the unexpected. The murderesses are two dear, sweet old ladies who delight in inviting lonely men back to tea where they poison them with elderberry wine laced with arsenic. Their brother, who is so crazy that he thinks he is still fighting the Spanish-American war in Cuba, buries the bodies in the cellar. All goes well until their nephew (Cary Grant, below left) turns up with even more corpses. Priscilla Lane is a nervous witness to the goings-on, but Peter Lorre (far right) and Raymond Massey enjoy the mayhem with subterranean relish.*

The movie was an uncharacteristic work for the sentimentally populist Capra. Cary Grant reckons this is his favorite among all the films in which he has appeared.

inevitable threesome of Bob Hope, Bing Crosby and Dorothy Lamour, were a shining exception, being built up loosely but reliably on the interplay of the known screen personalities of the stars, with, of course, Hope and Crosby always fighting over the favors of the unimpressed Lamour and a long string of often faintly surrealist gags. The series, which had begun in 1940 with **Road to Singapore**, reached its apogee in 1945 with the fourth, **Road to Utopia**, though it staggered on through three more, the last and least of which was **Road to Hong Kong** (1962).

Most of the nostalgia-escapist films were musicals or semi-musicals, and many of the musicals were to some extent escapes into other periods. In **Cover Girl** (1944), for instance, a flashback allowed Rita Hayworth to play her own grandmother, a musical star of an earlier era, while modern times were reflected in a number of lively routines choreographed by co-star Gene Kelly and a song for Phil Silvers – "Who's Complaining?" – which referred humorously to wartime rationing.

Above: "Like Webster's Dictionary we're Morocco bound", crooned Bob Hope (left) and Bing Crosby in **Road to Morocco** (1942). Crosby then sells Hope into slavery and woos Princess Shalmar (Dorothy Lamour) with the Johnny Burke/Jimmy Van Heusen number, "Moonlight Becomes You". Frank Butler and Don Hartman's witty script won an Academy Award nomination, and David Butler directed. This was the third in the very popular Paramount series of exotic excursions following trips to Singapore and Zanzibar. Next on the list is Yukon in the **Road to Utopia** (1945).

Right: Rita Hayworth poses for **Cover Girl** (1944), showing off her highly prized dancing legs. She started off as brunette Margarita Carmen Cansino, daughter of a Spanish dancer, switching to her mother's maiden name in 1937. Her husbands included Orson Welles and Aly Khan.

Music hath charms

Musical biographies of George Gershwin (**Rhapsody in Blue**, 1945), of Texas Guinan, queen of twenties nightclubs (**Incendiary Blonde**, 1945) and of **The Dolly Sisters** (1945) often did not take the re-creation of their period backgrounds very seriously, but at least looked backwards lovingly. And then there was a whole group of affectionate pieces of period Americana, set off seemingly by the enormous success of Vincente Minnelli's exquisitely stylish **Meet Me in St Louis** (1944), which had Judy Garland growing up amid the preparations for the great St Louis Exposition of 1904.

Among the films that immediately followed it were **State Fair** (1945), a remake with a new score by Rodgers and Hammerstein; **Centennial Summer** (1946), with a new score by Jerome Kern; and **Margie** (1946), in which Jeanne Crain suffered the pains and pleasures of a twenties adolescence, with enough music to remove the film from harsh reality, if not quite enough to transform it into a proper musical.

Meet Me in St Louis (1944) was based on a nostalgic serial in the New Yorker by Sally Benson, recalling the 1904 World Exposition in St Louis. It follows the life of the Smith family through four seasons, from summer 1903 to spring 1904, finding romance and fighting off a proposed move to New York. The lead part of Esther is played by Judy Garland **left** whose closest confidante is her elder sister Rose (Lucille Bremer, **above**). Her little sister Tootie (Margaret O'Brien, **right**) performs "The Cakewalk" with her at their brother's birthday party.

Top right: The film nears its climax on Christmas Eve when Esther gets a longed-for proposal of marriage from the boy next door.

Above and right: *On the Town* (1949) originated early in 1944 with a ballet, Fancy Free, by composer Leonard Bernstein and choreographer Jerome Robbins, later to be associated with **West Side Story** (1961). This tale of three sailors on 24 hours' shoreleave in New York was expanded into a Broadway show by writers Betty Comden and Adolph Green, and became a big hit. MGM owned the film rights but was in no hurry to use them. Finally innovative producer Arthur Freed permitted Gene Kelly and his co-choreographer Stanley Donen to direct it as their first entire film together. There were compromises, however. Most of the ballet sequences were dropped; so was much of Bernstein's music, replaced by Roger Edens' simpler, more commercial tunes. These — and the urban setting — made a superb base for MGM artifice and streetwise wit.

The cast could not have been bettered: the three sailors, Chip (Frank Sinatra), Ozzie (Jules Munshin) and Gabey (Gene Kelly); their girls, man-eating cabbie Brunhilde Esterhazy (Betty Garrett), sexy anthropologist Claire Huddesen (Ann Miller) and demure "Miss Turnstiles" Ivy Smith (Vera-Ellen); not to mention Florence Bates as a hard-drinking dance teacher and Alice Pearce as a comic-pathetic wallflower.

The contemporary scene was not entirely neglected, even in "proper" musicals. There were still sterling, if geographically vague, attempts to cement pan-American relations, and even vaguer nods to the war effort. Carmen Miranda was let loose on **Greenwich Village** (1944), and sent out to cheer the troops in **Four Jills in a Jeep** (1944), along with Alice Faye, Betty Grable and the "four Jills" themselves, played by Kay Francis, Carole Landis, Martha Raye and Mitzi Mayfair. **Bathing Beauty** (1944), the vehicle that launched Esther Williams, the new aquatic sensation, also featured the frantic comedy of Red Skelton and Xavier Cugat and a slew of explosive Latins such as the "famous Columbian baritone" Carlos Ramirez.

Even the film most indicative of the shape of musicals to come, **Anchors Aweigh** (1945), though primarily about a couple of sailors on leave in Hollywood, also could not resist getting Gene Kelly mixed up choreographically with some cutely ethnic Mexican children. This was sidestepping the film's prophetic quality, however, which lay in the happy combination of Kelly and Frank Sinatra, with Kelly's inventive dance direction, which beckoned towards **Take Me Out to the Ball Game** (1948) and the most influential musical of the decade, **On the Town** (1949).

Back to Reality 1946-7

Chapter 12

Naturally, before movie-making was sufficiently organized and industrialized to have spawned the studio system, movies were made largely in real places, or at least in stage-like settings built in natural light. But the cinema of the twenties and thirties thrived on illusion: the studios were the dream factories, and it was very rarely thought necessary to take film units away from Los Angeles on expensive and hazardous location adventures. A few semi-documentary exceptions were well publicized, but in the main the attitude to locations was that of the veteran producer who said: "A rock is a rock and a tree is a tree: shoot it in Griffith Park." (Griffith Park being a large, open, hilly area in the center of Los Angeles.) Immediately after the end of the war in 1945 ideas really began to change.

Street life

It is not easy to pin down the origins of the move towards realism in Hollywood movies after 1945. The bandwagon got rolling with a film that came out late in 1945, **The House on 92nd Street**, a tough thriller about spies in New York. A few film-makers in Hollywood had previously insisted on using real locations to give an extra realistic dimension to their films, notably the great French director Jean Renoir on his first American film, **Swamp Water** (1941), shot largely in the South, and on **The Southerner** (1945), shot in California but well away from Hollywood.

The producer of **The House on 92nd Street**, Louis de Rochemont, was the first to bring public attention to urban location shooting. His background had been in **The March of Time**, a famous series of topical documentaries in the thirties, and in factual films made for the American government and the various armed services during the war. He therefore had principles about eliminating the falsity he sensed in most Hollywood films, which would happily re-create New York, London or Paris on the studio backlot, and have stars react to hazy back-projections shot by a second unit in places they had never been. Though **The House on 92nd Street** was shot by an accomplished studio director, Henry Hathaway, and was probably not much closer to reality than dozens of other spy films of that era, it did gain in vividness by the "authentication" of real places in the background, and, most important, was a box-office success.

Right: *Exiled French director Jean Renoir's most "American" film was* **The Southerner** *(1945), in which he tried to catch the essence of rural Texas by showing a year in the life of a family of tenant farmers. This shot shows the children, Jot (Jay Gilpin) and Daisy (Jean Vanderbilt), Grandma (Beulah Bondi), Nona (Betty Field) and Sam Tucker (Zachary Scott). Despite the cruel weather and a mean-minded neighbor, they manage to survive, just.*

Inventing the truth

This, of course, was what principally encouraged the others. "Shot on the streets where it really happened" became an easy publicity tag, applied rapidly to all sorts of things that probably never came near to happening anywhere. Mark Hellinger, another producer with a background in journalism, was quick to see the advantages, and after producing such defiantly unrealistic works as **Thank Your Lucky Stars** (1943), one of the all-star revues to entertain the forces, and **The Horn Blows at Midnight** (1945), another comedy about celestial interference in the affairs of mankind, he suddenly made a gritty, realistic thriller, extensively shot on location, out of Ernest Hemingway's short story **The Killers**. The 1946 film uses Hemingway's story in the opening sequence, and then goes on to invent its own explanations, loosely tied to the theme of restlessness among demobilized veterans and the problems of fitting into civilian life again. (The difficulties of the returning soldier often provided a jumping-off point for thriller plots at this time – usually when he found his wife had been unfaithful or his non-combatant partner had taken over his business in his absence.) **The Killers** was directed by Robert Siodmak and is an interesting fusion of *film noir* with location-shooting technique; so were several of his later films, such as **Cry of the City** (1948) and **Criss-Cross** (1949).

Top: *Betty Field and Zachary Scott in* **The Southerner** *(1945).*

Above: ***The Killers*** *(1946), which derived from a 1927 short story by Ernest Hemingway. Swede Lunn (Burt Lancaster) waits resignedly for the hitmen to kill him while gazing into the eyes of the attractive and ambiguous Kitty Collins (Ava Gardner).*

Right: *Kitty is sane, bad and dangerous to know – the classic* femme fatale *of the* film noir. *She plays the girlfriend of a gang-leader, persuading Swede to join the gang and double-cross them after a robbery. But then she double-crosses Swede, returning to her lover with the money so destroying Swede's will to live. The film was remade in 1964 with Lee Marvin, Ronald Reagan, and Angie Dickinson.*

Below: *Henry Hathaway's* **Call Northside 777** *(1948) is the story of an investigation: a crime reporter, McNeal (James Stewart), discovers that a Polish woman, Tillie Wiecek (Kasia Orzaewski), has scrubbed floors for 11 years to get enough money to prove her imprisoned son Frank not guilty of murder. Impressed by her faith, McNeal takes up the task and a newspaper photograph wins the day.*

In the next couple of years both Louis de Rochemont and Mark Hellinger continued to develop the same kind of film and make capital out of location vividness: de Rochemont produced **13 Rue Madeleine** (1946) and **Boomerang** (1947), and Hellinger produced **Brute Force** (1947) and **The Naked City** (1948) before his premature death in 1947. By this time, too, influence had begun to come from another source: Italian neo-realism. This movement had originated in economic necessity. Towards the end of the war the Italian film industry virtually closed down as the major studios were marooned in fighting zones and physical resources for film-making were reduced to an absolute minimum. The only way of making films at all was by improvising on real locations. The first film made this way, Roberto Rossellini's **Rome, Open City** (1945), immediately won international acclaim, as did his **Paisan** and Vittorio De Sica's **Shoeshine** (both 1946) and **Bicycle Thieves** (1948) and the work of many of their contemporaries.

Though many Hollywood stalwarts would claim to be indifferent to highbrow critical enthusiasm, provided their films were successful at the box office, the younger generation of directors emerging in the late forties hankered more after critical laurels as well as commercial credibility, and accordingly the lesson of Italian neo-realism, reinforcing the ideas of de Rochemont and Hellinger, was not lost on them.

The documentary touch

There followed in Hollywood a spate of allegedly semi-documentary dramas, sometimes made by old dogs like Hathaway who had learnt new tricks (**Kiss of Death,** 1947; **Call Northside 777,** 1948) or William Keighley (**The Street With No Name**, 1948), but more often by newcomers. De Rochemont and Hellinger's own productions helped the careers of such new directors as Elia Kazan (**Boomerang**) and Jules Dassin (**Brute Force, The Naked City**), shortly to be

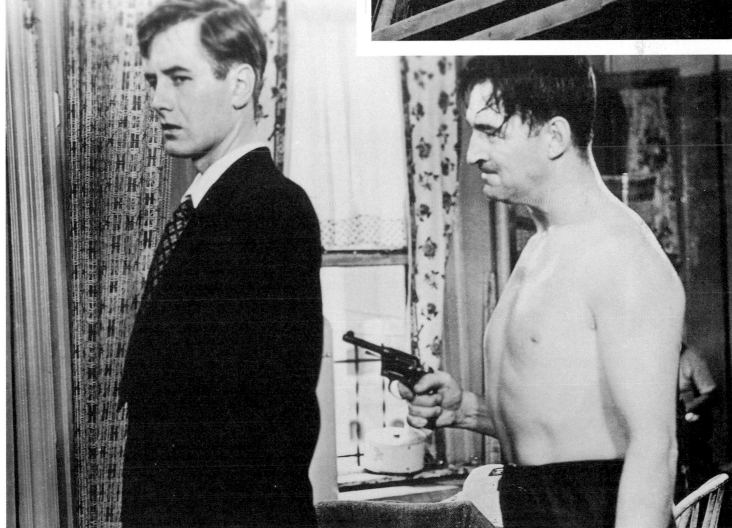

Left: *A new kind of violence, possibly influenced by the war, crept into the crime and prison films of the forties. In **Brute Force** (1947) an unwanted con is forced into a steam hammer with blowtorches and crushed to death. Howard Duff (second to right) is among the self-appointed executioners. Jules Dassin directed Mark Hellinger's production; the script was by Richard Brooks.*

Above and top: ***The Naked City*** *(1948), which spawned a long-running television series. A detective (Don Taylor), investigating the murder of a blonde, finds himself at the mercy of a fitness-freak killer (Ted de Corsia) and ends up by chasing the villain over a bridge, aided by the fast firing cops. This film was another collaboration between Hellinger and Dassin.*

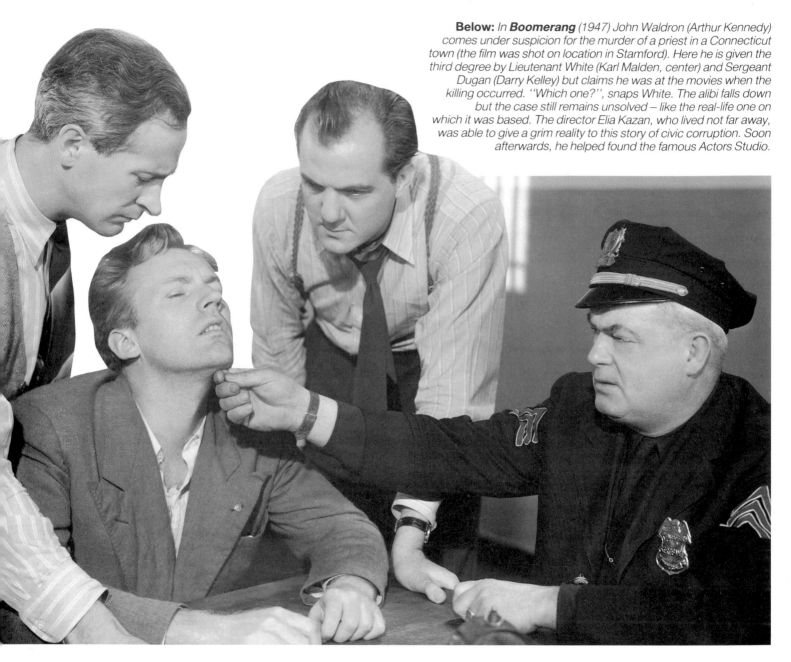

Below: In **Boomerang** (1947) John Waldron (Arthur Kennedy) comes under suspicion for the murder of a priest in a Connecticut town (the film was shot on location in Stamford). Here he is given the third degree by Lieutenant White (Karl Malden, center) and Sergeant Dugan (Darry Kelley) but claims he was at the movies when the killing occurred. ''Which one?'', snaps White. The alibi falls down but the case still remains unsolved – like the real-life one on which it was based. The director Elia Kazan, who lived not far away, was able to give a grim reality to this story of civic corruption. Soon afterwards, he helped found the famous Actors Studio.

followed into the big time by Nicholas Ray (**They Drive By Night**, 1948), Fred Zinnemann (**The Search**, 1948) and Joseph Losey (**The Boy With Green Hair**, 1948), all inspired at that time by a realist approach. In the long run, location-shooting became the norm in Hollywood, whether or not the subject was realistic or had any sort of social comment to make.

In the two years after the war, though, location shooting was still new and exciting, and was certainly promoted as such. In some respects it appeared diametrically opposed to the reigning genre, *film noir*, with its carefully controlled visual world of neo-Expressionistic studio-sets and lighting. But in other ways the distinction was not so clear as it seemed. The general tone of most of the location-shot films was tough and gloomy: exposing social injustice in such films as **Boomerang**, a grim, downbeat version of a real-life investigation into the New England murder of an Episcopalian minister, and Edward Dmytryk's **Crossfire** and Kazan's **Gentlemen's Agreement**, which probed the anti-Semitism latent beneath the cool, liberal exterior of American life. But **Crossfire** is particularly difficult to categorize: most of the key scenes take place at night, and the atmosphere of obsessional corruption that surrounds the character soon revealed as the Jew-killer is very typically *film noir*, while a number of the lesser characters are played by actors like Gloria Grahame and Paul Kelly, whose usual stamping-ground was the *film noir* proper. Nor is

Crossfire, like 1947's **Gentlemen's Agreement** (in which Gregory Peck masquerades as a Jew for a series of articles he is writing and finds out about anti-Semitism the hard way), overtly didactic: it makes its social point through atmosphere and psychology of the kinds that crop up throughout *film noir*.

Black satin

That movement, of course, continued on its unmerry way through 1946 and 1947. Some of the best examples, indeed, come from this time. Hitchcock's finest contribution to the genre, **Notorious** (1946) is a dark love story – in which the heroine (Ingrid Bergman) has to go to the edge of death itself in order to convince the hero (Cary Grant) that she loves him and is worthy of his love – disguised as a Rio-based espionage story about refugee Nazis. Rita Hayworth was incarnated as an especially bewitching *femme fatale* in Charles Vidor's **Gilda** (1946), another Latin American excursion in which she breaks up the attachment between her ex-lover Glenn Ford and her picturesquely sadistic present husband George Macreadly, as well as performing the extraordinary glove-striptease as she sings "Put the Blame on Mame" while clad in sheer black satin. A bit later, in 1948, her husband Orson Welles cut off her red locks and cast her as a blond and reptilian temptress, opposite himself, in his darkly haunting **The Lady from Shanghai**.

Left and below: *"There never was another woman like **Gilda**" (1946). Nor like red-headed Rita Hayworth. She sang "Put the Blame on Mame, Boys" while stripping only her gloves – a performance she parodied in **Pal Joey** (1957) with "Zip".*

COLUMBIA FILM S·A·B
présente
RITA
HAYWORTH
LA VEDETTE ATOMIQUE
dans
Gilda

AVEC
Glenn FORD
GEORGE MACREADY · JOSEPH CALLEIA

Mise en scène de CHARLES VIDOR

These films were made by dabblers in the form. Regular experts continued to work in their established fashion, too. Robert Siodmak made **The Dark Mirror** (1946), which featured a psychiatrist hero and twins (both Olivia de Havilland), one good, one bad – ah, but which is which? John Brahm went on from **Hangover Square** to **The Locket** (1946), an even more overwrought psychological drama about a beautiful bride (Laraine Day) who is an amnesiac and possibly a murderess. Fritz Lang continued his collaboration with Joan Bennett in **The Secret Beyond the Door** (1948), creating yet more dark dreams and forgotten mysteries. And *films noirs* as accomplished as **The Strange Love of Martha Ivers** (1946), **Dark Passage, The Unsuspected** and **Nightmare Alley** (all 1947), were produced on cue by solid craftsmen as various and versatile as, respectively, Delmer Daves, Michael Curtiz, Lewis Milestone and Edmund Goulding, all willingly and very capably falling in with the mood of the moment. Charles Chaplin meanwhile made the very, very black comedy **Monsieur Verdoux** (1947), in which his dapper wife-murderer replaced forever the little tramp.

Below: *Twin sisters, good and evil (ego and id?), became a popular symbol of psychological or moral ambiguity in the Freud-conscious forties. Director Robert Siodmak, having tried it out with Maria Montez in* **Cobra Woman** *(1944), gave it another whirl with Olivia de Havilland in* **The Dark Mirror** *(1946). Here is both of her. Which is guilty?*

Right: *The police lieutenant tries to find out by sifting through the evidence. In this case the paranoid Terry (Olivia de Havilland) can be trapped only by psychological testing according to the principles established by psychiatrist Lew Ayres.*

GI Joe comes home

Life, on the outside, continued as real and earnest as ever. By now the men who had served overseas were back in civilian life and having problems, as Hollywood reflected. In **Cornered** (1945), **The Blue Dahlia** (1946) and **Ride the Pink Horse** (1947), for instance, the hero is a returning GI who finds that back home there is something to sort out and someone to avenge – in the first two his wife has been murdered, in the third his best friend – and sets off through the night-world of *film noir* to do what he has to do. The fact that he is a GI back from war was irrelevant, however, and very few films faced up to the real questions of readjustment to civilian life. Those that did were frequently accused of returning culpably soft answers. The most famous, and most argued-over instance, was **The Best Years of Our Lives** (1946), produced by Samuel Goldwyn, directed by William Wyler, scripted by Robert Sherwood (from a verse novel, oddly enough), photographed by Gregg Toland (most famous for **Citizen Kane**) and starring a range of old and new stars. The film was immensely successful with critics and at the

box-office, cut a swathe through the year's Oscars, and was apparently loved by all. Then the reaction set in: it was accused of sweetening and sentimentalizing the book, of being hollow and pretentious, academic, unrealistic and out of touch with the present.

There is, undeniably, some truth in all of these strictures, but there was something new and unexpected about the film. Though the principal married couple is embodied by big established stars, Fredric March and Myrna Loy, and a newer arrival Dana Andrews, who plays the least satisfied war veteran (less even, curiously, than the genuinely handless Harold Russell), they do not, as stars, carry the film: they are used primarily as actors who are more or less at home in their roles. It was the beginning of the transition to the new kind of star who came in with the fifties – the kind who was too late to be systematically built up by a studio and have his or her own unquestioning following. The new breed of star had to make it performance by performance, one by one.

Although the star system was changing, for the moment you would not notice any change. Clark Gable was back, along with James Stewart, Robert Taylor and Henry Fonda, and none of them seemed to have too much trouble slipping again into their appointed places in the Hollywood hierarchy. There may have been some momentary uncertainty, perhaps, but major box-office success, as when James Stewart teamed up with Hitchcock for **Rope** (1948), and Robert Taylor got into fancy dress for **Quo Vadis** (1951), indicated that such stars were still as popular as ever. Others, however, were on their way out. Greer Garson proved more vulnerable than her beau, Gable, in **Adventure** (1945); Alice Faye was a falling star at Fox and her replacement, Betty Grable, was also a threat. And if Joan Crawford was riding high in her new career away from MGM at Warners following **Mildred Pierce**, Bette Davis was nearing the end of her fabulous first career at the same studio and being pushed into more and more unsuitable vehicles – before she bounced back in **All About Eve** (1950). Contracts were up, and stars like Veronica Lake and Ann Sheridan (the "oomph girl") were cast adrift far more disastrously than Bette Davis. Among the men who had not gone to war the longest established stars seemed the most secure: no one was really challenging the position of such pre-war favorites as Gary Cooper, Cary Grant, Spencer Tracy, James Cagney or Humphrey Bogart, and when the crop of new stars like Richard Widmark, Burt Lancaster, Kirk Douglas, Montgomery Clift and Robert Mitchum came up after the war, they were of a different enough generation not to provide direct competition.

Left: *Chaplin's **Monsieur Verdoux** (1947), the story of a ladykiller, was based on an idea by Orson Welles and on the infamous Landru case.*

Right: *A production shot of Lewis Milestone (leaning on camera) directing Lizabeth Scott in **The Strange Love of Martha Ivers** (1946) for Paramount.*

Creative lull?

What is notable in the immediately post-war years is a certain slackening of creative energy in Hollywood. Perhaps Hollywood had been having it too easy in the war years: after the nasty economic shocks caused by the advent of war in Europe, attendances for the movies had been soaring, and 1946 was indeed the most profitable year in the history of the American film industry. Television was yet a minor domestic toy, which could never rival the wonders of the big screen in the movie palace, while moves to break up the industry's production/distribution/exhibition monopoly via anti-trust laws were still to become a reality.

But if this was paradise, it turned out to be a fool's paradise. There were indications of disturbance already: industrial unrest in the studio unions in 1945 (with an eight-month closure in some cases), and in the laboratories in 1946, meant increasing costs and greater uncertainty. But Hollywood's real problems began with the imposition of a 75 per cent tax on foreign films by the British government in 1947. Britain was still the biggest single foreign market, so this cut foreign profits by nearly three-quarters, and the counter-move to boycott British markets altogether was only self-defeating. A sudden slump meant the elimination of many of the luxury trimmings that had always characterized Hollywood movies: a reduction of studio staff, a general tightening of belts and a new emphasis on efficiency in production. This mood also helped to reorientate Hollywood in the direction of location realism, small-scale production, and the encouragement of newer and less expensive talent. Films were in general less glossy, less inclined to conspicuous consumption, and more likely (by a somewhat obscure connexion of ideas) to have social content of some kind.

Red scare

To add to Hollywood's difficulties at this time, the House UnAmerican Activities Committee (HUAC) which, representing interests lying dormant since the preservation of neutrality had ceased to be an issue in 1941, sprang into life again in 1947 with new vigor, this time pursuing evidence of Communist infiltration into Hollywood. Since many people in the industry had flirted with left-wing politics in their youth, or belonged to Russian war-aid committees and even made pro-Russian films like **North Star** and **Mission to Moscow** (both 1943) when the Soviets were America's allies, this was often difficult to disprove. The general assumption of the committee was that you were guilty until you proved yourself innocent by suitable self-abasement and the naming of names.

The immediate result was, to put it mildly, a very nervous time in Hollywood, and the almost instant production of a group of vociferously anti-Communist films. Blacklists burgeoned, and lots of old personal scores were settled behind the scenes with secret denunciations. There was also, inevitably, the beginning of a significant brain-drain from Hollywood, as many who feared being witch-hunted left for Europe. In 1947 this was merely a trickle; by

Below: *The notorious communistic sympathies of studio bosses Jack L. Warner and his brothers emerged all too clearly in* **Mission to Moscow** *(1943), based on the memoirs of former ambassador Joseph E. Davies. Here Davies (Walter Huston) listens intently to the views of Comrade Stalin (Mannart Kippen) while the Soviet president (Vladimir Sokoloff) looks on benignly. The House UnAmerican Activities Committee did not like it at all.*

Above: *The Outlaw* was completed in 1941, briefly shown in 1943, given a limited release in 1946 (GB, 1947) but was not generally available until 1950. Jane Russell, seen here with Jack Buetel as Billy the Kid, fared the best, emerging from the film as a star.

Right: *The classic RKO poster marking the film's general release. Jane Russell, as the bosomy Rio, actually figured rather little in the plot, which mostly revolved around a protracted contest for a stolen horse between Billy the Kid and Doc Holliday (Walter Huston), egged on by Pat Garrett (Thomas Mitchell). Howard Hughes directed after firing Hawks.*

1949 it had become a flood — and worse was to come in the fifties with the arrival on the scene of Senator Joseph McCarthy.

All these disparate factors contributed to the instability of the studios themselves, which had for some years seemed a fixed and unchangeable quantity in Hollywood and American film-making. In 1946 the long-established Universal threw in its lot with the newer International Pictures to become Universal-International. David O. Selznick was making fewer and fewer films of his own, and finding the distribution company he had set up cumbersome and with little product to sell.

Howard Hughes had taken a fancy, during the making and remaking of **The Outlaw** (1941-50), which launched his new discovery Jane Russell, to control the whole film-making and marketing process, and had begun negotiating to buy RKO outright, a deal finally concluded in 1948. And other studios were in the throes of change, even the sacrosanct MGM, where Louis B. Mayer was gradually having to countenance the production of films that clashed with his own preference for sanitized, apple pie family entertainment. When the liberal Dore Schary was brought in as production head, with all the progressive ideas he had been trying to develop in pre-Hughes RKO, the old MGM image was changed forever. It had not yet lost quite all of its "more stars than there are in heaven", but most of them were fading fast. And if even MGM was changing, what was then left in Hollywood to rely on?

Brave New World 1948-9

Chapter 13

A practical belief has always been built into the Hollywood way of life – everyone knows that what goes up must come down, nothing lasts forever. This kind of pattern was expected in the career of the individual star, director or writer; in particular cycles of film types and subjects; even, perhaps in the history of major studios and production companies. And in the forties it happened to the industry as a whole. The decade started with an alarming slump due to the loss of European markets at the outbreak of World War II, although Hollywood managed to climb out of it partly because the entry of America into the war boosted the home market. There were war workers needing to be taken out of themselves and women and children feeling the absence of boyfriends, husbands and fathers.

Then in 1947 the roof fell in. Though something akin to panic had hit Hollywood, it was not necessarily apparent to the outside world: pictures, the publicity kept trumpeting, were bigger and better than ever, and more intelligent. Economic necessity pointed the way towards smaller films; depending on strong ideas rather than high production values, and so provided an opening for younger directors and writers with things to say. Accordingly new producers addressed themselves to social problems rather than, like Val Lewton in the war years, questions of style. Dore Schary at RKO, and from 1948 at MGM, specialized in small-budget and then progressively more expensive films with some kind of crusading point to be made. In 1948 an ex-writer and film editor called Stanley Kramer made a modest period piece, **So This Is New York**, as his first independent production, then went on immediately to make **Champion**, about corruption in boxing; **House of the Brave**, concerning the break-down of a black soldier through fear and anger over race prejudice back home; and **The Men**, about paraplegic veterans – a film that gave Marlon Brando his first leading film role. All of these films were solemn, literary and rather stodgy, but forced critics and at least a segment of the public to approve of them for their good intentions, and all of them went to swell the numbers of films in the currently fashionable social-problem cycle.

It was fortunate that some more experienced producers, like Darryl F. Zanuck, back from the war and in charge of 20th Century-Fox, should also be attracted to the idea of films that made some serious comment on social questions of current interest, and that some really talented directors like Elia Kazan and Fred Zinnemann should also be that way inclined, since no cycle could live by good intentions alone.

Right: *Future megastar Marlon Brando seen here as a wheelchair-bound ex-soldier in **The Men** (1950) with Teresa Wright as his girlfriend.*

Far right: *Pinky Johnson (Jeanne Crain) in **Pinky** (1949) with Granny Dicey Johnson (Ethel Waters) looking heavenward for help.*

Right: *Jean Simmons, an established star in Britain, made her first big impact on Hollywood in Otto Preminger's* **Angel Face** *(1952), strong in emotion and plot. Simmons plays Diane, who adores her father (Herbert Marshall) but detests her stepmother, whom she tries to kill — and eventually succeeds, but at the same time accidentally killing her father. Tried for murder with her accomplice Frank, she marries him, and gets off, but the plan backfires when he rejects her. In revenge she kills both Frank and herself in another crash. A fifties film with a forties flavor.*

Left: *Claude Jarman Jr makes friends with a fawn in* **The Yearling** *(1946), adapted from Marjorie Kinnan Rawlings' novel by Greta Garbo's favorite director, Clarence Brown. The boy won a special "child actor" Oscar.*

Ultimately, this type of film, so commonly seen from 1947 to 1950, depended not on the seriousness of their message but on their qualities as movie entertainment. But there was a disconcerting tendency on Hollywood's part to see all problems as interchangeable: the homosexual in the novel on which **Crossfire** was based could be changed into a Jew because that made the issue more acceptable in 1947, just as readily as the Jew in the original play **House of the Brave** could be changed into a black because in 1949 the Jewish problem was less newsworthy than the "black" problem.

A question of color

Racial problems were a burning issue in films in 1949. De Rochemont's contribution to the cycle, **Lost Boundaries**, and Zanuck's **Pinky** (directed by Kazan after John Ford left the production) concerned blacks passing for white who came to face the necessity of being true to themselves and finding their proper place in society. The stars concerned — Mel Ferrer in **Lost Boundaries**, Jeanne Crain in **Pinky** — could hardly look whiter if they tried, and while that is the essence of their characters' particular problem, it does also obscure the issue by making it almost entirely psychological. It also ensured that the racial subject matter did little for black actors. James Edwards in **House of the Brave** approximated closely to white standards of handsomeness, and so did the long-established Lena Horne and the next black stars to make it big, Harry Belafonte and Dorothy Dandridge in 1954's **Carmen Jones**.

But at least one very dynamic and quite obviously black actor was emerging: Sidney Poitier played his first major film role in the most uncompromising and intelligent of the first black cycle, Joseph L. Mankiewicz's **No Way Out**, an unsparing picture of reasoning racial bigotry that brought up the tail end of the series in 1950.

The best film of the group seemed to be there almost by accident. No doubt **Intruder in the Dust** was made at MGM largely because of Dore Schary's liberalizing presence, but in most respects it belonged to a long line of well-upholstered MGM adaptations of best-sellers and modern classics, rather self-consciously sold as such. "Class" was written all over this version of William Faulkner's novel, directed by Clarence Brown. It concerned a proud and intransigent old black farmer (Juano Hernandez) who refuses to "act black" when accused of murdering a white man, and creates more resentment by not bowing to the white bigots than by the crime of which he is unjustly accused. The main emphasis of the film is on the white boy who is one of the few to befriend and defend him, and probably the principal motive for making the film was to provide a suitable vehicle for MGM's most important juvenile star of the time, Claude Jarman Jr, who had won a special Academy Award for **The Yearling** in 1946.

Right: *Sorry Wrong Number* (1948) became the vehicle for a bravura performance by Barbara Stanwyck as a wealthy Sutton Place invalid, confined to bed with only the telephone as her outside contact. She becomes aware that she is the intended victim of a murder plot and desperately tries to summon help, at first not knowing who is behind the contract. But her struggles inexorably end in failure – flimsy expensive lace cannot protect her from the merciless leather glove of the assassin.

Husband Burt Lancaster, who was behind it all, at the last minute regrets his murderous plan as the police close in **below**. The old Hollywood system rarely allowed the murderer to succeed.

Above: *Celeste Holm (left) and Olivia de Havilland (second from right) as inmates of a hellish lunatic asylum in* **The Snake Pit** *(1949). Strong stuff in its day, it was said to have affected attitudes to mental illness and its treatment. But compared with the later revelations of ex-film star Frances Farmer of conditions around the same time, it now seems relatively tame. However,* **Sorry Wrong Number** *and* **The Snake Pit** *did give an undeniable and welcome touch of class to the otherwise merely competent (on the whole) career of Russian-born Anatole Litvak. His two somewhat divergent gifts, for documentary and for working well with top actresses, came together very effectively at this point.*

The darkest hour...

By 1948 the *film noir* cycle was drawing to a close, though there were occasional stragglers like Preminger's **Angel Face** or **Vicky**, a remake of 1941's **I Wake Up Screaming** with a significant change of emphasis. Some of the best examples in the late forties came from emigré directors still working in Hollywood. Anatole Litvak made two of the blackest contributions, both featuring virtuoso female performances in the central role. Barbara Stanwyck was the rich, menaced invalid whose only contact with the outside world is by telephone in **Sorry Wrong Number** (1948); and Olivia de Havilland was the woman who goes through the nightmare of a lunatic asylum in **The Snake Pit** (1949). The Austrian Max Ophüls was in Hollywood for a long time before he got a chance to show what he could do with the moody and elegant Viennese period piece **Letter from an Unknown Woman** in 1948, and the two distinctly black films he made afterwards, **Caught** and **The Reckless Moment**, both of which, as the titles indicate, picture a deterministic world where a momentary error can trap one for life.

An unexpected recruit to the ranks of *film noir* directors was King Vidor, famed since the twenties as one of Hollywood's great humanists. Possibly working on Selznick's sadistic super-Western **Duel in the Sun** in 1947 helped to change his view of things, but in 1949 he came up with two astonishing works, **The Fountainhead**, based on Ayn Rand's novel, about a megalomaniac architect (Gary Cooper) who reserves the right to destroy his own buildings if they do not come up to his required standards, and **Beyond the Forest**, Bette Davis' last film on her Warners contract. This had her wearing a Charles Addams fright-wig to portray a mid-western Emma Bovary who destroys everything about her to get on that train to Chicago but never quite succeeds. Meanwhile, less challenging was William Wyler's first film since **The Best Years of Our Lives**, a highly polished version of **The Heiress**, the matinee melodrama Ruth and Augustus Goetz had extracted from Henry James' richly ambiguous novel **Washington Square**.

Right and far right: *Beyond the Forest* (1949). Is Rosa Moline (Bette Davis) a mid-Western Emma Bovary or a burnt-out Warners star camping it up on her last assignment? Dr Lewis Moline (Joseph Cotten) puts up with it all, even when she practically falls under the outgoing Chicago train!

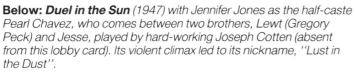

Below: *Duel in the Sun* (1947) with Jennifer Jones as the half-caste Pearl Chavez, who comes between two brothers, Lewt (Gregory Peck) and Jesse, played by hard-working Joseph Cotten (absent from this lobby card). Its violent climax led to its nickname, "Lust in the Dust".

This page: *Adam's Rib* (1949) was the first and possibly the best of George Cukor's half-dozen comedy collaborations with the husband and wife team of writer-director Garson Kanin and writer-actress Ruth Gordon: perhaps this was because it was the only one to include Spencer Tracy and Katharine Hepburn and Judy Holliday instead of just one or at most two of them.
The plot has a delightful range of comic possibilities with Adam Bonner (Tracy) as an assistant DA and his wife Amanda (Hepburn) as the defence lawyer in the case of a housewife so angered by seeing her husband with another woman that she takes a pot shot at him.

Left and below: *As the courtroom and domestic tensions increase in **Adam's Rib**; Amanda consoles herself in a mild flirtation with an old beau, Kip Lurie. Adam reacts violently, even though he has just been lambasting the defendant for behaving in the same jealous way. The movie delightfully explores sexist bias, even at one point dressing Doris as a man and her husband as a woman. Tom Ewell **below** on the carpet.*

Something old, something new

Other stalwarts were learning new tricks, or satisfactorily dusting off old forgotten ones. George Cukor, an accomplished director during MGM's heyday, suddenly showed a quite unsuspected flair for location shooting and the brisk, modern New York-based comedies written by Garson Kanin and Ruth Gordon. **Adam's Rib** (1949) was the first of a succession of hits starring Spencer Tracy and Katharine Hepburn or Judy Holliday or (in this case) both.

John Ford, whose version of the gunfight at the OK Corral myth, **My Darling Clementine** (1946), with Henry Fonda as Wyatt Earp and Victor Mature as Doc Holliday, was eccentric in its scope and star-power, fully revived the Western in the late forties with his "cavalry trilogy". **Fort Apache** (1948), **She Wore a Yellow Ribbon** (1949) and **Rio Grande** (1950) were films that poetically harnessed landscape – that of Ford's beloved Monument Valley – to storyline and also got the best from the director's stock company. They also consolidated John Wayne as a Western hero of noble stature – as did

Below and below right: *The battle of nature and culture is savagely taken up in* **My Darling Clementine** *(1946), whether on the battlefield of the OK Corral, the final showdown between the law-abiding Earps and the untamed Clantons or in the tonsorial parlor where Wyatt Earp (Henry Fonda) has his locks disciplined by the barber (Ben Hall). The good guys of Tombstone are: John Simpson (Russell Simpson), Doc Holliday (Victor Mature), Morgan Earp (Ward Bond), a decoy, and finally Wyatt himself. They will kill all but Old Man Clanton, played by Walter Brennan, who virtually commits suicide by drawing on Wyatt as he rides away. According to director John Ford, the real Wyatt Earp told him the whole story back in the early days, so it's practically a documentary!*

Howard Hawks' cattledrive epic **Red River** (1948), a masterpiece of storytelling. Ford's **The Wagonmaster** (1950), about a group of Mormon settlers heading West, was another excellent Western that helped usher the genre into its finest decade – although political overtones and psychological complexity would greatly alter its shape during the fifties.

Another great veteran who ended the decade by reverting to tried and trusted methods was Cecil B. DeMille. He had begun the forties with a spectacular "Western", **North West Mounted Police** (1940), starring Gary Cooper and Paulette Goddard, who also appeared together in the 1947 DeMille epic, **Unconquered**. He also made **Reap the Wild Wind** (1942), a Georgia-based seafaring drama with Goddard, Ray Milland, John Wayne and a giant squid, and his own flag-waving tribute to wartime American heroism, reliably personified by Cooper, in **The Story of Dr Wassell** (1944). But in 1949 DeMille fell back on the old formula of sex-and-sadism with a biblical excuse when he revamped an old thirties project as **Samson and Delilah**. If the idea of Hedy Lamarr and Victor Mature in the title roles filled the critics with unseemly mirth, the film at least reasserted DeMille's sure grasp of the taste of the public at large.

The last of Sturges

Comedies were, as usual, a staple of this period, though sadly the great comic discovery of the forties, writer/director Preston Sturges, was already burning himself out. His last satisfactory film was **Unfaithfully Yours** (1948), in which the conductor of an orchestra fantasizes various solutions to his current marital problems during a concert – and then tries confusedly to put all his ideas simultaneously into practice. Sturges' last Hollywood film, a Betty Grable vehicle called **The Beautiful Blonde From Bashful Bend** (1949), pleased no one. Frank Capra was nearing the end of his effective career. After a big success with his post-war comeback film, **It's a Wonderful Life** (1946), a Christmas fantasy in which a popular local hero (James Stewart) learns – with the help of an angel – how his little town would have suffered had he never lived, Capra changed his tone to something much tougher and more ruthless in **State of the Union** (1948), a political satire tailored to the requirements of the star team of Tracy and Hepburn.

Right: *Paulette Goddard played a Georgian belle in C. B. DeMille's* **Reap the Wild Wind** *(1942), fought over by John Wayne and Ray Milland. However, she missed out on the poster, being supplanted by the saucy Susan Hayward.*

Below: *Swiss-fathered Victor Mature and Viennese Hedy Lamarr make an odd yet appropriate couple as* **Samson and Delilah** *in DeMille's 1949 epic, which took a very respectable $11.5m in US rentals alone. Mature is big and hunky yet curiously soft and self-deprecating with an almost feminine streak. Lamarr is a hard little beauty, capable of cruelty. Ergo, perfect casting for a sado-masochistic biblical fantasy.*

Below: *Spencer Tracy and Katharine Hepburn made the fifth of their nine films together in 1948. Its punning title,* **State of the Union***, suggests a conflation of domestic and political themes. An estranged wife (Hepburn) rejoins her businessman husband (Tracy) when he is persuaded to run for the Presidency by a rich, ruthless lady newspaper publisher.*

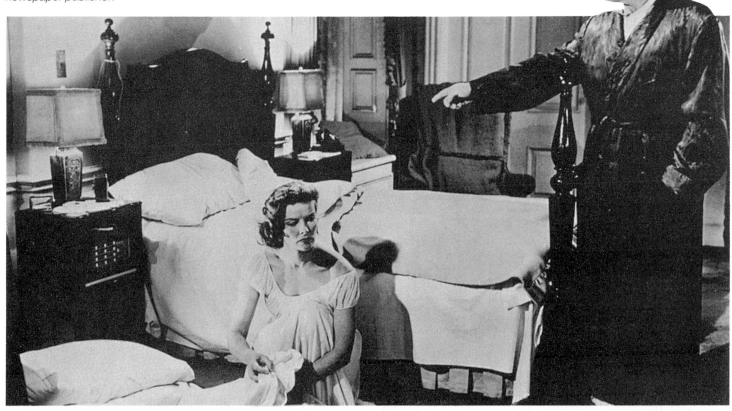

Above: ***The Beautiful Blonde from Bashful Bend*** *(1949) was not one of Betty Grable's best films and still less one of Preston Sturges' best. He was more at home with the raucous Betty Hutton; and this was to be his last American film. Grable (pointing the finger at Cesar Romero) is a tough saloon dancer out West, too handy with a gun. When she accidentally shoots a sheriff, she finds it convenient to hide out for a while and allow herself to be mistaken for a schoolmistress.*

Right: *John Wayne and Oliver Hardy in* **The Fighting Kentuckian** *(1949). Wayne was still the main prop of Republic Pictures, producing this one too, and accepting the inevitable Czech ex-ice skater Vera Ralston (not shown) as his co-star.*
Ollie's screen partnership with Stan had virtually ended, and in effect both were finished after 1940. Ollie made his last Hollywood film in 1950; the duo made their last in 1951. Ollie died in 1957, Stan in 1965.

Above: *Marilyn Monroe's first major role was not at her ''home'' studio, 20th Century-Fox, where she started and ended her fifteen-year career, but at Columbia.* **Ladies of the Chorus** *(1948) was the only film she made there – it gave her (center right) a glamorous mother (Adele Jergens, center left) less than nine years her senior. Unnerved by this anomaly (her real-life mother was problem enough) she falters in her pursuit of a rich husband . . . but only briefly.*

The shape of things to come

Other comic standbys were also vanishing from the scene. The **Bullfighters** (1945) was the last Hollywood film to star Laurel and Hardy together, though Hardy appeared with John Wayne in **The Fighting Kentuckian** in 1949 and made a final bow with Laurel in the French **Robinson Crusoeland** (1950). The last film in which Groucho, Chico and Harpo Marx appeared together was **Love Happy** (1950). This film showed off, in a short but spectacular bit part, a pretty young blonde – lusted after by Groucho – who in 1948 had played her first leading role in a small feature called **Ladies of the Chorus**. Her name was Marilyn Monroe, and very soon everyone in the world would have heard it. Already in 1950 she was being featured in major new films by the two most important directorial talents to confirm their Hollywood posititon in the late forties, John Huston and Joseph L. Mankiewicz.

Immediately before putting Monroe, as a gangster's moll, in the crime thriller **The Asphalt Jungle** (1950), Huston had made one of his best-respected misfires, **We Were Strangers** (1948), about a group of revolutionaries in Cuba, and one of his big successes, **The Treasure of the Sierra Madre** (1949), a harshly ironic prospecting adventure story starring Humphrey Bogart and Oscar-winning Walter Huston, the director's father. Mankiewicz, who gave Monroe a small part as the girl on George Sanders' arm in the classic bitchery of **All About Eve** (1950), had made a highly effective thriller/family drama, **House of Strangers** (1949); a contribution to the group of films concerned with racial prejudice, **No Way Out** (1950); and, most successfully of all, his brilliant episodic comedy drama **A Letter to Three Wives** (1949), in which he developed the elegant, witty "talk film" that was his speciality. Here three wives at a picnic receive a letter from an absentee fourth announcing she has run off with one of their husbands – but whose?

Above: *Mother (Adele Jergens) and daughter (Marilyn Monroe, right) in* **Ladies of the Chorus** *(1948). Mom was once married to a rich young man but was rejected by his family, who dissolved the marriage. She fears the same is about to happen to her girl: but Marilyn sings a couple of songs (including "Every Baby Needs a Da-Da-Daddy"), strips a little and soon wins over the snobs.*

223

Elsewhere in 1949 films such as Robert Wise's brutally laconic **The Set Up,** about a fixed prize-fight, and William Dieterle's **Portrait of Jennie**, which gave an ideal role to the ethereal Jennifer Jones in a magical story of ghosts, time-traveling and love conquering death, were widely appreciated. Even if, by the beginning of the year, there were more than two million television sets in the United States, it seemed like a time of promise and development for the cinema.

As if embodying this buoyant mood, the genre that was doing worst – despite the encouragement of producers eager to ingratiate themselves with the HUAC investigators – was the anti-communist series, which included such dull and alarmist diatribes as **Iron Curtain, The Red Menace** and **The Red Danube**, while the genre that was surging forward by leaps and bounds was the musical. Obviously the public just did not care for awful warnings, and did want to be taken out of itself with singing, dancing, raw energy and color by Technicolor.

Above: *Artist Eben Adams (Joseph Cotten) meets a girl (Jennifer Jones) in* **Portrait of Jennie** *(1949). She isn't all that she seems, however, having died long ago in a storm at sea. William Dieterle, with cinematographer Joseph August, experimented with tinted sequences to give a heightened romantic splendor to the rare encounters of the spiritual lovers. Delicate, refined Jennifer Jones surely found the proper atmosphere in this rarefied ethereal setting. Lillian Gish and Ethel Barrymore further added to the high tone.*

Above: *A typical 20th Century-Fox showbiz musical was* **Mother Wore Tights** *(1947). Vaudeville singer and dancer Myrtle McKinley Burt (Betty Grable) and her partner husband (Dan Dailey) are lovingly remembered by their younger daughter. The prolific Walter Lang directed.*

Foxy ladies

As usual, there were plenty of productions ready and willing to satisfy that need. At 20th Century-Fox a succession of luridly colored, artless but cheery musicals continued to emerge, without Alice Faye, who had retired from the screen in 1946, and without Carmen Miranda, who had moved on to fresh fields, but still with the irrepressible Betty Grable. She had just begun, in **Mother Wore Tights** (1947), a new and successful teaming with lanky song-and-dance man Dan Dailey and was to carry on as queen at Fox until finally replaced by Marilyn Monroe.

The studio had a constant supply of second-string musical ladies like June Haver and Vivian Blaine in reserve; one who did actually make real starring status, if only briefly, was Mitzi Gaynor, who made her debut in **My Blue Heaven** in 1950. Warners meanwhile had recently acquired Doris Day, and Paramount still kept up a series of brash semi-musicals starring Betty Hutton, who was introduced in **The Fleet's In** (1942) and had been barrelling her way through ever since. Paramount also had Bing Crosby, a law unto himself and perennially popular, whether on the road with Hope and Lamour or easing his way into the affections of each new generation with sentimental dramas like **Going My Way** and **The Bells of St Mary's**, or fully-fledged musicals like **Blue Skies, The Emperor**

Above: *Victor Schertzinger, who directed the first "Road" films for Paramount, sadly did not live to see the release of* **The Fleet's In** *(1942). A painfully shy sailor (William Holden, left) has to court a haughty nightclub singer (Dorothy Lamour) for a bet. He wins both bet and girl but his pal (Eddie Bracken) has a consolation prize – Betty Hutton (not shown) making her debut.*

Waltz and **A Connecticut Yankee in King Arthur's Court**. Bob Hope sang, too, and had one of his biggest successes singing "Buttons and Bows" in **The Paleface**, co-starring Jane Russell.

Metro's golden musicals

The real home of the musical, particularly in the forties, was MGM. Arthur Freed was in charge of the grandest MGM musicals right through from the beginning of the decade, when he was promoted from associate producer on **The Wizard of Oz** to full producer, to 1949 and beyond. Freed may have dominated MGM's musical output, but there were two other producers at the studio, Joe Pasternak and Jack Cummings, who regularly made musicals, and several others who occasionally dabbled in the form.

The big stars and frontline directors usually worked with Freed, though not inevitably – every now and then a star like Judy Garland might be thrown to a producer like Pasternak for **In the Good Old Summertime** (1949), where she replaced the pregnant June Allyson. Freed, though, dominated because he had a superior grasp of what constituted the best, and how best to showcase it. The stars got to know and trust this, and developed a regular relationship with the so-called "Freed Unit", while unknowns, speciality stars like Esther Williams and others who were being brought on slowly or let down gently usually worked with Pasternak or Cummings.

Left: In **The Paleface** (1948) Calamity Jane (Jane Russell) takes up with a nervous traveling dentist, Painless Potter (Bob Hope), while on an undercover mission and makes a marriage of convenience. After numerous adventures she decides that maybe she does love him after all. Meanwhile, he demonstrates his manhood by making passes at all the saloon girls **below left**. The song "Buttons and Bows" won an Academy Award. This was only Jane Russell's second (and last) forties film after **The Outlaw**; but never were two Westerns less alike.

Below: **The Good Old Summertime** (1949) was a rather brash Technicolor musical remake of Ernst Lubitsch's delicate romantic comedy, **The Shop Around the Corner** (1940). The tale of a shop manager and clerk who detest each other at work but unknowingly conduct an intense secret correspondence with each other was moved from Budapest to Chicago. Van Johnson and Judy Garland replaced James Stewart and Margaret Sullavan. But a dash of Hungarian atmosphere survived in the casting of S. Z. "Cuddles" Sakall as the store owner.

Left and above: *The Pirate* (1948) is, for good and ill, one of the most artificial musicals in the history of cinema. Nothing is real, nobody tells the truth until the end, all is fantasy, deception, theater and studio. It is both stifling and liberating, both empty and packed with noise and colors. On a Caribbean island, a young girl, Manuela (Judy Garland), dreams of the fearsome pirate Macoco and believes she has found him when she meets a wandering minstrel, Serafin (Gene Kelly). She fantasizes a dance in which he challenges and awakens her emerging sexuality.

At the same time, the lesser MGM musicals were far from negligible. It is easy now to appreciate the relatively unsophisticated charms of Esther Williams in **Neptune's Daughter** and **On an Island With You** or Jane Power in **A Date With Judy** and **Nancy Goes to Rio**. Moreover, **Three Little Words**, a biography of Kalmar and Ruby produced by Jack Cummings, is not really much inferior to **Words and Music**, a biography of Rodgers and Hart produced by Arthur Freed.

But in the final analysis, what we remember as really special nearly always turns out to have come from Freed. The years 1948-49 were probably the peak of his achievement in fusing together the studio's array of creative, technical and artistic talents. Rouben Mamoulian's **Summer Holiday**; Vincente Minnelli's **The Pirate**, with Judy Garland and Gene Kelly; **Words and Music** with just about everybody; **Easter Parade**, which brought Fred Astaire out of premature retirement and teamed him with Judy Garland; **Take Me Out to the Ball Game**, which, under Busby Berkeley's supervision, at last gave Gene Kelly and Stanley Donen their choreographic and directorial chance; **The Barkleys of Broadway**, which reunited Fred Astaire and Ginger Rogers; and especially **On the Town** — all these were masterminded by Freed.

On the Town has frequently been tagged the key musical in the history of MGM, as important to the film musical as **Oklahoma!** was to the stage. This is hardly overstating the case: when Kelly and Donen let their three sailors (Kelly himself, Frank Sinatra and Jules Munshin) loose for 24 hours in New York, and brought them together with their matching girls (Vera-Ellen, Betty Garrett, Ann Miller), they created a new, freer world where song, dance and dialogue flow effortlessly into and out of one another. **On the Town** was not the first musical to shoot numbers in the open air, or to attempt an integration of this sort, but in no film previously had everything hung together with such ease, or been driven forward with such total,

uninhibited energy. There were to be many successors in the fifties, some of which – **An American in Paris** (1951), **Singin' in the Rain** (1952), **The Band Wagon** (1953), and **Silk Stockings** (1957) – might be more to the taste of this moviegoer or that. But nowhere does one get quite so unmistakably the feeling of "Bliss was it in that dawn to be alive".

Hollywood was already in a difficult position, and was not to find it improved much in 1950, a year that added to mankind's store of experience the Korean War, the rise of Senator McCarthy and the explosion of the first hydrogen bomb. Many further indignities were in store. But for the moment **On the Town** is the perfect place for us to bow out of the forties, convinced every time we see it that movies were then better than ever, and that Hollywood – even on location in New York – was at that point immortal.

*The climax of **Easter Parade** (1948) is, of course, the Fifth Avenue Easter Parade of, in particular, new hats ("In your Easter bonnet . . ."). Don Hewes (Fred Astaire) and his new vaudeville dancing partner (Judy Garland) are in love – and the music is by Irving Berlin. Who could ask for anything more?*

Adrian Turner

Hollywood 1950s

Marilyn Monroe

Reel Lives

Chapter 14

Although it is convenient to divide periods of history into decades, the mood or definitive character of one particular decade may only become apparent a few years into it and that mood may persist well into the following decade. This is certainly true of the Hollywood cinema and, as far as the 1950s is concerned, it is possible to trace its character back to 1947 and forward to 1963.

Climate of vitality

The most profitable year in Hollywood's history was 1946. The war had ended and families were reunited but there was little general affluence; the cinema offered a cheap form of entertainment and an effective way of resuming a normal pattern of life. By 1948 the American economy was booming, turning cinemagoers into consumers and parents. The sales of automobiles and household appliances cut deeply into the money spent on moviegoing and the baby boom required that young married couples mostly stay at home. By 1950 television had become well established. All these factors had a dramatic effect on cinema attendances and the major studios became increasingly competitive and international in their outlook since they could no longer rely on a film recovering its production costs in North America alone.

At the same time, the anti-Communist witch hunts initiated by the House of Representatives' Un-American Activities Committee (HUAC) in the late 1940s lingered on through the early 1950s. Several notable writers and directors, including Carl Foreman, Jules Dassin and Joseph Losey, went into exile in Europe while others remained in America and worked under pseudonyms. Eventually, the loathsome blacklist slowly began to fall apart when Dalton Trumbo won an Academy Award in 1956 for the screenplay of **The Brave One**, which he had written under the name of "Robert Rich". In 1960, Trumbo became the first blacklisted writer within the USA to receive an open screen credit.

The concurrent war against Communism in Korea produced a rash of movies which generally lacked the critical perspective that characterized Hollywood's later screen treatment of the Vietnam war. Nevertheless, the war in Korea, McCarthy's purges and the development of the hydrogen bomb created a mood of political suspicion and uncertainty that permeated many dramas, thrillers, science-fiction films and even Westerns.

Right: *In George Cukor's classic **A Star is Born** (1954), James Mason is the big-time star who marries chorine Judy Garland and then, gradually destroyed by drink, watches her career take off before he dies, a suicide by drowning.*

Despite the oppressive political climate there was a marked relaxation in censorship codes, permitting a more sophisticated approach to social issues such as sexuality, adolescence, urban violence and drug addiction. In part this was due to the growing influence of the European cinema but also reflected the concerns of major American dramatists like Tennessee Williams, Arthur Miller, William Inge and Paddy Chayefsky. Just as the European cinema — especially the Italian — was committed to realism, so American literature, theater and cinema became more naturalistic, and new styles of acting emerged to give the movement powerful expression.

These political, social and creative tensions produced one of the most fascinating periods in Hollywood's 75-year history. The 1950s was a decade that saw the best Westerns, the best musicals, the best dramas, and the best chariot race ever filmed; great directors such as John Ford, Howard Hawks, Alfred Hitchcock and Billy Wilder made their finest films; major new directors such as Samuel Fuller, Stanley Kubrick, Sidney Lumet and Robert Aldrich effectively began their careers; established stars like John Wayne, Gary Cooper and James Stewart gave some of their most distinctive performances;

Far left: *Judy Garland as rising film star Vicki Lester in a production number from* **A Star is Born** *(1954).*

Below: *Joe Gillis (William Holden) and Norma Desmond (Gloria Swanson) settle down to watch Swanson's own* **Queen Kelly** *(1928) in* **Sunset Boulevard** *(1950). Desmond hires Joe to write her comeback picture; but when he finally decides to walk out on her . . . .*

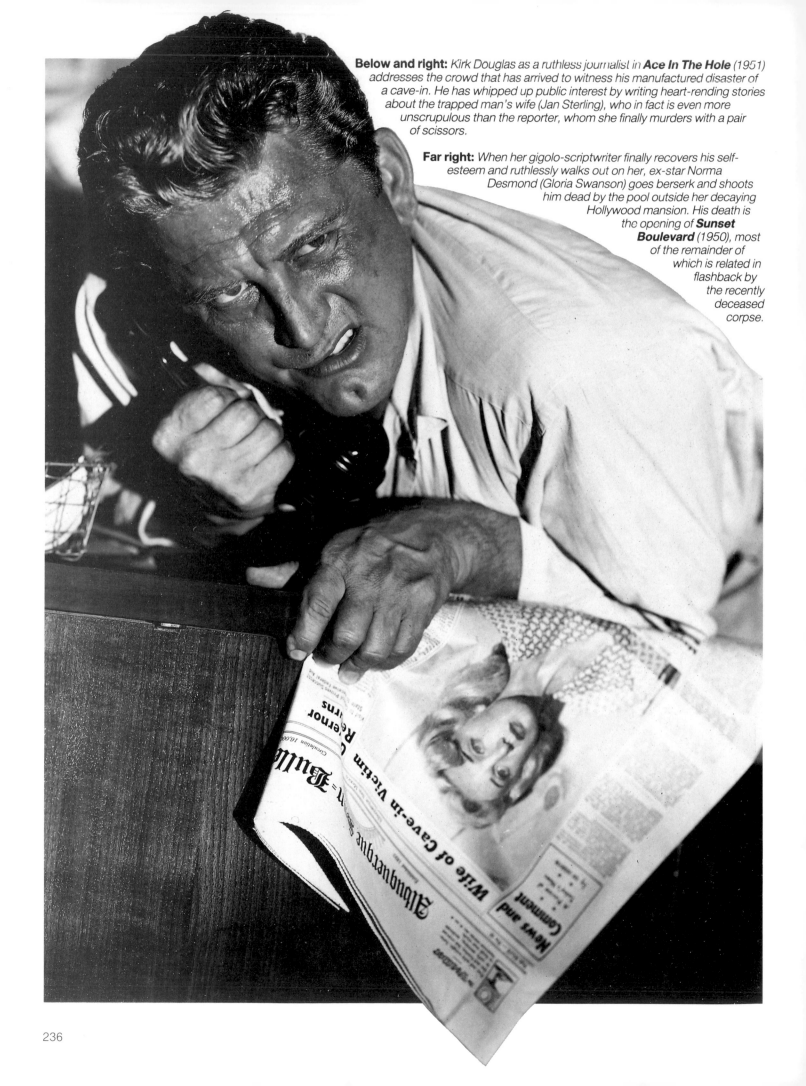

Below and right: *Kirk Douglas as a ruthless journalist in* **Ace In The Hole** *(1951) addresses the crowd that has arrived to witness his manufactured disaster of a cave-in. He has whipped up public interest by writing heart-rending stories about the trapped man's wife (Jan Sterling), who in fact is even more unscrupulous than the reporter, whom she finally murders with a pair of scissors.*

Far right: *When her gigolo-scriptwriter finally recovers his self-esteem and ruthlessly walks out on her, ex-star Norma Desmond (Gloria Swanson) goes berserk and shoots him dead by the pool outside her decaying Hollywood mansion. His death is the opening of* **Sunset Boulevard** *(1950), most of the remainder of which is related in flashback by the recently deceased corpse.*

brilliant new stars like Marlon Brando, James Dean, Paul Newman, Audrey Hepburn and Marilyn Monroe began to emerge; screens expanded and sound went stereophonic.

And yet, despite this extraordinary vitality, the 1950s can be regarded as Hollywood's final decade as a living reality. It was the decade which saw the passing of Hollywood's founding fathers, the immigrant moguls. Louis B. Mayer, Samuel Goldwyn, Harry Cohn and David O. Selznick either died, retired or grudgingly relinquished control of their studios. The decade ended in the summer of 1963 with the release of a film that seemed to summarize and symbolize all the exigencies and excesses of the period: after **Cleopatra**, Hollywood ceased to be a reality. Thereafter it was pure myth.

Hollywood self-portraits

Hollywood has always liked to make films about itself, presumably in the belief that the factory is of equal interest to the automobiles it produces. Until the 1950s these self-portraits were invariably affectionate and romantic, although **What Price Hollywood?** (1932)

Left and above: *"Fasten your seat belts, it's going to be a bumpy night,"* warns aging actress Margo Channing (Bette Davis) when she hosts a Broadway party. Her playwright lover (Gary Merrill, left) and her producer (Gregory Ratoff) are among the guests in **All About Eve** (1950). Other guests include rising actress Eve Harrington (Anne Baxter), who later achieves the success she had sought so desperately, and acidulous critic Addison DeWitt (George Sanders), who blackmails her into becoming his mistress.

Top left: *"Match me, Sidney"* is a much-quoted catchline from **Sweet Smell of Success** (1957) and brutally implies the dependence of smalltime agent Sidney Falco (Tony Curtis) on powerful gossip columnist J. J. Hunsecker (Burt Lancaster), even if he sometimes uses a Zippo lighter instead of the requested match.

and its near remake, the first **A Star is Born** (1937), did allow a degree of criticism of Hollywood's sybaritic and sycophantic enclave. A sharply-written satire like **Bombshell** (1933), however, cast its real-life characters as no more than zany "movie people". Significantly, the toughest earlier works about Hollywood were novels: Horace McCoy's *They Shoot Horses, Don't They?* (1935) and *I Should Have Stayed Home* (1938), Nathanael West's *The Day of the Locust* (1939), Budd Schulberg's *What Makes Sammy Run?* (1940), F. Scott Fitzgerald's *The Last Tycoon* (1941).

Billy Wilder's magnificent **Sunset Boulevard** (1950) changed all that, paving the way for a remarkable series of inward-looking films that may not have dominated the 1950s but certainly provide a richly expressive and prophetic context for the most turbulent decade since the 1920s when sound recording shattered the silents.

Consider a scene in **Sunset Boulevard** when Gloria Swanson as a faded and demented old movie queen and William Holden as a brash and ambitious screenwriter settle down to watch an old movie in Swanson's mansion, littered with memories and baroque extravagances. The film is Swanson's own **Queen Kelly** (1928) and her butler-cum-projectionist is played by Erich von Stroheim, the director of **Queen Kelly** until Swanson closed the picture down. Holden, casually dressed, is bored by the show but Swanson, dressed for a premiere, is enthralled by the images of herself. "Still wonderful, isn't it?" she says, "And no dialogue. We didn't need dialogue. We had

faces." The line is a rebuke to the writer beside her; as Swanson says later, "You made a rope of words and strangled this business." And when Holden first meets this living Medusa he says, "You're Norma Desmond. You used to be in silent pictures. You used to be big." Swanson then straightens herself imperiously and delivers one of the most famous lines in all of movie history, "I *am* big. It's the pictures that got small."

Sunset Boulevard is an appropriate starting point for a survey of the 1950s since it is both a deeply-felt tribute to the grandeur of Hollywood's past, embodied by Swanson's performance, and a bitter foretaste of the Hollywood to come, evoked by Holden's cynicism and the tawdry world of yes-men (who, however, say no to him), uncultured executives and callous gossip columnists who swarm like flies to gloat over Norma Desmond's descent into madness and murder.

Top: *When a Hollywood girl (Gloria Grahame) starts to suspect that her alcoholic lover (Humphrey Bogart) may be a murderer, their relationship founders on mistrust and both end up* **In a Lonely Place**. *Santana, Bogart's own company, produced the film in 1950.*

Above: *Kirk Douglas surpasses even Marlon Brando as the 1950s' most masochistic actor, losing an ear in* **Lust for Life** *(1956), a finger in* **The Big Sky** *(1952), an eye in* **The Vikings** *(1958) and his mind in many other films, including* **The Bad and the Beautiful** *(1952), in which he played a film producer. Lana Turner portrayed a famous actor's alcoholic daughter, pushed to stardom by the producer's ruthless determination.*

Alexander Mackendrick's **Sweet Smell of Success** (1957) is a blood-brother of **Ace in the Hole**, again not a Hollywood story but revealing, in its sordid world of New York gossip columnists and blackmailing press agents, the precariousness of celebrity which can be made or broken at the strike of a match. Burt Lancaster's awesomely slimy performance as the Broadway columnist J. J. Hunsecker and Tony Curtis's ingratiating press agent Sidney Falco might be Hollywood's East Coast nightmare. The same could be said of Joseph L. Mankiewicz's glitteringly witty **All About Eve** (1950), in which Broadway star Margo Channing (Bette Davis) is threatened by the ambition of newcomer Eve Harrington (Anne Baxter), but the mood is much lighter, despite George Sanders' splendidly menacing role as an all-powerful critic.

Bette Davis also took on the role of **The Star** (1952), an aging Hollywood actress (modeled on Joan Crawford) long out of the limelight who, after a drunken night with her Oscar and a disastrous screen test for a comeback, is finally reconciled to an ordinary life with boat-builder Sterling Hayden. The film lacks tension, despite a full-blooded performance by Davis, but it remains an interesting specimen of how film stars are perceived by their producers and public, and is more optimistic than the biopic **Jeanne Eagels** (1957) in which Kim Novak as the stage and silent movie queen dies in a haze of drinks and drugs at the age of thirty-five.

After **All About Eve** Joseph Mankiewicz made a torrid Hollywood story, **The Barefoot Contessa** (1954), in which Humphrey Bogart played a disillusioned American director who attends the funeral of his Spanish discovery, the sensuous Ava Gardner, and reflects on her career from childhood during the Spanish Civil War, to overnight Hollywood stardom, through sundry affairs until her violent death at the hands of her aristocratic Italian husband (Rossano Brazzi) whose war wounds have rendered him impotent. The film is hopelessly overwrought but compelling, and beneath its operatic exterior perhaps lurks oblique political comment in its Civil War references (a cause for Hollywood's left-wingers), its fascistic millionaire and its decaying splendor.

More explicit in regard to Hollywood's local problems is Nicholas Ray's **In a Lonely Place** (1950), in which Bogart plays a screenwriter blacklisted for his alcohol-induced temper who becomes a murder suspect, which leads to the destruction of his personal life. Although the film is a murder mystery, its evocation of Hollywood as an uncaring, distant world is disturbing, a long-shot of the milieu of **Sunset Boulevard**. Meanwhile, Vincente Minnelli's **The Bad and the Beautiful** (1952) cast Kirk Douglas as a producer trying to reclaim a successful career while colleagues Dick Powell, Walter Pidgeon and Lana Turner (as the requisite alcoholic) nostalgically recall their hatred for him. The film's overblown view of Hollywood's capacity for self-pity and self-destruction is very much in accordance with the prevailing mood of the period, as evidenced also by the drunken decline of film star Norman Maine (James Mason) in George Cukor's superb **A Star is Born** (1954). This film stands a discreet distance away from the seductive glamour of Hollywood and celebrates Judy Garland's greatest (but now most painful) performance as Vicki Lester, Maine's wife and protegée, who uses her own sudden stardom to create a monument to her husband's memory by announcing herself as "Mrs Norman Maine".

The poisoned pen

On the surface Wilder's next film, **Ace in the Hole** (1951), has nothing to do with Hollywood at all, being about an ambitious reporter (Kirk Douglas) who deliberately prolongs the ordeal of a man trapped in a mountain cave in order to fabricate a dramatic news story. The setting is the arid desert but the story works brilliantly as an allegory about Hollywood and the public's morbid appetite for sensation and suffering. As Douglas's story builds, the public and the media swarm to the disaster site, lining up their cars as at a drive-in cinema, complete with box-office, candy stall and adjoining fairground. Douglas stands on the craggy mountain top — a mischievous corruption of Paramount's own corporate logo — surrounded by the cranes, scaffolding and lights that resemble a film set, and addresses the crowd like a Cecil B. DeMille showman. There is no more potent metaphor for the crises that afflicted Hollywood in the coming years.

Dark mirrors

Robert Aldrich's **The Big Knife** (1955) is possibly the cruelest portrait of Hollywood in the 1950s; it is also the hammiest, like Aldrich's subsequent and sadistic **What Ever Happened to Baby Jane?** (1962) in which Bette Davis and Joan Crawford's spirit is savagely betrayed. Based on a play by Clifford Odets, **The Big Knife** is a ruthless parody of a self-righteous studio mogul, allegedly based in part on Columbia's Harry Cohn, and played by Rod Steiger with the same manic intensity he brought to his roles as **Al Capone** (1958), Napoleon and Mussolini. Jack Palance is the unfortunate star within the mogul's power, haunted by the memory of a drunken car accident in which he killed a pedestrian but escaped punishment by virtue of a studio frame-up. When Palance refuses to renew his contract, he is blackmailed by Steiger and following the murder of a friend, designed to make the contract into an offer he can't refuse, he

Above: *The excellent Kim Stanley, who made only a handful of films before becoming a drama teacher, played an insecure screen actress in* **The Goddess** *(1958). She falls for and marries Lloyd Bridges (real-life father of three acting sons, Beau, Jeff and James), whose character bears a passing resemblance to baseball star Joe DiMaggio, Marilyn Monroe's second husband.*

Top left: *In* **The Bad and the Beautiful** *(1952), Kirk Douglas is the Bad guy, a ruthless Hollywood producer who makes a Beautiful but alcoholic actress (Lana Turner) his mistress in order to use her in his new film. But when she has the illusion that he loves her, he soon straightens her out about that.*

Left: *In Robert Aldrich's rancid drama* **The Big Knife** *(1955), Hollywood star Charles Castle (Jack Palance, left) demands to be released from his contract to studio boss Stanley Hoff (Rod Steiger), a request that leads to Castle's suicide.*

slits his own wrists. Despite its almost *film-noir* grandiloquence, **The Big Knife** is deeply dispiriting. At one point Steiger raises his arm in a quasi-fascist salute and pointedly says, "Hail Columbia!" while Palance's suicide, performed in his bath like a Roman patrician fallen foul of the Emperor, projects Hollywood as an unholy empire ruled by gangsters.

By contrast, **The Goddess** (1958), written by Paddy Chayefsky, is almost restrained and brings the cycle of movies to a close, drawing heavily on the life story of Marilyn Monroe in its account of a vulnerable girl unable to cope with the pressures of success and performance even though that is the only life available to her. She is public property, cast forever in the same role. In the film, the actress, played by the excellent Kim Stanley, manages somehow to survive. The reality was often more painful, as the lives and deaths of James Dean, Judy Garland, Monroe and others testify.

As Gloria Swanson playing Norma Desmond says at the end of **Sunset Boulevard**, "You see, this is my life. It always will be, there's nothing else. Just us. The camera and those wonderful people out there in the dark." But we must not confuse the actress with the role.

Breaking Taboos

Chapter 15

In 1952 the Academy Award for Best Picture went to Cecil B. DeMille's old-fashioned circus spectacular, **The Greatest Show on Earth**, and in 1956 the award went to Mike Todd's all-star extravaganza **Around the World in 80 Days**. But in 1953, **From Here to Eternity** won Oscars for Best Picture, Best Director and Best Screenplay; in 1954 **On the Waterfront** collected a similar trio of awards, as did **Marty** in 1955. DeMille, who had been deposed as all but titular head of the Screen Directors Guild for his own purge on left-wing or Communist members, had given way to a new Hollywood, and, for three years, during the opening salvos in the CinemaScope assault on television, the Academy of Motion Picture Arts and Sciences closed ranks behind three serious, small-scale black-and-white dramas.

There is perhaps nothing unusual in this — witness **Gandhi**'s Oscar triumph over **E.T. The Extra-Terrestrial** in 1982 — but in the early 1950s there was more than a token display of liberal conscience involved. It was a time to take sides, and the preponderance of heavy dramas gradually broke down the barriers of accepted morality and ideology.

New freedoms, new techniques

Fred Zinnemann's **From Here to Eternity** is a landmark movie, not easy to classify as a war film since the climactic Japanese attack on Pearl Harbor is seen as a deus ex machina which shakes the characters out of their promiscuous indolence and insane bigotry. Montgomery Clift's powerful and original performance as the idealistic bugler who refuses to join his unit's boxing team, and Frank Sinatra's recruit killed for his innocent exuberance, become metaphors of political conscience while Burt Lancaster's affair with Deborah Kerr, culminating with their passionate embrace in the pounding surf, broke new ground in the realistic depiction of sex, especially since Kerr was hitherto typecast in virginal roles.

In the same year, Otto Preminger's **The Moon is Blue** became the first film to be released without a seal of approval from the Production Code, established in 1930 and enforced from 1934 as an ethical and moral watchdog. **The Moon is Blue** is an unfunny sex comedy, but its flouting of taboo words like "virgin" played a prominent role in weakening censorship, as did Preminger's subsequent **The Man with the Golden Arm** (1955) in which Frank Sinatra gave a devastating performance as a drug-addicted jazz musician (a few years earlier he would have been a mere alcoholic). Even in 1959 the

Right: *In Cecil B. DeMille's Oscar-winning **The Greatest Show on Earth** (1952), Charlton Heston runs a gigantic circus that stars Betty Hutton as a trapeze artist. The film relied heavily on star appeal and guest appearances – but for Hutton it was virtually the Last Show. After one more minor film, she walked out on her Paramount contract.*

bombastic Preminger was able to stir up controversy by introducing the clinical details of rape — and Lee Remick's underwear as evidence — in the gripping courtroom drama **Anatomy of a Murder**, while in Richard Fleischer's courtroom drama, **Compulsion** (1959), homosexuality came out of the closet in the story of the Leopold and Loeb case which had formed the basis of Hitchcock's **Rope** (1948). But it wasn't until Sidney Lumet's harrowing **The Pawnbroker** (1965), in which a (black) girl exposes her breasts, that censorship really came to an end.

However, this more liberated approach to drama brought with it a new kind of star and a new kind of acting. Every actor will admit to a personal method or technique but not every actor was equipped with "The Method". In 1947 the stage and film director Elia Kazan founded the Actors Studio in New York and from it evolved a new theory of acting, derived in part from the Russian stage director Konstantin Stanislavski, and stressing the importance of collaboration between actors, writers and directors, and a psychological understanding of character. Important playwrights like Tennessee Williams and Arthur Miller, who challenged the conventions of Broadway, found themselves in easy alliance with the talents at the Actors Studio.

The technique, which became known as "The Method", was defined by Kazan as developing from that of the left-wing Group Theatre with which he had worked, initially as an actor himself, in the thirties: "It was exactly the opposite of the then British tradition

246

Left: *Marlon Brando (center) and Karl Malden in the greatest screen monument to The Actors Studio's Method,* **On the Waterfront** *(1954), a heady mixture of Catholicism, gangsterism and romance set in the dockyards of Hoboken, New Jersey, just across the Hudson River from Manhattan.*

Bottom far left: *Originally a TV play, Paddy Chayefsky's* **Marty** *(1955) starred the usually macho Ernest Borgnine as a shy Bronx butcher who falls in love with a lonely teacher, played by Betsy Blair. Borgnine won an Oscar for his performance.*

Below: *This scene in* **From Here to Eternity**, *when Burt Lancaster and Deborah Kerr make love in the pounding Hawaiian surf (the beach location is now on every round-island tour), amazed audiences in 1953 by its frankness, and was thereafter much imitated and parodied, notably by Billy Wilder in* **The Seven Year Itch** *(1955).*

©D-1271-264

248

Left: *This distinctive poster for* **The Man With the Golden Arm** *(1955) was designed by Saul Bass, whose posters and credit title sequences for this film as well as* **The Seven Year Itch** *(1955),* **Around the World in 80 Days** *(1956),* **Vertigo** *(1958) and* **Anatomy of a Murder** *(1959) and many others influenced a whole generation of graphic artists and designers.*

Bottom left: *James Stewart as the small-town lawyer in* **Anatomy of a Murder** *(1959) gingerly handles Lee Remick's torn underwear in his battle of wits against the big-time prosecutor (George C. Scott). The witness (Kathryn Grant) is the murder victim's alleged mistress, actually his daughter.*

Below: *James Dean's three starring roles were largely autobiographical: he was brought up by foster parents and ran away from home at an early age. In* **Rebel Without a Cause** *(1955) he turns his back on his family and study for mindless switchblade knife fights and death-defying car challenges. Dennis Hopper (extreme right) is enjoying the fun.*

[whereby] a person would study the external manifestations of a certain experience or emotion and imitate them. The Group actors would induce the actual emotion within themselves. We would get ourselves *into* the role rather than imitate the externals of the role." The Method had an enormous influence on world theater and cinema and among the talents trained at the Actors Studio were many of the major stars of the 1950s: Montgomery Clift, James Dean, Paul Newman, Rod Steiger, Karl Malden, Eli Wallach, Anthony Quinn, Carroll Baker, Julie Harris, Shelley Winters and Joanne Woodward; Marilyn Monroe took a brief postgraduate course towards the end of her career.

Marlon's method

But the principal advocate of The Method and the most important male star of the decade is Marlon Brando, in whose performances can be seen the advantages (as well as the deficiencies) of the system, resulting in a greater degree of naturalism but also an introspection which led Brando to be known as the great mumbler. Yet, even at his most incoherently sullen (when perhaps the character eludes him, turning technique into trickery), Brando is never less than magnetic, expressing all the pent-up fury of confused and inarticulate modern heroes.

Brando was brought to Hollywood by the producer Stanley Kramer to play a paraplegic soldier in **The Men** (1950), directed by Fred Zinnemann and written by Carl Foreman. It is a remarkably studied performance in a strangely compromised film; but as Stanley Kowalski in **A Streetcar Named Desire** (1951), directed by Kazan and adapted from his own play by Tennessee Williams, Brando's physical power was overwhelming, forcing itself upon Vivien Leigh's fragile and demented Blanche DuBois, metaphorically stripping her of the last vestiges of a romanticism that belonged to another era. In **Viva Zapata!** (1952), again with Kazan, Brando was the Mexican

Left and above: *In Marlon Brando's only film as a director,* **One-Eyed Jacks** *(1961), he also stars as an outlaw who is viciously flogged by his former partner (Karl Malden), known for Freudian reasons as Dad, and has his gun-hand smashed, leading to a convalescence by the sea, a symbolically quasi-incestuous love affair with Malden's stepdaughter (Pina Pellicer) and final, bloody revenge.*

Right: *Despite its period setting before and during World War I,* **East of Eden** *(1955) struck a chord with American teenagers of the 1950s. It was James Dean's first starring role after bit parts in B-movies including Fuller's* **Fixed Bayonets** *(1951) and Sirk's* **Has Anybody Seen My Gal?** *(1952).*

peasant revolutionary on whose shoulders The Method sat exposed as the mannered mouthpiece of contemporary political parallels. **On the Waterfront** (1954) is a triumph of social realism laced with melodrama, with Brando's crude and repressed Terry Malloy smashing the corrupt longshoremen's union by ratting on his friends, a resolution which some saw as the expiation of Kazan's guilt at having testified before the House Un-American Activities Committee.

Kazan's direction and Budd Schulberg's script whip the film into a frenzied *film noir*, a showcase for both The Method and liberalism, with Karl Malden as the working-class parish priest, Rod Steiger as Brando's crooked elder brother, Eva Marie Saint as Brando's conscience and Lee J. Cobb as the corrupt dockside union boss all giving memorable performances.

On the Waterfront was Brando's last film for Kazan but he worked again for Kramer in Laslo Benedek's **The Wild One** (1954), an archetypal 1950s social protest picture with the star in black leather and chains as the leader of a motorcycle gang which destroys a peaceful but complacent Californian community. The film was banned in Britain (except in the university city of Cambridge) for many years because of its apparent incitement to violence but, along with James Dean's equivalent in **Rebel Without a Cause** (1955), Brando's missionary zeal to deprave and corrupt ("What are you rebelling against?" he is asked, to which he laconically replies, "What

have you got?") was immortalized as a scowling one-sheet poster which hung and still hangs above every alienated teenager's bed. In Joseph L. Mankiewicz's Shakespearean political thriller **Julius Caesar** (1953), Brando is a brooding Mark Antony, a New Yorker-upon-Avon with John Gielgud and James Mason and surely meeting the most demanding test The Method ever had.

For Brando, **On the Waterfront** was an apogee of sorts and he drifted into character roles and caricatures — as Napoleon in **Desiree** (1954), as Sky Masterson in Mankiewicz's musical **Guys and Dolls** (1955), as the Japanese interpreter Sakini in **Teahouse of the August Moon** (1956), totally bewildering US Captain Glenn Ford, and as a Nazi in Edward Dmytryk's **The Young Lions** (1958). He was reclaimed by director Sidney Lumet for Tennessee Williams' **The Fugitive Kind** (1960) before plunging into his premature mausoleum as both actor and director, the brilliant and grandiloquent **One-Eyed Jacks** (1961), the last of the 1950s Westerns which paved the way

for spaghetti-director Sergio Leone, Clint Eastwood and Sam Peckinpah.

Despite the triumph of **The Godfather** (1972) and the soul-baring of **Last Tango in Paris** (1972), Brando's career frittered away into self-indulgent cameos. It is our loss; perhaps not his. But James Dean's career ended in the twisted wreck of a Porsche coupe, leaving behind three starring roles, an undying legend and speculation about an unresolved talent. Apart from **The Wild One**, Brando's films were for intellectuals and the middle class. But James Dean, even in Kazan's **East of Eden** (1955), struck a universal chord with his scared face and jittery pulse; he gave the world tight-fitting jeans and a misfit mentality that prefigured rock 'n' roll.

Bottom left: *A characteristic James Dean expression in **East of Eden** (1954), a sensitive face scarred with pain as he quarrels with his father (Raymond Massey).*

Below: *Anne Francis, one of Glenn Ford's more understanding students, sympathizes with him after his high-school class of young hoodlums have beaten him up in Richard Brooks' **The Blackboard Jungle** (1955).*

Young rebels

Every film of Dean's was an inarticulate cry against authority and parental influence: in **East of Eden**, from John Steinbeck's vast novel, he is stranded in CinemaScope's empty spaces, set apart from his father (Raymond Massey) and his Abel-like brother (Richard Davalos). In Nicholas Ray's **Rebel Without a Cause**, the quintessential movie of the 1950s despite its limitations, Dean is the speed-obsessed teenage son of a couple who fear the publicity his escapades might bring them. His only friends, Sal Mineo and Natalie Wood (who, as well as Dean, would all meet violent real-life deaths) are the products of broken and bickering homes and the film drives inexorably towards tragedy in the magical, escapist setting of a planetarium. By contrast, Richard Brooks' **The Blackboard Jungle** (1955), with Glenn Ford as a schoolteacher viciously persecuted by his pupils, and John Frankenheimer's first feature **The Young Stranger** (1956), about the wayward son of a movie executive, have dated badly, lacking the neurotic focus of a Dean. **Giant** (1956) was Dean's last movie, an epic panorama of Texas spanning two generations of a dynastic ranching family who become oil magnates. Beside the solid if uninspired performances of Rock Hudson and Elizabeth Taylor, Dean's introspection is accentuated, though director George Stevens gives him one transcendent extrovert moment when he strikes oil.

Giant was released after Dean's death and perhaps his mantle was assumed by Paul Newman as the boxer Rocky Marciano in **Somebody Up There Likes Me** (1956), which was to have been Dean's next role: it is feasible to see Dean in the role of Billy the Kid, which Newman played in Arthur Penn's first feature **The Left-Handed Gun** (1958), a psychological drama about a social misfit. The critic David Thomson has pondered the possibility of Dean in **Last Tango in Paris** but a more persuasive projection, perhaps,

Bottom far left: In ***The Caine Mutiny*** *(1954), based on Herman Wouk's best-seller, the paranoid harsh disciplinarian Capt. Queeg (Humphrey Bogart, left) commands a minesweeper, the USS* Caine. *But when he loses his nerve in a storm, Lt. Maryk (Van Johnson, center) assumes command because the only alternative, he believes, is allowing the ship to sink, a too drastic way of proving the captain's inadequacy.*

Left: *In Stanley Kramer's **The Defiant Ones** (1958), Tony Curtis (left) and Sidney Poitier played two escaped convicts who are shackled together in an obvious allegory of American racism.*

would have been the successor of Paul Newman's **Hud** (1963), or his own Jett Rink in **Giant**, the corrupt J. R. Ewing in the TV series *Dallas*.

Even without Brando or Dean, Stanley Kramer and Elia Kazan made important films. Kramer's production of Arthur Miller's **Death of a Salesman** (1951), directed by Laslo Benedek, with Fredric March as America's most resonant failure, Willy Loman, was sadly little more than a film record of a great play. Kramer's **The Caine Mutiny** (1954), directed by the formerly blacklisted Edward Dmytryk, contains Humphrey Bogart's last truly major performance — as the paranoid captain of a naval ship. Kramer then became a director and left subtlety if not sincerity behind: the medical drama **Not as a Stranger** (1955), with Robert Mitchum, is a terrible film and **The Defiant Ones** (1958), with Tony Curtis and Sidney Poitier as convicts chained together, was a ten-gallon antiracist message in a pint bottle. Kazan's **Baby Doll** (1956), from an original screenplay by Tennessee Williams, is a deliriously Gothic comedy of sexual repression, with Carroll Baker as Karl Malden's teenage wife who will remain a virgin until she is twenty, except that Silva (Eli Wallach) cannot resist Baker's blatant invitations as she abstractedly sucks her thumb and reclines on a swing-couch like a leopard in heat. **Baby Doll** is a major film, superbly acted and photographed (by Boris Kaufman). It was roundly condemned as immoral, and slightly cut, at the time of its release — which, intriguingly, coincided with Vladimir Nabokov's novel *Lolita* and, in France, with Brigitte Bardot's nakedness in Roger Vadim's **And God Created Woman** (1956), an innocent stroll through the Garden of Eden financed by Columbia Pictures. But Baker in **Baby Doll** was all-American and threatening, with the primordial waters of the Mississippi Delta seemingly oozing from her body.

Left: *Carroll Baker in **Baby Doll** (1956), one of the American cinema's finest (and funniest) depictions of sexuality. In only her second major role, she was Oscar-nominated at 25, her finest hour. Though directed twice in sympathetic parts by John Ford, she then went down the path indicated by **The Carpetbaggers** (1964) and **Harlow** (1965), becoming an exiled sex-queen in Italian exploitation pix. In the late 70s she returned to Anglo-American productions.*

Below: *While America gasped at Lancaster and Kerr in **From Here to Eternity** (1953) or Frank Sinatra's drug addiction in **The Man with the Golden Arm** (1956), Brigitte Bardot in Roger Vadim's **And God Created Woman** (1956) was playing a latterday Eve who delighted rather than shocked.*

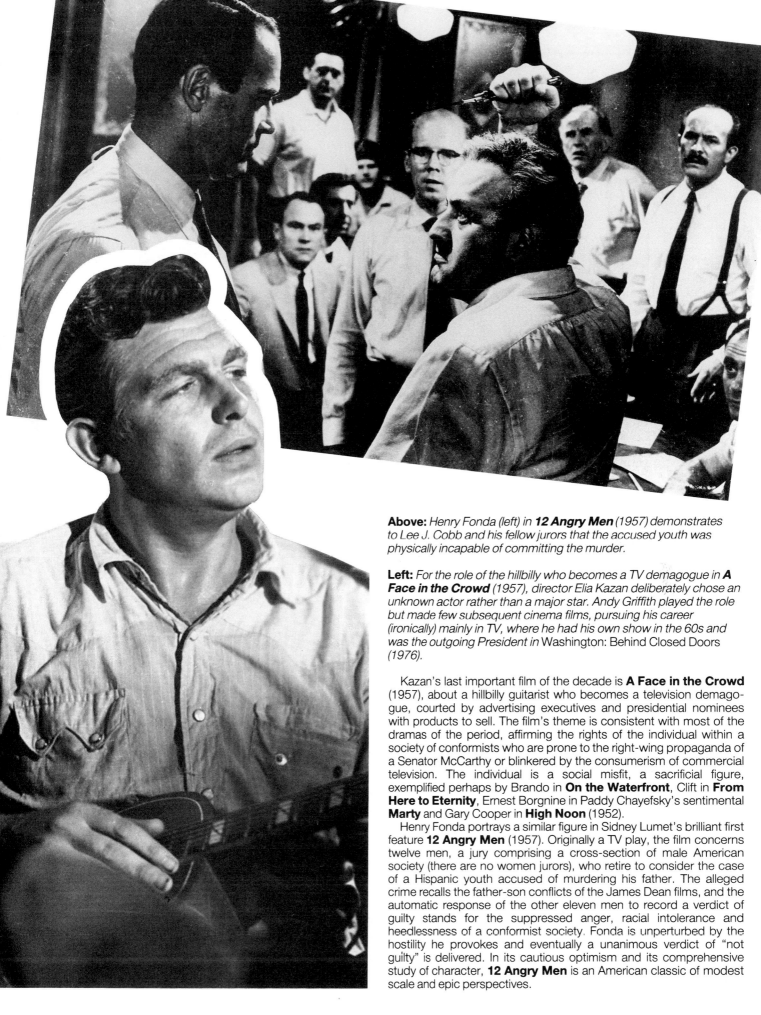

Above: *Henry Fonda (left) in* **12 Angry Men** *(1957) demonstrates to Lee J. Cobb and his fellow jurors that the accused youth was physically incapable of committing the murder.*

Left: *For the role of the hillbilly who becomes a TV demagogue in* **A Face in the Crowd** *(1957), director Elia Kazan deliberately chose an unknown actor rather than a major star. Andy Griffith played the role but made few subsequent cinema films, pursuing his career (ironically) mainly in TV, where he had his own show in the 60s and was the outgoing President in* Washington: Behind Closed Doors *(1976).*

Kazan's last important film of the decade is **A Face in the Crowd** (1957), about a hillbilly guitarist who becomes a television demagogue, courted by advertising executives and presidential nominees with products to sell. The film's theme is consistent with most of the dramas of the period, affirming the rights of the individual within a society of conformists who are prone to the right-wing propaganda of a Senator McCarthy or blinkered by the consumerism of commercial television. The individual is a social misfit, a sacrificial figure, exemplified perhaps by Brando in **On the Waterfront**, Clift in **From Here to Eternity**, Ernest Borgnine in Paddy Chayefsky's sentimental **Marty** and Gary Cooper in **High Noon** (1952).

Henry Fonda portrays a similar figure in Sidney Lumet's brilliant first feature **12 Angry Men** (1957). Originally a TV play, the film concerns twelve men, a jury comprising a cross-section of male American society (there are no women jurors), who retire to consider the case of a Hispanic youth accused of murdering his father. The alleged crime recalls the father-son conflicts of the James Dean films, and the automatic response of the other eleven men to record a verdict of guilty stands for the suppressed anger, racial intolerance and heedlessness of a conformist society. Fonda is unperturbed by the hostility he provokes and eventually a unanimous verdict of "not guilty" is delivered. In its cautious optimism and its comprehensive study of character, **12 Angry Men** is an American classic of modest scale and epic perspectives.

War, Hot and Cold

Chapter 16

On June 25, 1950 the Communist forces of North Korea crossed the 38th parallel and captured Seoul, the capital of South Korea. The Americans responded immediately and, for more than two years, were embroiled in their first fruitless war in Asia. By this time the entire Chinese mainland had fallen to the Communist forces of Mao Tse-tung, while in Vietnam the French were fighting Ho Chi Minh, who had once been the recipient of limited American Aid. President Harry Truman announced that the American policy of "containment", originally directed against Soviet expansion in Europe, would be extended to all of Asia.

In Washington, both HUAC and Senator McCarthy exploited the tense situation in Asia by campaigns against suspected Communists in America. As in 1947, one of HUAC's main targets was Hollywood and its writers, directors and actors. Chairman John S. Wood claimed that Hollywood was giving Communist Party members access to prestige, power and wealth. Although McCarthy himself was eventually censured by the Senate in December 1954 (he died two and a half years later), blacklisting was extremely effective throughout the Fifties and well into the Sixties, destroying many careers and forever changing others.

At the same time, on November 6, 1952, the second phase of the nuclear age was born with the detonation of America's first hydrogen bomb in the Pacific. After America had withdrawn its forces from Korea in 1953, leaving an austere Stalinist state in the North and a capitalist puppet regime in the South, the temperature dropped. Winston Churchill had already coined a phrase for it in 1948: the Cold War.

Fields of conflict

Hollywood war films veered from the self-conscious liberalism of **Paths of Glory** (1957) and **The Bridge on the River Kwai** (1957) to the jingoistic **The Steel Helmet** (1950) and **Retreat, Hell!** (1952), the last two set in Korea. The moral perspective and historical distance were important: the Germans and, to a slightly lesser extent, the Japanese, had become allies, trading partners, and bastions against Communism. World War II films became adventure dramas and even comedies. The common enemy was Communism, with its

Right: Kirk Douglas about to lead the futile attack in **Paths of Glory** (1957) which director Stanley Kubrick filmed in a series of elaborate tracking shots through the trenches and into no-man's-land.

Left: The platoon that fights the communist North Koreans in Samuel Fuller's **The Steel Helmet** (1950) was led by Japanese-American actor Richard Loo and included Lynn Stalmaster who subsequently became the head of Hollywood's major casting agency.

threat of nuclear oblivion, and this paranoid atmosphere produced the Red Scare picture which infiltrated the thriller and the science fiction genres. Thirty years later, it was equally inevitable that the fervently anti-Communist Reagan administration would inspire its own rash of Red Scare films such as **Firefox** (1980), **Red Dawn** (1984), **White Nights** (1985) and **Invasion USA** (1985).

The ideological softening of the World War II film can be seen in **The Desert Fox** (1951), directed by Henry Hathaway and starring James Mason as Field Marshal Rommel, portrayed as a professional soldier rather than a raving Nazi. After the superbly staged battle of El Alamein, Rommel emerges defeated yet worthy of respect, becoming a participant in the plot to overthrow Hitler. The same impulse can be detected in John Huston's **Heaven Knows, Mr Allison** (1957) in which an Irish nun (Deborah Kerr) and a boozy American marine (Robert Mitchum) are stranded on a Pacific atoll; but their developing, comic relationship defuses the background of war and Mitchum's fight against an occupying unit of Japanese troops. And who really remembers Huston's **The African Queen** (1951), with Humphrey Bogart and Katharine Hepburn joyously upstaging each other, as a World War I picture?

Billy Wilder's **Stalag 17** (1953) is only ostensibly a World War II picture, using a German prisoner-of-war camp setting for a corrosively funny comment on cut-throat capitalism. William Holden's Oscar-winning performance as J. J. Sefton is an unrelieved portrait in dehumanized man yet, despicable as he is, Sefton is the only dynamic character in the film. Wilder, throughout his career, saw this as one of the essential contradictions of the American character —

the same equivocation attends Kirk Douglas in **Ace in the Hole** — and of course Sefton's fellow-prisoners are torn between hatred and admiration. Sefton's crazy, profit-motivated schemes, like his rat-race and his books on escape attempts, are compellingly cynical, somewhat against the grain of his own escape. But then, as one character suggests, "Maybe he just wanted to steal our wire-cutters."

Nicholas Ray's **Flying Leathernecks** (1951), on the other hand, used the war in the Pacific as a vehicle for John Wayne's heroics and as moral support for the forces in Korea, while **To Hell and Back** (1955) starred Audie Murphy in his own story as the most decorated GI of World War II. These were simple-minded action movies, miles from Wilder's social criticism or the ambiguous treatment of war in a film like Robert Aldrich's **Attack!** (1955).

Attack! brought an acute sense of 1950s paranoia to its story about a platoon in the Ardennes which is led by cowards, psychotics and political opportunists. **Attack!** is by no means a comedy, yet there is a vivid sense of the absurd about it, as there is in Aldrich's **Too Late the Hero** (1970), a Vietnam parable set in World War II. The men of the platoon in **Attack!** are spokesmen for the Eisenhower era — Eddie Albert as the captain with shot nerves and dead men on his conscience, Lee Marvin as a colonel who depends on the captain's political connections once the war is over, and Jack Palance as a lieutenant whose concern for his men ends in a heroic death, forcing the elimination of the captain and a cover-up to preserve the status quo.

Attack! is perhaps the most brutal — and brutally honest — war film of the decade, its ambiguities outreaching those of **Paths of**

Bottom left: *Alec Guinness as the politely demented Colonel Nicholson and Sessua Hayakawa as the Japanese officer in David Lean's hugely successful* **Bridge on the River Kwai** *(1957). Their battle of wills was viewed with disdain by James Donald, in the background as the British medical officer.*

Below: *There is nothing like a bestselling biography and a True Story to add luster to a movie. But the publicists of* **The Desert Fox** *(1951) tactfully overlooked the fact that the film's hero, Field Marshal Rommel, had a mere nine years earlier been second only to Hitler as the Allies' most formidable adversary.*

Glory. This is not to dismiss Stanley Kubrick's film, which many critics have compared to such pacifist masterpieces as King Vidor's **The Big Parade** (1925) and Lewis Milestone's **All Quiet on the Western Front** (1930). Set on the French and German front during World War I, the film is eloquent in its antimilitarism but the dice are loaded. Despite the fine acting of Kirk Douglas as the defense counsel, there is no argument, only the inevitability of a firing squad for the three men accused of cowardice when in fact they are the scapegoats of a corrupt officer (George Macready). The film's liberal credentials are impeccable (executive producer Kirk Douglas was later to hire the blacklisted writer Dalton Trumbo for **Spartacus**, 1960) but against Douglas's humanitarian crusade is Kubrick's darker fascination with the timelessness of evil as represented by Macready's general.

Yellow peril

The most successful war film of the 1950s was David Lean's **The Bridge on the River Kwai**, a hugely expensive adventure epic set in a Japanese POW camp where the prisoners are forced to work on the railway that would link India and Singapore. Written under a pseudonym (Pierre Boulle, French-speaking author of the original novel) by the blacklisted Carl Foreman and Michael Wilson, the film portrays the futility of war by cutting between the construction of the bridge, signifying order and civilization, and a mission to destroy it.

Left: *Aboard* **The African Queen** *are Humphrey Bogart and Katharine Hepburn in John Huston's 1951 version of C. S. Forester's novel, scripted by James Agee.*

Bottom left: *James Mason as Field Marshal Rommel endeavoring to snatch victory from the jaws of defeat in Henry Hathaway's exciting World War II adventure* **The Desert Fox** *(1951).*

Below: *The combination of Robert Mitchum's rugged world-weariness and Deborah Kerr's delicate charm was beautifully explored by John Huston in* **Heaven Knows, Mr Allison** *(1957), a wartime adventure set on a South Pacific island but actually made, for logistical reasons, on Tobago in the West Indies.*

The performances by William Holden, in a role not unlike Sefton in **Stalag 17**, Jack Hawkins as a neurotic commando and, especially, Alec Guinness as the British officer who unwittingly aids the enemy by ensuring that the bridge will become a monument to the morale of his men, are of a very high caliber, as are Lean's direction and Jack Hildyard's photography which brilliantly conveys the heat and fecundity of the location. However, the greatness of **Kwai** lies not in its portrayal of the war as such but in its Conradian portrait of the end of the British Empire.

When America went to war in Korea, so did Hollywood, and the first into battle was Samuel Fuller's **The Steel Helmet**, about a platoon behind enemy lines who kill commies like something out of *Mad Magazine.* Fuller ended the picture with a dire warning — "This Story Has No End" — and proved it with **Fixed Bayonets** (1951), behind enemy lines again with another platoon of rednecks. Both films have a rough-hewn intensity which has led Fuller's Marxist admirers to label him an anarchist, though **The Steel Helmet** and **Fixed Bayonets** hardly undermined the war effort. Neither did **One Minute to Zero** (1952), with Robert Mitchum ordering the slaughter of a refugee column who might be harboring Communist guerillas. Joseph H. Lewis's threadbare **Retreat, Hell!** said everything in its title. However, the American forces were shown in retreat in Richard Brooks' **Battle Circus** (1952) in which Humphrey Bogart played an embittered officer brought to his senses by a tearfully patriotic June Allyson in the setting of a Mobile Army Surgical Hospital, later the locale of the satirical hit and Vietnam parable **M*A*S*H** (1970).

Right: *Humphrey Bogart as the drunken Charlie Allnutt and Katharine Hepburn as the prim Rose in John Huston's classic adventure yarn* **The African Queen** *(1951). Bogart eventually blows up a German gunboat but it was Bogart and Hepburn's verbal and romantic sparring that made the film enduringly popular.*

Far right: *Baby-faced and ready for another medal, Audie Murphy played himself in* **To Hell and Back** *(1955). Murphy's film career foundered in the 1960s and he was declared bankrupt before his death in a plane crash in 1971.*

After the Korean war had ended, Karl Malden's only film as a director, **Time Limit** (1957), took the new line of disillusionment in its story of a McCarthy-like tribunal investigating an officer (Richard Basehart) who collaborated with the North Koreans when he was their prisoner. The tribunal, led by Richard Widmark, subsequently learns that Basehart's actions were designed to prevent the slaughter of his men, one of whom had given in under torture and described an escape plan. Arnold Laven's **The Rack** (1956), based on Rod Serling's TV play and starring Paul Newman and Lee Marvin, had a similar plot and an atmospheric depiction of post-Korean American society. In Lewis Milestone's **Pork Chop Hill** (1959) Gregory Peck is an officer who orders his men to take a strategically worthless hill so that the American side of the peace negotiations will be in a stronger bargaining position. But the best of the post-Korean dramas is

Anthony Mann's **Men in War** (1956), which dealt with the dignity of retreat as Robert Ryan and Aldo Ray lead a platoon, plus a shell-shocked colonel, through enemy lines to rejoin their unit, realizing that their only chance is to attack a well-defended North Korean position. The attack is successful but very costly in lives, leaving a powerful expression of individual heroism and group solidarity against the tragedy of men dying miles from home in someone else's war. This last aspect of the war — its civilian aftermath — can be detected in a few films, though it was not until Vietnam that the traumas of readjustment became a major preoccupation. In Richard Fleischer's **Violent Saturday** (1954) a young man feels guilty at not being awarded a medal but confirms his bravery by foiling a bank robbery, and in Lewis Allen's little-known but superb thriller **Suddenly** (1954), a family held hostage by Frank Sinatra's would-be Presidential assassin are deeply scarred by their Korean experiences.

Reds under the bed

The Cold War brought about the Red Scare films which began in the late 1940s with **The Red Menace** (1949), **The Big Lift** (1949), about the Berlin Blockade, and **I Married a Communist** (1949) by Robert Stevenson, the future director of **Mary Poppins** (1964). Samuel Fuller's **Pickup on South Street** (1953) is often cited in this respect for its portrayal of Communist agents as Mafia-style gangsters, but more to the point are the hysterical **The Red Danube** (1950), in which Russian citizens in Austria are forced to return to Russia; **I Was a Communist for the FBI** (1951), in which a Federal agent infiltrates the Pittsburgh steel mills to weed out subversives; **Big Jim McLain** (1952), in which John Wayne made plain his political allegiances by energetically conducting a McCarthyist campaign in Hawaii; **Red Planet Mars** (1952), which imagined that the deeply religious and utopian Martians might inspire a revolution in Russia, replacing the Bolsheviks with Bible-Belt fanatics; **The 27th Day** (1957), in which Communism is wiped out by using a suicide pill acquired from a doomed alien planet whose inhabitants are subsequently invited to Earth to establish a commie-free, peace-loving community.

The paranoia of the period was readily assimilated into the science-fiction genre. America was under siege from allegorical monsters, sentient vegetables and irradiated and overgrown insects. **The Day the Earth Stood Still** (1951), **When Worlds Collide** (1951) and **The War of the Worlds** (1953) took a cosmic view of earthly strife and intervened, both politically and religiously. In Howard Hawks' production **The Thing** (1951), credited to editor Christian Nyby as director, American scientists discover a UFO in the Antarctic, accidentally thaw the monster and discover it is a vegetable, giving rise to the line, "An intellectual carrot, the mind boggles!" The poor thing then creates havoc until it is incinerated with a flamethrower, leaving a horrified radio reporter to urge Americans to "Watch the

Right: *Richard Widmark, one of Hollywood's most consistent performers, and Dolores Michaels in the post-Korean drama* **Time Limit** *(1957), directed by Karl Malden.*

Bottom far right: *In the British sector of postwar Vienna, an English officer (Peter Lawford) falls in love with a defecting Russian ballerina (Janet Leigh). The strident Red Scare picture* **The Red Danube** *(1950) was directed by George Sidney, who prefers to be remembered for his musicals.*

Below: *Robert Ryan in* **Men in War** *(1956). Ryan was one of the American cinema's finest actors, never quite a major box-office star and at his very best in uniform or on the wrong side of the law.*

skies!" **The Thing**, with its closely-knit male characters and assertive female so similar to Hawks' work as director, is a classic of its kind.

So, too, is **Them!** (1954) in which H-bomb tests in the New Mexico desert have produced a strain of giant ants which is destroyed when the queen is trapped and killed in a Los Angeles sewer. This exciting and well-made film, directed by Gordon Douglas, has been interpreted as a Red Scare film with armies of Communists overrunning America, but its basis in nuclear anxieties seems sufficiently allegorical, as was the earlier **The Beast From 20,000 Fathoms** (1953), based on a story by Ray Bradbury about a dinosaur awakened and thawed out by an atomic blast, prompting it to return to its home — which now happens to be New York City.

The mood of the times was also caught by **I Married a Monster From Outer Space** (1958) which is a subtle film in every respect except its title. Here the allegorical red is not under the bed but literally in it, kidnapping grooms on the eve of their weddings and replacing them with humanoid aliens who impregnate the brides to keep alive their endangered species, flying the babies away in spaceships. It is an ingenious idea of sexual indoctrination by monsters with phallic tendrils, with serious considerations for the nuclear American family. Even more disturbing is Don Siegel's masterly **Invasion of the Body Snatchers** (1956), a classic example of how an established fictional genre could accommodate a political argument, even though its precise nature remains ambiguous. Some have seen the alien vegetable pods who implant themselves into humans as Communists whilst others regard the characters who refuse to conform as the left-wingers. Siegel himself seems to identify the pods with Hollywood studio executives, among many others. The film's *noir* imagery and Kevin McCarthy's paranoid hero evoke an enclosed world from which there is no escape. It is an oppressive film that paints a dark picture of American society where freedom of expression and individuality are at risk.

*Before he made his name as Marshal Matt Dillon in the long-running TV series Gunsmoke, James Arness's 6 foot 6 inch bulk was well cast as the thawed-out vegetable monster known as **The Thing** (1951).*

Above: *For the 1953 film version of H.G. Wells'* **The War of the Worlds***, the setting was changed from Victorian London to modern Los Angeles. The invading Martians withstand atomic retaliation but succumb to the Earth's bacteria.*

Left: *In* **The Day the Earth Stood Still** *(1951) an alien lands in Washington to warn us petty-minded earthlings of the futility and dangers of international tension. The director Robert Wise was a former editor who had worked on* **Citizen Kane** *(1941), had the luckless job of recutting Orson Welles'* **The Magnificent Ambersons** *(1942), and later won four Oscars for producing and directing* **West Side Story** *(1961) and* **The Sound of Music** *(1965).*

After the bomb

A world beyond risk was shown in Stanley Kramer's **On the Beach** (1959), the first major post-holocaust film, realistic in its scenes of Australian cities slowly poisoned by fall-out and a deserted San Francisco. But the film is dramatically feeble, with Gregory Peck as a submarine commander, Ava Gardner as a Melbourne socialite, and a non-dancing Fred Astaire as a racing driver who kills himself with carbon monoxide gas rather than wait for the cloud of fall-out to arrive. Only in the sequence when Peck sails to California in search of a mysterious radio signal does the film convey the real horror of the situation since the signal is merely a morse key tied to a flapping window cord. Otherwise, the script bludgeons its audience and Ernest Gold's music offers endless variations of "Waltzing Matilda".

The film which drew all these social and political strands into a combustible whole was Robert Aldrich's **Kiss Me Deadly** (1955), based on one of Mickey Spillane's Mike Hammer novels but encompassing the Red Scare, the Cold War and the Bomb. Aldrich is one of the key directors of the 1950s, beginning his career as assistant to such notable left-wingers as Charles Chaplin, Abraham Polonsky and Joseph Losey. His first feature, **The Big Leaguer** (1953), was a gutsy baseball yarn, but his second film, **World for Ransom** (1953), is a post-Korean war story of international espionage in the Far East, a much sourer view of things to come than the corruption of Graham Greene's anti-American French Vietnam novel **The Quiet American**, filmed as anti-Communist propaganda by Joseph L. Mankiewicz in 1957 with Audie Murphy.

Right from the credit titles which are run back to front (ie, **Deadly Kiss Me**), Aldrich's film charts a nihilistic world beyond the brink of

Below: *James Arness as an FBI agent and Joan Weldon face one of the giant ants in **Them!** (1954).*

274

moral collapse. In Spillane's novel the story was a search for narcotics but in the film everyone is seeking the "great whatsit", a box containing a radioactive device. There is a murdered scientist, foreign agents, a confused FBI and a strange girl (Cloris Leachman's debut) who flags down Mike Hammer's car, crashing him into an unwanted case (he normally does divorces, spying on moonlighting women). Hammer (Ralph Meeker) is a blunt instrument possessed by arrogance and supercharged by violence, weaving way out of his depth through false trails and lost characters. **Kiss Me Deadly** is a film of unusual pessimism, relieved by flashes of sour wit, and Aldrich's intense direction leads us through a world of shadows until the end, when Pandora's box is opened to bathe the world in a radioactive glow. With **Kiss Me Deadly**, *film noir* was transformed into apocalypse *noir*.

Below: *In Don Siegel's masterly science-fiction thriller **Invasion of the Body Snatchers** (1956) an entire Californian community's cheery complacency is destroyed by the arrival of the 'pods', a vegetable growth that takes over human thought.*

Old Forms, New Directions

Chapter 17

THRILLERS

The 1940s cast long and menacing shadows in the genre called *film noir*. The darkness persisted throughout the 1950s, lightened somewhat in the 1960s and darkened again in the paranoid 1970s, providing an illusory refuge for the haunted and the hunted, and for illicit lovers nervously plotting spousal murder.

In the 1940s *film noir* was lustrous and seductive. There was Barbara Stanwyck's anklet in **Double Indemnity** (1944), Robert Mitchum's compelling fatalism in **Out of the Past** (1947), Rita Hayworth putting "the blame on Mame" in **Gilda** (1946), and the shimmering mystery of who killed **Laura** (1944). In the 1950s *film noir* became apocalyptic, as in **Kiss Me Deadly**, or excessively violent as in Fritz Lang's **The Big Heat** (1953), in which Lee Marvin throws a pot of scalding coffee into Gloria Grahame's face, or assumed the mythic grandeur of Shakespearean or Jacobean tragedy as in Orson Welles' **Touch of Evil** (1958).

Cheap but chilling

A director could often achieve more on a shoestring than with a big budget. Joseph H. Lewis's **Gun Crazy** (1950) and **The Big Combo** (1955) are economic miracles to place well ahead of the same director's B-Westerns **The Halliday Brand** (1957) and the cult favorite **Terror in a Texas Town** (1958). Lewis had neither the time (both literally and figuratively) nor the money to indulge in distracting subplots; he got straight to the point with clear narratives, finely drawn characters and well-choreographed action. **Gun Crazy** in particular is a masterly exploration of sexual and violent ritual, played out by a doomed romantic couple on the run from the law and inhibition, recalling the lovers in **They Live by Night** (1949) and prefiguring **Bonnie and Clyde** (1967).

The thriller, like the one- and two-reel Westerns of the 1920s and the exploitation films of Roger Corman, provided a valuable training ground for new directors. The form had an inbuilt potential for visual

Right: *All the pent-up arrogance and violence of Robert Aldrich's **Kiss Me Deadly** (1955) is contained in Ralph Meeker's malevolent expression in his portrayal of Mickey Spillane's sleazy private-eye Mike Hammer. He is threatening the crooked Dr Soberlin (Albert Dekker), whose robe is a clear film-noir sign of decadence.*

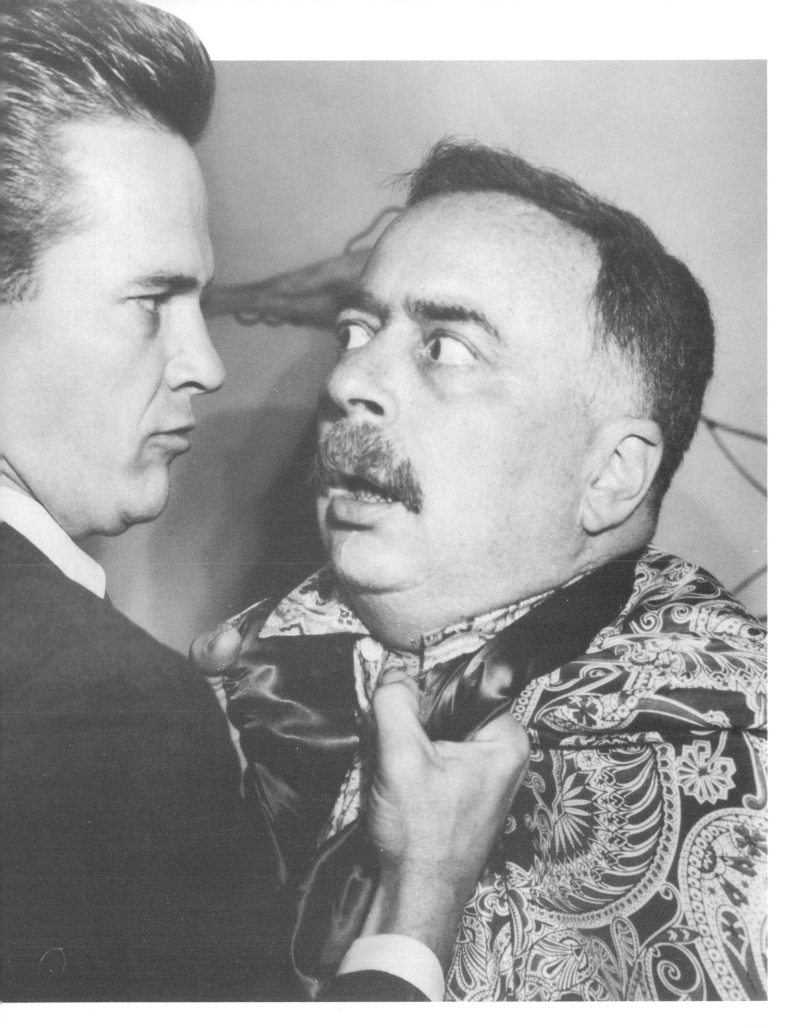

Above left and above: *Lee Marvin was the 1950s most compelling sadistic brute, seen in Fritz Lang's* **The Big Heat** *(1953) examining his handiwork on Gloria Grahame's face after he has thrown a pot of boiling coffee at her.*

Left: *Orson Welles as the corrupt cop in* **Touch of Evil** *(1958). Mexican policeman's bride Janet Leigh is unconscious and mobster Akim Tamiroff is about to get strangled with her stocking.*

experimentation which caught the eye of critics and studio executives. Richard Fleischer, who would later direct the Walt Disney studio's best live-action feature, **20,000 Leagues Under the Sea** (1954), and the historical adventure **The Vikings** (1958), began his career directing **March of Time** newsreels, and incorporated documentary techniques into his low-budget thrillers **Armored Car Robbery** (1950) and the superb **The Narrow Margin** (1952), about

a detective's relationship with a racketeer's widow whom he is escorting by train to an important trial. Working under severe budgetary restraints, Fleischer conveyed a powerful impression of a desolate and indifferent America. The quality that most characterizes these early Fleischer films — as well as Fred Zinnemann's **Kid Glove Killer** (1942) and **Act of Violence** (1948), and also John Sturges' **Mystery Street** (1950) and **Jeopardy** (1953), a little-known gem of a crime film — is their modest, crisp assurance which, critics might argue, disappeared when these directors graduated to conventionally weightier material.

Before 2001

Some critics might claim the same deterioration in the work of Stanley Kubrick, the most important and idiosyncratic director to have emerged in the 1950s, and Joseph Losey. Before he achieved international recognition for **Paths of Glory**, Kubrick had privately funded a now tantalizingly unavailable war allegory called **Fear and Desire** (1953) and then made two cheap and immensely stylish *noir* thrillers for United Artists. **Killer's Kiss** (1955) is an essentially ordinary tale of a boxer's involvement with a girl with gangland connections but Kubrick's visual flair transforms documentary-style shots of New York streets into nightmarish labyrinths, and a climactic fight in a warehouse filled with tailors' dummies pushes the film into pure surrealism.

The Killing (1956) stars the estimable Sterling Hayden, who masterminds a racetrack robbery. The film recalls John Huston's neat thriller **The Asphalt Jungle** (1950), in which Hayden is the heavy in a jewel robbery, but Kubrick disrupts the chronology of the story, charging it with irony as we watch the plan disintegrate. The gallery of flawed and vulnerable characters, notably Elisha Cook Jr's timid husband driven to crime by faithless blonde Marie Windsor, gives **The Killing** a grim realism that makes it a minor classic.

Kubrick now regards these early films as little more than competent and, following his experience on the epic **Spartacus** (1960), he moved to Britain where in 1961–2 he filmed the most controversial American novel of the 1950s, Vladimir Nabokov's **Lolita**, replacing the novel's explicit sexuality with mordant humor and surreal imagery.

Joseph Losey also forged an outstanding career in Britain after he was blacklisted. Like Kubrick, Losey is the antithesis of the genre director and where Kubrick's ambitions were fulfilled by such audacious films as **2001: A Space Odyssey** (1968) and **Barry Lyndon** (1975), Losey became the most articulate satirist of the British class system with **The Servant** (1963), **Accident** (1967) and **The Go-Between** (1971), all scripted by playwright Harold Pinter. At the same time, Losey's World War I drama, **King and Country** (1964), is every bit the equal of **Paths of Glory** in the power of its antimilitarist stance.

And like Kubrick, Losey, too, had served his apprenticeship in the American B-movie thriller: **The Prowler** (1951), written by blacklisted writers Dalton Trumbo and Hugo Butler, and with Robert Aldrich as assistant director, is a stark commentary on the sterility of American life as a cop answers the distress call of a lonely, childless wife and later pretends to be a prowler to engineer the husband's death. **M** (1951) is a remake of the Fritz Lang 1931 classic and transposed its indictment of German mob mentality to modern American society. **The Big Night** (1951), about an alienated teenager drifting towards murder, concluded an amazingly productive year for Losey and proved to be his last American picture.

Unlike Kubrick and Losey, Samuel Fuller preferred to remain a genre director, refining his peculiar art within its restraints. Fuller is Hollywood's tabloid muckraker whose films burst with energy in a way that implies that only the toughest will survive. **Park Row** (1952) is Fuller's tribute to the early newspaper industry, shot through a glass darkly and one of the best period films ever made. **House of Bamboo** (1955) and **The Crimson Kimono** (1959) both dealt with the cultural collision between America and its former enemy but then economic competitor, Japan, in the guise of gangbusting thrillers and **Underworld USA** (1961) was almost an epic of corruption in America. These are crude yet dynamic works, alight with Fuller's passion for movies and vexed questions.

Touch of evil

In exalted Hollywood circles Orson Welles and Fritz Lang might have been regarded with some disdain, great artists descended into genre movies. Welles' **Mr Arkadin** (aka **Confidential Report**, 1955) is a bizarre remake in Spain of **Citizen Kane** (1941), badly acted and technically uneven, yet the murderous investigation into a rich man's murky past evokes a world of limitless corruption. **Mr Arkadin** is an

Top right: *In **The Killing** (1956), Sterling Hayden overpowers a guard in the racetrack booking hall at the start of the robbery.*

Right: *Peggy Cummins, a Welsh actress who made too few films, and John Dall as the doomed romantic couple in Joseph H. Lewis's influential B-movie **Gun Crazy** (1950).*

Far right: *Lewis's **The Big Combo** (1955) lacked **Gun Crazy**'s violent eroticism but contained some striking imagery on a low budget. Seen in silhouette are Jean Wallace as a gangster's girlfriend and Cornel Wilde as the cop she falls for.*

NO ADMIT

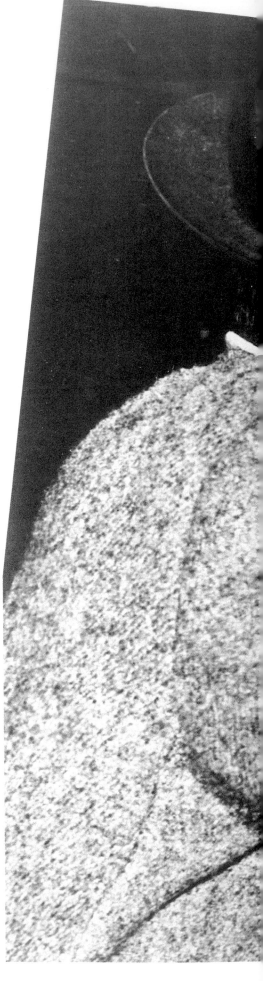

enjoyable, baroque doodle; **Touch of Evil** is a formidable achievement, poetic and flamboyant and beginning with a three-minute shot which tracks and cranes through a decaying, soulless American border town. Welles casts himself as a mountain of twisted law enforcement who clashes with a virtuous Mexican detective (Charlton Heston) until, like a rogue elephant, Welles is shot by his appalled partner, dying on the banks of a filthy river and leaving Marlene Dietrich to improvise a corny yet exact epitaph, "He was some kind of a man." The studio, Universal, wanting a conventional thriller, cut this grandiose meditation on fate by some ten minutes — restored in later years — and Welles never completed another film in America.

Fritz Lang had been one of the key directors of the German cinema in the age of Expressionism. After leaving Hitler's Germany he became a principal exponent of *film noir*. His Hollywood thrillers of the 1950s are deeply pessimistic, rarely relieved by the humor of a Wilder or a Hitchcock, nor as technically adventurous. Yet Lang's work is that of a classicist, portraying America as a nightmare founded on power, not unlike the repressive world shown in his futuristic **Metropolis** (1927).

The Big Heat is Lang's greatest film of the 1950s, a story of jealousy and betrayal in which a good-natured detective (Glenn Ford)

Far left: *Marilyn Monroe draped across the Niagara Falls was one of the decade's most imaginative artworks and contributed significantly to her rising fame. In* **Niagara** *(1953), a Hitchcock-style thriller, she plots the murder of her weakling husband (Joseph Cotten).*

Above: *Joseph Cotten gets to grips with faithless wife Marilyn Monroe in* **Niagara**. *Cotten, who made his name in* **Citizen Kane** *(1941), specialized in weak or flawed characters, which is possibly why he never became a major star.*

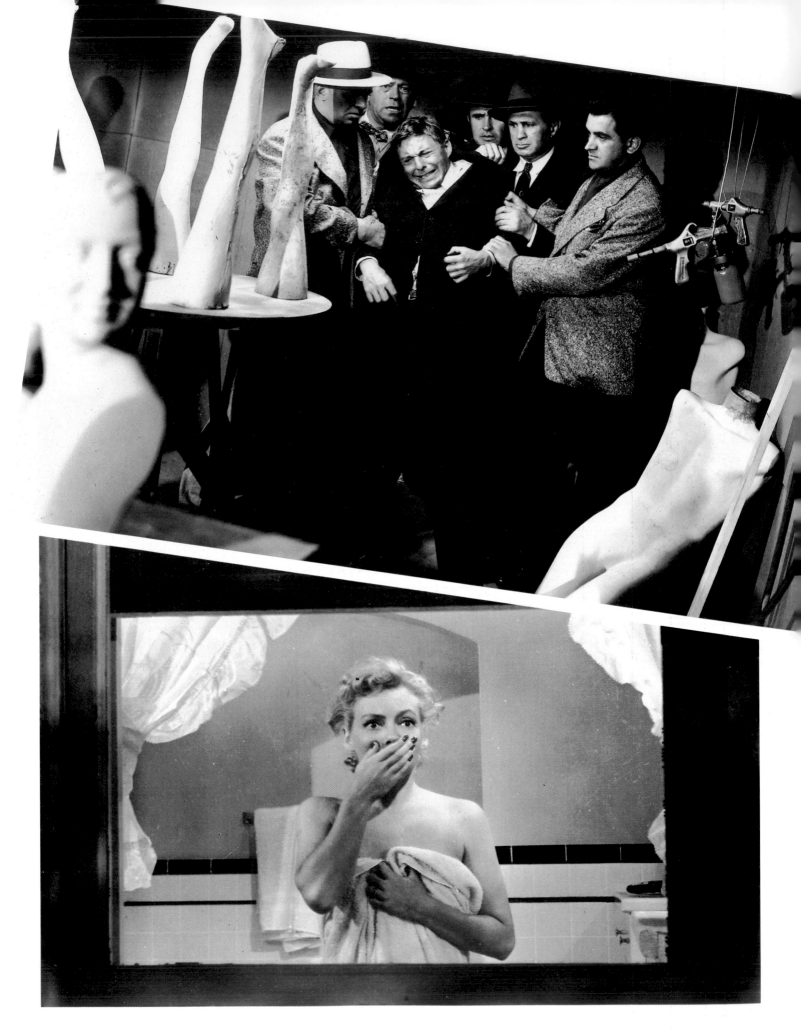

Above: *A boy sees his father being murdered in an alley and grows up with a mission of revenge. An archetypal film noir image, evoking a world of shadowy violence, from Samuel Fuller's most ambitious crime film* **Underworld USA** *(1961).*

Top left: *Joseph Losey's 1951 remake of Fritz Lang's* **M** *had a surreal atmosphere, notably this scene in which David Wayne as the child murderer is captured by the mob and taken to a contemporary chamber of horrors.*

Left: *Evelyn Keyes spots a Peeping Tom outside her bathroom window in Joseph Losey's disturbing crime drama* **The Prowler** *(1951).*

is slowly and unwittingly transformed into a vengeful killer as he comes up against the all-powerful syndicate. The film glitters like steel, cold yet alluring, and is charged with violence, totally uncompromised in its view of a society beyond redemption. **Clash by Night** (1952), from a play by Clifford Odets, **The Blue Gardenia** (1953), **Human Desire** (1954), a remake of Jean Renoir's **La Bête Humaine** (1938) from Zola's novel, **While the City Sleeps** (1956) and **Beyond a Reasonable Doubt** (1956) are lesser films, perhaps, but correspond in their shadowy dramas to a quotation from Democrates that Lang admired, "Everywhere man blames nature and fate, yet his fate is mostly but the echo of his character and passions, his mistakes and weaknesses."

After completing **Beyond a Reasonable Doubt** Lang left America and he made his last film in Germany, a return to the satanic world of Dr Mabuse, the hero of Lang's 1922 classic whose evil, it seems, permeates every film Lang made in Hollywood.

Perhaps the most bizarre and unexpected thriller of the 1950s is the only film directed by Charles Laughton, **The Night of the Hunter** (1955), financed by the most enterprising of the studios, United Artists, which was responsible for many of the radical dramas of the decade as well. Perhaps Laughton's film is not a thriller at all since it occupies a dreamlike realm of its own. Laughton does not appear in the film; instead there is Robert Mitchum in his most challenging and greatest role as a psychopathic preacher who specializes in murdering widows and donating their fortunes to the Lord. On his fingers are tattoos proclaiming "love" and "hate" and in his face is a deranged serenity. He murders his new wife (Shelley Winters) because he believes she has a hoard of stolen money, and is prepared to murder his two stepchildren but, after a long chase through the swamps, a lonely spinster (Lillian Gish) suffers the little children to come unto her and calls the cops. **The Night of the Hunter** is a unique achievement, both nightmare and dream, full of poetic imagery, a study in repression where there may be allegories, and an evocation of childhood like no other.

Master of Suspense

There remains Alfred Hitchcock whose name is synonymous with the thriller. The 1950s were unquestionably his most creative period, beginning with **Strangers on a Train** (1951) and ending with **North by Northwest** (1959), two of his most enduringly popular films. Hitchcock also took a most unexpected and audacious leap into the cinema's archenemy, television, by introducing in those lugubrious tones of his – and occasionally directing – the series **Alfred Hitchcock Presents** (1955-1962) which earned him more fame than ever before and helped to promote his feature films. Hitchcock's familiar profile on scores of paperbacks and mystery magazines, all

Above: *Cary Grant dead? No, Eva Marie Saint used blanks in order to fool masterspy James Mason, henchman Martin Landau and Mount Rushmore's tourists in Alfred Hitchcock's **North by Northwest** (1959).*

Top left: *Charles Laughton's masterpiece **The Night of the Hunter** (1955) owed much to the lighting effects of famed cinematographer Stanley Cortez, creating here a distorted church out of shadows and bare sets, as crazy preacher Harry Powell (Robert Mitchum) prepares to murder his new wife (Shelley Winters), the last of many susceptible widows.*

controlled by him, added to his fame and remains unique in the marketing of a film director, but perhaps this detracted from the serious consideration of his work. After all, Hitchcock never won a Best Director Oscar.

Strangers on a Train is Hitchcock's final full-fledged *film noir*, a remarkable study of sexual psychopathy with a father-hating playboy (Robert Walker) who proposes swapping murders with a politically ambitious tennis player (Farley Granger) who needs to get rid of his sluttish suburban wife. Yet there is an overt schematism to the film that diminishes much of the tension — the famous sequence which intercuts a tennis match with Robert Walker's desperate attempts to retrieve an incriminating cigarette lighter from a drain proclaims its tension without ever achieving it. **I Confess** (1953), with Montgomery Clift as a priest whose faith is tested by a confession of murder, is again overly schematic. **Dial M For Murder** (1954), originally made in 3-D, is rather more than a straight adaptation of a play but still a minor work, as is the French Riviera holiday of **To Catch a Thief** (1955) with Cary Grant and Grace Kelly and a shot, worthy of Spanish surrealist director Luis Buñuel, of a cigarette stubbed out in a fried egg. **The Man Who Knew Too Much** (1956) is now regarded by

Above: *Robert Walker (on top) and Farley Granger in Hitchcock's* **Strangers on a Train** *(1951), which ends with a lethal fight aboard a fairground carousel that runs out of control after the police accidentally kill the operator.*

Right: *A happy marriage? Spoilt rich kid Robert Stack keeps a gun under the pillow – one of the quieter scenes from Douglas Sirk's* **Written on the Wind** *(1956).*

Far right: *Canned again – the weak and possibly infertile son (Robert Stack) of a domineering father (Robert Keith, right) is brought home by his best friend (Rock Hudson), who is secretly in love with his wife (Lauren Bacall) but loyally suppresses his feelings – which are ultimately reciprocated. The misery of the Texas rich is vividly depicted in* **Written on the Wind**, *anticipating and surpassing* Dallas.

many critics as superior to the 1934 version and is a forerunner of **North by Northwest** in its mordant view of international espionage. **The Trouble With Harry** (1955) is perhaps Hitchcock's most bizarre experiment, a jet-black comedy about a body that won't lie down, set in a gloriously photographed Vermont autumn (much of it re-created in a studio) and Hitchcock's only real commercial disaster.

But the creator of **Rear Window** (1954), **The Wrong Man** (1956), **Vertigo** (1958) and **North by Northwest** within six years might well have retired on his laurels, except that **Psycho** (1960), **The Birds** (1963) and **Marnie** (1964) were still to come and the fact that **Rear Window**, **The Wrong Man**, **Vertigo** and **North by Northwest** were regarded as little more than superior entertainments. All four films are masterpieces (even if **Rear Window** is afflicted by the schematism of **Strangers on a Train**) and are mesmerizing commentaries on the nature of watching movies, taking three of Hollywood's most entrenched star personas and undermining them: James Stewart, Henry Fonda and Cary Grant, or The Good, The Better Than Good and the Urbane.

In both **Rear Window** and **Vertigo** Stewart is neurotic and prone to waking nightmares. In **Rear Window** he is imprisoned in his apartment by virtue of a broken leg. He has nothing to do all day except peer through his binoculars and telephoto lens at his neighbors, one of whom he is convinced has murdered his wife. Stewart's impotence, the macabre humor of his visiting nurse (Thelma Ritter) and the sexual taunts of his girlfriend (Grace Kelly) constitute a perfect essay in voyeurism. The tone of **Rear Window** is surprisingly light but **Vertigo** is another matter, an almost Wagnerian (thanks to Bernard Herrmann's music score) account of romantic obsession. The film opens as Stewart fails to prevent a police colleague from falling to his death and thereafter Stewart has a fear of heights, a sickness exploited by a friend planning murder. Stewart is duped into believing in the intended victim's double (Kim Novak) whom he grows to love. The plot is totally implausible, which led to dismissive reviews at the time; but what matters is the inescapable conviction of Stewart's obsession and its visual expression. Perhaps **Vertigo** is no more profound a moral tale than Douglas Sirk's florid melodramas such as **Magnificent Obsession** (1954), **Written on the Wind** (1956) and **Imitation of Life** (1959), but the Hollywood cinema has never produced another film of such disturbing and unbridled passion.

Identity crisis

The Wrong Man was something of an experiment for Hitchcock, based on a true story and shot like a documentary, with Fonda as the staunchly Catholic victim of mistaken identity, whose faith is tested when he is plunged into the Kafkaesque nightmare of a possible life sentence. He is saved by a lucky chance speciously presented as a "miracle", but not before his wife (Vera Miles) has collapsed into madness. If Hitchcock's universe is essentially determined by fear, then **The Wrong Man** is his most austere exploration of it.

North by Northwest is another story of mistaken identity but the tone this time is flippant. Yet beneath the film's dazzling surface texture and wordplay there is a dark and prophetic vision of American ruthlessness and its power in the world. Cary Grant is a facile advertising man whose life is a cocktail party until he is mistaken for a nonexistent CIA agent by foreign spies. The CIA discover the mistake

but callously allow him to be their unwitting decoy, hoping he will stay alive long enough to lead them to the supercool master-spy (James Mason).

The film charts a northwesterly course from New York to Chicago to South Dakota, and as a thriller it works brilliantly, leaving the viewer no time to consider logic in the headlong rush from one Hitchcockian set-piece to another: the drunken car ride intended to kill Grant; the murder at the United Nations; Grant's encounter with a crop-dusting plane and the climactic, cliff-hanging scene at Mount Rushmore. At the very end of the 1950s, as America moved towards the Kennedy era and beyond, there were few more moving sights than Cary Grant's growing humanity as his Madison Avenue shallowness gives way to a deep concern over the fate of Eva Marie Saint's cool undercover agent, nor many sharper political insights than the CIA's dirty work being fought over the "Shrine of Democracy", the stony, impassive faces of Washington, Jefferson, Lincoln and Theodore Roosevelt.

Above: *Actress Lana Turner finds that a tactical affair with an important agent (Robert Alda) helps her career in **Imitation of Life** (1959), Douglas Sirk's last Hollywood film.*

Top right: *Passing-for-white showgirl Susan Kohner (left) in **Imitation of Life** breaks her black mother's heart – and later regrets it at her spectacular funeral.*

Right: *Henry Fonda made comparatively few films in the 1950s but his portrayal of **The Wrong Man** (1956) was one of his very finest performances. Vera Miles was his distraught wife, who loses her sanity.*

290

WESTERNS

Between Fred Zinnemann's **High Noon** in 1952 and Howard Hawks' **Rio Bravo** in 1959 is a collection of the best Westerns ever made; certainly the most complex and contradictory. **High Noon**, produced by Stanley Kramer and written by Carl Foreman, was not the first politicized Western — **Broken Arrow** and **The Gunfighter** (both 1950) had ideas beyond the familiar Indian slaughter and fancy gunplay: the former portrayed Indians as belonging to an intricate culture, the latter was an exercise in pacifism. But **High Noon** was implicitly a condemnation of McCarthyism that might have been usable as evidence in HUAC's case against Foreman.

Gary Cooper, in his most charismatic role, is a proud marshal who fails to win the support of his community when four gunmen with a grudge arrive to kill him. The film resembles a mythical ballad, accompanied by Dimitri Tiomkin's "Do Not Forsake Me, Oh My Darlin'" and running 85 minutes, the amount of time Cooper has before sacrificing himself to prove a moral point. Of course, Cooper succeeds in killing the gunmen, aided by his pacifist Quaker wife (Grace Kelly) who has a last-minute change of heart, but his final gesture of throwing his star into the dust is surely a defeat.

A woman's touch

Grace Kelly saves Cooper's life by shooting through a window and killing one of the gunmen. In **Rio Bravo**, Angie Dickinson helps John Wayne's plan by throwing a flowerpot through a window, creating a

diversion that enables Wayne to reach for his rifle.·It is important that Wayne does the actual killing which, as sheriff, he has been appointed to do. For Hawks made **Rio Bravo** in response to **High Noon**, which he thought was unrealistic and politically dubious. His plot is virtually identical except in one crucial respect: Wayne refuses all amateur offers of help from his community of men and women determined to eradicate lawlessness from their civilization created out of the wilderness.

Instead of Zinnemann's crisp, mechanized 85 minutes, **Rio Bravo** is extraordinarily relaxed, drifting along for 141 minutes and finding time for a few songs in the besieged sheriff's office. Yet **Rio Bravo** is a masterpiece, with a richness of character based on professionalism and interdependence, vividly expressed through Wayne's role as a surrogate father to a drunken deputy (Dean Martin), a crippled

Below left and far left: *One of the most famous shoot-outs ever filmed was in **High Noon** (1952), with Gary Cooper as the isolated marshal helped in the nick of time by his Quaker wife (Grace Kelly) who shoots badman Robert Wilke in the back. Audiences accepted this, but Cooper of course would never stoop so low.*

Below: *Before teaming up with director Budd Boetticher, Randolph Scott made several lesser films, including **Fort Worth** (1951) in which he played a gunfighter turned newspaperman who opposes a landowner.*

Above: ***Broken Arrow*** *(1950), if not a great film, was certainly an influential one in its treatment of the Indians. James Stewart marries an Indian princess (Debra Paget) who is killed by white men. Jeff Chandler played Cochise, who becomes Stewart's blood brother.*

Right: *Gunslinger's moll Janet Leigh and corrupt officer Ralph Meeker in Anthony Mann's* ***The Naked Spur*** *(1953), perhaps the most brutal and unstable of Mann's great series of Westerns.*

jailkeeper (Walter Brennan) and a callow gunslinger (Ricky Nelson) conducting his own vendetta. Only the thrillingly resourceful gambler Feathers (Angie Dickinson) undermines Wayne's indomitability.

Although Cooper and Wayne made other important Westerns in the 1950s, the genre was dominated by two other stars, Randolph Scott and James Stewart. Scott was a star of the B-Western; he became one of the wealthiest men in Hollywood on that modest basis. He was an undistinguished actor but his lined face and slow, deliberate gestures had unshakable integrity. His Westerns of the early 1950s were seldom more than routine but **Seven Men From Now** (1956) teamed him with director Budd Boetticher and writer Burt Kennedy (later a director) and their collaborations are minor classics.

Apart from an acute sense of irony, Boetticher was a living Hemingway hero who, before making films, had done it all. Boetticher's early work was uneven, but with Scott's middle-aged imperturbability he found a star able to embody his unique vision of treachery and heroic vengeance in the scorching desert. In **Seven Men From Now**, **The Tall T** (1957), **Decision at Sundown** (1957), **Buchanan Rides Alone** (1958), **Ride Lonesome** (1959), **Westbound** (1959) and **Comanche Station** (1960) there is a remarkable

continuity in Scott's ambiguous relationship to the community, where he invariably settles a personal score or lends a sympathetic gunhand before riding off alone into the desert only to reappear, with another name, in the next picture.

Of the Hollywood stars established during the 1930s, James Stewart might justifiably claim the 1950s as his decade. Consider Stewart's non-Western roles: as **Harvey** (1950); in **Rear Window**, **The Man Who Knew Too Much** and **Vertigo** for Hitchcock; as American heroes Glenn Miller, and Charles Lindbergh in the underrated **The Spirit of St Louis** (1957); as the lawyer in **Anatomy of a Murder**. Such roles veered between moral righteousness and neurosis. When we add the Westerns such as **Broken Arrow**, in which he marries an Indian princess, and particularly those directed by Anthony Mann, Stewart's achievement is unparalleled in its variety and complexity.

Mann of the West

Unlike the low budgets and arid deserts of Boetticher's work, Anthony Mann's films, mostly made for Universal, were expensive and set in unplowed prairies, forests and, occasionally, snow-covered mountains. The films are visually arresting, pantheistic externalizations of the inner rages that possess his characters. One of Mann's lesser Westerns, **The Furies** (1950), is derived from Greek myth, and all of his stories are parables about man's destiny, patriarchy and the presence or absence of God, a philosophical argument that the director later defined as a "trilemma" in **The Fall of the Roman Empire** (1964). And at the time of his death in 1967, Mann was preparing a Western version of *King Lear*. This may make the films seem solemn and portentous but they are exhilarating pieces of cinema.

In the first of his pictures for Mann, **Winchester 73** (1950), Stewart sets out to kill his brother who has killed their father; in **Bend of the River** (1952) Stewart is an ex-outlaw seeking redemption as a homesteader but becomes a vengeful killer after his partner betrays the farmers and leaves Stewart to die on a mountain top; in **The Naked Spur** (1953), perhaps the greatest of the series, Stewart is a crazed bounty hunter; in **The Far Country** (1955) he delivers a mining community from tyranny, but only as a side-effect of vengeance for his murdered partner Walter Brennan; in **The Man from Laramie** (1955), the last and most extreme of the series, he blunders into a bitterly divided ranching family (based in part, no

Right: *Wyatt Earp (Burt Lancaster) shoots it out with the Clantons in* **Gunfight at the OK Corral** *(1957).*

Below: *Vengeful James Stewart (right) faces killer Arthur Kennedy in* **The Man from Laramie** *(1955), one of Anthony Mann's studies of men under stress, set against the scenic grandeur of the American West.*

From left, Kirk Douglas as
Doc Holliday, Burt Lancaster as
Wyatt Earp, Kenneth Tobey as Bat
Masterson and DeForest Kelley as
Morgan Earp pace the deserted
streets of Tombstone on October
26, 1881, when they routed the
Clanton gang in one of the West's
legendary shoot-outs, the
Gunfight at the OK Corral
(1957).

doubt consciously, on the Gloucester subplot in *King Lear*), in which the rebellious younger generation is gunrunning for the Indians who killed the kid brother of the aptly named Will Lockhart (Stewart). He is brutally shot through the hand by the weakling legitimate son, who is later murdered in a quarrel by his own bastard brother (Arthur Kennedy). This tangled knot is abruptly cut by the Indians, who kill the murderous brother, freeing Lockhart from the burden of revenge.

Mann's next Western, **The Tin Star** (1957), with Henry Fonda as a bounty hunter and former lawman who instructs an inexperienced sheriff (Anthony Perkins) in controlled violence, lacked the allegorical intensity of the Stewart films, but **Man of the West** (1958) might be Mann's greatest and gravest film, a synthesis of his work to date. It opens with Gary Cooper leaving his peaceful community to hire a schoolteacher, but his train is ambushed. He traces the outlaws to their hideout and discovers his old gang of surrogate father (Lee J. Cobb) and his vicious "sons". Cobb exerts a considerable influence over Cooper whose inner struggle assumes biblical proportions, finally resolved when one by one he kills his "family" and returns home with a reformed saloon singer who will become the schoolmarm. What makes the film so disturbing is the price Cooper pays: his reaffirmation of moral values and his commitment to the community has devitalized him.

Bottom: *A classic Western image from Samuel Fuller's **Run of the Arrow** (1957) which was otherwise extremely unconventional, with Irishman Rod Steiger preferring to become a Sioux Indian after the Confederates lose the Civil War. Steiger's delusion that he could do an Irish accent persisted through several films.*

Below: *In William Wyler's epic **The Big Country** (1958) Gregory Peck preferred to keep his riding, fighting and dueling abilities private until the end when Chuck Connors pushes him too far.*

BC(191-6)B

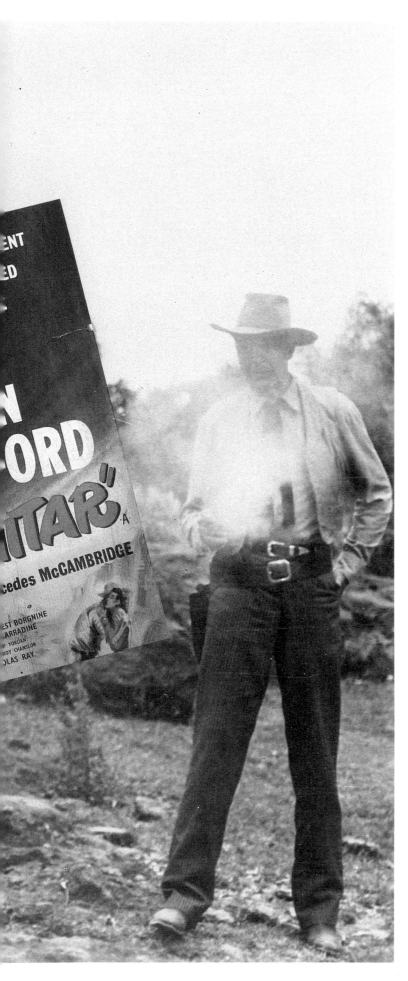

Heroes and hero-worship

It took some years before Mann's films were accorded the status they deserve. George Stevens' **Shane** (1953) was instantly hailed as a classic of the genre, and its images of the buckskinned Alan Ladd against a blue sky, idolized by a young farmer's boy, have a genuine mythic power. Every gesture and every frame is but preparation for the moment when Shane, having killed Jack Palance's maniacal hired gunman, rides off into the boy's memory. It is an unforgettable moment, but the film is a stacked deck devoid of the jittery intensity of the Mann films or the spontaneity of a Hawks.

In the same category of solid craftsmanship are John Sturges' **Gunfight at the OK Corral** (1957), with Burt Lancaster as Wyatt Earp and Kirk Douglas as a consumptive Doc Holliday upstaging each other before the splendidly realized shoot-out with the Clanton gang; William Wyler's **The Big Country** (1958) with Gregory Peck as a greenhorn rancher who clashes with Charlton Heston's ramrod in perhaps the most protracted fistfight ever filmed; and Delmer Daves' **3.10 to Yuma** (1957) with Glenn Ford as an outlaw escorted to jail by Van Heflin's farmer in a psychodrama that seemed ashamed of its generic roots. **The Big Country** has a grandeur lacking in the others — and an evocative, stirring score by Jerome Moross — but their influence was more commercial than creative.

More striking, though variously flawed, are Samuel Fuller's characteristically vigorous **Run of the Arrow** (1957), with Irish-accented Method-acting Rod Steiger becoming an adoptive Sioux Indian rather than a Confederate prisoner of the Union Army, and **Forty Guns** (1957) with Barbara Stanwyck as a rancher involved in a family feud. Robert Aldrich's **Vera Cruz** (1954) looks like a premature spaghetti Western, with Burt Lancaster only one step removed from his swashbuckling **Crimson Pirate** (1952), double- and triple-crossing Gary Cooper over Mexican gold. Fritz Lang's **Rancho Notorious** (1952) was a slice of Expressionism in an outlaws' hideout called Chuckaluck where, ageless at fifty, Marlene Dietrich sings mournful ballads to revenge-crazed men. But even Lang's melodrama seems conventional when placed beside Nicholas Ray's **Johnny Guitar** (1954), the most eccentric and baroque Western of the 1950s. This incredible Freudian drama was financed by Republic Pictures, home of worn-out costumes and ideas, and photographed in lurid Trucolor with Joan Crawford and Mercedes McCambridge as murderously bitter rivals and Sterling Hayden, Scott Brady, Ward Bond and Ernest Borgnine as screen tough-guys reduced here to passive spectators. **Johnny Guitar** is an acquired taste which the French, notably François Truffaut — who paid it due tribute in **Mississippi Mermaid** (1968) — pronounced a delicacy; but British and American critics, dismayed and embarrassed by its blatant sexuality, had no difficulty in spitting it out.

Main picture: *Burt Lancaster is beaten to the draw by his treacherous buddy Gary Cooper in Robert Aldrich's flamboyant **Vera Cruz** (1954).*

Inset: *Nicholas Ray's **Johnny Guitar** (1954) is certainly the weirdest film ever made at Republic Studios, founded in 1935 by Herbert J. Yates as a factory for B-Westerns with John Wayne, Gene Autry and Roy Rogers. Sterling Hayden played the title role and uttered the line, 'I'm a stranger here myself,' which became Ray's motto. But Joan Crawford and Mercedes McCambridge scarcely gave him a look-in otherwise.*

920.179

In search of H-O-M-E

But if only one Western of the 1950s could be preserved, it should be John Ford's **The Searchers** (1956). Largely dismissed at the time of its release as an aberration on Ford's part, **The Searchers** contains in John Wayne's character, Ethan Edwards, the quintessential American hero, torn between independence and society, the pioneer and the settler. It is, unequivocally, a study in racism as Wayne sets out on an obsessive, five-year quest for a niece who has been kidnapped by Indians. Once he discovers her he kills her Indian captor, Scar, who has become his alter ego but he cannot kill the girl (Natalie Wood) or the Indian within her. Instead, he abruptly lifts her into his arms and takes her home. Yet Ethan is unable to enter the house that burned so many years ago in the Indian attack and the door closes, excluding him from the community which must forever remain an ideal. He walks off into the desert, condemned to the life of a nomad. He prefers it that way. (In a later film **Cheyenne Autumn**, 1964, Ford depicts the Indians as excluded from the H-O-M-E that their children know only as a spelled-out word.)

Set against the majestic, cathedral spires of Monument Valley, yet having the intimate quality of a ballad, **The Searchers** is perhaps the most influential American film since Orson Welles' **Citizen Kane** (1941), inspiring an entire generation of American directors and finding echoes in such diverse films as Francis Coppola's **The Godfather** (1972), George Lucas's **Star Wars** (1977) and Paul Schrader's **Hardcore** (1979).

Top: *Mercedes McCambridge as the cattle owner and Joan Crawford (center) as the saloon owner in Nicholas Ray's bizarre* **Johnny Guitar** *(1954). Crawford survives the necktie party to fight a final duel.*

Left: *Clark Gable ran into a furious Jane Russell in* **The Tall Men** *(1955), a typically gritty Raoul Walsh film.*

COMEDIES

The 1950s were no laughing matter. If anything superseded the slapstick of the 1920s, the innuendo of the 1930s and the sarcasm of the 1940s, it was prurience. Marilyn Monroe's skirts were sent billowing by a subway train, she kept her undies in the icebox, and a lasciviously prompt plumber found her with a toe stuck in the overflow of her bath. These famous moments from **The Seven Year Itch** (1955) perhaps summarize the prevalent mood in which everyone itched but few scratched.

The hapless hero of George Axelrod's screenplay, Monroe's downstairs neighbor (Tom Ewell), is so intimidated by her unaffected sexuality — her body straining to break free of her clothes, her mouth an open invitation to infidelity — that he ceases to function rationally, drawing on movie imagery such as the beach scene in **From Here to Eternity** to harden his resolve but returning to his office where he censors the lurid dustjackets of the paperbacks he sells. Because of this inconsequence, the movie — unquestionably Billy Wilder's worst — has no comic resonance. There is only Monroe and an attendant, post-Kinsey sociological interest. It was the era of dumb blondes and even dumber men.

Top far left: *Judy Holliday as the pin-headed mistress of Broderick Crawford in George Cukor's sparkling comedy* **Born Yesterday** *(1950).*

Left: *In Billy Wilder's romantic comedy* **Love in the Afternoon** *(1957), Gary Cooper played an aging playboy with a suite at the Ritz Hotel in Paris, where he understandably succumbs to the charms of Audrey Hepburn.*

MARILYN MONROE *and her bosom companions* TONY CURTIS JACK LEMMON

in a BILLY WILDER *Production* "SOME LIKE IT HOT"

CO-STARRING GEORGE RAFT · PAT O'BRIEN · JOE E. BROWN · SCREEN PLAY BY BILLY WILDER and I. A. L. DIAMOND · DIRECTED BY BILLY WILDER

Above: *In* **Some Like It Hot** *(1959), Marilyn Monroe is the singer with an all-girl band; Tony Curtis and Jack Lemmon, jazz musicians on the run after accidentally witnessing the St Valentine's Day massacre, become 'girls' to join the band for a Florida booking. But the gangsters are holding a convention in the same hotel . . . and love adds a further complication.*

Left: *Marilyn Monroe's hapless costar in* **The Seven Year Itch** *(1955) was Tom Ewell, who had played the role of the errant husband on Broadway in 1952 and made his screen debut in* **Adam's Rib** *(1949), opposite Judy Holliday, Katharine Hepburn and Spencer Tracy. He became famous for his TV show but was never a major film actor.*

Wilder shores of love

McCarthyism, Korea (where Monroe entertained the troops), the Bomb, the Cold War and the dull, paternalistic years (1953-60) of the Eisenhower presidency (an aging war hero in an era of burgeoning youth) seemed to cast a spell over Hollywood's best humorists which they have never fully exorcised. In 1961, Wilder made **One, Two, Three**, a devastating Cold War satire; John Frankenheimer's **The Manchurian Candidate** (1962), written by Axelrod as a comedy, turned Korean veterans into brainwashed assassins; Stanley Kubrick's **Dr Strangelove, or How I Learned to Stop Worrying and Love the Bomb** (1963) turned the nuclear age into a huge joke and made it twice as frightening. Perhaps the freer and insistently youthful Kennedy presidency created a climate for these films but his death in 1963 certainly ended it and gave these films an appalling dimension of irony.

There are other elements in the equation. The death of producer-director Ernst Lubitsch in 1947 brought an entire comic universe to a close. So, too, did the retirement of Preston Sturges in 1949 and the hibernation of Frank Capra throughout two-thirds of the decade. There was no American equivalent of the Ealing comedies being made in Britain, which celebrated quirkiness, upheld the virtues of postwar austerity and championed the corner shopkeeper in his fight against the supermarket chain. This had no place in America: consumerism was too important to laugh about. In **The Seven Year Itch** Monroe was the perfect embodiment of the Eisenhower ideology, playing a TV model who believes totally in the soapy products she sells.

After Lubitsch, there were Wilder and George Cukor to keep the comic flag flying above half-mast. If **The Seven Year Itch** was a failure (or now reveals itself to be one), Wilder's dramas like **Sunset Boulevard** and **Ace in the Hole** were rich in humor, as were **Sweet Smell of Success** and **Baby Doll**, all difficult to classify as comedies. But Wilder's **Sabrina** (1954) and **Love in the Afternoon**

309

GLADYS GLOVER

WENDY BARRIE

©D-1285

(1957) are near-masterpieces, both bitter-sweet romances which significantly find humane and life-affirming qualities in Europe as against the impersonal and acquisitive mood of America. Humphrey Bogart in **Sabrina** and Gary Cooper in **Love in the Afternoon**, both criticized for being too old for their parts when that is precisely the point (both men having outgrown the childish pursuits of money and mercenary sex), are educated in the wiser ways of the world by Audrey Hepburn. The tone is unmistakably Lubitschean, with champagne seductions and gypsy bands, but Wilder adopts a more expressive and politicized context.

Wilder ended the decade with **Some Like it Hot** (1959), which many regard as the greatest comedy since the 1930s. Reunited with Monroe, he casts her as a buxom blond vocalist with a hip-flask in an all-girl band, given heart-breaking ballads like "I'm Thru With Love" which she sang as if she meant it. The comedy derived from Tony Curtis and Jack Lemmon as two jazz musicians who inadvertently witness the St Valentine's Day Massacre, disguise themselves as women and join Monroe's band for the season at a Florida hotel. The 1929 setting, aflame with gangsters and speakeasies, has a vitality that Wilder found lacking in the late 1950s, conjuring up a bygone age of both innocence and sexual challenge: unlike the hero of **The Seven Year Itch**, Tony Curtis only feigns impotence, while disguised as a Cary Grant playboy ("Nobody talks like that!" says Lemmon), to

earn Monroe's sympathy and miracle cure. **Some Like it Hot** was an exercise in brinkmanship and also a nightmare to make, since Monroe was at her most vulnerable, primed by coach Paula Strasberg and The Method but unable to exploit its disciplines, and turning Wilder's customarily buoyant set into a crucible of frustration.

George Cukor was less fortunate than Wilder with Monroe. Cukor's dismal **Let's Make Love** (1960) trapped her again as a singer who falls prey to a millionaire. After John Huston's drama **The Misfits** (1961), which was written by Monroe's third husband Arthur Miller and became a bizarre requiem to her as well as Clark Gable and Montgomery Clift, she was fired from Cukor's unfinished **Something's Got to Give** in 1962 and died a month after.

The not-so-dumb blonde

In the 1940s Cukor had directed a wonderful series of comedies starring Spencer Tracy and Katharine Hepburn. **Pat and Mike** (1952) was the last of them, and used a prolonged round of golf for a round of sexual politics. In the earlier and much better **Adam's Rib** (1949), Tracy and Hepburn were supported by the Broadway actress Judy Holliday who played a dumb-blonde wife accused of (ineffectively) shooting her two-timing husband. It is thought that the close-knit team of Cukor, Tracy and Hepburn highlighted Holliday's role in order to persuade Columbia's president, Harry Cohn, to agree to Cukor's

Left: In **Limelight** (1952), Charles Chaplin played the failed music-hall comic Calvero, who makes one final comeback – and dies at the moment of his last triumph.

Top far left: In **It Should Happen To You** (1954) Gladys Glover (Judy Holliday) becomes an overnight celebrity just by having her name in lights. Here, at the height of her fame, she steamrollers Wendy Barrie (playing herself) during a TV game show.

Far left: Gregory Peck as an American journalist taking a **Roman Holiday** (1953), during which he suddenly finds himself sharing his apartment with a runaway princess (Audrey Hepburn).

casting her in **Born Yesterday** (1950), which she had played on Broadway. There is no other reason why Hepburn allows herself to be upstaged so blatantly by Holliday in **Adam's Rib**.

Judy Holliday was an offer Harry Cohn could not refuse and she won an Oscar for **Born Yesterday** as junk dealer Broderick Crawford's dim-witted mistress who is educated, in the manner of Pygmalion, by William Holden. Cukor directed her again in **The Marrying Kind** (1952), almost a comedy of divorce with Aldo Ray, and in **It Should Happen to You** (1954), the best of the three films, about a dumb blonde who wants her name in lights and has to choose between a clever documentary film-maker (Jack Lemmon in his screen debut) and a detergent manufacturer (Peter Lawford). The film has much of the satirical bite that **The Seven Year Itch** lacked and contains Holliday's most wholly satisfying performance. In the unpronounceable **Phffft!** (1954) she starred opposite Lemmon in a strained George Axelrod farce about divorce and remarriage and, in Richard Quine's **The Solid Gold Cadillac** (1956), she was amusing as a boardroom executive.

Holliday was a real discovery, but her retirement in 1960 and her untimely death at 43 from cancer in 1965 did not rob the cinema of a major, developing talent. In private life a classic New York-Jewish intellectual, highly intelligent and almost intimidatingly well-read, she was brilliant as a stereotype but lacked Monroe's emotional complexity and appeal. A Holliday performance was a mechanism and she made one aware of each cog, gear and wheel. She acted with her brain, with a hint of condescension, whereas Monroe acted with her heart.

Laughter in the dark

Affectionately remembered also are William Wyler's **Roman Holiday** (1952) and Howard Hawks' **Monkey Business** (1952). As a director, Wyler was hardly noted for his sense of humor (in fact, he was an extremely witty man) and **Roman Holiday** is more like a Wilder film than anything else, dealing with an ambitious American newspaperman in Rome (Gregory Peck) who suddenly stumbles upon a runaway princess (Audrey Hepburn in her first starring role) and a

Far left: Danny Kaye starred opposite Pier Angeli and child star Clive Hodgson in **Merry Andrew** (1958), a musical comedy with a circus setting.

Top left: In Frank Tashlin's **The Girl Can't Help It** (1955) Tom Ewell (left) is a drunken Broadway agent assigned the task of turning gangster's moll Jayne Mansfield into a star.

Below: Tom Ewell is clearly intimidated by Jayne Mansfield's hilarious and blatantly symbolic milk bottles in **The Girl Can't Help It**. She complains, 'Nobody thinks I'm equipped for motherhood.'

front page story. The film is tender and funny, projecting the gorgeous, elfin Hepburn as an actress capable of transforming all of Hollywood's most established stars – Peck, Bogart, Cooper, Astaire and Cary Grant all succumbed on-screen to her European charms.

Hawks' **Monkey Business** was noted at the time only for the brief appearance of Monroe as Charles Coburn's dim secretary who momentarily catches Cary Grant's eye. It is now widely regarded as one of Hawks' most characteristic films, as screwball as his 1938 classic **Bringing Up Baby** of which it is almost a sequel, cowritten by I. A. L. Diamond, who later became Billy Wilder's collaborator. Grant plays an absentminded professor who takes a rejuvenating drug which undermines his stable marriage to Ginger Rogers. The film is often hilarious, but its wholehearted celebration of regression and irresponsibility strikes a remarkably subversive note in heralding the bland Eisenhower era.

Without the grace and sophistication of Wilder and Cukor, the talents of Monroe, Holliday and Lemmon, as well as Wyler's and Hawks' only comedies of the decade, the 1950s would have been grim indeed. Charles Chaplin fashioned his last masterpiece in **Limelight** (1952) but it was a deeply elegiac tragicomedy about his roots in the British music halls, intensely moving and with the added bonuses of Claire Bloom's Hollywood debut and a stage routine teaming Chaplin with Buster Keaton. **A King in New York** (1957) was Chaplin's final starring role and intended as a satire on American customs and manners, but it was seriously flawed by Chaplin's own bitterness as a political exile.

Bob and Jerry

Bob Hope's most influential films were **Road to Bali** (1952) and **Son of Paleface** (1952). Hope's brand of humor found its way on to American TV and it was here, rather than in the cinema, that the new generation of writers and comedians were serving their appren-

ticeships. Television series such as Sid Caesar's *Your Show of Shows* and Phil Silvers' *Sergeant Bilko* were voracious consumers of good scripts, and writers like Neil Simon, Mel Brooks and Woody Allen provided some of them. They were to be the pre-eminent American humorists of the 1960s and beyond.

Having noted the name of Danny Kaye, we shall pass over his eight titles of the decade in silence. But Jerry Lewis is another matter, a comedian of the grotesque and perhaps an American equivalent of the British Norman Wisdom, a clown too prone to sentimentality and self-pity. Lewis's pictures, especially those directed by Frank Tashlin – **Artists and Models** (1955) and **Hollywood or Bust** (1956) which costarred Dean Martin – have a tawdry glamor and invention that appealed to the French critics who were on the threshold of careers as directors. François Truffaut found Lewis "more and more delightful with every picture," while Jean-Luc Godard, reviewing **Hollywood or Bust**, declared that comedies should henceforth be described as "Tashlinesque" and not "Chaplinesque" and that Jerry Lewis's face is where "the height of artifice blends at times with the nobility of true documentary". In America and Britain the French critics eventually won more or less unanimous verdicts in their cases for Hitchcock, Hawks, Nicholas Ray, Samuel Fuller and Robert Aldrich. In the case for Jerry Lewis, the jury is still out.

Left: *In **Limelight** (1952), the music-hall career of Calvero (Charles Chaplin) has been ruined by alcoholism (like that of Chaplin's own father). He befriends a young ballet dancer (Claire Bloom), whom he helps to walk again after being crippled by a psychosomatic illness. She in turn helps him to make a comeback.*

Above: *Bob Hope in the arms of a none-too-convincing gorilla in the penultimate ''Road'' film, **Road to Bali** (1952).*

MUSICALS

When, in 1949, Gene Kelly, Frank Sinatra and Jules Munshin ran excitedly from their battleship to enjoy a day's shore leave in New York, it is difficult to say whether they were initiating a whole new era for the musical or merely completing a cycle. **On the Town** is a milestone if not quite a masterpiece, for it was the first truly integrated musical, in which plot was driven by song and dance rather than temporarily suspended by it. **On the Town** certainly gave star Gene Kelly and his codirector Stanley Donen considerably more power and independence and led, in the 1950s, to even better work.

Whilst the musicals of the 1950s lay claim to being the best ever made, the decade also saw the decline of the genre, the increasing and deadening reliance on transposing Broadway hits and, in the nature of things, the aging of many of the genre's finest stars who were not being replaced by comparable younger talent schooled in the studio machine.

Freed-om at MGM

One man in particular created the modern musical, Arthur Freed. Born in 1894, Freed began as a lyricist and first went to Hollywood to compose the score for **The Broadway Melody** (1929). Freed stayed at MGM until he retired in 1962, never abandoning his old art of songwriting, but becoming the musical's greatest and most prolific producer. He turned down the honor of running MGM in order to run his own virtually autonomous Freed Unit within it. Freed surrounded himself with an array of ambitious artists — Kelly and Donen, scriptwriters Betty Comden and Adolph Green, choreographer Michael Kidd and composer/arranger-plus-associate producer Roger Edens. More than any other type of film, the musical is the result of teamwork and Arthur Freed's team was unbeatable.

After starring opposite Judy Garland in **Summer Stock** (1950), which proved to be her last film at MGM, Kelly plunged into **An American in Paris** (1951), not the tour de force it was thought to be at the time, but perhaps the most arrogant work of the Freed Unit intellectual wing. As with certain sections of **On the Town**, **Singin' in the Rain** (1952), **The Band Wagon** (1953) and **Silk Stockings** (1957), **An American in Paris** draws insistent comparisons between popular Hollywood culture and the fine arts and literature. Directed by Vincente Minnelli, **An American in Paris** takes George Gershwin's quintessentially American music and sets it in a Paris as imagined by Van Gogh, Rousseau, Dufy and Lautrec. The touching love affair between Kelly's painter and Leslie Caron's shop assistant escalates into an 18-minute ballet that cost $450,000 to make and is undeniably thrilling, but belongs in another movie.

An American in Paris won six Academy Awards, including Best Picture, but Kelly's next major work, codirected by Donen, is the greatest musical ever made, **Singin' in the Rain**. What makes the film so remarkable and cherishable is its funny and vivid depiction of Hollywood as it entered the sound era. If **Sunset Boulevard**, **In a Lonely Place** and **The Bad and the Beautiful** presented Hollywood as a nightmare, **Singin' in the Rain** let the light in but still found room to expose philistine executives and maniacal stars.

Top left: *Three sailors and their girls go **On the Town** in MGM's 1949 production, directed by Stanley Donen and Gene Kelly. From left: Frank Sinatra, Betty Garrett, Jules Munshin, Ann Miller, Gene Kelly, Vera-Ellen.*

Main picture: *Against a Toulouse-Lautrec background, Gene Kelly (left) and Leslie Caron perform the spectacular, climactic ballet in the Oscar-winning **An American in Paris** (1951).*

Singin' in the Rain is nothing less than a history of the genre, charting the Kelly character's typical rise from vaudevillian to Hollywood stuntman to silent matinee idol. When production of a costume drama, "The Duelling Cavalier", is halted by the arrival of sound, the decision to turn it into a talkie and then a musical is hampered by the squeaky voice of the leading lady, unforgettably played by Jean Hagen. A small-time chorine (Debbie Reynolds) enters Kelly's life and a solution emerges when Reynolds' voice is dubbed on to Hagen's lip-movements. At the premiere of "The Dancing Cavalier", in a scene of exquisite maliciousness, the curtain is raised on the deception, turning Hagen into a silent-movie has-been and Reynolds into an overnight sensation.

Certain sequences, notably Kelly's rendition of the title number on a deluged street lined with boutiques, pharmacies and antiquarian bookstores, Kelly's courting of Reynolds in an empty studio, the climactic "Broadway Melody" ballet (itself a compendium of the genre), and Donald O'Connor's breathtaking solo number, "Make 'em Laugh", have an inspirational brilliance that subsequent Kelly projects never equaled. **Brigadoon** (1954) was an awkward exercise in Scottish whimsy; **It's Always Fair Weather** (1955) was a half-hearted, unofficial sequel to **On the Town**; and **Invitation to the Dance** (1956), Kelly's virtuoso tribute to the world of dance, was a

pretentious failure, shortened by the studio. After the indigestible whipped cream of George Cukor's **Les Girls** (1957), Kelly virtually retired from musicals, turning to dramas and comedies but directing Barbra Streisand in the gargantuan **Hello, Dolly!** (1969), 20th Century-Fox's musical equivalent of **Cleopatra**.

That's entertainment

Only Vincente Minnelli's **The Band Wagon** (1953) comes close to matching **Singln' in the Rain**. Here the cultural parallels are dominant but uninsistent; pretension is the theme rather than the

Above: In **Singin' in the Rain** (1952), movie star Don Lockwood (Gene Kelly) gives reporters a prudently edited account of how he rose from humble vaudevillian to featuring in the Follies (seen here) and then to Hollywood, emphasizing that his motto was "Dignity, always dignity".

Far left: Gene Kelly sings and dances the classic title number in **Singin' in the Rain.**

Above: *The lavish dance sequences in **Silk Stockings** include this send-up of Napoleon's wife Josephine by Janis Paige, a minor musical star whose greatest success was on Broadway.*

Top left: *Janis Paige as a swimming star of movie musicals, and Fred Astaire as a film director dazzle the press with the wonders of the wide screen and 'Stereophonic Sound' in **Silk Stockings** (1957), the only CinemaScope film of Russian-Armenian/American director Rouben Mamoulian.*

Left: *Fred Astaire (left), Nanette Fabray and Jack Buchanan perform the hilarious 'Triplets' number in **The Band Wagon** (1953). As precocious brats in frocks, they were aided in the routine by short false legs that made them look like prematurely aged infants.*

tone. Fred Astaire, in an autobiographical role of great depth and sensitivity, is a faded Hollywood star who arrives in New York to revive his career in a Broadway show, a musical version of *Faust* directed by Jack Buchanan. The show is jeered on opening night as a pretentious bore and Buchanan (whose role was a comic send-up of José Ferrer and Orson Welles) loses his artistic resolve, leaving Astaire, with Nanette Fabray and Oscar Levant (self-portraits by Betty Comden and Adolph Green), to transform the show into a musical comedy which becomes a smash-hit. The theme song, "That's Entertainment", is Arthur Freed's policy statement, and Astaire's dance with the scintillating Cyd Charisse in Central Park, "Dancing in the Dark", is regarded by Gene Kelly as the greatest dance sequence ever placed on film.

Running alongside the Freed Unit's intellectual wing was the populist wing, producing more conventional hymns to Americana, remakes of earlier successes and musical fantasies. **Annie Get Your Gun** (1950) is a smashing film, bursting with Betty Hutton and great numbers; **Showboat** (1951), with Kathryn Grayson and, as an octoroon singer, Ava Gardner, was a richly nostalgic trip down the Mississippi; Stanley Donen's **Seven Brides for Seven Brothers** (1955) was exuberance personified; **High Society** (1956), a musical remake of **The Philadelphia Story** (1940), contained performances

by Bing Crosby and Frank Sinatra of such luxuriant indolence that they transcended professionalism and mutual respect; **Silk Stockings**, the musical version of Lubitsch's **Ninotchka** (1939), with Astaire and Charisse, was Rouben Mamoulian's final film and a stylistic tour de force. Esther Williams swam through **Million Dollar Mermaid** (1952), **Dangerous When Wet** (1953) and **Jupiter's Darling** (1955), the last an apotheosis of kitsch resembling an underwater **Quo Vadis** that has to be seen to be believed.

Best of the rest

Outside the heady creative environment of the Freed Unit at MGM, the musical was much less certain of itself, though Paramount's **Funny Face** (1957), directed by Donen and produced by Roger Edens, can be regarded as an MGM film in all but corporate logo. A satire on the world of high fashion, it is set mainly in Paris, where photographer Astaire is commissioned to promote the "new look" as represented by Audrey Hepburn's rebellious Greenwich Village bookstore assistant, and explores the dichotomy between popular culture and fine arts, even at one point rhyming "Montmartre" with "Jean-Paul Sartre". Donen's use of color filters and split-screen effects is audacious and Astaire's number, "Bonjour, Paris", takes the opening sequence of **On the Town** many stages further.

Funny Face was exceptional. More conventional were Paramount's **White Christmas** (1954), with Bing Crosby and Danny Kaye, and the series of musical comedies with Dean Martin and Jerry Lewis which delighted downmarket American audiences and the French intellectuals. Columbia produced **Pal Joey** (1957) with Sinatra, Rita Hayworth and Kim Novak, which resembled a Method-style drama set to music — and the same might be said of Joseph L. Mankiewicz's Goldwyn/MGM production, **Guys and Dolls**, with Sinatra, Marlon Brando and Jean Simmons. Columbia also discovered rock 'n' roll in the person of Bill Haley and the Comets. More cogently, Elvis Presley's early films, **Love Me Tender** (Fox, 1956), **Loving You** (Paramount, 1957) and **Jailhouse Rock** (MGM, 1957), heralded a new form of teenage musical — which Presley's own 1960s movies failed to deliver. Warner Bros.' most significant musical was **A Star is Born**, which functioned equally powerfully as a drama. Warner Bros. also felt that a remake of their epoch-making **The Jazz Singer** (1953) was in order and updated the story to include post-Korean disenchantment, but audiences rejected its heavy sentimentality. Perhaps the sprightliest Warner musicals were **Calamity Jane** (1953) and **The Pajama Game** (1957), both starring Doris Day, the former full of great songs such as "Secret Love" and "The Deadwood Stage" and the latter a Broadway hit musical treatment of industrial relations. Universal contributed most spectacularly with **The Glenn Miller Story** (1954), a moving biography of the bandleader with James Stewart and June Allyson going dewy-eyed over each other.

Marilyn

But only 20th Century-Fox could be considered in any way a rival to MGM although, compared to the Freed unit's work, Fox's musicals are tinny, brash and much less innovative. Fox pressed on, as they had in the 1940s, with recycled vehicles for Betty Grable and June Haver, and scored a raucous success with **Call Me Madam** (1953) with Ethel Merman. But the same year Fox struck lucky: they suddenly realized the potential of a contract player called Marilyn Monroe and might have invented CinemaScope expressly to accommodate her.

Monroe was the major female star of the decade, combining the glamor of the 1940s pin-up and the postwar angst of a New York radical. Monroe's tragic odyssey from an impoverished orphan, through a marriage at sixteen to an aircraft worker who joined the marines, a second marriage to a baseball star and a third to playwright and guru Arthur Miller, to alleged affairs with John and Robert Kennedy, to immortalization as an Andy Warhol silkscreen, was perhaps not without precedent, but no less enthralling and symbolic of the pain that attaches to stardom. She was a brilliant comedienne, impossible to work with and irresistible to watch; her

Far left: *Replete with gyrating pelvis, Elvis Presley was perhaps the musical equivalent of James Dean, embodying teenage rebellion in his early films, such as* **Jailhouse Rock** *(1957).*

Above: *Blonde Marilyn Monroe and brunette Jane Russell were two little, gold-digging girls from Little Rock, Arkansas, in* **Gentlemen Prefer Blondes** *(1953), Howard Hawks' musical version of Anita Loos' 1925 novel.*

Below: *Doris Day as the trade unionist fighting for a raise of 7.5 cents an hour in* **The Pajama Game** *(1957), choreographed by Bob Fosse, the future director of* **Sweet Charity** *(1969) and* **Cabaret** *(1972).*

body was voluptuous and ridiculous, her face a blank negative on which male fantasies of rape and impotence were printed. She was projected as an icon, but only dimly comprehended the meaning, possibilities and dangers that lurked within the cinematic ray of light. Her roles cast her in search of the ideal man but she invariably ended up with the "fuzzy end of the lollipop" or the "squeezed-out tube of toothpaste", as the script of **Some Like it Hot** suggestively put it. The strain was too much and she killed herself in 1962, bequeathing to her public an eternal rage of controversy about murder, tapped telephones, false autopsies and Presidential cover-ups – all the morbid paraphernalia that attends a person transformed into myth.

Her musicals for Fox, let it be said, are not very good: **Gentlemen Prefer Blondes** (1953) and **There's No Business Like Show Business** (1954) would be nothing without her. They have their moments, to be sure, including some lively classic numbers such as "Diamonds Are a Girl's Best Friend". The largely non-musical comedy **How to Marry a Millionaire** (1953) offers a strange fascination in the sight of Fox's greatest musical star, Betty Grable, waning before Monroe's wistful beauty. Monroe, who frequently played singers even in non-musicals, was better exploited in Billy Wilder's comedies **The Seven Year Itch** and **Some Like it Hot** and as a nightclub

Above left: *Marilyn Monroe preparing to snare a rich husband in* **How to Marry a Millionaire** *(1953).*

Above right: *Donald O'Connor, Ethel Merman, Dan Dailey, Mitzi Gaynor and Johnnie Ray as the vaudevillian family The Five Donahues in* **There's No Business Like Show Business** *(1954), which centers on O'Connor's romance with Marilyn Monroe (not shown).*

"chantoose" (torturing her vowels in "That Old Black Magic") in Joshua Logan's torrid **Bus Stop** (1956), based on a play by William Inge.

There was still another kind of musical which emerged in the 1950s, the blockbuster, made possible by the development of wide-screen processes such as CinemaScope and Todd-AO. Because of the heavy investments involved, these were lavish transcriptions of Broadway hits, exemplified by **Oklahoma!** (1955), **The King and I** (1956), **Carousel** (1956) and **South Pacific** (1958). All have their virtues, specifically the scores by Rodgers and Hammerstein in which there is hardly a number that has not become a standard. The films were not innovative — like their equivalent, the historical epic, the investment precluded any genuine risk-taking — but **South Pacific**, in the midst of its lurid color-washes, treated the themes of miscegenation and sexual promiscuity among American marines and South Sea islanders with remarkable frankness.

I remember it well

The last major studio musical was a screen original, **Gigi** (1958), produced at MGM by Arthur Freed, directed by Vincente Minnelli, with a Lerner and Loewe score and enchanting performances by Maurice Chevalier, Leslie Caron and Louis Jourdan. The film was based on a tart little French novel by Colette; but, in tone and its *fin de siècle* setting, it recalls Minnelli's 1944 classic **Meet Me in St Louis**,

evoking an adolescent's notion of a perfectly ordered world on the brink of change but preserved like the St Louis family's ketchup or an old master in gilt-edged frames. **Gigi** was a museum piece on the day of its release.

The musical never died, despite numerous suicide attempts in the 1960s (the colossal success in 1965 of **The Sound of Music** produced a bubble that burst over every studio), but the 1950s was its final flowering as a key component of what we think of as Hollywood. The collapse of the studio system brought to an end the essential infrastructure of orchestras, choreographers, chorus lines and designers.

The best musicals — and even the weaker among them — had style, humor, life-affirming qualities and "dignity, always dignity".

Left: In **Oklahoma!** (1955), mean, ornery Jud Fry (Rod Steiger, not shown) gets fried while Laurie (Shirley Jones) and Curly (Gordon MacRae) look on helplessly. The good old Southern tradition of barn-burning, as practiced by Judd himself, paves the way for a happy ending. While the film, directed with Teutonic heaviness rather than Viennese flair by Fred Zinnemann, was of little interest, the original 1943 stage production by Rouben Mamoulian was a major breakthrough in the American musical theater.

Bottom left: One of the decade's most successful musicals, **The King and I** (1956) starred Yul Brynner as the King of Siam and Deborah Kerr as Anna, the English governess to his children. Brynner was playing the role on Broadway at the time of his death in 1985.

Below: A reflective moment from **South Pacific** (1958) in which Rossano Brazzi, as a French planter, finds his independence undermined by American nurse Nellie Forbush (Mitzi Gaynor) who cannot get Brazzi out of her hair.

The Fall of the Empire

Chapter 18

On September 30, 1952 a film opened in New York that had a major influence on the decade ahead. The film had no stars, not even a director. It was a travelogue of uneven quality that began with a ride on a rollercoaster and ended with an aerial tour of America's scenic wonders. Its three 35mm projectors, giant curved screen and eight loudspeakers rendered all questions about artistic worth superfluous. The film was **This is Cinerama** and it was a sensation.

Running concurrently was a film called **Bwana Devil**, a terrible adventure picture set in darkest Africa and directed by Arch Oboler. **Bwana Devil** was shown in a process called Natural Vision, quickly simplified (by showbiz weekly *Variety*) to 3-D, a process which required two 35mm projectors running simultaneously to produce an image that, when viewed through special cardboard spectacles, seemed three-dimensional. The advertising campaign promised customers the dubious thrill of "A Lion in Your Lap". Thousands queued up for the experience.

Epic battles

A year later a Roman epic, **The Robe** (1953), heralded in another new process patented by 20th Century-Fox and called Cinema-Scope. **The Robe** was projected on to an extra-wide screen that soon became known as a letter-box. This film, too, was a huge success at the box-office.

So began several years of intense competition between the major studios as to which of them could produce the biggest film on the biggest screen. But, despite their rivalry, the studios had a common enemy — a small box that had begun in the late 1940s to appear in living rooms across the country. Television had arrived and Hollywood frantically sought ways of preserving its regular audience in the face of home entertainment at the push of a button. Bigger screens were the studios' immediate panacea and enormous investments were made in re-equipping cinemas.

Ever since the movies began scientists, directors and producers have striven to achieve greater realism through increasing technical sophistication. The advent of television merely intensified something that was innate. At the Paris Exhibition of 1900 the pioneer cinematographer Louis Lumière projected moving pictures on a screen that measured 63 × 45 feet (19 × 14m), and the inventor Raoul Grimoin-Sanson presented his elaborate Cinéorama process which called for ten projectors and a circular screen of ten panels.

Right: *After a brief prologue on a standard-sized screen,* **This is Cinerama** *(1952) began with a rollercoaster ride that was only marginally less exciting than the real thing. By the late 1960s most Cinerama theaters had been converted into multi-units but Cinerama's influence can be felt at Disneyland and Disney World.*

Above: *The Odeon, Leicester Square, London, on November 19, 1953, when Europeans took their first look at CinemaScope at the premiere of* **The Robe***. Note the CinemaScope-shaped marquee and the spirited counter-attack on 3-D by assuring audiences that CinemaScope can be appreciated without cardboard spectacles. The CinemaScope logo, designed by 20th Century-Fox, was to feature prominently on many films of the 1950s, often printed larger than the stars' names.*

Right: *House of Wax (1953) is à fine horror film in any version and audiences lined up to provide a welcoming lap for Vincent Price's victim, Phyllis Kirk . Director André de Toth, blind in one eye, never saw his own 3-D effects.*

Left and below: *Richard Burton confronts Jay Robinson as Caligula in the final scene from* **The Robe** *(1953). Two versions of the same scene show the additional width of CinemaScope.*

Cinéorama was banned by the police as a public safety hazard after only three performances but the Russian Circlorama of the 1960s and a current Disneyland attraction are virtual copies of Grimoin-Sanson's process. In 1927 the exuberant French director Abel Gance devised a forerunner of Cinerama called Polyvision for the final reel of his five-hour **Napoleon** in which the Emperor's armies and the French tricolor spread across three screens. Also in 1927, Henri Chrétien, a physicist and professor of Optics at the Sorbonne, developed an anamorphic lens that squashed the image sideways in taking a wide-angle picture and restretched it in wide-screen projection. This was later bought by 20th Century-Fox as the technical basis for CinemaScope. In 1930 the Fox studio produced an epic Western called **The Big Trail**, starring an unknown John Wayne and shown in Grandeur 70, using film twice the normal width and a wide screen. However, all these early innovations remained embryonic since few theaters could accommodate the technical equipment and the large screens without major structural alterations (it was not until 1980, for instance, that Gance's **Napoleon** was shown again in its original Polyvision version). But in the early 1950s, television changed all that.

Following the initial successes of Cinerama, 3-D and Cinema-Scope, Paramount developed VistaVision, Warner Bros. developed their own Warnerscope and producer Michael Todd and the American Optical Company combined to produce a 65mm process called Todd-AO. Stranger and short-lived systems included Cine-miracle, Thrillerama, and even Smellovision which was intended to enhance specific scenes with appropriate aromas but ended up with a terrible mixture of stinks.

The Cinerama process remained little more than a circus-like stunt until 1962 when the first dramatic films — **How the West Was Won** and **The Wonderful World of the Brothers Grimm** — were released. In 1963 the cumbersome three-screen, three-projector system was abandoned in favor of single-lens 70mm but perhaps only Stanley Kubrick's 1968 Super Panavision 70 film **2001: A Space Odyssey** really came to terms with the giant Cinerama screen. Films made in 3-D enjoyed only limited success because of technical difficulties and audience resistance to wearing glasses, and such prestige films as **Kiss Me Kate** (1953) and Hitchcock's **Dial M For Murder**, though photographed in 3-D, were released in "flat" versions. By the mid-1950s only CinemaScope, VistaVision (which ran the film sideways through the camera for a wide, high-quality image) and Todd-AO were recognized as viable formats and these remained until the early 1960s when, like Cinerama, they gave way to 35mm or 70mm varieties of Panavision.

Twice as large, half as good . . .?

When CinemaScope first appeared it attracted a good deal of comment, much of it caustic which, we should recall, was the response to sound in 1927. After seeing his first CinemaScope film, Jean Cocteau is reputed to have said, "The next time I write a poem I'll use a large sheet of paper." Leon Shamroy, who photographed **The Robe**, thought CinemaScope "wrecked the art of the film for a decade". The director Rouben Mamoulian thought it "the worst shape ever devised" but went on to compose some wonderful CinemaScope imagery in **Silk Stockings**. Sam Goldwyn quipped, "A wide screen makes a bad film twice as bad."

There is more than a grain of truth in Goldwyn's remark. The increased width did create problems for many directors, especially for close-ups and dialogue sequences, and the early CinemaScope lenses were less flexible in their focal range. But directors learned how to deal with the additional width very quickly and some early CinemaScope films, such as John Sturges' **Bad Day at Black Rock** (1955) and Nicholas Ray's **Rebel Without a Cause**, are visually powerful.

Although many dramas, Westerns, comedies and thrillers were made in the various widescreen systems, two genres in particular gained from the increased size and enhanced sound — the musical and the historical epic, both marketed as prestige films with separate performances and seats bookable at inflated prices. We have already discussed the musicals of the 1950s so it falls to the epic to bring the curtain down on the decade. It is appropriate that it does so, for there is no more expensive type of film to make and one of them was to bring about the decline of the studio system that had lasted for more than forty years.

When in Rome . . .

Cecil B. DeMille's **Samson and Delilah** (1949) had been a commercial success and, faced with the threat from television, MGM decided to make a version of Henryk Sienkiewicz' novel *Quo Vadis?*, which dealt with the Roman Empire under Nero, the fire of Rome and the persecution of the Christians who became the Emperor's handy scapegoats. An Italian version of 1912 had become the first international blockbuster and a second Italian version of 1924 rivaled MGM's silent **Ben-Hur** (1925). Since then Hollywood has had a lasting if intermittent love affair with the intrigues of the Caesars and their world. One only has to look at the inauguration of any American president to appreciate how much of the Republican structure and Roman architectural form has been assimilated in our own century. And as Peter Ustinov once remarked, "I've always thought that only the Americans can do Ancient Rome pictures. Both cultures have the same kind of relaxed, rangy pomp. Both have exactly the same kind of bad taste."

Quo Vadis (1951) contains all the virtues and failings that characterize the genre. The hapless Christians, the slaves and the good Roman soldier (Robert Taylor) are little more than ciphers given the most overblown and sanctimonious dialogue. The Romans, on the other hand, are the achievers, the instigators, the most compelling characters. A role like Nero is a gift from the Gods and, as the matricidal, incendiary emperor, Peter Ustinov was superb, leering through a ruby eyeglass as the Christians are eaten or burned alive and whimpering like a spoilt child as he faces oblivion. The script — originally by John Huston but reworked by less able writers — even found room for an attack on McCarthyism when Nero's "arbiter of elegance" Gaius Petronius (Leo Genn) kills himself. In a final letter, Petronius pardons Nero for his murders and perversions but castigates him for his artistic pretensions: "Mutilate your subjects if you must; but with my last breath I beg you, do not mutilate the arts."

The Robe and its hastily-made sequel **Demetrius and the Gladiators** (1954) tread the same territory, beginning with Christ's crucifixion and charting the growth of Christianity through the vessels of converted Romans and stateless slaves. Again Richard Burton, Jean Simmons and Victor Mature cope bravely with weak material, and Jay Robinson is a convincingly insane Caligula. Although **The Robe** and **Demetrius and the Gladiators** are not as spectacular as **Quo Vadis**, their CinemaScope imagery more than compensates. **Quo Vadis** and **The Robe** were immense box-office successes, not only prompting every major Hollywood studio to make historical epics but reviving the Italians' taste for them. Many of Hollywood's epics were made in Italy (notably **Quo Vadis** and **Ben-Hur**, 1959) and the Italians began to produce literally hundreds of cheaply-made but often extremely stylish interpretations of Greek myths and Roman history.

Hollywood's pharaohs

Fox delved deeper back into history for **The Egyptian** (1954), directed by Michael Curtiz and starring the lackluster Edmund Purdom, Jean Simmons and the all-purpose historical hunk Victor Mature. **The Egyptian** was mostly risible and served Sam Goldwyn's adage well, but Howard Hawks' excursion into Ancient Egypt, **Land of the Pharaohs** (1955), had a sure grasp of narrative, turning a pharaoh's obsessional construction of a pyramidal mausoleum into a compelling drama. For **Land of the Pharaohs** Hawks devised some CinemaScope vivid compositions of men dwarfed by their self-glorifying monuments.

Hollywood's flirtation with Ancient Egypt culminated in Cecil B. DeMille's **The Ten Commandments** (1956). DeMille had made an

Left: *Mitzi Gaynor singing 'I'm Gonna Wash That Man Right Outa My Hair' in* **South Pacific** *(1958). The Todd-AO process used a six-track sound system similar to Cinerama's but the single 65mm negative (blown up to 70mm projection prints) avoided Cinerama's distortions.*

Right: *The immensely complicated and labor-intensive Cinerama process could only be fully appreciated from a seat in the middle of the stalls. From other viewing positions both the picture and sound seemed distorted and a constant problem were the points where the separate images joined. But the effect of Cinerama was undeniably thrilling and by the early 1960s most major American and European cities had at least one Cinerama theater.*

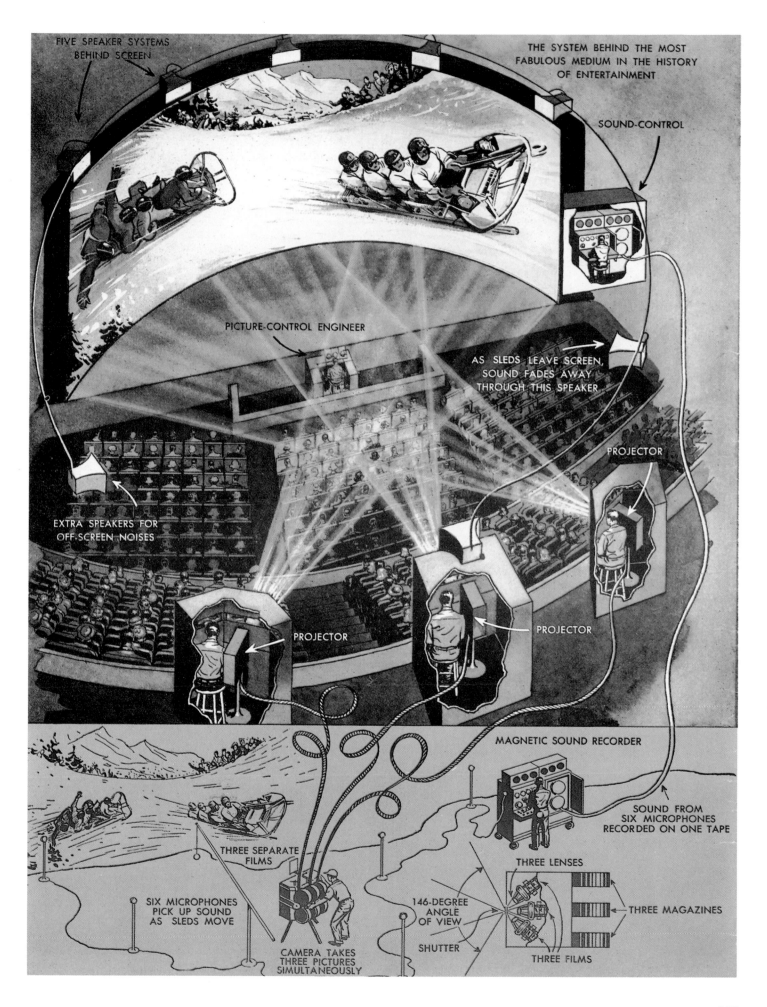

earlier version in 1923 but a remake in VistaVision was an attractive proposition. DeMille was one of Hollywood's greatest self-publicists and a fine director (though his fizzy comedies of the 1920s are largely forgotten). He was able to condemn all forms of moral perversion whilst relishing their cinematic possibilities, without a trace of irony or self-consciousness; no one could stage an orgy and frown upon it quite like DeMille. Such was his flair for showmanship that the original prints of **The Ten Commandments** included a five-minute homily by the director, standing before a giant red curtain, where he endorsed his film's sense of moral purpose, enlisted the support of God and the Holy Scriptures and finally announced a running time of three hours and forty-three minutes and that an interval had thoughtfully been provided for our comfort.

The Ten Commandments is a turgid film with a faltering grasp of narrative as the years drift by and the beards grow longer and grayer. There are some startling moments: the parting of the Red Sea, enabling the Jews to escape, and the erection of an obelisk are special-effects tours de force. Charlton Heston in his first epic role as Moses somehow conveys the terrible God-given burden that weighs upon his shoulders, Anne Baxter is a venomous Queen after she realizes that Moses has other things on his mind, and Yul Brynner is a fine young Pharaoh. For the most part the script veers from Midwestern contemporary to that strange invented language called

Hollywood Archaic which can produce a dialogue exchange like, "Why aren't you kneeling at the feet of a princess?" "I'm afraid the mud pits have stiffened my knees, royal one." On the other hand some relatively simple lines – such as Yul Brynner's "His God is God" – are poetic and evoke all the uncomprehending rage of a mere mortal.

Spectacles in frame

The Ten Commandments was a prestige picture in every respect. Somewhat lower down the scale were **The Silver Chalice** (1954) which was advertised as "The Mightiest Story of Tyranny and Temptation Ever Lived – Ever Written – Ever Produced!" But few agreed, including Paul Newman who made his debut as a silversmith called Basil. **Helen of Troy** (1955), directed in Italy by Robert Wise with a British, French and Italian cast, was a comparatively rare Hollywood excursion into Ancient Greece, beautifully photographed but in all other respects (despite a fleeting appearance by Brigitte Bardot) totally without interest. Robert Rossen's biopic **Alexander the Great** (1956), starring Richard Burton and Claire Bloom, saw Alexander as a visionary who might unite the world in both political and spiritual terms, but United Artists cut the film by over an hour, leaving little more than a remarkable performance by Burton – who seems to be playing a combination of Henry V and Hamlet. King

Far right: *Jack Hawkins as the Egyptian Pharaoh and Joan Collins as his overambitious wife in Howard Hawks'* **Land of the Pharaohs** *(1954). Collins made several Hollywood films in the 1950s before returning as the dragon-queen in the TV soap opera Dynasty.*

Above: *Michael Wilding as the Pharaoh Akhnaton (center left) lays down the law to Gene Tierney (center right) and Victor Mature in* **The Egyptian** *(1954), directed by Michael Curtiz whose talents were better suited to modern stories such as* **Casablanca** *(1943). Polish-born, Paris-bred Danuck protegée Bella Darvi (left) is inscrutable as usual – indeed, she was rarely scrutable in a brief film career.*

Vidor's final film, **Solomon and Sheba** (1959), with Gina Lollobrigida, was blighted by the death of Tyrone Power halfway through production (he was replaced by Yul Brynner, though Power can still be seen in long-shot) but contains some fine spectacle. But the great Vidor, whose previous film was a gargantuan and thoroughly respectable adaptation of **War and Peace** (1956), found himself too compromised by the demands of the blockbuster and, unable to finance smaller and more personal films, he retired (and died in 1982).

The responsibilities of making a historical epic were considerable. So too were the compromises. With an international public in mind, care had to be taken not to offend any religious group; and directors

with a reputation for flamboyance were seldom chosen to account for several million dollars. Once MGM had made the decision to remake their silent epic **Ben-Hur**, the search for a director was governed by reliability and professionalism above all other considerations. The choice fell upon William Wyler, who had been one of many assistant directors on the chariot race sequence of the silent film. He was a classical stylist who specialized in serious dramas and had the reputation of being the most demanding and fastidious director of actors in Hollywood. **Ben-Hur** proved to be his masterpiece.

Ben-Hur triumphant

At $14.5 million, **Ben-Hur** was then the most expensive film ever made; but it quickly became one of the most commercially successful films of all time, and won a still unbroken record of eleven Academy Awards. MGM gambled everything on **Ben-Hur** and won.

Wyler was shrewd enough to appreciate the deficiencies of other historical epics, and engaged the American novelist Gore Vidal and the British playwright Christopher Fry to transform the original script into something approaching blank verse. **Ben-Hur** has none of the vulgarity, anachronisms or the plain crassness of many epics. It is literate, lucid and has the density of a novel by Tolstoy or Dickens with a magnificent narrative sweep and a gallery of richly defined characters, all of whom intersect and offer striking symbolic contrasts.

The story is simple: an aristocratic Jew, Judah Ben-Hur (Charlton Heston), is condemned to be a galley slave by his former boyhood friend, the Roman tribune Messala (Stephen Boyd), but after a miraculous adoption by a Roman commander (Jack Hawkins), Judah returns to exact revenge on Messala in the breathtakingly filmed chariot race. Ben-Hur is seen as a secular equivalent of Christ, whose

life runs parallel to Ben-Hur's and at three specific points intersects — Christ gives Ben-Hur life-saving water during his desert march to the galleys; faced with a choice of business with Rome or listening to Christ deliver his Sermon on the Mount, Ben-Hur walks diagonally across Christ's line of vision; on the way to Calvary, Ben-Hur gives Christ water to drink.

Ben-Hur depicts life as a trial of strength. Judah Ben-Hur begins as a character of some arrogance who is required to experience life as a living hell before he realizes spiritual salvation. Wyler's principal achievement was never to lose sight of the human drama amidst the spectacle and, in terms of direction, script and performance (especially Heston, and Stephen Boyd whose evil permeates the entire film), **Ben-Hur** is in a class of its own.

Following the success of **The Ten Commandments** and encouraged by MGM's commitment to **Ben-Hur**, two further Roman epics began production in 1959: Universal's **Spartacus** (1960) and 20th Century-Fox's **Cleopatra**. **Spartacus**, based on a Communist novel by Howard Fast, told the story of the Slave Revolt of 73–71BC which

ended in disaster as thousands of slaves, led by a Thracian gladiator, were crucified along the Appian Way. As far as Rome was concerned, Spartacus's rebellion was little more than a fleabite but his symbolic stand against repression has made him a hero in socialist countries. Kirk Douglas played Spartacus, Jean Simmons was his wife, Laurence Olivier was his nemesis and Charles Laughton and Peter Ustinov played Romans with heart and a sense of humor. **Spartacus** began shooting under the direction of Anthony Mann.

Cleopatra had a more illustrious pedigree with a well-documented historical basis and plays by Shakespeare and Shaw. Elizabeth Taylor was to play the Egyptian Queen and, when shooting began, Peter Finch was Julius Caesar, Stephen Boyd was Mark Antony and the director was Rouben Mamoulian. **Spartacus** was made entirely in California but **Cleopatra** began production in Britain.

By coincidence both Mann and Mamoulian were replaced early on. Stanley Kubrick took over **Spartacus** which made him, at 31, the youngest director ever to control such a lavish production. Although Kubrick was subsequently to disown **Spartacus,** claiming that

Top center: *One of the cinema's greatest special effects sequences, the parting of the Red Sea in* **The Ten Commandments** *(1956). The effect was achieved by filling a tank with two torrents of water, running the film backwards and matting-in the suitably awed Jews and God's storm clouds.*

Left: *Gina Lollobrigida models the latest in 9th-century BC fashion in* **Solomon and Sheba** *(1959). "La Lollo", as she was called, was one of many European beauties courted by Hollywood but only in comedies did she really excel, lacking the dramatic weight of Sophia Loren, her main rival.*

Right: *The original advertisements for* **Cleopatra** *(1963) were to have featured only a supine Elizabeth Taylor and an attentive Richard Burton but their costar Rex Harrison objected so he was subsequently incorporated into the artwork, lurking behind the potted palm. Taylor and Burton's real-life romance had made the film so famous that its title and main credits were deemed unnecessary: the first advertisements simply carried the legend, "The Film The Whole World Is Waiting To See".*

executive producer/star Kirk Douglas allowed him little independence, it is an impressive and exciting film, but perhaps not quite for the reasons that Douglas would have liked. His role as Spartacus never rises above the stock requirements of Christlike martyrdom, but the triumvirate of British actors — Olivier, Laughton, Ustinov — work wonders with an often simplistic screenplay. Apart from the film's visual and visceral bravura, for which Kubrick must take the credit, **Spartacus** earns a footnote in history as one of two 1960 films scripted openly by the blacklisted writer Dalton Trumbo. His other film, Otto Preminger's **Exodus**, a paean to the creation of Israel, is echoed in his script for **Spartacus** which contains more than an undercurrent of Zionist fervor.

Burton and Taylor

Despite the change in director, **Spartacus** was a trouble-free production and a profitable film. **Cleopatra** was another matter. Shortly after production began in Britain, Elizabeth Taylor became ill and Fox decided to replace Mamoulian, Finch and Boyd. The new director and writer was Joseph L. Mankiewicz, who had made **Julius Caesar** and would emphasize character and political struggle over spectacle. Rex Harrison became Julius Caesar and Richard Burton, who had starred in Fox's first 1950s Roman epic **The Robe**, took over as Mark Antony. The production shifted to Italy, where Mankiewicz was directing by day and writing by night, and for three years **Cleopatra** dominated the front pages of the world's newspapers owing to the public romance between Taylor and Burton. By the time shooting was completed, **Cleopatra** had become the most expensive film ever made at around $43 million and Elizabeth Taylor had broken the magic $1 million fee (plus expenses and a share of the profits). Mankiewicz edited the film in Paris where he devised a two-part film running five and a half hours. At the same time, Darryl F. Zanuck deposed Spyros P. Skouras as president of 20th Century-Fox; he took over the editing of **Cleopatra** and reduced it to a single film running four hours. After its initial showings its running time was shortened again.

Cleopatra became the first modern film to be more famous for its production circumstances than for its own merits as a movie. In a way, it hardly matters that the very rarely-shown 243-minute version is a magnificent achievement — literate, witty and with a fine sense of history on the move as Rome shifts from Republic to Empire, quite different from the skeletal 190-minute version now available. **Cleopatra** became the byword for Hollywood excess in the same way that Michael Cimino's masterpiece **Heaven's Gate** became in 1980. Neither does it really matter that **Cleopatra** was an enormous commercial hit by any standards except its own. The film had cost so much to make and to advertise that a profit was impossible to achieve in the short run, though secondary income may eventually have covered most of the losses directly chargeable to production and distribution.

End of an era

Cleopatra almost bankrupted 20th Century-Fox and it created shockwaves throughout the boardrooms of Hollywood, heralding an era (which remains to this day) of short-lived executives and uncertain production policy. The fee awarded to Elizabeth Taylor quickly became accepted — and overtaken — and the stars acquired creative independence, using the studios merely as a production facility and distributor. The age of the director as *auteur* had arrived. Without the moguls running the studios — they began to be replaced by the agents of the stars and directors or Wall Street accountants — the studios lost their identities and eventually were taken over by conglomerates. **Cleopatra** was both the end and a new beginning. It was the last film of the 1950s and Hollywood would never be the same again.

Douglas Jarvis

Hollywood 1900s

Brigitte Bardot

Blockbusters

Chapter 19

*The climactic scene from **The Greatest Story Ever Told** (1965).*

Everything changed for Hollywood in the Sixties, and Hollywood didn't like it. In its 50-year existence, the American film industry had surmounted two major upheavals. The first of these was the coming of sound in 1927, an innovation resisted by a community not noted for its forward-looking attitudes. Yet the public soon decreed that silent movies were dead, and the talkies eventually proved to be a shot in the arm for the film capital of the world.

The second crisis was the divorce of exhibition from production and distribution. The Hollywood majors believed in their inalienable right not only to distribute the films their studios made but also to show them in their own theaters, but the American government stood firm in its move to break the industry's monopoly. The battle, interrupted by the war, lasted 20 years. But from 1948 to 1959 antitrust laws compelled the major companies to divorce their studios from their cinema chains and cease block-booking; the last major to capitulate was Loew's/MGM.

Pessimists predicted that these laws would kill the film industry. Needless to say it survived, and despite the strong threat from television. The threat took two forms. The first struck in January 1960 when the Screen section of the Writers' Guild went on strike for a share of the profits of movies sold by the studios to television. The actors' and directors' organizations followed suit. The second — that television kept potential audiences at home — was rejected by the industry, which argued that audiences were still flocking to the movies, not least to see 1959's big hit, **Ben-Hur**.

This epic was shot, of course, in one of the wide-screen processes considered to be the answer to any threat from television. The most ambitious process was Cinerama, but by 1960 the novelty had worn off: Cinerama's cameras had filmed most of the world's natural wonders and were now running out of places to show on the giant wrap-around screen. Audiences too were tiring of these travelogues (as well as the inevitable flickering between the three projected images). Cinerama executives believed that the rot could be stopped if they combined spectacle with a story and, thinking back to the kind of profits earned by **Around the World in 80 Days** (1956) they signed an agreement with MGM to cooperate on **How the West Was Won** (1962).

The big screen

Winning the West gave opportunities for an all-star cast — including John Wayne, Gregory Peck, James Stewart, Henry Fonda, Richard

Widmark, Debbie Reynolds and Robert Preston — to shoot the rapids, fight, and indulge in train and horse chases. Audiences approved, though few were inclined to experience **The Wonderful World of the Brothers Grimm** (1962), a second cooperation between the two companies which proved that Cinerama in itself was no attraction. Nor was its less than all-star cast, including Laurence Harvey, Claire Bloom and Karl Boehm.

But there were 20 comic talents, plus Spencer Tracy, in **It's a Mad, Mad, Mad, Mad World** (1963), which, with one screen and one projector, had the added attraction of eliminating those maddening wobbly lines, and was supposed to make the audience take Cinerama to their hearts once again. A three-hour knockabout comedy concerning a search for buried treasure over much of California and Nevada, the film was produced and directed for United Artists by Stanley Kramer, who could not resist the sort of message conveyed in his more serious films — this one, naturally, underlining the evils of greed.

Cinerama was saved, and United Artists gathered yet another all-star cast, including Charlton Heston, Sidney Poitier, Pat Boone and Dorothy McGuire, for a Cinerama version of Fulton Oursler's best-selling interpretation of the life of Christ, **The Greatest Story Ever Told** (1965), directed by the much-respected George Stevens. Christ was played by Max von Sydow, the superb Swedish actor known from his work in Ingmar Bergman's films, and even John Wayne showed up for one line: "This truly was the son of God."

The film seemed likely to be a big box-office success. **Ben-Hur** had reaffirmed the popularity of the religious spectacle and had brought fresh laurels to the veteran director William Wyler, who had accepted the challenge of breathing new life into an old tale. Stevens, like Wyler, belonged to that group of film-makers admired by critics and able to win Oscars, which was why they had achieved a degree of independence; the studio moguls were not too happy about this, but were forced to agree that these were the talents most likely to bring them prestige and respectable financial returns.

The Greatest Story Ever Told, however, was not a studio project but one of Stevens' own; 20th Century-Fox turned it down as costs mounted, but United Artists was happy to be associated with a director who had received acclaim in the Fifties for **A Place in the Sun** (1951), **Shane** (1953) and **Giant** (1956). That acclaim was not forthcoming on this occasion. The much-vaunted all-star casts of **How the West Was Won** and **It's a Mad, Mad, Mad, Mad World** had enabled both to sell tickets despite poor notices, but when the public spurned **The Greatest Story Ever Told**, Cinerama was doomed. The film, much cut, played most of its engagements in a CinemaScope print. CinemaScope was also doomed, but that was only because its place was taken by an identical but much cheaper anamorphic wide-screen process, 35mm Panavision.

Below left: *Some of the cast of thousands welcome Christ into Jerusalem in* **The Greatest Story Every Told** *(1965).*

Bottom: *A spectacular scene from the multi-million dollar Technirama 70 Roman epic* **Spartacus** *(1960) with Kirk Douglas (center) in the title role. Also in the all-star cast were Laurence Olivier, Jean Simmons, Tony Curtis, Charles Laughton and Peter Ustinov.*

Below: *Kirk Douglas (foreground) as* **Spartacus** *brandishes a stave as he leads the revolt of the slaves (among them John Ireland and Harold J. Stone just behind him) in the Ancient Rome of 73 BC, as imagined by director Stanley Kubrick.*

The wider screens, especially when enhanced with color and stereophonic sound, had revitalized cinemagoing during the Fifties. The small black-and-white screen at home couldn't compete with movies which were clearly events, and which had temporarily revived the old concept of "roadshow exhibition".

Rivaling Broadway

By 1960 the industry was geared to producing a handful of movies — or roadshows — annually which were as much of a night out as a big Broadway show. The public booked ahead at advanced prices for the "event", which was preceded by an overture and was sufficiently lengthy to require a profitable interval. An all-color souvenir book was available for those wishing to relive the magic, while a soundtrack album for a wide range of films, not just musicals, could be bought in record shops.

But the "big night out" treatment didn't always work. John Wayne's **The Alamo** (1960), which he starred in and produced, was his personal statement and account of the famous battle of 1836, which he believed every American would want to see. He couldn't have been more wrong. Instead the public flocked to the Roman epic **Spartacus** (1960). This was also produced by an actor as a vehicle for himself, Kirk Douglas, but whereas Wayne's only big co-star was Richard Widmark, Douglas had the sense to include two top box-office names, Tony Curtis and Jean Simmons, plus Laurence Olivier, Charles Laughton and Peter Ustinov to commend the

Above: *The $750,000 motor-operated reproduction of HMS* Bounty *constructed for* **Mutiny on the Bounty** *(1962) was only part of the $19-million cost of the movie, ten times that of the 1935 version.*

Right: *Marlon Brando (right) put on an English accent for his foppish Fletcher Christian, playing opposite Trevor Howard (left) as Captain Bligh in* **Mutiny on the Bounty**. *While on location in Tahiti, Brando met Tarita, a Tahitian with whom he has two children.*

enterprise to the critics. Moreover, **Spartacus** was entertaining and **The Alamo** wasn't — largely owing to their screenplays and, to a lesser extent, their direction. When no major film-maker had showed interest in making **The Alamo**, Wayne decided to direct it himself, although he hoped until well into the production that the job would be taken over as a favor to him by his friend John Ford, master director of the Western.

Spartacus began with Anthony Mann in the directorial chair but, after a dispute with him, Douglas called upon Hollywood's brightest new talent, Stanley Kubrick. He agreed to tackle the job partly as a return favor to Douglas whose decision to take on the star part in **Paths of Glory** (1957) attracted much needed financial backing.

Star power

Some stars carried a lot of weight in the early Sixties. Throughout Hollywood history, they had snatched at power. The studio tycoons had blenched at the clout attained in the Twenties by Charles Chaplin, Mary Pickford and Douglas Fairbanks, and vowed not to let any such thing happen again. Nor did it until the studio system broke down in the early Fifties.

Left: *'The Rivers' episode from the first fiction film to be presented in Cinerama,* **How the West Was Won** *(1962). Fighting the rapids are Debbie Reynolds (left), Agnes Moorehead (center), Carroll Baker (right) and Karl Malden (background).*

Below: *A scene from the Civil War interlude of* **How the West Was Won***, directed by John Ford and featuring his favorite actor John Wayne (left). The other four episodes in this all-star Cinerama Western were directed by two other stalwarts of the genre, Henry Hathaway and George Marshall.*

Above: *Richard Burton (in plumed helmet) as Mark Antony fights to save his war galley from being taken over by Octavian's legionaries in Joseph L. Mankiewicz's* **Cleopatra***, the picture that almost bankrupted 20th Century-Fox.*

Above right: *The $37-million* **Cleopatra** *(1963) was described as being 'conceived in a state of emergency, shot in confusion and winding up in blind panic'. It did, however, provide gossip columnists with copy on the off-screen love affair between Elizabeth Taylor (center) as the Queen of Egypt and Richard Burton.*

Right: *'She makes hungry where most she satisfies.'*

One of the surviving moguls, Darryl F. Zanuck, publicly criticized John Wayne for taking unto himself the powers of producer and director, but it was a naive statement. Although their names only appeared on the cast lists, some stars controlled every aspect of their vehicles — and in the early Sixties these included Charlton Heston, William Holden, Gregory Peck, Frank Sinatra, Burt Lancaster and Cary Grant, the only one of the pre-war stars who was also in all but name his own producer.

Anthony Quinn and Paul Newman soon acquired the same degree of autonomy; Yul Brynner held it briefly, as did Glenn Ford, until it was taken from both because of box-office failures — in Ford's case after two expensive remakes of old Hollywood favorites, **Cimarron** (1960) and **The Four Horsemen of the Apocalypse** (1962). In between these two, Ford appeared in another remake, **Pocketful of Miracles** (1961), Frank Capra's revised version of his own **Lady for a Day** (1933). Incidentally, Capra's autobiography, *The Name Above the Title*, contains an eloquent account of Ford's whims and tantrums when he subjected the great veteran director to constant humiliations. After similar experiences with John Wayne's advisers, when he was preparing to direct Wayne in **Circus World** (1964), Capra decided to leave the industry he had served so magnificently.

Among the most powerful stars was Marlon Brando, acknowledged as both a superb actor and a box-office favorite. All his projects received wide press coverage, and with this in mind Paramount gave him total control on **One-Eyed Jacks** (1961), as

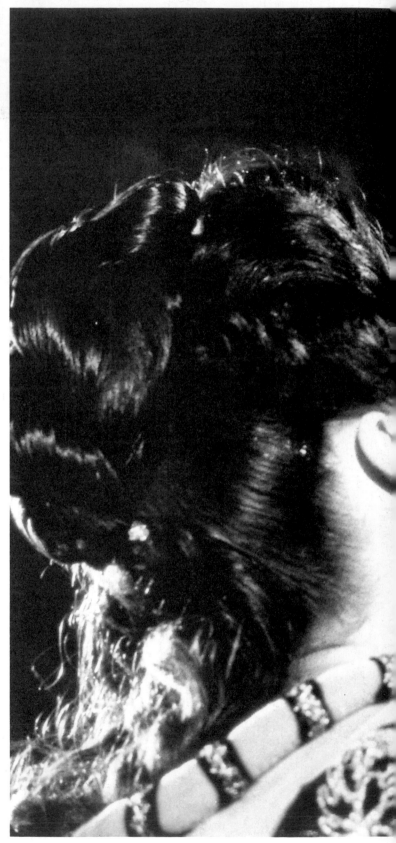

well as all profits after the cost had been recouped. Not long after shooting began, Brando began to fall out with the director, Stanley Kubrick, who subsequently left the film. Brando took over as director and acquitted himself so honorably on this harsh Western that it is a pity that he hasn't accepted that responsibility since.

Search for the blockbuster

Subsequently Brando wielded even greater power at MGM. Several times in its history MGM's fortunes had been restored by pouring its resources into one costly film – as with the silent **Ben-Hur** (1926), a cogent consideration when they contemplated the 1959 remake. Receipts from that remake and a reissue of **Gone With the Wind** convinced executives that they needed another blockbuster, one with reissue potential if times got tough. They decided that the old MGM success most demanding a new treatment was **Mutiny on the Bounty** (1935), about a half-forgotten incident in British naval history.

Asked to play the evil Captain Bligh in the 1962 version, Brando refused, but added that he might be interested in playing Fletcher Christian, the leader of the mutineers. The opportunity of getting Brando sent MGM's executives into delirium – in the end the star walked away with an unprecedented $1¼ million, which included bonuses when the film went over schedule (on account of delays for which he himself was often responsible). Brando had been given complete control over production, which may be why Britain's respected Carol Reed was replaced as director by the veteran Russian-American Lewis Milestone, although in the event Milestone loathed working with Brando. The cost of the film escalated to an astounding $19 million, but with final North American rental takings of less than $10 million, Brando could not claim the share of the profits agreed in his contract. It was 18 years before he worked for MGM again.

Simultaneously, 20th Century-Fox was committed to paying a vast

salary to Elizabeth Taylor for **Cleopatra** (1963); announced as $1 million by the publicity department, it was, in fact, somewhat less, but large sums were guaranteed if shooting went over schedule. It was not her fault that production in London was shut down and restarted in Rome, with Richard Burton and Rex Harrison respectively replacing Stephen Boyd and Peter Finch, and with a new director, Joseph L. Mankiewicz, who was compelled to rewrite the script as filming progressed.

As costs mounted to $36 million, the studio called for its lawyers, and among the many suits flying about was one accusing Taylor and Burton — enjoying a much-publicized affair — of moral conduct likely to alienate the public. Few of those who eventually saw the film felt that the events on screen were as dramatic as those in the journalists' version of "real life". Apart from Mankiewicz, the only major figure to emerge from the fiasco with credit was Harrison, who played Julius Caesar; critics found Burton monotonous as Mark Antony and Taylor inadequate in the title-role. The critics put forward no pressing reason for seeing the film, and many for avoiding it; though it was easily the top box-office hit of the year and eventually took $26 million in domestic rentals alone, there was no question of this hugely expensive movie recovering its costs in the short run favored by movie accounting, though US and worldwide TV and video income may eventually have soaked up most of the red ink.

Burton and Taylor recovered from this setback to their careers by appearing quickly and quietly in a British movie, **The VIPs** (1963), which enjoyed moderate popularity. Brando behaved similarly (by making the medium-budgeted **The Ugly American**, 1963), so silencing those who wanted him and Taylor thrown out of Hollywood. The truth was that no one individual was responsible for those spiraling budgets. Those to blame were the executives who had allowed these players such power and had then turned a blind eye to the circumstances in which they wielded it.

The blockbuster mentality was revitalized by **Lawrence of Arabia** (1962), produced by Sam Spiegel, who had established a substantial

Above: *Omar Sharif made a sensational debut in English-speaking films (he had previously made Egyptian and French pictures) as Sherif Ali in David Lean's intelligent, brilliantly photographed desert epic,* **Lawrence of Arabia** *(1962).*

Above: *David Lean's* **Lawrence of Arabia** *(1962) – the first of three epics using a Robert Bolt screenplay – attempted some psychological insight into the complex character of T.E. Lawrence as portrayed by Peter O'Toole (with Anthony Quinn, right).*

Right: *Lawrence of Arabia* (1962) alias Peter O'Toole (in white Arab dress) gazes mystically into the beyond as he leads his Bedouin army against the Turks with Omar Sharif, as his friend Sherif Ali ibn el Kharish, by his side.

reputation with such films as **The African Queen** (1951), **On the Waterfront** (1954) and **The Bridge on the River Kwai** (1957). The last-named had been directed by Britain's David Lean, and the two teamed up again for an epic biographical study of the enigmatic Arabist, soldier and writer T.E. Lawrence.

Lawrence of Arabia provided many opportunities for action, spectacular desert photography and a big role (turned down by Brando) for the then relatively unknown Peter O'Toole and almost equally fine parts for newcomer Omar Sharif, Anthony Quinn, Alec Guinness, José Ferrer, Claude Rains and Anthony Quayle. While avoiding any suggestions of homosexuality or masochism, it also intimated that Lawrence was a poseur and discreetly hinted that he had been sexually assaulted while in a Turkish jail, two reasons why the film was regarded as "the thinking man's epic". This was the first film in the history of the cinema which presented a hero in this ambivalent way.

Reliving the past

In the Sixties there was a fascination with films about historical characters, in keeping with the cinema's yearning for intellectual respectability. Charlton Heston, who had been John the Baptist in **The Greatest Story Ever Told**, also played the painter Michelangelo in **The Agony and the Ecstasy** (1965), the title-role of the semi-legendary Spanish warrior in **El Cid** (1961), and the Victorian General Gordon in **Khartoum** (1966), all of which were roadshown. The producer of **El Cid** was Samuel Bronston, who tried to build a career out of epics.

In the Fifties, the American film industry discovered not only that Britain and Italy possessed first-class production facilities, but that filming there was cheaper than at home. Moreover, the pool of talent available in Britain was more suitable to historic tales because of the more "starchy" accent considered essential, and was cheaper to transport to, say, Italy than having a cast brought over from

Above: *A typical 'cast of thousands' scene from Anthony Mann's* **The Fall of the Roman Empire** *(1964), shot at Samuel Bronston's studio in Spain. The same year, Bronston's empire fell when he was forced to suspend production because of heavy debts.*

Right: **The Fall of the Roman Empire** *had its longueurs, but it also contained stunning visuals, an impeccable performance from Alec Guinness as Marcus Aurelius, and the beautiful Sophia Loren (illustrated) as his daughter.*

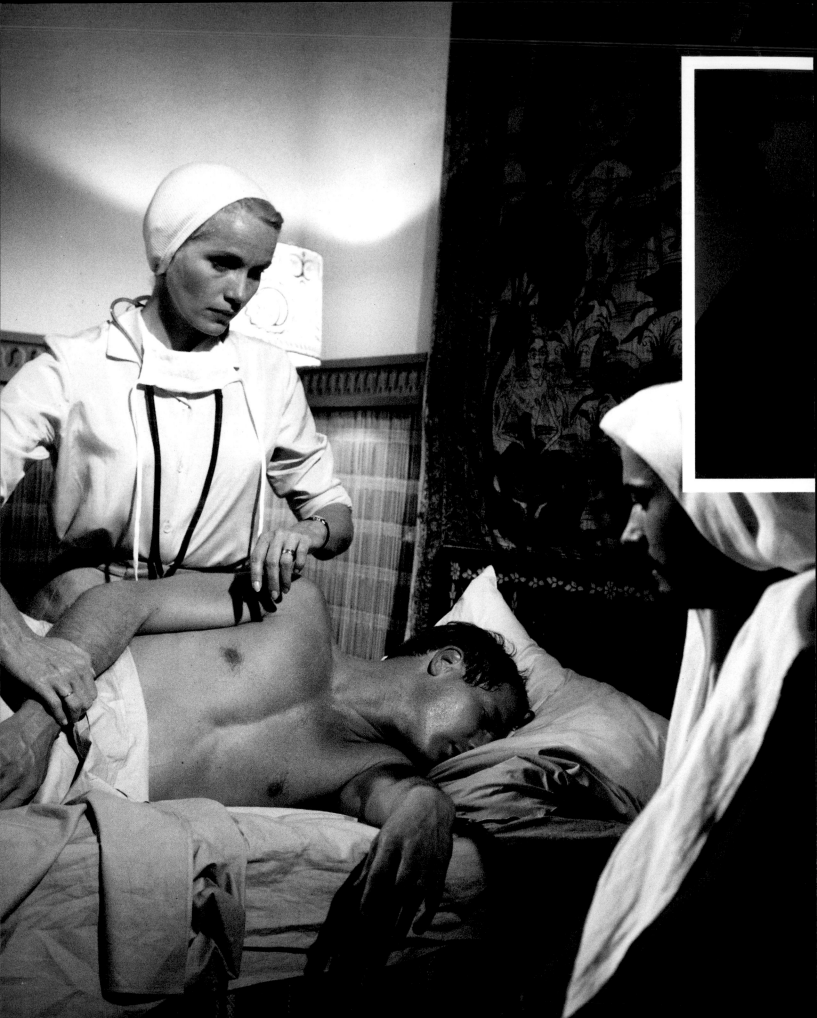

Hollywood. Bronston homed in on Spain and imported supporting players from Britain; while Spanish studios left much to be desired, their personnel came cheap. It was therefore possible to assemble "casts of thousands" by using non-unionized extras at minimal rates. Bronston started with Nicholas Ray's **King of Kings** (1961), a life of Christ, and followed it with Anthony Mann's **El Cid**, Ray's **55 Days at Peking** (1963), a tale of the Boxer Rebellion starring Heston again, Ava Gardner and David Niven, and Mann's **The Fall of the Roman Empire** (1964), with a cast headed by Sophia Loren, James Mason and Alec Guinness. Nicholas Ray and Anthony Mann were skilled commercial film-makers who, much admired by French intellectuals, were later critically acclaimed.

El Cid and **The Fall of the Roman Empire** had particularly impressive visuals, but audiences were less interested in the Boxers battling against the International Settlement in Peking or the Visigoths at the gates of a Roman outpost than heroes like Jesus and the Cid. Bronston, in fact, was helping audiences to kick the blockbuster habit. Roadshow plans were abandoned for his next film, **Circus World** (1964), and takings were not enough to shore up the tottering Bronston empire, which now included a vast new studio complex near Madrid. Bronston's debts were a clear warning: size was not enough.

Yet once again the roadshow concept received a fillip from another spectacle made in Spain, **Doctor Zhivago** (1965), produced by Carlo Ponti, who with his former colleague Dino De Laurentiis had pioneered the international super-production in the Fifties. Both producers had since left Italy for Hollywood and gone their separate

Above center: *Spencer Tracy as the American judge at the* **Judgment at Nuremberg** *(1961) listens intently as 'star' witnesses such as Judy Garland, Montgomery Clift and Marlene Dietrich give evidence in Stanley Kramer's well-meaning drama.*

Left: *American nurse Eva Marie Saint attends to wounded resistance leader Paul Newman while his Arab friend John Derek looks on anxiously in Otto Preminger's mammoth 220-minute* **Exodus** *(1960).*

Above: *Katharine Hepburn gained the second of her four Oscars for* **Guess Who's Coming to Dinner** *(1967), the last of the nine movies she made with her beloved Spencer Tracy.*

ways, but each maintained his interest in blockbusters, and Ponti decided that Boris Pasternak's epic novel of the Russian Revolution was ripe for such treatment. Fresh from their triumph with **Lawrence of Arabia**, David Lean and Robert Bolt were brought in to direct and write, while the title-role was given to Omar Sharif, whose performance in **Lawrence** had made him an international star. **Doctor Zhivago** also featured Julie Christie, Ralph Richardson, Rod Steiger and Alec Guinness. The result was lashings of prestige and five Oscars.

The more serious among the other big movies of the time had mixed receptions. **Judgment at Nuremberg** (1961) was produced and directed by Stanley Kramer, who assembled a cast including Spencer Tracy as the judge, Burt Lancaster as one of the accused Nazis, Maximilian Schell and Richard Widmark for and against the defense, Marlene Dietrich as spokesperson for the good Germans and, in cameo roles, Judy Garland and Montgomery Clift as Nazi victims. **Exodus** (1960), Otto Preminger's film on the founding of the state of Israel, also required an all-star cast: Paul Newman, Eva Marie Saint and Lee J. Cobb. Like Kramer, Otto Preminger was drawn to challenging subjects, especially when based on controversial best-sellers or Broadway hits — in this case Leon Uris's massive Zionist novel.

Both Kramer and Preminger had established their reputations in the Fifties, when their work was praised by the influential critic of the *New York Times*, Bosley Crowther. Individually, they had hits in the Sixties, Preminger with **Advise and Consent** (1962) and Kramer

Left: *One of the many visually impressive scenes from David Lean's 197-minute epic* **Doctor Zhivago** *(1965): the wintry Russian landscape was actually shot in Spain.*

Below: *Omar Sharif as the idealistic Russian doctor-poet in* **Doctor Zhivago** *stares out of his iced-up window with soulful eyes as he dreams of his lost love, Lara.*

with **Guess Who's Coming to Dinner** (1967), and later a run of flops. **Advise and Consent** was based on Allen Drury's political bestseller, and included Henry Fonda, Don Murray, Charles Laughton and Gene Tierney, though the film's strength derived from its narrative rather than its star cast.

Guess Who's Coming to Dinner was based on an original screenplay by William Rose, concerning the reaction of a white couple — played by Spencer Tracy and Katharine Hepburn — to their daughter's impending marriage to a black man — Sidney Poitier.

Columbia released both movies — but roadshowed neither since one was an intimate comedy-drama and the other was a doubtful proposition, for few political films had ever succeeded at the box office. It was also made in black-and-white, as was **Judgment at Nuremberg**, for Hollywood still believed that Technicolor was too frivolous for serious drama. But the black-and-white **The Longest Day** (1962), Darryl F. Zanuck's elaborate all-star reconstruction of the landings in Normandy in 1944, which required the insertion of newsreel material of the period, was roadshowed. It was also Hollywood's last big-budget black-and-white film, as color finally became indispensable during the decade. There were by now many cheaper color systems than Technicolor, and except in the rare instances noted audiences expected color in all major films. After all color was universal in television by the mid-Sixties in the USA and by the end of the decade in the major countries of Europe too.

Left: *The Allied landings in Normandy on June 6, 1944 were the subject of the lengthy (180-minute) Darryl F. Zanuck production* **The Longest Day** *(1962). A Who's Who of international stars took cameo roles, among them John Wayne (illustrated).*

Above: *The Germans defend the beaches of Normandy in* **The Longest Day**. *The huge 20th Century-Fox production had three directors, each dealing with their own armies — Ken Annakin (British), Andrew Marton (American) and Bernhard Wicki (German).*

Right: *Washington politicians were put under the microscope in Otto Preminger's all-star* **Advise and Consent** *(1962). One of them, Don Murray (left foreground), finds himself in a gay bar.*

Musical profits

In the late Thirties when Technicolor was prohibitively expensive except on certain box-office successes, its use had been restricted chiefly to musicals and historical subjects. A musical in black and white was unthinkable by 1950, and for the next few years the combination of song-and-dance and color guaranteed good box-office returns, often for unimaginative versions of Broadway shows.

Chronologically, the first blockbuster of the Sixties was a musical, **Can-Can** (1960). Its producers, 20th Century-Fox, saw no great need to adhere to the original (first staged in 1953), which was not one of Cole Porter's biggest hits, despite having one of his finest scores. That now was cut and supplemented by some of his most hackneyed songs; the material was changed to accommodate

Maurice Chevalier and Louis Jourdan reprising their double-act from **Gigi**, and bowdlerized, curiously, to suit Shirley MacLaine and Frank Sinatra – thus losing its piquancy. The film did not live up to box-office expectations.

MGM, considered the market leader in musicals, meanwhile had only modest successes with **Bells Are Ringing** (1960), in which Judy Holliday repeated her Broadway triumph; **The Unsinkable Molly Brown** (1964), starring Debbie Reynolds; and **Billy Rose's Jumbo** (1962), with Doris Day. Only the last of these was from an *old* (and indeed half-forgotten) Broadway show, but Doris Day, America's favorite female star, was expected to atone for that. Yet the film failed and MGM lost interest in making musicals.

If, however, people were selective in choosing movie musicals, this

Above left: *The bravura high-kicking* **Can-Can**, *the central theme of the 1960 Cole Porter musical of that title. The story of café owner Shirley MacLaine's fight to allow the 'lewd' dance to be performed at her establishment lacked the verve of the title routine.*

Above: *A scene from* **West Side Story** *(1961) which had galvanic dances, exciting music by Leonard Bernstein, and some social consciousness, even if seen in radical-chic showbiz terms. Though the members of the street gangs were meant to be in their teens, the ages of the clean-cut cast ranged from 22 to 30.*

Right: *Natalie Wood and Richard Beymer as Maria and Tony, a contemporary New York Romeo and Juliet, in the most fêted musical film ever, Robert Wise and Jerome Robbins'* **West Side Story**.

Above: *David Tomlinson looks astonished as his son and daughter (Matthew Garber and Karen Dotrice) descend the stairs with their magical governess who arrived by umbrella. Julie Andrews won an Oscar for her remarkable screen debut in* **Mary Poppins** *(1964) in the role of P. L. Travers' nanny.*

Right: *Julie Andrews as* **Mary Poppins** *walks through a Walt Disney cartoon land with her cockney beau Dick Van Dyke.*

was an era in which every Broadway original-cast record album was assured huge sales throughout the country; and indeed, in New York itself the musical had never been healthier. The critics and the public had adored a trailblazing show that switched the story of *Romeo and Juliet* to the contemporary slums of New York, and **West Side Story** (1961) was swiftly brought to the screen by United Artists. They were rewarded with fine notices, a fistful of Oscars and excellent business the world over.

One of the problems of making musicals was that their costs were rising and, because of television, the domestic market was shrinking. This meant a greater dependence on foreign returns, but there were some important foreign markets – notably France – which remained indifferent to the American musical. **West Side Story**, with its electrifying Leonard Bernstein score and direction by Jerome Robbins (who had staged the show on Broadway) and Robert Wise, appeared to signal that there were new audiences for musicals.

Accordingly, Warner Brothers brought **The Music Man** (1962) to the screen, despite its folksy, very American theme. As on Broadway, Morton Da Costa directed and Robert Preston – deemed irreplaceable as the fast-talking traveling salesman who cons a small Iowa

town into starting up a boys' orchestra — played the title role. But the film did poorly in many foreign territories to the extent that Warners' French office didn't bother to open it at all. Preston was not, after all, a big name. And neither was Ethel Merman, which was why Warners did not invite her to repeat her Broadway triumph in **Gypsy** (1962), as the stage-crazy mother of a vaudeville kid (Natalie Wood), whom she turns into a striptease "artist". Although the almost equally raucous Rosalind Russell replaced Merman, Mervyn LeRoy's film lacked the spark of the exhilarating stage original.

My Fair Lady (1964) presented fewer problems for Jack L. Warner, the last of the movie-making brothers, who wanted to finish his career on a high note. With book and lyrics by Alan Jay Lerner and music by Frederick Loewe, this version of Bernard Shaw's *Pygmalion* had been the most acclaimed musical in Broadway history. Its New York run had survived many changes of cast and after eight years was drawing to a close only because its sponsors felt that Warners should start to get a return on the record-breaking $5½ million they paid for the rights — the film couldn't open until the show closed.

Moreover, the show had repeated its Broadway success in every country in which it had been staged – which did not include France, for the impresario who owned the rights hesitated until the film version was upon him. In New York, and subsequently in London, the play had been a triumph for its stars: Rex Harrison as the arrogant Professor Higgins, who teaches a cockney flower girl to speak properly and thereby transforms her into a "lady"; Julie Andrews as Eliza Doolittle and Stanley Holloway as her reprobate father.

Cary Grant was approached to play the Harrison role in the film,

but replied that not only would he not play it, but if Harrison wasn't cast, he wouldn't even go and see it. Warner offered the Holloway role to James Cagney, who refused it; Holloway was the only other possible choice. The beautiful and talented Audrey Hepburn replaced Julie Andrews, who had not then made a movie, and George Cukor, a master-director of civilized art and skilled handler of musical numbers, was asked to make the film. The Warners directive was to reproduce the stage hit.

My Fair Lady, though popular, could not recover its high costs at the box-office, but it might have done better if Julie Andrews had played Eliza, since she was about to become a major star thanks to Walt Disney, who made her the perfect all-purpose flying British nanny in Robert Stevenson's **Mary Poppins** (1964). This was the

Far left: *'Wouldn't It Be Luverly' sings Audrey Hepburn as the cockney guttersnipe Eliza Doolittle in George Cukor's* **My Fair Lady** *(1964) in the huge Covent Garden set. Actually, Marni Nixon dubbed Audrey's singing for her.*

Left: *Rex Harrison, as the arrogant Professor Higgins in* **My Fair Lady**, *subjects Eliza to the tortures of elocution.*

Below: *Barbra Streisand (right), making her Oscar-winning screen debut in* **Funny Girl** *(1968), tries to stay upright during the 'Roller Skate Rag'. Barbra forced audiences to reassess their preconceived notions of beauty.*

Above: *Julie Andrews (center, with hat), reached stardom as the singing governess to the Trapp children in the chocolate-box-office hit* **The Sound of Music** *(1965).*

Left: *Julie Andrews finally conquers the heart of Captain von Trapp (Christopher Plummer) and audiences almost everywhere in* **The Sound of Music** *helping the film to gross over $80 million.*

Below: *Ninety-nine helpless puppies, without their parents, cringe in terror as two evil kidnappers (or dognappers) search for them in* **One Hundred And One Dalmatians** *(1961).*

only important original screen musical of the decade, although because of its animated sequence and high whimsical content, it is more to be considered alongside Disney's cartoon features. Since each one of these was an event, and despite the fact that **One Hundred and One Dalmatians** (1961) had been one of the best and most popular, Disney refused to consider roadshowing **Mary Poppins** — which nevertheless proved the biggest financial success of any Disney production.

Disney knew a good thing when he saw it, and was so impressed with the rushes of **Mary Poppins** that he invited other producers to view them. Before the film was released and won Andrews the Best Actress Oscar, she had signed for several more. One of these was **The Sound of Music** (1965), a mixture of nuns, Nazis and children, which had earned a reputation for being too saccharine during its 1959 Broadway run. The Rodgers and Hammerstein songs were the chief attraction for Hollywood and Rodgers struck a deal with 20th Century-Fox. William Wyler accepted the assignment and then changed his mind and it was given to Robert Wise on the strength of his **West Side Story** success. The screenplay was assigned to Ernest Lehman, who likewise had shown little affinity with screen sentiment. Even so, the cast and crew worked throughout in an attempt to rob the piece of its inherent stickiness, but it must be said that they weren't entirely successful. It may be because of its obvious faults that **The Sound of Music**'s virtues are all the more apparent, however. By far the greatest of these is Julie Andrews, who imbued her songs, lines and character with as much charm, merriment and wit as they would allow.

It was soon equally clear that the public loved **The Sound of Music** as they had loved no other film since **Gone With the Wind** a quarter of a century earlier. Just as **Doctor Zhivago**'s grosses wiped out MGM's memories of **Mutiny on the Bounty**, so was Fox able to forget **Cleopatra**. Even France liked **The Sound of Music**. As it knocked box-office records sideways, the industry breathed again. All it had to do — and it couldn't be too difficult, could it? — was to find a few more hits like **The Sound of Music**.

The Europeans

Chapter 20

The blockbuster habit was one of several reasons why attitudes to movies polarized in the Sixties: the art-houses were now booming and the trickle of films on television soon became a flood. The term "movie buff" was coined (replacing "fan"), and as likely as not the movies and the stars that buffs cared about came from Hollywood's past and Europe's present — in both cases without benefit of overtures, intervals and Technicolor.

The sweet life

In 1960, three impressive films arrived from Italy: Luchino Visconti's **Rocco and His Brothers**, Federico Fellini's **La Dolce Vita** and Michelangelo Antonioni's **L'Avventura**. All three directors had been making films since the Forties, but only Fellini was well known in America — although that does not explain why **La Dolce Vita** became the first foreign-language movie to appear among the top ten US box-office hits (if admittedly dubbed in many bookings) and, at $8 million rentals, remained unsurpassed until **I Am Curious — Yellow** (1967), not seen in the USA until 1969 for censorship reasons. It was an attraction for the increasing number of Americans who had spent their vacations in Europe — and had found it decadent. That had always been the message imparted by the Continental cinema, but the tourist industry gave it new impetus; **La Dolce Vita** confirmed the American view that Europeans were jaded, likely to consort with prostitutes and given to spending their evenings at joyless orgies.

The outlook of the other two films were equally bleak and just as pungently expressed. All three confirmed to critics and buffs the elementary fact that what the cinema needed was not wide screens but film-makers of vision and intelligence.

In France this view had emerged in the Fifties as the *auteur* theory, in which the most esteemed directors were those whose individual tastes and interests were discernible in their work. Alfred Hitchcock, for example, was accorded *auteur* status because he made thrillers with recurrent themes. Many of the most admired Hollywood film-makers of the time were quick to point out, however, that American movies were made, in collaboration, for worldwide mass consumption.

Elsewhere, however, there was a consistent individual tone to the work of certain directors, particularly those who wrote or contributed to their screenplays and sometimes did their own editing — among them Antonioni, Visconti, Fellini, Sweden's Ingmar Bergman, India's Satyajit Ray and the Spaniard Luis Buñuel.

*Taking an unconventional shower in the Trevi fountain is tall, voluptuous Swede Anita Ekberg, placed in a key position in Federico Fellini's frieze of decadent modern Rome, **La Dolce Vita** (1960).*

French inspiration

Those French critics who had evolved the theory in their writings were meanwhile putting it into practice by making movies on low budgets – a group that would be known as the *nouvelle vague*, or New Wave. Their films were chiefly made on location and with new or little-known talent – but the waves that resulted were very big. Francois Truffaut with **The 400 Blows** (1959), Jean-Luc Godard with **Breathless** (1960), Claude Chabrol with **Les Cousins** (1959), Alain Resnais with **Hiroshima Mon Amour** (1959) and Louis Malle with **The Lovers** (1958) tackled the job of movie-making with a vitality not to be found in Hollywood, and with only a fraction of Hollywood's resources – which suggested to some Americans that they might do the same.

The barrier to independent film-making in the USA had been the refusal of theaters to book any such movies; the Hollywood-owned circuits ignored "runaway" productions, while independent exhibitors were disinclined to offend Hollywood, their main suppliers. But the pattern of exhibition was now changing since there were sufficient art-house theaters for an independently produced movie to return its costs from them alone, provided those costs were low enough.

The producer Lewis M. Allen was the driving-force behind **The Connection** (1961) and **The Balcony** (1963), made for an average of $166,000, the latter with an investment from Walter Reade, a distributor of foreign movies, and with the participation of a Hollywood name, Shelley Winters, who received a share of the

Left: Peter Falk (left), later 'Columbo', and Leonard Nimoy, later 'Mr. Spock', as very plain-clothed policemen in **The Balcony** (1963), based on Jean Genet's scurrilous play set in a brothel.

Above: Melina Mercouri, surrounded by friends and clients, used her mercurial temperament and ouzo-soaked voice to play one of the screen's first happy hookers in **Never on Sunday** (1960).

Above: *Anthony Quinn (illustrated with Eleni Anousaki as a city prostitute) was the 'life force' hero* **Zorba the Greek**, *a role that seemed written for his ebullient personality.*

Left: *In* **Zorba the Greek** *(1964), set in Crete, a widow (Irene Papas) begins an affair with a visiting Englishman, and is murdered by the savage villagers, who blame her for the suicide of a lovesick and unsuccessful young suitor.*

profits. Both films were based on stage plays of minority appeal: **The Connection** was about drug-addicts waiting for their "fix"; **The Balcony** concerned the activities in a Continental brothel while a revolution waged outside. They did not point the way forward for independent American cinema, but two other films, Frank Perry's **David and Lisa** (1962) and Larry Peerce's **One Potato, Two Potato** (1964), did. The first was a tale of a young couple (Janet Margolin, Keir Dullea) falling in love in a mental home, and the second examined the difficulties affecting a mixed marriage.

In the age of blockbusters, these two low-key, starless, black-and-white dramas appealed to large numbers of moviegoers. Hollywood simply did not make movies like this any more — nor like **Never on Sunday** (1960), directed in Greece for $150,000 by an expatriate American, Jules Dassin, who also played one of the two leading roles, that of a prudish tourist who learns a thing or two about life from a happy hooker (Melina Mercouri, later Dassin's wife). The Cypriot director Michael Cacoyannis also made a Greek film — **Zorba the Greek** (1964) — in English, which was so popular that it appealed to audiences beyond the art-houses, partly due to the presence of Anthony Quinn in the title-role. Adapted from a novel by Nikos Kazantzakis, it featured Alan Bates as a prissy Anglo-Saxon who learns that there is a Mediterranean way of doing things — joyfully and extrovertedly — from an unconventional tutor, Zorba. Quinn's presence encouraged 20th Century-Fox to invest in the film; but Hollywood's interest in Europe was also due in part to an Italian actress who had become an international star.

After only a moderate success in Hollywood, Sophia Loren had returned to her native Italy at the start of the Sixties. Her husband, Carlo Ponti, had turned himself into one of the new Hollywood tycoons — and one whose main interest was in promoting Loren's international career. To that end he decided that she should make an Italian-speaking movie under the direction of Vittorio De Sica, the first Italian film-maker to achieve international fame.

Two Women (1961) was not on the level of such earlier De Sica masterpieces as **The Bicycle Thieves** (1948) and **Umberto D** (1952), but it was a fine portrait of a woman managing to survive World War II. Loren received a Best Actress Oscar for her performance, perhaps because a dubbed version was widely seen in the US, but it was unprecedented for a non-American actress in a foreign-language film to receive that highest of prizes. Loren remained in Italy for two De Sica comedies co-starring Marcello Mastroianni, a ''name'' in the USA since he appeared in **La Dolce Vita**. In dubbed versions **Yesterday, Today and Tomorrow** (1964) and **Marriage – Italian Style** (1964) were well received in America, enabling Loren to return to Hollywood a much bigger star.

Below left: *Sylva Koscina manages to get her arms around muscleman Steve Reeves in* **Hercules Unchained** *(1960). The vogue for this type of film petered out in the mid-Sixties, to be replaced by the Spaghetti Western.*

Below: *After having been Mr America, Mr World and Mr Universe, it was natural that Steve Reeves (left) should flex his muscles in the title role of* **Hercules Unchained**, *one of a series of Italian-made torso-and-toga epics.*

379

The Italian way

Those three Loren movies were handled in the USA by a new, thrusting entrepreneur, Joseph E. Levine, who had made his reputation by buying the Stateside rights to a series of Italian epics starring an American muscle man, Steve Reeves, as the ancient Greek hero Hercules. **Hercules Unchained** (1960) was mediocre as spectacle or action-adventure, but Levine spent a million dollars to promote it — which paid dividends. Italian producers subsequently turned their attention to making more of these "sword-and-sandal" epics, and on the strength of their box-office success were able to lure such Hollywood names as Alan Ladd, Victor Mature, Guy Madison, Orson Welles, Lex Barker, Jeffrey Hunter, Debra Paget and Jeanne Crain to appear in them. But few of these stars were still greatly in demand out on the West Coast — and they were certainly not powerful enough to keep the series afloat when the paying public lost interest.

The Italian film industry had dreamed of beating Hollywood at its own game ever since the remarkable international success of the neorealist (and Communist) **The Bicycle Thieves** in 1948, although it was a film that the Italian government and moguls both loathed; now

Top: *The Bible (1966) contained some superb photography as in the scene from the 'Tower of Babel' episode illustrated.*

Above: *Richard Harris as Cain suffers the wrath of God or that of director John Huston in* **The Bible***, which tackled only the first 22 chapters of Genesis. Huston himself played Noah.*

Right: *Sophia Loren and Marlon Brando in a compromising situation on board an ocean liner in* **A Countess from Hong Kong** *(1967), the last film to be directed by Charles Chaplin. His ten-second appearance as a ship's steward was the best moment in the crude and unfunny comedy.*

Left: *Jane Fonda as the 40th-century astronaut **Barbarella** in the arms of angel John Phillip Law. Jane's then husband Roger Vadim managed to find various ways of getting his wife's clothes torn off during this 1968 comic-book extravaganza.*

Above: *Clint Eastwood made a name for himself as the taciturn 'Man with No Name' in Sergio Leone's first Spaghetti Western **A Fistful of Dollars** (1964), which took no less than $4.2 million in NA rentals.*

Left: *Louis Malle's second film **The Lovers** (1958) helped wreck sexual censorship the world over. The shots of an adulterous couple (Jeanne Moreau and Jean-Marc Bory) making love caused a sensation.*

they were conquering world markets with other movies which were very different. Some of the most popular came about as a result of Italian producers trying a few Westerns, shooting in Spain, where the scenery resembled the American West or Mexico. Second-rank stars such as Barker and Madison were easily persuaded to take lead roles. All these films were later named "Spaghetti Westerns".

The brighter producers realized that yesterday's movie stars were liable to be less attractive to audiences than current television heroes. Exported American Western series such as **Gunsmoke**, **Have Gun, Will Travel** and **Rawhide** were the rage throughout the Continent, and it was thought that Europeans would turn out to see their favorites in color and on the large screen.

From **Rawhide** came Clint Eastwood, who had not gone very far in Hollywood movies, but after playing the deadly, monosyllabic gunfighter, the Man With No Name, for director Sergio Leone in three violent Westerns — **A Fistful of Dollars** (1964), **For a Few Dollars More** (1965) and **The Good, the Bad and the Ugly** (1966) — he was able to return to Hollywood as a major box-office star, eventually overtaking the likes of John Wayne and Steve McQueen.

Jane's comic strip

Another star to emerge at this time was Jane Fonda. Not yet having discovered politics or the extent of her talent, she was at first molded by the French director Roger Vadim (then her husband) into a sex object, in such films as the sci-fi spoof **Barbarella** (1968), based on a popular French comic strip. This was one of the typical "international"

Above: *French sex symbol Brigitte Bardot, known to the world simply as BB, pretty and kittenish as an unlikely revolutionary in Central America for Louis Malle's* **Viva Maria!** *(1965).*
Left: *Bardot and Jeanne Moreau (right) combined to sparkling effect in* **Viva Maria!** *As both girls were called Maria, the title referred to the two of them.*

movies of the decade, a co-production in English between Italy and France, with some money from Paramount, in return for US distribution rights.

The producer of **Barbarella** was Dino De Laurentiis, who was very active in this field. Having enjoyed a mild success with **Barabbas** (1962), a biblical epic directed by Richard Fleischer with Anthony Quinn heading the cast, De Laurentiis announced that he was tackling the Bible itself, in a film to be made by a consortium of directors, each handling a portion of his own choice — among them Orson Welles, Ingmar Bergman, Federico Fellini, Robert Bresson and John Huston.

In the event Huston tackled the whole project with a cast including George C. Scott, Ava Gardner, Peter O'Toole, Richard Harris and Huston himself as Noah — the guiding craftsmanship and imagination were of such a high order that **The Bible ... in the Beginning** (1966) was not unworthy to stand with Huston's finest work.

One episode depicted the Old Testament story of the Tower of Babel, whose image might be said to symbolize such coproductions at their worst. For instance, in De Sica's **The Condemned of Altona** (1963), one German family consisted of the American Fredric March and Robert Wagner, the Italian Sophia Loren, the Austrian-born Swiss Maximilian Schell and the French Françoise Prévost, all speaking with their own native accents. Based on a play by Jean-Paul Sartre, the film was an almost total disaster, as was the

Above: *Julie Christie as the vain advertising model soars up the social ladder by using men such as TV interviewer Dirk Bogarde in John Schlesinger's cynical morality tale **Darling** (1965)...*
Right: *In **The Spy Who Came in from the Cold** (1965), British agent Leamas (Richard Burton), after a sentence in Wormwood Scrubs to embellish his track record as a drunken malcontent, is greeted by naive Communist librarian Liz (Claire Bloom), whom he also embroils in the plot — with fatal results.*

German director Bernhard Wicki's 1964 adaptation of Friedrich Dürrenmatt's **The Visit**, starring Ingrid Bergman and Anthony Quinn.

René Clément's **Is Paris Burning?** (1966), France's one attempt at an international blockbuster at this time, fared little better. An account of the Allies' recapture of Paris, it at least allowed its American actors, including Glenn Ford, Kirk Douglas and Anthony Perkins, to speak English, while the French players, including Leslie Caron, Simone Signoret and Jean-Paul Belmondo, were given the benefit of subtitles. Undeterred by the film's reception, Clément imported Charles Bronson for a thriller, **Rider on the Rain** (1969), but wiser French film-makers decided that the simplest way to succeed in the international market was to make intrinsically French films — such as Claude Lelouch's love story **A Man and a Woman** (1966), which became (until **La Cage aux Folles**, 1979) the highest-grossing French-language movie ever to play in American theaters.

Viva Maria! (1965) attracted immediate international attention because it teamed France's contrasting sex-symbols, Brigitte Bardot and the intellectual's favorite, Jeanne Moreau. United Artists supplied some of the budget and the leading man, George Hamilton, but Louis Malle's film with the two ladies scampering about Mexico during one or other of its revolutions, was a damp squib. Another New Wave director, François Truffaut, turned up in Britain because no French producer would finance his version of Ray Bradbury's **Fahrenheit 451** (1966), but despite the presence of Julie Christie in two roles, Universal did not get a hefty return on its investment.

The British bubble

Britain, in fact, was where the action was. American producers,

directors, writers and actors poured into the UK to help in the revival of the British film industry, which was being spearheaded by Woodfall, the company founded by director Tony Richardson and playwright John Osborne. The public endorsed two Woodfall productions, **Saturday Night and Sunday Morning** (1960) and **A Taste of Honey** (1961), the first of which brought the forceful young proletarian actor Albert Finney to the fore. Woodfall decided Finney was ideal for the title-role of **Tom Jones** (1963), based on Henry Fielding's bawdy eighteenth-century novel. This ambitious historical subject required a bigger budget than Woodfall was used to, but when none was forthcoming from British sources United Artists stepped in. **Tom Jones** opened in the USA to critical acclaim, played to capacity houses and went on to win Oscars for Best Film, Best Director (Richardson) and Best Screenplay (Osborne).

Those Oscars were the final shots in the Woodfall revolution. British cinema would never be the same again, although Hollywood was keen enough to back movies about the British working class, many of which were very bad. Two which were extremely good – made

Right: *Albert Finney (right) as* **Tom Jones** *with Diane Cilento (then the wife of Sean Connery) in one of the many amorous adventures rollickingly portrayed in Tony Richardson's 1963 Oscar-winning British triumph.*

Below: *Finney in one of the few quiet and chaste moments with Susannah York as Sophia Western, the girl he marries after his wild oats are sown.*

without American backing — were directed by John Schlesinger, **A Kind of Loving** (1962) and **Billy Liar** (1963), which respectively starred Alan Bates and Tom Courtenay.

The latter film also contained the first major appearance of a pretty, friendly blonde girl, Julie Christie, who proved to be ideal for Schlesinger's next film, **Darling . . .** (1965), the story of a London model scripted by Frederic Raphael. Dirk Bogarde was hired as her costar but not until a part was written in for Laurence Harvey — an English actor who had attracted some attention in America — was backing secured, partly because this exposé of the morals of London's fashion world was not quite what was expected of British movies at this time. In the event, Christie's performance as the promiscuous heroine won her the Best Actress Oscar, and Schlesinger had no difficulty finding backing for his next venture, **Far From the Madding Crowd** (1967), a version of Thomas Hardy's novel. Bates, Christie, Peter Finch and Terence Stamp were cast and MGM put up the money, but the film was not a great success in the USA.

Lynn and Vanessa Redgrave competed for Oscars for their roles in two of the better post-Woodfall films. Karel Reisz's **Morgan: a Suitable Case for Treatment** (1966), starring Vanessa as a society

Left: *Terence Stamp, resplendent in his scarlet sergeant's uniform, greets Julie Christie as Bathsheba in* **Far from the Madding Crowd** *(1967), John Schlesinger's picturesque illustration of the Thomas Hardy novel.*

Above: *Little Mary McGregor (Jane Carr) comes across her unconventional schoolteacher Jean Brodie (Maggie Smith) presumably giving art teacher Teddy Lloyd (Robert Stephens, Miss Smith's real-life husband) a kissing lesson in* **The Prime of Miss Jean Brodie** *(1969).*

wife, has dated badly, however. American audiences were just not interested in the character of her husband, crazy Morgan (David Warner). But they loved **Georgy Girl** (1966) – featuring Lynn as an ugly duckling who blossoms when she realizes that she's found attractive by both her elderly guardian (James Mason) and the cast-off lover (Alan Bates) of her bitchy flat-mate (Charlotte Rampling). The film's frank treatment of sex was one reason why it became a top-ten box-office hit in the US. Backed by Paramount, **Alfie** (1966), in which a cockney layabout (Michael Caine) uses a number of women before tossing them aside like Kleenex, echoed its box-office success.

Although Shelley Winters was brought over to Britain for **Alfie**, it wasn't intended for the international market in quite the same way as the two movies that made Michael Caine a star, **Zulu** (1963), a spectacular re-creation of the battle of Rorke's Drift filmed in South Africa with Stanley Baker and Jack Hawkins, and **The Ipcress File** (1965). The latter, a spy thriller, was set in London, but it was the kind of glossy entertainment that had previously been the domain of Hollywood. It typified a trend in the Sixties for location-shooting in Europe, the Americans taking full advantage of the skills available in the British industry in particular.

Also, the American film industry liked the new generation of British stars. Hollywood had always poached talent from wherever it could be found, and had assimilated many British stars and character

Right: *Sean Connery as British agent James Bond in* **Dr. No** *(1962) in the first of a string of car chases that were to become a staple ingredient of the seemingly endless series.*

Below: *32-year-old Sean Connery gained international stardom in* **Dr. No**, *the first of over a dozen James Bond pictures, the most durable of all long-running, money-spinning movie series. Twenty-one years later, Connery was again playing 007.*

actors through the years. What is more puzzling is why Hollywood liked British directors, few of whom carried much prestige. Clearly, Hollywood had first call on big names like Carol Reed, David Lean and later John Schlesinger, but many other Brits had long careers working for the Americans without managing more than a couple of box-office hits apiece. Columbia employed J. Lee Thompson to direct **The Guns of Navarone** (1961) and 20th Century-Fox gave **Those Magnificent Men in Their Flying Machines** (1965) to Ken Annakin, perhaps on the precedent of Michael Anderson directing **Around the World in 80 Days** (1956). Both movies owed their popularity to their powerful casts: Gregory Peck, David Niven, Anthony Quayle, Anthony Quinn and Stanley Baker in **Navarone**, a tale of saboteurs working in Greece during the German occupation; and Sarah Miles, Stuart Whitman, James Fox, Robert Morley among many more in **Those Magnificent Men**, a lavish — but unamusing — comedy about the 1910 London to Paris air race. Few critics would go to bat for Terence Young, who directed the first James Bond film, **Doctor No** (1962), which, unlike the two films just mentioned was not expected to do more than moderately well.

The greatest Bond

The 007 series, however, became the most successful in the history of the cinema. Bond, an urbane, well-dressed secret service man often pitted against other agents in exotic locales, and with a taste for fast cars and fast women, had been introduced by novelist Ian Fleming in 1952, but was not an immediate success. Each of the Bond books, though, did better than the one before, and they were enjoying respectable sales by the end of the decade. The decision to make a Bond movie was taken by producers Harry Saltzman, a Canadian who had provided Woodfall's finance, and Albert ("Cubby") Broccoli, an American who had been making mediocre action films in Britain for a few years. Young, best known for violent melodramas, was hired to direct.

Among the actors who turned down the role of Bond were Trevor Howard, Peter Finch and David Niven. It went to Sean Connery, who lacked the necessary suavity and polish but acquired these qualities as time went by. **Dr No**, a surprise hit, made major stars of him and Ursula Andress, and necessitated another 007 vehicle, **From Russia With Love** (1964) — and with that America joined Britain in Bond fever. **Goldfinger** (1964), **Thunderball** (1965) and **You Only Live Twice** (1967) were all box-office bonanzas, although Connery griped against the producers' greed and refused to do **On Her Majesty's Secret Service** (1969). He was replaced by George Lazenby, an Australian who was unknown then and has been ever since. Saltzman and Broccoli were soon petitioning Connery to return.

Saltzman had also produced **The Ipcress File**, whose secret service hero Harry Palmer was, as played by Michael Caine and more

*Below: **Help!** (1965) was an Eastmancolor package for the Beatles, full of visual tricks displayed by director Richard Lester, and crammed with some of their best numbers.*

Below: *'All You Need Is Love', one of the many Beatles' hits animated in* **Yellow Submarine** *(1968).*

Left: *Peter Sellers demonstrated his versatility in a triple role in* **Dr. Strangelove or How I Learned to Stop Worrying and Love the Bomb** *(1963) as an RAF officer, the US President and the mad nuclear scientist (illustrated) of the title.*

Below: **The Guns of Navarone** *(1961). Playing a team of saboteurs were (from left to right) Anthony Quinn, Gia Scala (as a traitor), Stanley Baker, Gregory Peck, David Niven and James Darren.*

realistically written by Len Deighton, the antithesis of Bond; two sequels, **Funeral in Berlin** (1966) and **Billion Dollar Brain** (1967), did respectably, but while Bond carried on Harry Palmer was quietly put out to grass.

In the pink

A further series began with **The Pink Panther** (1963), directed by Blake Edwards and starring Peter Sellers as Inspector Clouseau. This bumbling French police detective took the public fancy sufficiently for Edwards to incorporate the character in **A Shot in the Dark** (1964), which was an even bigger success. Neither Edwards nor Sellers had anything to do with **Inspector Clouseau** (1969), in which the role was played by Alan Arkin for director Bud Yorkin, but they gave the character a whirl in the Seventies when their careers weren't going too well, with profitable results.

Along with **Lawrence of Arabia** and Julie Andrews, Sellers — a comic with a gift for mimicry — was a factor in Hollywood's interest in Britain in the Sixties, but the biggest attractions were Woodfall, **Tom Jones**, James Bond and the Beatles. Although the Liverpool pop group appeared in only two fictional features, **A Hard Day's Night** (1964) and **Help!** (1965), both directed by the American Richard Lester, the first of these was a worldwide hit, which emphasized the growing appeal of movies for the young (as older audiences fell away) at this time.

Below left: *The age of Vladimir Nabokov's nymphet **Lolita** (1962) was raised, thus giving 16-year-old Sue Lyon the chance to make her screen debut opposite James Mason and Peter Sellers.*

Below right: *'How could they make a movie of **Lolita**?' asked the posters. Stanley Kubrick managed very well, and the takings were boosted by pictures like this one of Sue Lyon in the title role.*

Below: *James Mason as Nabokov's Humbert Humbert helps to satisfy his 'perverse passion' for young girls by painting the toenails of Sue Lyon as **Lolita**.*

396

Above: *The only British-born-and-bred musical to win the Best Picture Oscar was **Oliver!** (1968), Carol Reed's well-scrubbed version of the musical based on Dickens, starring Oliver Reed (foreground left, the director's nephew) as Bill Sikes, Shani Wallis (center) as Nancy and nine-year-old Mark Lester in the title role.*

Far left: *British stage actor Paul Scofield, in only his fourth film in 12 years, as Sir Thomas More, Chancellor of England, in **A Man for All Seasons** (1966). Orson Welles played Cardinal Wolsey.*

Left: *Paul Scofield (right) as Sir Thomas More, a man of conscience, confronts Robert Shaw's King Henry VIII in Fred Zinnemann's well-acted historical drama.*

Another American active in Britain was Stanley Donen, whose **Two for the Road** (1967) engagingly shunted Albert Finney and Audrey Hepburn around France as a couple falling in and out of love and marriage. Stanley Kubrick's film of Nabokov's novel **Lolita** (1962), starring James Mason as the middle-aged hero with a penchant for under-age girls, was made in Britain because its risqué subject matter might mean low box-office returns and costs therefore had to be kept down. Kubrick wasn't entirely successful in making the Home Counties look like the Midwest, but he stayed on for one of the decade's critical triumphs, **Dr Strangelove, or How I Learned to Stop Worrying and Love the Bomb** (1963), an anti-nuclear black comedy mostly set in America and featuring George C. Scott with Peter Sellers in three roles. When Fred Zinnemann left Hollywood to settle in Britain, he directed **A Man for All Seasons** (1966), based on Robert Bolt's historical play about the clash between Sir Thomas More (Paul Scofield) and Henry VIII (Robert Shaw). It won the Best Film Oscar, Zinnemann was voted Best Director and Scofield was Best Actor.

In 1968, Carol Reed's musical **Oliver!**, made in Britain, won the Best Film Oscar and Reed the Best Director. He was followed a year later by fellow-Londoner John Schlesinger, but for a film made in New York — **Midnight Cowboy**, also chosen as Best Film of its year.

American stars who worked in England in the Sixties included Judy Garland, making her final bow playing an American singer appearing at the London Palladium in Ronald Neame's **I Could Go On Singing** (1963); and Bahamian Sidney Poitier, who became a British West Indian teacher at an East End school in **To Sir, With Love** (1967). Charles Chaplin directed Marlon Brando — an unhappy collaboration — and Sophia Loren in **A Countess From Hong Kong** (1967), although the result was in inverse proportion to the publicity engendered. The Polish director Roman Polanski set the French actress Catherine Deneuve in South Kensington for the decade's most disturbing horror story, **Repulsion** (1965).

Franco Zeffirelli's **Romeo and Juliet** (1968) was shot in his native Italy but it was otherwise a British film with a British cast. Michelangelo Antonioni came to London, however, for **Blow-Up** (1967), another youth movie that found a warm reception wherever it was shown. Starring David Hemmings as a successful photographer discovering the emptiness of his "Swinging London" existence, **Blow-Up** — in its mixture of chic, disillusion, mystery and sexual experimentation — may be the quintessential movie of the Sixties; surprisingly, it is also one of the least dated.

Left: *The legendary Judy Garland making her final screen appearance in the hackneyed British musical* **I Could Go On Singing** *(1963), almost a parody of her own private and public life.*

Right: *A scene from Franco Zeffirelli's bustling, energetic, and colorful 1968 version of Shakespeare's* **Romeo and Juliet**.

Below: *Jane Birkin (right) and Gillian Hills (left) romp in the nude with 'Swinging London' photographer David Hemmings in Michelangelo Antonioni's trendy puzzler* **Blow-Up** *(1967).*

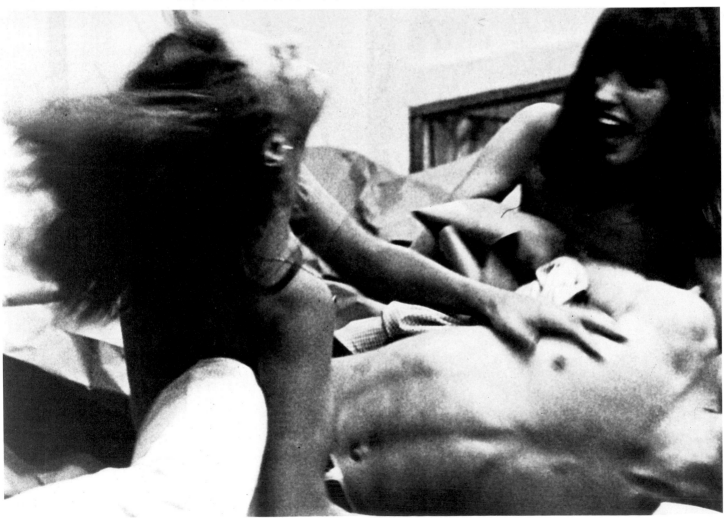

Pillow Talk

Chapter 21

Sex, from **La Dolce Vita** to **Blow-Up**, and not forgetting Brigitte Bardot, **The Lovers**, **Georgy Girl** and **Alfie**, was a European phenomenon – despite the inroads made by Hollywood into the greater American consciousness in the Fifties. Films were made of Broadway plays and bestselling novels, with their producers fighting every step of the way to preserve the sexual frankness that in many cases had been the reason for their popularity. The Motion Picture Association of America (MPAA), guardian of the movies' morals since the effective implementation of the Hays Code in 1934, was beginning to give ground, to the extent that, for the first time since then, it was clear that when a man chased a woman on the screen he was more interested in bedding than wedding her.

Bachelor boys

In comedy, it was the time of the swinging bachelor, invariably equipped with a luxurious pad replete with a vast bed and a stock of champagne in the icebox. Lovers and would-be lovers included Frank Sinatra, Dean Martin, Jack Lemmon, Tony Curtis and most notably Rock Hudson, whose pictures with Doris Day – **Pillow Talk** (1959), **Lover Come Back** (1961), **Send Me No Flowers** (1964) – were among the biggest hits of the era. She also costarred with Cary Grant (**That Touch of Mink**, 1962), James Garner (**The Thrill of It All** and **Move Over Darling**, both 1963) and Rod Taylor (**The Glass Bottom Boat**, 1966) and eventually became the butt of many a nightclub comic's joke for retaining her virginity through so many pictures. There was rough justice in this, despite her natural personality and comic skill, for the tone of these films is at best bland and at worst salacious – an anesthetized *Playboy* view of sex. Jane Fonda, Shirley MacLaine and Natalie Wood were among the girls tempted to toss away their virginity in movies: Peter Tewkesbury's **Sunday in New York** (1964), starring Fonda, is virtually the sole film of this time and type which doesn't leer or smirk.

Two serious films with a comic point of view were Blake Edwards' **Breakfast at Tiffany's** (1961), in which Audrey Hepburn is a kookie New Yorker available at the right price, and Arthur Hiller's **The Americanization of Emily** (1964), with Julie Andrews as a British girl wondering how best to please an American soldier (James Garner) in wartime. The best sex comedy of the period was Billy Wilder's **The Apartment** (1960), full of inspired comic lines and sadness. Both Jack Lemmon, as a junior executive hoping for advancement by loaning his superiors the key to his rooms, and

Right: *Rock Hudson and Doris Day in* **Send Me No Flowers** *(1964), the last of three fluffy comedies they made together. In the light of Hudson's death in 1985, the plot about a husband who believes he's dying, and determines to find his wife another mate, has lost some of its humor.*

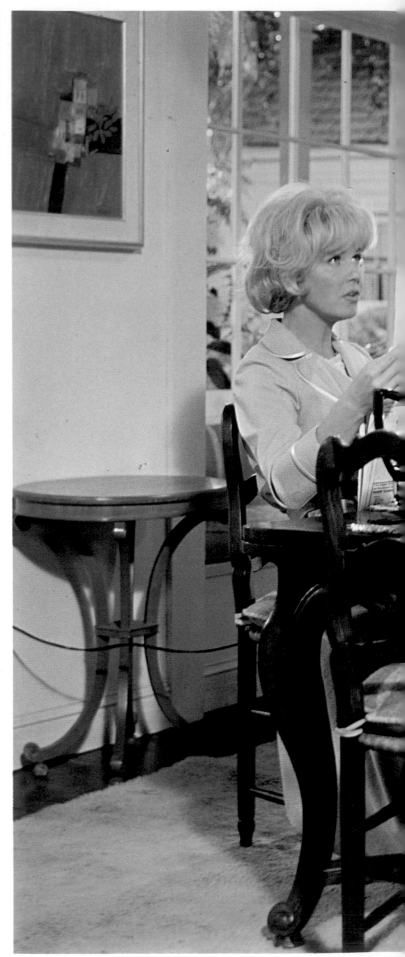

Shirley MacLaine, as one of the girls being taken there, surpassed themselves in this highly popular film, winner of the Best Film, Best Director and Best Original Screenplay Oscars.

For many years, Wilder and fellow Hollywood directors like William Wyler and George Stevens had been fighting against the restrictions of the MPAA — but none more so than Wilder, who used the triumph of **The Apartment** and 1959's **Some Like It Hot** to smooth the way for the filming of **Irma La Douce** (1963), a comedy about a Parisian hooker (MacLaine) and her policeman lover (Lemmon), whose baby she bears on the church steps just after they've married. The subject was sanctioned inasmuch as the original show had been a great success in Paris, London and New York. The public loved the film — ironically, for it is one of Wilder's poorest movies, while his next two, among his most brilliant work, were rejected.

Critics thought he had gone too far with **Kiss Me Stupid** (1964) and panned it; it shares with **The Fortune Cookie** (1966) a cynical view of American society which Lyndon B. Johnson's America found unpalatable. In the first, a small town amateur songwriter (Ray Walston) so wants to make it big that he is prepared to offer a hooker (Kim Novak), masquerading as his wife, to a visiting TV celebrity (Dean Martin) — only his real wife changes place with her. The second film is less overtly sexual, but concludes with a white man (Lemmon) and a black football player going off into the sunset together; they aren't necessarily in love, but the black guy has shown no interest in women, while Lemmon's wife is portrayed as viciously greedy.

Below: *Nebbish executive Jack Lemmon (left) drowns his sorrows in Billy Wilder's brilliant acid comedy* **The Apartment** *(1960) while waiting to get home. He lends his apartment to his superiors to entertain their lady friends. The film was the last black-and-white movie to win the Best Picture Oscar.*

Right: *Audrey Hepburn is carried away by George Peppard in* **Breakfast at Tiffany's** *(1961), a rather sugary version by Blake Edwards of the Truman Capote novella.*

Gays were beginning to be portrayed in movies, if only tentatively. Homosexuality in someone's past was the key to blackmail in two political dramas, **Advise and Consent** and **The Best Man** (1964), while lesbianism was an accusation thrown about in Wyler's **The Children's Hour** (1962), with Audrey Hepburn and Shirley Mac-Laine. (When Wyler had originally filmed Lillian Hellman's play, as **These Three** in 1936, a heterosexual premarital affair substituted for lesbianism.) The film's failure to find a public seemed to suggest that the public didn't wish to see "deviant" behavior on the screen — and it wasn't until **The Group** (1966) that an affair between two women was explicitly acknowledged. The film's director was Sidney Lumet, who also persuaded the MPAA to allow him to show a woman baring her breasts in **The Pawnbroker** (1965) — the first time such a sight had been seen in an American film since the ethnic **Tabu** in 1931. The cause on this occasion was serious, for the picture was a harsh and powerful study of the survivor of a Nazi concentration camp.

Above and right: *Rod Steiger in his favorite role as* **The Pawnbroker** *(1965) an ex-concentration camp victim now living in Spanish Harlem and tortured by his memories. It was shot on location in New York by Sidney Lumet.*

Left: *Anne Jackson and Walter Matthau in* **The Secret Life of an American Wife** *(1968), a sharp satire on surburban American mores. Jackson, primarily a stage actress, appears as a bored housewife seeking extramarital kicks with a movie star.*

Above: *The highest paid and most publicized couple in the movies, Elizabeth Taylor and Richard Burton, as the foul-mouthed and self-loathing George and Martha in the best of the ten films they made together,* **Who's Afraid Of Virginia Woolf?** *(1966).*

Far left: *The tragic and lovely Marilyn Monroe on the set of her last completed film,* **The Misfits** *(1961). A week before the opening, she divorced Arthur Miller, who wrote the script.*

Left: *Susannah York as one of the exhausted contestants of the Hollywood dance marathons held during the Depression evoked by Sydney Pollack in* **They Shoot Horses Don't They?** *(1969).*

In the meantime, Natalie Wood had starred in two films which dealt with premarital sex, as it affected high school kids in the Twenties in Elia Kazan's **Splendor in the Grass** (1961), and as a Macy's clerk who reluctantly plans an abortion until prevented at the last minute by her repentant lover (Steve McQueen) in Robert Mulligan's **Love With the Proper Stranger** (1963). Nor could there be any doubt that Clark Gable and Marilyn Monroe were playing lovers in the full sense of the word in John Huston's **The Misfits** (1961). Her last completed film, it was written by her then husband Arthur Miller, whose Broadway contemporaries, notably Tennessee Williams, had contributed to Hollywood's losing its prudishness during the Fifties. Williams' **Sweet Bird of Youth** (1962), directed by Richard Brooks, was not the equal of his earlier films like **A Streetcar Named Desire** (1951) and **Suddenly Last Summer** (1959), but its aging actress heroine (Geraldine Page) *is* allowed her gigolo (Paul Newman). Similarly, **Breakfast at Tiffany's** had a hero (George Peppard) being kept by an older woman (Patricia Neal).

Breaking taboos

Irving Wallace, who wrote the novel on which **The Chapman Report** (1962) was based, was no Tennessee Williams or Arthur Miller, but the film's director, George Cukor, was one of the Hollywood elite, and its producer, Darryl F. Zanuck, was determined to repeat the success of an earlier filmed bestseller, **Peyton Place** (1957), by retaining its raciness. The report in question concerned sexual behavior, and the film was able to deal with the rare topics of frigidity, nymphomania, adultery and gang-rape.

Another important Broadway dramatist, Edward Albee, provided four-letter-word-littered dialogue in **Who's Afraid of Virginia Woolf?** (1966), as a professor (Richard Burton) and his wife (Elizabeth Taylor) hurl abuse at each other throughout one long drunken night. Mike Nichols directed this watershed film, and he went on to make **The Graduate** (1967), in which a young man (Dustin Hoffman), returning from college, is seduced by a friend (Anne Bancroft) of his parents. **The Graduate** was not raunchy; but its frankness and dialogue would not have been permitted even a few years earlier.

Below: *After eight years of struggle to make a living out of acting, 30-year-old Dustin Hoffman (right) became a star overnight as 20-year-old Benjamin Braddock,* **The Graduate** *in Mike Nichols' 1967 film. Ben falls in love with the daughter (Katharine Ross) of the woman who seduced him, and pursues her to Berkeley with offers of marriage.* **Left:** *Middle-class college kids went for the story in a big way, the boys identifying with rebel Hoffman, who rescues Ross from a respectable marriage in the nick of time.*

As audiences everywhere reveled in this new freedom, it was clear that the MPAA restrictions had to be removed. The huge popularity of **Bonnie and Clyde** (1967) was another contributory factor to this, for Arthur Penn's clever gangster thriller, starring Warren Beatty and Faye Dunaway, contained more blood and violence than had been seen before in a major movie.

The point is that audiences were leaving their TV sets to see these films, as well as British equivalents like **Georgy Girl** and **Alfie**. They also gave a warm welcome to **Rachel, Rachel** (1968), directed by Paul Newman and starring his wife Joanne Woodward as a small-town teacher who has a last sexual fling before settling into spinsterhood; lesbianism was hinted at in this film, too.

The public meanwhile gave a more guarded reception to **The Killing of Sister George** (1968); based on a British play which had enjoyed a long run on Broadway, it was the story of a bossy radio soap-opera queen (Beryl Reid) who loses her girlfriend (Susannah York) to a predatory BBC executive (Coral Browne).

Left: *The Killing of Sister George* (1968) dealt with a lesbian relationship between Beryl Reid (left) as a bad-tempered soap-opera actress and Susannah York (right) as her child-like lover.

Right: Paul Newman's first film as director, *Rachel, Rachel* (1968) was the perfect vehicle for his wife Joanne Woodward, as a repressed Connecticut schoolteacher.

Below: Faye Dunaway and Warren Beatty as bank robbers *Bonnie and Clyde* (1967). Caught in an ambush, they barely escape with their lives — but they will be less lucky next time.

414

Two discreet films on male homosexuality failed to attract viewers, however. John Huston's **Reflections in a Golden Eye** (1967), based on the novel by Carson McCullers and set in the Deep South, and John Flynn's **The Sergeant** (1968), set in northern France and very different in tone, share the theme of an officer conceiving an almighty passion for an enlisted man. Marlon Brando played the man obsessed in Huston's film, where matters are complicated by the fact that he has a wife (Elizabeth Taylor).

By this time, the MPAA had scrapped its regulations. Much had happened to American film-making since that flurry of independent production in the early Sixties. The independents were supplying movies in English to both art-houses and the seedy exploitation theaters which had become starved of product since TV had forced the closure of Hollywood's Poverty Row studios; Westerns and other action films had been replaced by what often amounted to soft

Left: *23-year-old Jane Fonda, making her screen debut in **Tall Story** (1960), is shocked to find an unclothed Tom Laughlin, team mate of her basketball star husband Anthony Perkins (right), in their apartment. It was a far cry from Ms Fonda's later roles.*

Bottom left: *A dramatic moment from John Huston's **Reflections In A Golden Eye** (1967) as Elizabeth Taylor lashes at her husband Marlon Brando, who has been out trying to ride his wife's stallion to prove his virility. Brando's lack of horsemanship is linked to the character's closet homosexuality.*

Right: *Curvacious American sex-symbol of the 60s Raquel Welch used her anatomy to effect in the grunt 'n' groan prehistoric saga **One Million Years B.C.** (1966), wearing a Stone-Age designer bikini.*

pornography. In the Fifties, only a handful of maverick exhibitors were prepared to show movies denied the MPAA seal of approval, but such films had multiplied and were bringing customers back to the theaters.

The MPAA bravely announced that it was renouncing the Code because patrons were now sufficiently sophisticated to decide what they and their children could be permitted to see, but the truth was that sex had always sold tickets and was doing so more than ever when the cinema was in desperate need of support. Chancing their arms, the owners of exploitation houses offered hardcore pornography, and when they weren't prosecuted this became a staple diet — if for a while creating havoc in newspaper offices as discussions raged as to whether such films should be reviewed or advertised.

For Hollywood this was a bewildering time, but it eventually came up with three eminently respectable films with a strong sexual content. Larry Peerce's **Goodbye, Columbus** (1969), based on Philip Roth's novel, starred Richard Benjamin and Ali MacGraw as a young, unmarried Jewish couple who enjoy their lovemaking (and discuss contraception); Paul Mazursky's **Bob & Carol & Ted & Alice** (1969) had two couples abortively engaged in wife-swapping after

Top left: *Bette Davis (right) as a drunken ex-child star gets her kicks by slowly torturing her crippled sister Joan Crawford (left) in Robert Aldrich's* **What Ever Happened to Baby Jane?** *(1962). It was the only time the two former Warner Bros. stars appeared together.*

Left: *Clive Donner's now dated hit* **What's New, Pussycat?** *(1965) is notable as Woody Allen's debut as writer and performer. Peter O'Toole, as an English playboy and editor of a fashion magazine, is engaged to be married but is constantly distracted by leggy ladies such as aviatrix Ursula Andress.* **Above:** *Professional stripper Paula Prentiss and enthusiastic amateur O'Toole entertain at Paris's Crazy Horse Saloon in* **What's New, Pussycat?**

trying a little adultery on the side; and John Schlesinger's **Midnight Cowboy** (1969) starred Dustin Hoffman as a tubercular hustler and Jon Voight as a country boy who comes to New York to set himself up as a gigolo for Park Avenue ladies, but finds his only paying customers are gays.

All three films were enormously popular, as was Dennis Hopper's **Easy Rider** (1969), which followed two drugged-up hippies (Hopper and Peter Fonda) as they travel across the country, ostensibly to deliver drugs but in fact on a voyage of discovery. They have a psychedelic trip while making love to two girls (Karen Black and Toni

Left: *Tennessee Williams' plays were often adapted to the screen in the 60s, and John Huston's* **The Night Of The Iguana** *(1964) was an engrossing example. Among the cast were Richard Burton (left) and Sue Lyon (right).*

Right: *Richard Benjamin and Ali MacGraw take a shower in* **Goodbye, Columbus** *(1969), based on Philip Roth's stinging portrait of Jewish life in the Bronx in the 1950s.*

Below: ***Bob & Carol & Ted & Alice*** *(1969) was a comedy about surburban wife-swapping in which the two couples realize that love and fidelity are more important than sex. Here Elliott Gould and an air hostess plan adultery in the air.*

Above: *Paul Newman (right) as the cynical, irresponsible **Hud** (1963), billed as 'the man with the barbed wire soul!' Here he gets his teenage brother Brandon de Wilde drunk before returning to their declining cattle ranch.*

Left: *Jon Voight, a young hustler from Texas, the **Midnight Cowboy** (1969) of the title, thinks he has it made when he services the wealthy lady, Sylvia Miles, he meets on 5th Avenue.* **Top near left:** *Dustin Hoffman took on the character role of Ratso, the petty conman. With his greasy hair, pallid complexion, bad teeth and gammy leg, he merged perfectly into the seamy New York setting of the movie.*

Top far left: *In her decaying Hollywood mansion, Bette Davis as the demented ex-child star Jane Hudson tries to answer the question of the title, **What Ever Happened to Baby Jane?** (1962), by rehearsing her comeback act with the portly Victor Buono, making his film debut, at the piano.*

Basil) in a cemetery, encounter a mild-mannered lawyer (Jack Nicholson) who finds their lifestyle irresistible, and discover that the *real* America belongs to rednecks only too eager to cut down anyone not conforming to *their* way of life.

Hopper, who directed with feeling, and Fonda were known to have adopted a hippie existence offscreen. Public curiosity about that lifestyle, together with the innate romanticism of the film, may have been why it was so popular.

It was easy to understand why a whole generation of young Americans had revolted against their parents' values. Despite the Vietnam War and the assassinations of John Kennedy, Bobby Kennedy and Martin Luther King, institutional America was well content with itself. Yet the young did not care for its materialism, for the bland, dishonest pap always available on the home screen, and above all for US involvement in Vietnam. In New York, the rallying cry came from a rock musical, *Hair*; **Easy Rider** too spoke to hippies everywhere.

Hair owed much of its notoriety to the fact that it climaxed with naked girls and boys dancing on the stage. The sex scenes in **Easy Rider** were not so explicit, nor even erotic, involving casual couplings with glamorized hookers rather than the grand romances of Bogart and Bergman, Garbo and Taylor, or Gable and Crawford, the staple diet of the Thirties and Forties. Hollywood was very uncertain about its new license to show overt sexual acts.

As the industry studied the film's relatively huge receipts (ultimate domestic rentals alone of over $19 million on a derisory outlay of $400,000, a percentage profit virtually unheard of in Hollywood history), the future seemed clear ... and simple. **Easy Rider** was no great work of art; neither was Hopper a Wyler or a Cukor. Surely it would not be difficult to make better films to pull in even bigger profits. But, in fact, apart from its pleasing if comparatively anodyne stepchild **American Graffiti** (1973) — which actually took almost three times as much at the box-office — **Easy Rider** remained a tantalizing one-off. The other imitations were abysmal flops and artistic disasters.

The Secret of Success

Chapter 22

While Hollywood wondered how best to keep its audiences, Walt Disney's studio had no such problems. Disney turned out a series of live-action family comedies which one after the other rang box-office bells – from **The Absent-Minded Professor** (1961) to **The Love Bug** (1969), the adventures of an independent-minded Volkswagen. By the end of the decade, however, a Disney movie was no longer guaranteed to be a hit. Family audiences had disappeared.

Shock waves

The greatest shock waves followed in the wake of **The Sound of Music**. Two family movies, **Dr Dolittle** (1967) and **Chitty Chitty Bang Bang** (1968), promptly failed. Julie Andrews had a big success with a frothy musical set in the Twenties, **Thoroughly Modern Millie** (1967), but audiences quickly fell away for both **Star!** (1968), in which she played the temperamental stage actress Gertrude Lawrence, and **Darling Lili** (1969), a World War I spy spoof, costarring Rock Hudson. In both instances the quality of the material was in doubt, and **Darling Lili** in particular was a long, lumbering yawn as directed by Blake Edwards.

As the leading lady of musicals, Andrews had a new challenger in Barbra Streisand, who scored a big hit when she re-created her Broadway role of comedienne Fanny Brice in **Funny Girl** (1968), directed by William Wyler. But her next film, **Hello Dolly!**, another adaptation from Broadway, failed to recoup its very high budget.

British singer Petula Clark, whose records were hot sellers throughout Europe, played opposite Peter O'Toole in a musical version of **Goodbye Mr Chips** (1969), and starred with Fred Astaire and Tommy Steele in **Finian's Rainbow** (1968); the first did badly after undeservedly poor notices, but the second did only average business after very good ones.

Clark's popularity in Europe was expected to compensate for the Continent's indifference to musicals, and on that principle Jean Seberg was cast in **Paint Your Wagon** (1969), which, like **My Fair Lady**, was based on an old Lerner-Loewe Broadway show. Seberg was an American actress who had found fame in such French movies as **Breathless**, and was therefore expected to guarantee the success of the film in Europe. Starring with her were two box-office giants, Clint Eastwood and Lee Marvin, but **Paint Your Wagon** still took less than $15 million in US rentals – though in Britain Marvin had a Number 1 hit single with "Wandering Star" (ironically, since it was put together syllable by syllable from Marvin's

Right: *Audiences were pleased to say* **Goodbye Mr Chips** *(1969), after 147 minutes of this big budget musical weepie. Peter O'Toole and Petula Clark (among the boatered boys) could in no way replace Robert Donat and Greer Garson of the 1939 version.*

innumerable attempts at singing it for the soundtrack). This was, indeed, an era when musicals were likely to include stars who could neither sing nor dance — Vanessa Redgrave, for example, in another film of a Lerner-Loewe Broadway musical, **Camelot** (1967), which did only moderately well ($14 million). But the biggest flop of all, **Sweet Charity** (1969), starred a popular and very talented singer-dancer, Shirley MacLaine, and ironically received sparkling notices! The public was right, however — the last half-hour of **Sweet Charity** is a real downer, likely to send even the greatest optimist out into the street depressed.

The failure or half-failure of this batch of musicals may be attributable to a dozen different reasons, from the dreary scores of **Dr Dolittle** and **Goodbye Mr Chips** to the fact that the public didn't care to see Julie Andrews playing a vamp. Perhaps the main reason was that they generally lacked the élan and high spirits of Hollywood's musicals of the Thirties and Forties. Also, the musical was a form that had become dangerously expensive — so that if a musical couldn't succeed in roadshow engagements, it couldn't succeed at all. During the Seventies, Hollywood ventured to make only a handful of musicals, none of which revived the genre.

Perhaps the last successful non-musical roadshow was **Hawaii** (1966), again with Julie Andrews; but no one considered showing the sequel, **The Hawaiians** (1970), in this way. **The Sand Pebbles** (1966) was quickly withdrawn from roadshow release, despite the

Top Left: *Camelot* had plenty of spectacular scenes on the Technicolor and Panavision screen, such as the chivalric one illustrated, but it was a costly flop. However, John Truscott's costumes made from coarse linen and raw silk won an Oscar.

Bottom left: Lancelot (Franco Nero, in armor), King Arthur (Richard Harris, kneeling right) and his wife Guinevere (Vanessa Redgrave, right) in Joshua Logan's $15 million *Camelot* (1967), Lerner and Loewe's musical version of the classic Round Table love triangle.

Right: 'If They Could See Me Now' sings dynamic taxi dancer Shirley MacLaine in former dancer and choreographer Bob Fosse's first film *Sweet Charity* (1969), a rather strident and gaudy version of the hit Broadway musical.

Below: Sammy Davis Jr (center), in a guest spot in *Sweet Charity*, belts out a pseudo-religious rock song entitled 'Rhythm of Life'.

presence of Steve McQueen. It did not do nearly as well ($13.5 million) as the record-breaking actioner **The Dirty Dozen** (1967), with Lee Marvin ($20.3 million). The trouble was that the public expected something special from a blockbuster and when they didn't get it they were inclined to tell their friends not to go and see it, or so the industry thought.

Vision of things to come

MGM did roadshow **2001: A Space Odyssey** (1968) in some engagements, sometimes utilizing those theaters that had been used for Cinerama. The special effects of this sci-fi epic had cost a small fortune, and had been undertaken only because the director, Stanley Kubrick, had an impressive record with critics and young audiences. The former did not much care for **2001**, but the latter did and **2001** was in the long run a huge moneymaker, as to a lesser extent was **Planet of the Apes** (1968). With the exception of Disney's **20,000 Leagues Under the Sea** (1954), these were the first occasions on which Hollywood had allocated large budgets to science-fiction movies, traditionally a cheap genre, although it was not until the Seventies that the sci-fi explosion began.

Still, it was obvious that audience loyalties were shifting. Westerns began to die out − despite the lesser or greater popularity of some memorable ones: **The Magnificent Seven** (1960), with Yul Brynner

Left: *Lee Marvin and Charles Bronson (foreground on floor), two of* **The Dirty Dozen** *(1967), lose their trousers in a tense moment from Robert Aldrich's violent and rugged wartime adventure that spawned dozens of imitations.*

Right: *The grand-daddy of space operas: Stanley Kubrick's* **2001: A Space Odyssey** *(1968) set new standards in special effects.*

Below left: *Set during the California Gold Rush,* **Paint Your Wagon** *(1969) starred Clint Eastwood and Lee Marvin as two prospectors who set up a Mormon menage with the same wife (Jean Seberg).*

Below: *Non-singers Eastwood (left) and Marvin (right) each got to sing in the sluggish musical* **Paint Your Wagon**. *Eastwood warbled 'I Talk To The Trees', and Marvin scored a hit by croaking 'Wandrin' Star'.*

427

Ryan, Edmond O'Brien and Ernest Borgnine, the reviews were fair to good, and much publicity accrued from accusations of excessive violence, but the public still mostly stayed away.

Safety first

Comedies and thrillers were safer box-office bets than Westerns — provided the jokes and the thrills were there. Two versions of Neil Simon's Broadway comedy plays did well — **Barefoot in the Park** (1967), with Redford and Jane Fonda ($9 million); and **The Odd Couple** (1968), with Jack Lemmon and Walter Matthau ($20 million): and two cleverly plotted thrillers, **The Thomas Crown Affair** (1968) and **Bullitt** (1968), scored a double for Steve McQueen. The screen's pre-eminent exponent of the thriller, Alfred Hitchcock, had wowed audiences with **Psycho** (1960) and, to a lesser extent, **The Birds** (1963). But **Torn Curtain** (1966), a Cold War suspenser starring Paul Newman and Julie Andrews, and **Topaz** (1969) perhaps showed him

Above: *Audrey Hepburn made a leap from gamine to cosmopolitan sophisticate in Stanley Donen's flashy Hitchcockian thriller **Charade** (1963) opposite suave Cary Grant. It was their only film together, though Grant was offered Professor Higgins in **My Fair Lady** (1964).*

Right: *In between playing Mr Tough Guy in Don Siegel's **Coogan's Bluff** (1968), Clint Eastwood becomes tender with New York social worker Susan Clark, while remaining impassive and laconic.*

430

432

at his least effective.

Failures by other leading directors towards the end of the decade included Elia Kazan with **The Arrangement** (1969), Joseph L. Mankiewicz with **There Was a Crooked Man . . .** (1970), George Stevens with **The Only Game in Town** (1970) and William Wyler with **The Liberation of L.B. Jones** (1970). Between them they had provided the American cinema with some of its greatest films; now they all walked away from it.

The stars of the Stevens film were Warren Beatty and Elizabeth Taylor, supposedly hot properties although Taylor, still drawing a large salary, was embarking on a long run of flops, as was her husband Richard Burton. In fact, one of the reasons for the huge losses sustained by the Hollywood studios in 1969-70 was due to the

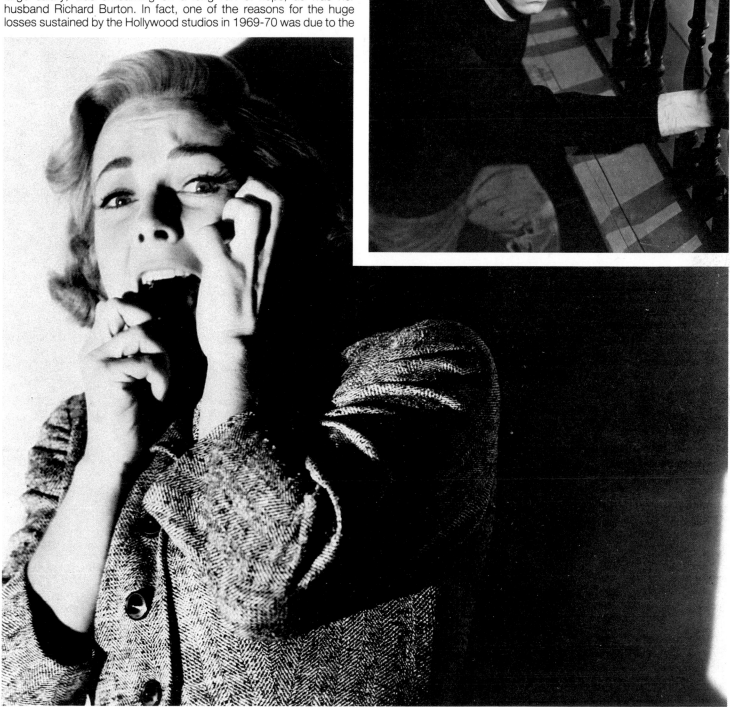

Left: *Rod Taylor, already pretty pecked, faces another of his feathered enemies in Alfred Hitchcock's ornithophobic* **The Birds** *(1963), a superb transformation of the mundane into the nightmarish.*

Above: *After Janet Leigh is disposed of in a celebrated, bloody manner in the shower in Alfred Hitchcock's first real horror movie*

*Psycho (1960), another 'cool blonde' Vera Miles (illustrated) appears to search for her missing sister. The same film starred Anthony Perkins **(top)** in his memorable role as the maniac motel keeper Norman Bates. Just as Norman identified with this dead mother, so Perkins has always been identified with the character he created.*

433

colossal fees they were paying performers who were no longer box-office draws.

There were 13 names in the box-office top-ten lists of 1960 and 1961, and only John Wayne and Jack Lemmon survived to the top tens of 1969 and 1970. Of the others, Cary Grant had retired; Doris Day had gone into television after some movie failures; Sandra Dee had disappeared after some flops; audiences were no longer interested in Rock Hudson, Frank Sinatra, William Holden or Elvis Presley; Debbie Reynolds was to make no more films; and Jerry Lewis and Elizabeth Taylor were both box-office liabilities. Apart from Wayne and Lemmon, the names in the 1969 and 1970 top tens are Paul Newman, Dustin Hoffman, Steve McQueen, Clint Eastwood,

Lee Marvin, Sidney Poitier, Elliott Gould, Barbra Streisand, Katharine Hepburn and Walter Matthau. A couple of years later, only half of these would still be box-office attractions. In other words, for the first time in Hollywood's history stars no longer guaranteed success.

These years saw some surprising box-office hits. They included Roman Polanski's **Rosemary's Baby** (1968), a thriller involving

Left and above: *Julie Andrews trying bravely to be convincing as Gertrude Lawrence in* **Star!** *(1968), an old-hat biopic that cost $12 million. After its failure on first release, it was re-released under the title* **Those Were the Happy Days**. *It flopped again.*

Above: *Freshly divorced from Frank Sinatra, Mia Farrow scored her first major screen success with* **Rosemary's Baby** *(1968), a lurid adaptation of Ira Levin's novel about Satanic practices in New York.*

Left: *Jane Fonda in the title role of* **Cat Ballou** *(1965), a school marm in the Wild West who hires a gunfighter to get the man who shot her father. In the same year, Fonda married French director Roger Vadim, who tried to make her into another Bardot.*

and **Woodstock** (1970), a documentary record of the huge rock festival in upstate New York which signified the apogee of hippiedom.

The flops were many and varied, and there is little point in listing them, since some failed so completely that they have no revival value — even on late-night television. The great Hollywood studios had begun to change hands during the Sixties, being either swallowed up by conglomerates or absorbed by new, ambitious companies with show-business interests. After some doubts, they retained their famous old names, so that in the 1969-70 period we can see Paramount announcing a loss of $22 million, MGM $35 million, United Artists $50 million, Warner Bros. $59 million and 20th Century-Fox over $100 million. Columbia waited a couple of years before noting a write-off of $82 million (along with Universal, it was the only studio not to acquire new owners — and, indeed, Universal was very well managed by MCA).

Above: *Oversized leprechaun Tommy Steele and Irish immigrant Petula Clark in **Finian's Rainbow** (1968), set in a mythical Mississippi. This indigestible musical blend of blarney and social comment was the second movie directed by Francis Ford Coppola, a far cry from his **Godfather** pictures.*

Right: *Lee Marvin (right) and Burt Lancaster (left) as two mercenaries hired by a millionaire to bring back his wife Claudia Cardinale, kidnapped by a Mexican bandit in **The Professionals** (1966), Richard Brooks' ochre-colored Western.*

The industry reeled, not knowing where to turn. The public could not be relied upon for clues. Variously during the Sixties it wanted nuns, kids and songs; pornography; old-fashioned Disney fun; James Bond; hippies on a drug trip; blood and jokes in an operating theater; Shakespeare; spaceships hurtling through the universe; devils; and parents debating whether their daughter should marry a black man. The public had never signaled in the past that it wanted to see such films, and if the studios now offered anything similar they were just as likely to be greeted by empty theaters, as occurred with the countless attempts to recapture the audiences of **Easy Rider**. Formula movies seemed as moribund as the studio system and the star system, except that in 1970 Universal presented **Airport**, a portmanteau

Right and below: *The popular tandem of Paul Newman (right in main picture) and Robert Redford as* **Butch Cassidy and the Sundance Kid** *(1969), legendary outlaws who finished their days in the dusty towns of Bolivia.*

442

446

Top left: *Nice locations, shame about the plot. Elvis Presley in his salad days in* **Blue Hawaii** *(1961).*

Bottom left: *Not one of The Duke's greatest roles, but John Wayne won a sentimental Oscar for his role as the boozing, one-eyed marshal in* **True Grit** *(1969).*

Below: *Steve McQueen in one of his most memorable roles as the rebel POW in* **The Great Escape** *(1963). McQueen pulled off all his motorcycle stunts himself.*

Back to the future?

Pleasing the audience in 1968 was another revival of **Gone With the Wind**. The decade of blockbusters produced a desperate search for another almighty hit — unexpectedly found in **The Sound of Music**. That proved a false dawn, certifiably a throwback when the "family" entertainments that followed it all flopped. Cinemas continued to close, so that censorship was relaxed in an attempt to persuade people to emerge from their homes to see the sort of product not shown on the television screen, but that was no long-term solution. From 1969 to 1970 Hollywood was fighting for its survival.

Which is where we came in, except that in 1960 the film industry refused to see how desperate the struggle would be. Yet the battle for survival was won — excepting one casualty of the Fifties, RKO, all the major studios still existed (and still do). Furthermore the decade had produced a wide range of enduring movies — from **The Misfits** to **Coogan's Bluff** (1968), from **The Magnificent Seven** to **Midnight Cowboy**, from **The Hustler** (1961) to **True Grit**, from **The Apartment** to **Easy Rider**. Come to think of it, there aren't many films of the Seventies or Eighties that you'd swop for these, or **2001: A Space Odyssey**, **Psycho**, **How to Succeed in Business Without Really Trying** (1967), **The Deadly Affair** (1967), **Cat Ballou** (1965), **Charade** (1963), **Dr Strangelove**, **The Hill** (1965), **One, Two, Three** (1961). And there's hardly a blockbuster among them.

Clint Eastwood as a deputy sheriff from Arizona in New York in **Coogan's Bluff** *(1968) 'interviews' a suspect in his own subtle way. The film was Eastwood's first collaboration with director Don Siegel with whom he made four others, including* **Dirty Harry** *(1971).*

David Castell

Hollywood 1970s

Clint Eastwood

Tombstone California

Chapter 23

In the late Fifties the prescient wise men of the motion picture business realized that Hollywood, as both the spiritual capital of the movies and the geographical hub of the industry, was entering its twilight years.

Ben Hecht's 1957 prophecy that, before the end of the century, Hollywood would be "just another tourist spot like Tombstone, Arizona," is already well on the way to being fulfilled: I made my first and only visit there in 1985 when, of sixteen interviews that had been arranged, only one took place in a working studio (and that with an actor-producer preparing a project that has still to come to fruition). Everyone else was working from home, from independent production offices or on location.

At Universal the tourists are not only catered for but actively wooed. Their celebrated studio tour (which earns enough each year by way of admissions to finance two modest feature films) is a glum monument to a vanished age. Not that it isn't modest fun when Bruce, the killer shark from Steven Spielberg's **Jaws** (1975) lurches out of a lake at the tourists. But the film itself was very properly shot at sea, and the stranding even of a mechanical relic in a studio tank has undertones of zoological indignity.

Mementos of studio-made pictures are few, for the age that many insist on calling golden slips deeper and deeper into the past. The Victorian-Gothic mansion from which Anthony Perkins once looked down at the Bates motel in Alfred Hitchcock's **Psycho** (1960) stands gaunt against the Californian haze, but so much of the mystique of film-making is now deliberately exploded by behind-the-scenes documentaries that nobody is much surprised when the relentlessly cheerful tour guide exposes the trickery.

"You see, this building is just a facade," she explains, adding thoughtfully that, "facade is a French word meaning false front." And Hollywood, of course, built its reputation on being the American word for false front. The dream factories of Warners and Columbia, Paramount and Universal, MGM, 20th Century-Fox and others now forgotten by all but devotees of late-night movies peddled their wares for decades with only internal hiccups to disturb them. But the advent of television and its bushfire spread through the consumer world in the Fifties was to be a delayed trauma for the motion picture industry.

Producer David O. Selznick summed up the size of the threat to the film-making Establishment while he was supervising the location filming of his ill-fated **A Farewell to Arms** (1957). "Hollywood is like Egypt, full of crumbling pyramids," he said. "It will never come back; it will just keep crumbling until the wind blows the last studio props across the sand."

Right: *Jack Nicholson gave an eye-catching performance in Bob Rafelson's* **Five Easy Pieces** *(1970) as a middle-class drifter who cuts loose from family ties, finding more vitality in working-class company while still retaining his snobbish sense of superiority.*

Selznick's wind of change was then already groaning in the rigging and stirring the sails of Hollywood, but the studios resolutely declined to change course. They had control of the way a film looked, by dint of the four-wall imprisonment within their sound stages; they had control of the way it sounded, by dint of a voluntary pre-censorship that, even in the mid-Sixties, was offering under the guise of risqué sex comedies countless variations on the theme of the middle-aged virgin pursued by playful middle-aged bachelors who packed a wedding ring as surely as the Ringo Kid carried a rifle.

So the major companies simply marked time, doing what they had always done, but doing it more expensively and with less commercial success. Financial contraction meant that they made economies, often in the areas in which expenditure was most prudent (script development, the training of the young actors and actresses who had been put under contract for their looks rather than any natural acting abilities). A side-effect of this last measure was that, while contract artists of the Fifties such as Rock Hudson and Robert Wagner went on to become household names and box-office champions, new projects had to rely on the interest of one of no more than a dozen top stars on whose name and track record finance could be raised. Many a script, like that of **Butch Cassidy and the Sundance Kid** (1969), arrived at its final destination dog-eared and marked with the fingerprints of other major stars who had turned it down.

Bottom left: *Mike Nichols' **Carnal Knowledge** (1971), scripted by Jules Feiffer, broke sexual taboos in the frankness with which it tackled its study of two college room-mates and the changes in their sexual attitudes. The action spanned their schooldays in the late Forties up to middle-age in the early Seventies. Jack Nicholson was the lawyer who has a stormy relationship with his mistress (Ann-Margret); Art Garfunkel and Candice Bergen played the couple who opt for marriage.*

Below: *People wept while standing in line to see **Love Story** (1970), Arthur Hiller's maudlin tale (taken from Erich Segal's tearful best-seller) of a dislikable preppie (Ryan O'Neal) who marries the lower-class fellow student (Ali MacGraw) who is dying of cancer. The weepie of the decade; astonishingly popular worldwide.*

453

something that television could not, it had to resort to extremes of violence, language and sexual behavior. And, as the studios slipped from the control of film-sated tycoons and into the hands of conglomerates and multinationals, that polarization extended to finance as well as content.

Those who wanted a nice little profit from a safe little movie found that the film world had progressed without them. The gap between success and failure was a yawning chasm into which many took a fatal tumble, and a Las Vegas gaming table mentality swept the cinema. Stars were paid bigger and bigger salaries (Marlon Brando earned a sum in excess of $4 million plus 11.3 percent of the profits of **Superman the Movie** (1978) in exchange for just twelve days' work) to lure larger and larger audiences. It wasn't so much that fewer people were going to the cinema: the same people were going, but less frequently. If yours was one of the dozen or so pictures a year that captured the international imagination you could make a substantial killing, but only one film in eight made a profit.

Above: Bruce Lee, superstar of the Hong Kong-based kung-fu movies (nicknamed "chop socky" by Variety) starred in Hollywood's first venture into the genre, **Enter the Dragon** (1973), in which a martial arts master helps British Intelligence corner opium smugglers. Lee died in 1973, the year of the film's release.

Far right: Most grueling of the "buddy" movies was **Papillon** (1973), the unrelenting film that Franklin J. Schaffner made from Henri Charrière's account of life in and escape from the penal colony on Devil's Island. Steve McQueen was the French safecracker imprisoned there; Dustin Hoffman played the fellow-convict with whom he forms a bond.

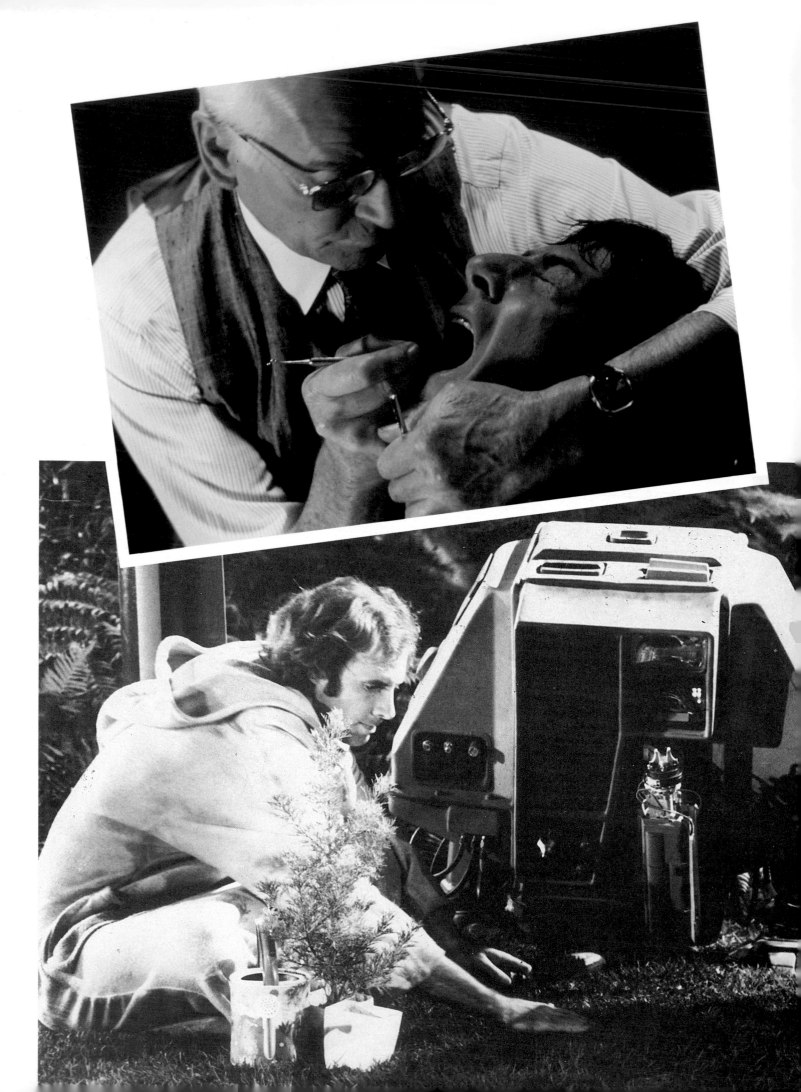

Left: *Dustin Hoffman starred in John Schlesinger's taut thriller* **Marathon Man** *(1976) as a Jewish student who stumbles into Nazis in modern New York. Laurence Olivier was memorable as their leader, a polite sadist whose way of extracting information is to tour his victim's mouth with a dentist's drill.*

Bottom left: *Douglas Trumbull's* **Silent Running** *(1972) was an unsung science fiction movie set aboard a huge space freighter on a long-term mission. The little droids prefigure R2-D2 and C-3PO of the* **Star Wars** *cycle. They are actually planting trees in this ecological tract, but they might as well be sowing the seeds for Spielberg's* **Close Encounters of the Third Kind** *(1977), for which movie Trumbull was later to design the effects. Bruce Dern was the lonely pioneer who preferred plants to people.*

Right: *Robert Redford and Jane Fonda were tellingly cast in Sydney Pollack's* **The Electric Horseman** *(1979), he as a former rodeo champion now reduced to advertising breakfast cereals, she as a reporter who follows his trail when he steals a champion horse and heads for the wide open spaces.*

The state-of-the-art special effects that marked Stanley Kubrick's **2001: A Space Odyssey** (1968) — along with those in Douglas Trumbull's comparatively unsung **Silent Running** (1972) — set the standards for the decade, while the "Star Wars" cycle and Spielberg's **Close Encounters of the Third Kind** (1977) brought into the live-action cinema the kind of magic for which audiences had hitherto looked to the Disney animators. It was the vogue for fantasy and science-fiction features that restored the studios themselves to favor, for the swing to location filming in the early Seventies had resulted not only in significant financial savings but in a fresh realism that audiences clearly found appealing.

459

Formula for success

As the risks and potential rewards for film-makers became greater, there was a marked reluctance to abandon successful formulas. Whereas series had always been popular with audiences – from "Lassie" to the Andy Hardy pictures – the sequel or continuation was now doubly attractive to the backers.

Not only could the same audience probably be induced back into the cinema once more, but there were also budgetary advantages. Alexander and Ilya Salkind, wizards of international financing who prospered in the Seventies, went to Spain to make **The Three Musketeers** (1973) and came back with enough footage to justify two features. Up to that point the choice would have seemed to have been between two options: edit the film right back and leave some of the most expensive scenes on the cutting-room floor, or release it in a three-hour-plus version that might have audiences wriggling in their seats and which would in any event dent the movie's earning power since fewer performances a day means less revenue. The Salkinds hit on a new solution. With only a few irate agents to face, they edited

Above: *Nostalgia for the heyday of the Hollywood musical was catered to by an admirable compilation,* **That's Entertainment** *(1974), which included highlights from MGM movies from the previous half-century.*

Top left: *Sidney Lumet's* **Network** *(1976), a sharp-toothed satire of network television and the ratings war (Paddy Chayefsky wrote the screenplay) won Oscars both for Faye Dunaway as the power-hungry executive and for Peter Finch (who died before he could receive the award) as the paranoid presenter whose mental breakdown was presented nightly as segments of prime-time entertainment.*

Bottom far left: *Constance (Raquel Welch), a respectable bourgeois wife, is not entirely constant by nature and has to hide her Musketeer lover when the Cardinal's Men pay an early-morning call in* **The Three Musketeers** *(1973), Richard Lester's send-up of the Dumas novel and, so he claims, "the best Panamanian film ever made," since the production company was registered for convenience under the flag of Panama.*

Below: *Richard Attenborough's* **A Bridge Too Far** *(1977) was one of the very few World War II films to surface in the Seventies. Immaculately made and extravagantly cast, it was a no-expense-spared reconstruction of the events leading up to the tragic defeat of the airborne Allied troops at Arnhem in 1944.*

461

their footage into two separate films, **The Three Musketeers** and **The Four Musketeers** (1975). The Salkinds followed their own example in shooting key scenes for **Superman II** (1981) while they had the cast and component parts assembled for **Superman the Movie** (although a legal-minded Brando ensured that his own out-takes never saw the light of day in the second installment).

The reluctance to abandon a winning formula was never more understandable than in the case of **Rocky** (1976). Sylvester Stallone had written the character (of a none-too-bright boxer who gets a crack at the world title) with himself in mind. Even though films with a sporting theme were supposedly anathema, he found several producers willing to gamble on the script, but none who would accept him in the role of the Philadelphia southpaw. Finally he got the ending his Cinderella story deserved when **Rocky** took the Best Film Oscar and vindicated his faith in the project. John G. Avildsen had

Left: *In the opening sequence of **Superman the Movie** (1978) the destruction of the planet Krypton forces Marlon Brando and Susannah York to send their son to Earth for safety....*

Right: *Clint Eastwood's first Western as director was the diabolic **High Plains Drifter** (1973) (later reworked in **Pale Rider** (1985)) in which he cast himself as a former lawman who comes back from the dead to take revenge on the townspeople who deserted him in his hour of need. It showed the influence of Sergio Leone, the Italian director of the Dollars Westerns, but nevertheless suggested that Eastwood's own visual style was a remarkable one.*

Bottom left: *In **Smokey and the Bandit**(1978), former stuntman Hal Needham directed his friend Burt Reynolds in a two-dimensional, cartoon-like chase. (Jackie Gleason was the incompetent lawman pursuing Reynolds' bootlegger.) A sequel followed, by which time Needham and Reynolds were pandering unashamedly to a redneck audience of good ole boys who just wanted to burn rubber and down beers.*

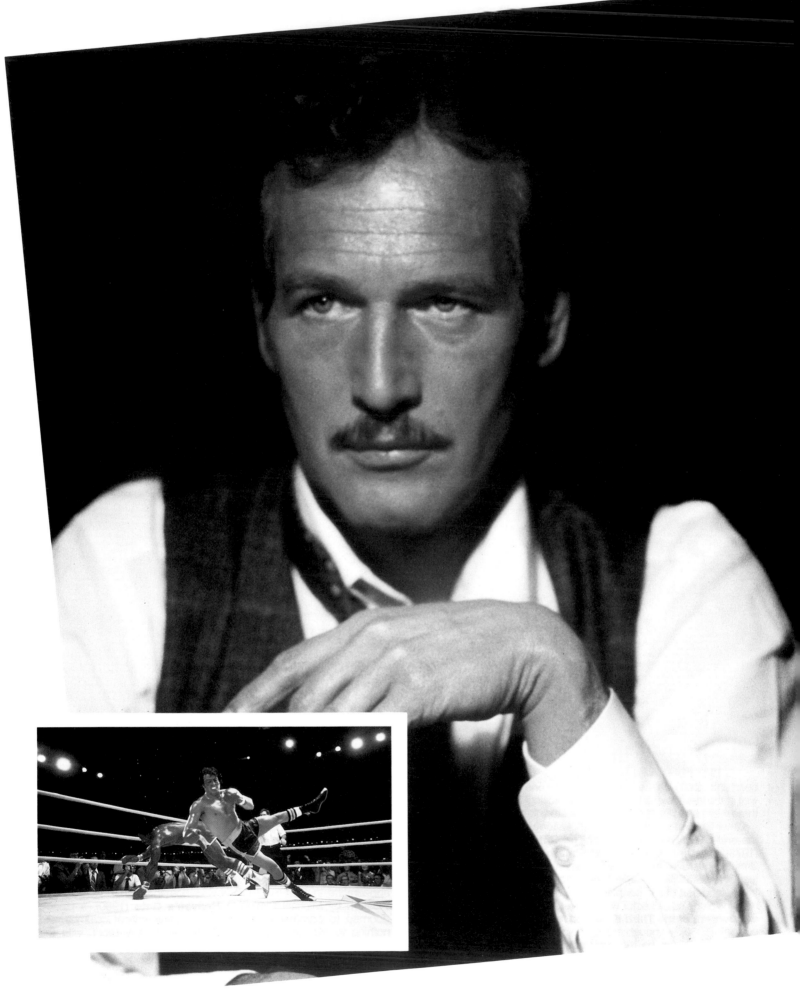

had exchanged his horse for a motorcycle as early as **Coogan's Bluff** (1968) while **Dirty Harry** (1971) gave him, after the poncho-clad Man with No Name from the Sergio Leone Westerns, the second of his great screen characters.

The war film also petered out, though the intelligent and intimate epic **Patton** (1970) drew audiences (and won a rejected Oscar for its star, George C. Scott). Later in the decade **Midway** (1976), a conventional World War II story, looked for success in Sensurround but without much luck or profit. The more recent war in Vietnam tended to be examined through the trauma of homecoming veterans (**Taxi Driver** (1976) and **The Deer Hunter** (1978) represented the

fiercer face of this drama) rather than through scenes of the conflict itself. It wasn't until the watershed of Francis Ford Coppola's **Apocalypse Now** (1979) that the scales tipped: the Reaganite bullishness of karate-chopping Chuck Norris and of Stallone's **First Blood** (1982) and **Rambo: First Blood Part II** (1985) still lay in the future.

For the purpose of easy analysis it is maddening that no discernible trend emerges from the list of box-office champions of the Seventies, yet for this we must be thankful since their variety argues the public's refusal to be pigeonholed. Were it otherwise, Hollywood would surely be as predictable as a factory conveyor belt. **Star Wars** (1977) was

Left: *Capitalizing on the phenomenally successful teaming of Paul Newman and Robert Redford in* **Butch Cassidy and the Sundance Kid** *(1969), George Roy Hill's confidence trickster comedy* **The Sting** *(1973) reunited the actors in a twisty Thirties tale of bluff and double-bluff. Marvin Hamlisch's arrangements immortalized the hitherto little-known piano rags of Scott Joplin. Newman plays Henry Gondorff, gambler and conman extraordinaire.*

Bottom left: *At the end of* **Rocky II** *(1979), Rocky (Sylvester Stallone) fights a rematch with Apollo Creed (Carl Weathers) and both men go down for the count — but Rocky is the first up, at 10.*

Right: *The three friends (Robert De Niro, Christopher Walken and John Savage) have escaped from Vietcong captivity, but their troubles are far from over in* **The Deer Hunter** *(1978).*

Below: *Francis Coppola's* **Apocalypse Now** *(1979) was a vast undertaking that nearly bankrupted this maverick director. Costs escalated; a leading actor (Martin Sheen) suffered a heart attack; typhoons wrecked one vast set. Coppola showed the movie to the Cannes Film Festival as a "work in progress" and admitted that he had had to mortgage his home to safeguard a final budget that was in excess of $30 million. Yet the film was its own vindication, drawing (uncredited) on Joseph Conrad's novella Heart of Darkness to provide an electrifying picture of the madness and monstrosity of the Vietnam war.*

the undisputed leader: otherwise there was one science-fiction film, a thriller, two musicals, a horror film, a crime thriller and two comedies. With the exceptions of **Grease** (1978), **The Sting** (1973) and **National Lampoon's Animal House** (1978), they are all intense pictures that would be diminished considerably by home viewing. Only three rely on stars for their appeal, **The Sting**, **Grease** and **Saturday Night Fever**, the last two leaning heavily on the talents of a contemporary phenomenon, John Travolta. **National Lampoon's Animal House** owes its popularity to the evergreen appeal of sophomore humor, while some would claim that the success of **The Godfather** (1972) was due in part to the reputation of Mario Puzo's book. Personally, I think the film developed its own "must-see" mystique, just as **The Exorcist** outgrew entirely the attractions of William Peter Blatty's novel.

Films were more attractively packaged, from the consumer's standpoint, and more aggressively marketed in the Seventies. Studio complacency and a system by which films earned automatic release had been banished and, in considering films as individual items for specialized treatment, target marketing was now becoming a reality. The increased showings of film on television and the boom in video recorders meant that the appetite for and awareness of movies was probably larger than at any previous point in the history of the cinema. Only the cinemas were letting the industry down. In the richer, leisure-oriented countries, prospective cinemagoers were moving away from the city centers which contained the old picture palaces. Only once or twice a year would audiences abandon the home screen to go to the cinema.

Above: *Sophomore humor was given its head of steam in John Landis's **National Lampoon's Animal House** (1978), set in 1962 and pitting Delta fraternity slobs against the Omega elite, as well as the hard-pressed faculty. Pretty girls decorate the scene – but the frat-house boys have most of the fun.*

Right: *In **The Sting** (1973), the aptly named conman Johnny Hooker (Robert Redford) shares his luck with his first partner (Robert Earl Jones), who is about to be killed by a big-time gangster. The rest of the picture turns on a revenge plot to even the score, though by extracting money instead of blood it hurts the bad guy more. Ironically Redford was Oscar-nominated for this role, though he missed out with his superior performance in **Butch Cassidy and the Sundance Kid** (1969).*

Above: *Richard Rush's high-octane thriller-farce,* **Freebie and the Bean** *(1974), cast James Caan and Alan Arkin as cop-buddies whose relationship is one of love-hate. The film tacked comic mayhem on to the* **Dirty Harry** *ethos, an uneasiness of styles that is summed up in the finale in which Caan is ambushed in a lavatory by a transvestite killer.*

Right: *Michael Winner's* **Death Wish** *(1974) certainly struck a chord at the right moment with the American cinemagoing public who cheered loudly whenever Charles Bronson's self-appointed judge, jury and executioner took a potshot at one of the hoodlums or muggers who persistently menace him.*

having been given a foretaste in Arthur Penn's **The Left-Handed Gun** (1958) and **Bonnie and Clyde** (1967) and Sam Peckinpah's **The Wild Bunch** (1969) and **Straw Dogs** (1971). What was new in the Seventies was the kung-fu movie, whose success was intimately bound up with Bruce Lee-style violence.

Movies like Robert Aldrich's **The Longest Yard** (1974) and Norman Jewison's **Rollerball** (1975) mirrored the violence in sport while, once police fallibility had been acknowledged, a sickening flood of law-and-order statements followed, most of which advocated private citizens' taking the law into their own hands. Clarence Darrow's statement that "the failure of justice itself may be more damaging to society than the crime" had never seemed truer. **Walking Tall** (1973), **Death Wish** and **Freebie and the Bean** (1974) were movies that put their tap roots down into the pool of anxiety over this issue. And there were, of course, the inimitable "Dirty Harry" movies. . . .

Below: *Even at his daughter's wedding, Don Vito Corleone (Marlon Brando), **The Godfather** in the 1972 adaptation of Mario Puzo's epic novel, is willing to listen to requests for favors or to right wrongs — but only for those who show "respect", which he values more than money.*

Bottom: *Opening with a huge close-up of keys hammering a sheet of paper, a striking metaphor for assassination by typewriter, **All the President's Men** (1976) was an always intelligent and resourceful filming of the Watergate investigations of Woodward and Bernstein. Robert Redford (right) and Dustin Hoffman added star luster to the roles of the crusading reporters, but the success was really that of the director, Alan J. Pakula.*

Dirty Harry was variously hailed and hated as a right-wing hymn to law and order, and it certainly spelled out with unarguable clarity the fact that the police often have to live by the rules of a brutal society if they are successfully to control it. But **Magnum Force** (1973), the film's sequel, pitted Harry against a cell of vigilante cops (the then comparatively unknown David Soul among their number) who act as judge, jury and executioner in exasperation over the number of felons escaping punishment from the congested and toothless courts. Harry makes his own violent stand against these miscreants, but too late — the vigilante was well on the way to becoming the Seventies' new screen hero.

One real-life model was Sheriff Buford Pusser of McNairy County, Tennessee, whose life (and death) was celebrated in a trilogy of movies, the first of which was **Walking Tall**. When appointed to office, Pusser believed absolutely in the axiom "Talk softly and carry a big stick." The election platform of the former wrestler had been the efficiency with which he had coped with a contretemps in a local casino. Pusser had had a major win that so displeased the management that they sent in their hired men to beat up Pusser and reclaim his winnings. When he had recovered, he took a home-made club and smashed his way back into the casino. "I fractured everybody's arms," he said proudly. "They tried me for armed robbery and acquitted me." He was promptly given a badge and the tacit license to fight fire with fire. Society saw him as a fitting hero; so did Hollywood and put the burly Joe Don Baker into **Walking Tall**.

The real Pusser suffered fifteen plastic surgery operations, the shooting away of part of his jaw and 200 stitches in his face following an ambush by those opposed to his regime. He died in a car crash while preparing to play himself in the second of the films, **Part 2, Walking Tall** (1975). The part was subsequently played by the Swedish actor Bo Svenson, who was also seen as Robert Redford's costar in **The Great Waldo Pepper** (1975). What had once had some pretense to being civic-minded action of a violent nature went on to become a vendetta of fury when Pusser's wife was killed in an

Right: James Caan played the violent, unpredictable Sonny Corleone, son of Brando's Mafia dynasty chieftain in **The Godfather** (1972), Francis Coppola's powerful epic saga of organized crime from the mid-Forties to the mid-Fifties. Here Sonny deals with his wife-beating brother-in-law (Gianni Russo), a traitor to the Family who will shortly draw him into a fatal trap.

Left: Michael Cimino's powerful drama of Vietnam and its aftermath, **The Deer Hunter** (1978), contained an exceptionally controlled performance by Robert De Niro as the focal member of a group of friends altered by the war and reunited back on American soil. John Savage was the soldier maimed in the holocaust.

Right: One of the best conspiracy thrillers of the Seventies. Alan J. Pakula's **The Parallax View** (1974) starred Warren Beatty as a crusading journalist trying to stop the domino killings of the witnesses to a political assassination.

Bottom right: A lively conspiracy thriller distinguished by fine acting, **The China Syndrome** (1979) starred Jack Lemmon (on floor) as an employee who spills the beans about a near-meltdown at a nuclear plant and Jane Fonda and Michael Douglas as the media crusaders who alert America to the deceit and the danger. The accident at Three Mile Island almost coincided with the film's release which certainly broadened the box-office appeal of a worthy thriller. James Bridges directed.

ambush. "What's right is right, and you're the one that's gotta draw the line," is the encapsulation of the Pusser philosophy in the second film, an oversimplified statement that echoes the cliches of the traditional Westerns, "A man's gotta do what a man's gotta do" and "There are some things a man just can't walk around."

Despite the Pusser movies and such titles as **Gordon's War** (1973), **Vigilante Force** (1976) and **White Line Fever** (1975), the biggest international success of this group was Michael Winner's **Death Wish**, which had American audiences cheering in the cinemas as Charles Bronson takes his gun to snatch power from the impotent New York police, gunning down the muggers who hang around Central Park. He seeks revenge for his wife's murder and daughter's rape — yet when the police finally catch up with him they have to let him go since he has become a public hero. **Death Wish** inspired two sequels (both in the Eighties), by which time copycat vigilante violence had occurred on the New York subway.

Exterminating angel

The vigilante film reached its apotheosis with Martin Scorsese's excellent **Taxi Driver**. Robert De Niro's insomniac Vietnam veteran turns to taxi driving but is sickened and appalled by the seamy world that he sees through his windshield. Literally, a taxi driver is a man who will take anyone anywhere for money. No questions, no responsibility, no involvement; an embodiment of the spirit of urban alienation. But Scorsese is at pains to make his character mythic. He

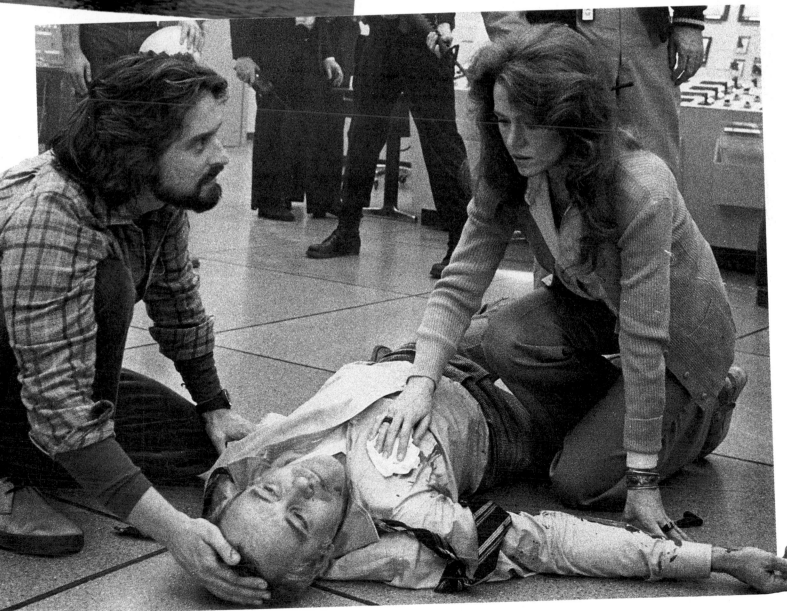

is an avenging angel, his cab a yellow chariot. He weighs the politicians and finds them wanting, he tries personal relationships and is rejected. Finally he retreats into his inner self, training and preparing for a conflict that is as apocalyptic as anything in the Book of Revelations.

De Niro kills and is himself seemingly killed, a bullet in his neck. But as the camera pans over the detritus of the mayhem, the walls as blood-spattered as those of an abattoir, Scorsese shifts gear and continues with a pan over a cleaner wall, this time decorated with newspaper cuttings acclaiming De Niro a hero for his night of massacre. The film ends with his rebirth when, for the first time, he establishes rapport with his fellow drivers, and ironically is able to feel coolly superior to the girl who spurned him. It is through the catharsis of operatic violence that a paranoid psychotic can finally achieve the status of hero.

The cinema of the Seventies was keen to debase the notion that the vigilante is someone who protects his own or society's interests in an imperfectly organized world. Active violence and bloodshed has a stronger box-office appeal than the chivalrous conduct of a sidewalk Superman. Yet the most notable vigilante action of this century was

Below: *While clearly deriving from the much superior* **Rosemary's Baby** *(1968),* **The Exorcist** *(1973) itself spawned not only a sequel (1977) but a shortlived host of imitations. The demonic possession of a young girl, Regan (Linda Blair) — named after King Lear's most wicked daughter — surely reflects US anxieties about the family, the generation gap, youthful rebellion and, above all, drugs — which "possessed" so many in the long aftermath of the hippie period, not yet concluded. Since much youthful protest was over the Vietnam War — which destroyed or distorted so many young lives (not all of them Vietnamese) — perhaps parents thought their children were also "possessed" by Communist sympathies, while young people enjoyed the spectacle of parents and priests disturbed and frightened.*

Right and bottom right: *A stylish remake of the Don Siegel classic of the Fifties, Philip Kaufman's* **Invasion of the Body Snatchers** *(1978) set the takeover of humans by seed-pods from another planet in contemporary San Francisco and cast Donald Sutherland, Brooke Adams, Jeff Goldblum and Veronica Cartwright as the quartet fighting the extra-terrestrial menace.*

Above: *Best and most ambitious of the group jeopardy thrillers was* **The Towering Inferno** *(1974), in which a skyscraper goes ablaze during the inauguration ceremony and a host of VIPs are trapped on the 136th floor. Decent architect Paul Newman comes to the rescue (aided by Fire Chief Steve McQueen).*

Above: *Charlton Heston was one of the more mature actors who had to contend with the natural demolition of California in* Earthquake *(1974), the disaster movie that introduced Sensurround, an emission of low-frequency sound that gave the audience a headache almost as bad as the one inflicted by the script. British-born veteran matte artist Albert Whitlock, who worked on some of Hitchcock's later films, supervised the special effects photography, creating many of the backgrounds.*

prematurely-titled **Airport 1975** ("You mean the stewardess is flying the plane?" cried a terrified passenger, thereby laying the foundation of the satirical comedy film **Airplane!** (1980)); Charlton Heston and fellow stars fought against the complete annihilation of California by **Earthquake**; fireman Steve McQueen teamed up with architect Paul Newman to save trapped celebrities from **The Towering Inferno**, a huge 136-story skyscraper that goes ablaze during the inauguration ceremony. And in the same year as this woe-laden trio, the British cinema also weighed in with Richard Lester's **Juggernaut**, about a terrorist bomb planted aboard a storm-lashed cruise liner.

However robust the beginnings of this cycle, it was to fizzle out ingloriously with half-baked spectacles such as **Avalanche** (1978) and the decline of producer Irwin Allen in **The Swarm** (1978) (killer bees destroying Houston), **Beyond the Poseidon Adventure** (1979) (a mistaken return to the watery scene of former glories) and the papier-maché volcano drama, **When Time Ran Out** (1980).

The disaster movie and the conspiracy thriller are joined by Steven Spielberg's monster hit, **Jaws,** which built Peter Benchley's best-selling novel about a marauding killer shark and the reactions of the townspeople whose tourist beaches the hungry beast is depopulating, into a masterpiece of terror-suspense. This hugely successful film not only opened the trilogy of watery Benchley thrillers to be filmed — **The Deep** (1977) and **The Island** (1980) were the two that followed — but rewarded Hollywood's faith in the young Steven Spielberg, who had previously made only one feature, **The Sugarland Express** (1974): all his earlier work had been television films, including **Duel** (1971), in which he had turned a story of a motorist being menaced by a giant truck into a similarly abstract exercise in terror.

Far left: *Second of a watery trilogy of films deriving from the novels of Peter Benchley -* **Jaws** *(1975) came before it,* **The Island** *(1980) after.* **The Deep** *(1977) starred Jacqueline Bisset and Nick Nolte as treasure-seekers who became entangled in voodoo and drug-smuggling off the coast of Bermuda. Peter Yates directed with misplaced conviction.*

Left: *The world's tallest building lights up the San Francisco sky in* **The Towering Inferno** *(1974) – giving the contract (for electrical wiring) to the lowest bidder does not always pay, as architect Richard Chamberlain discovers at the cost of his life.*

491

A Funny Sense of Humour

Chapter 25

Comedy came out of the closet in the Seventies, out of the family den and into a less constrained and more adult area. Carefully assembled comedy packages were replaced by the highly personal output of a number of former television gagsmiths – Carl Reiner, Mel Brooks and Woody Allen among them – who had labored for Sid Caesar on television's legendary *Your Show of Shows*.

Their work swept away the svelte bedroom comedies that had kept Rock Hudson, Doris Day and Cary Grant in almost constant employment during the first half of the previous decade. Nothing risqué was ever allowed to erupt through the mirrored calm of those Universal fantasies. That would have been as unthinkable as Doris Day going to bed in curlers or waking up without a fresh coat of lipstick. It was simply impossible for audiences any longer to accept the rigid sexual propriety of these impossibly well-bred and well-behaved characters.

America was heading for social, sexual and moral precipices. Landmarks along that route were pointed out by iconoclastic but isolated movies such as **Bob & Carol & Ted & Alice** (1969) (psychological), **M∗A∗S∗H** (1970) (sociological) and the later **Shampoo** (1975) (sexual and political). In the face of this ruthless advance, former box-office comedy champions like Bob Hope and Jerry Lewis retired gracefully. The "family" comedy remained in the phenomenally successful domain of the disaster-prone Inspector Clouseau, a character created by Peter Sellers in the Blake Edwards film **The Pink Panther** in 1963. The role had been planned for Peter Ustinov, but Sellers took over as a last-minute replacement, growing a Victorian moustache as a sign of self-asserted masculinity that gave him the key to the bumbling Sûreté detective. The series, which continued until (and by some tasteless use of out-takes even after) Sellers' death, became the James Bond of comedy, a sequence of ever brasher and ever more expensive productions that became mechanical with time, although the Seventies saw huge box-office receipts for **The Return of the Pink Panther** (1974), **The Pink Panther Strikes Again** (1976) and **The Revenge of the Pink Panther** (1978).

Even though he rarely stretched his comic genius in his later years, Sellers was a uniquely gifted actor and mimic in the manner of his idol, Sir Alec Guinness, and a box-office champion whose endorsement could and did help a film like Mel Brooks' **The Producers** (1968) get off the ground. He called it "the ultimate film . . . the essence of all great comedy combined in a single picture . . . tragedy-comedy, comedy-tragedy, pity, fear, hysteria and a largesse

Right: *In the Neil Simon parody of **Casablanca** (1943) and **The Maltese Falcon** (1941), **The Cheap Detective** (1978), private-eye Lou (Peter Falk) interviews crippled millionaire Ezra Dezire (Sid Caesar) and his voluptuous wife Jezebel (Ann-Margret).*

493

In his next film, **Sleeper** (1973), the hero wakes from hypersleep 200 years hence, worrying about the arrears of his Social Security payments while facing a bizarre new world in which sex remains his greatest problem. The subsequent **Love and Death** (1975) was set in the Russia of 1812 with Woody as a man condemned to death and reviewing the slapstick folly of his life in a pleasing parody of Tolstoy's *War and Peace*. These were art movies, unusual since they were comedies at a time when the art circuit rarely rocked with laughter; nor could Allen even be described as a box-office star. A straight acting role in Martin Ritt's passionate film **The Front** (1976), a study of the effects of McCarthy's anti-Communist hysterics on the witch-hunted television writers, did nothing to boost his broad appeal. It wasn't until the sublime **Annie Hall** took the Best Film, Director and Actress Oscars (Woody preferred to play jazz with his cronies in New York rather than fly out to the Californian society he satirized in the film) that there was a real shift of gears in his career and that of Diane Keaton, the starring actress on whom the character of Annie was loosely based. He followed that with **Interiors** (1978), a determinedly straight-faced study of a disturbed and self-destructive

Bottom left: Neil Simon exercised his dry wit in a 1978 portmanteau comedy, *California Suite* (a companion piece to his 1971 Manhattan-based **Plaza Suite**) and this time came up with four separate stories linked by the Los Angeles hotel in which the characters are staying. The final episode involved the trouble-plagued holiday of two black couples, the husbands played by Bill Cosby and Richard Pryor.

Below: One of the most spectacular of Woody Allen's comedies and one of the most consistently funny was **Love and Death** (1975), set in the Russia of the Napoleonic wars and casting the bespectacled comic as an anachronistically neurotic and anxious condemned man reviewing his life after an assassination attempt (unsuccessful, of course, since he kills a lookalike) on Napoleon himself. Since his chilly wife and cousin Sonia (played by Diane Keaton) habitually served meals made of snow and consistently avoided sex – at least, with him – perhaps execution could be considered something of a relief.

503

Right: *Ryan O'Neal makes an ingenious quick getaway in* **Nickelodeon** *(1976). Peter Bogdanovich's comedy about the early days of moviemaking paid affectionate tribute to the Golden Age of silent comedy; this scene is reminiscent of Buster Keaton's classic short* **Neighbors** *(1920).*

Bottom right: *Significantly posed against a poster for a movie by his role-model Ingmar Bergman, Woody Allen and Diane Keaton were soon to win 1977 Oscars (he as Best Director, she as Best Actress) for* **Annie Hall**, *a sweet-and-sour examination of a relationship not unlike their own.*

Far right: *In the office comedy* **Nine to Five** *(1980), a tyrannical boss (Dabney Coleman) gets his comeuppance from a trio of formidable women. Blond country singer Dolly Parton made a debut as one of them (the other two were Jane Fonda and Lily Tomlin). She was also Oscar-nominated for the theme song, which she wrote and performed. The film sparked off a TV series in which three different actresses took the roles — but executive producer Jane Fonda made an occasional guest appearance.*

family that severely disappointed many of his newly acquired fans. **Manhattan** (1979) arguably became his best single film to date, magically bringing together the maypole strands of his talent.

Neuroses in New York

Less candidly autobiographical than **Annie Hall**, **Manhattan** mirrored honestly the joys, sorrows and dangers of being a 42-year-old New Yorker. Allen plays a writer of fatuous television sitcoms who impulsively quits his job to attempt to write a novel based on characters from among his coterie of modish Manhattanites. Right up to and including **Annie Hall**, Allen had used his witty one-liners as crutches to support what was still fundamentally the act of a stand-up comic. His need to raise a laugh and be loved may have been abandoned during the glum posturings of **Interiors**, but **Manhattan** drained off much of the cuteness from his act and gave it the hard edge of truth. The jokes were no longer jumping out seeking approval; they now rose organically from the characters and lay rooted in their haphazard, chaotic lives.

This was the promised comic masterpiece, the sweeter for the time it had been in coming. It was indeed everything we always wanted to know that Woody Allen could do but were afraid to ask of him.

If Allen's was the one comic talent that came to perfect fruition in the Seventies, there were others that cropped heavily. Carl Reiner started the decade by offering the monstrous black comedy **Where's Poppa?** (1970), which had an almost demonic energy in the way it drew up the battle lines between George Segal and his impossible Jewish mother, played to the hilt by Ruth Gordon. This fine actress, then well into her seventies, also played opposite the whey-faced young Bud Cort in the comparably dark **Harold and Maude** (1971). Reiner went on to incur the uncomfortable displeasure of the religious lobby by casting George Burns as the Almighty in

Joking with genre

Brooks' next four films were parodies of specific film genres that went beyond the delight of buffs and *aficionados* to score more strongly with the public than did the films of his *Your Show of Shows* cowriter, Woody Allen. Broader meant better at the box-office and **Blazing Saddles** (1973) was a literally flatulent explosion of the clichés of the Western film, attacked by one American critic for a plot that sagged like a tenement washing line. But Brooks' very style was more and more to create a revue-style parody and pack it haphazardly with gags, rather like cramming students into a telephone box. Narrative never is and never was his prime concern.

Wilder played the alcoholic Waco Kid in **Blazing Saddles** and then went on to star in Brooks' best and most disciplined picture, **Young Frankenstein** (1974), shot in black and white, which used many of the original settings from Universal's Thirties Frankenstein films and which sent up the original James Whale picture with transparent affection. Anachronism was the key here rather than a rude explosion of the traditions of the horror film, and the character of the demented scientist gave Gene Wilder a fresh license for his rages. Meanwhile Peter Boyle was genuinely touching as the Creature who longs to don white tie and tails and dance "Puttin' on the Ritz" with his creator.

Silent Movie (1976) (in which the only spoken word falls from the lips of the great French mime Marcel Marceau) and **High Anxiety** (1977), a spoof of Hitchcock set-pieces that probably looked a lot better on paper than it does on celluloid, completed a quartet of films that fed off other films. Thereafter Brooks moved on to a no less controversial field of comedy with **History of the World Part I** (1981) and became a serious behind-the-scenes patron-producer with **The Elephant Man** (1980).

Mel Brooks' **Blazing Saddles** (1973) was the commercial breakthrough film for the gloriously unstable writer-director of **The Producers** (1968). Guying the traditions and clichés of the Western, it starred Gene Wilder as the Waco Kid and Cleavon Little as the West's first black sheriff. In the film's madcap finale the pair accidentally (and anachronistically) gatecrash a film studio where a big musical production number is being filmed.

Brooks' career without Wilder (they parted company after **Young Frankenstein**) continued in robust overdrive, but the actor's sputtered and stalled when he turned to direction with **The Adventure of Sherlock Holmes's Smarter Brother** (1975) and **The World's Greatest Lover** (1977) (which pounded the same beat as **Silent Movie**). Yet his performances continued to impress, especially in the railroad train thriller **Silver Streak** (1976) and opposite Harrison Ford in **The Frisco Kid** (1979).

The Seventies had seen comedy become a far more direct and personal statement: the knotty problems of relationships were now the banana skins and verbal abuse replaced the custard pie. The key figures in the predominantly Jewish comedy of the decade gave us reflections of themselves in their work, however risky that initially seemed in terms of acceptability by a public bred on mechanical comic formulas.

"I look at my films," said Mel Brooks, "and I think, 'Am I *that* vulgar, *that* Jewish?' And the answer is, 'Yes.' You can only be your true self in a film these days. I give you myself; you give me the price of admission. That's the deal."

Above and top: *Made in black and white and utilizing the set designed for the 1931 James Whale original,* **Young Frankenstein** *(1974) presented Mel Brooks at his least frantic and most film-reverent. Gene Wilder was the new-generation resurrectionist, Peter Boyle his gauche creature and the late Marty Feldman the requisite lab assistant who can't be trusted to use his brains.*

Right: *The third of Mel Brooks' four Hollywood spoofs,* **Silent Movie** *(1976) was a picture with only one word of dialogue (and, perversely, that is spoken by the French mime Marcel Marceau). The film gave a starring role to a manic stalwart of the Brooks repertory company, Dom DeLuise.*

6 Months Dead

The Sounds of Music

Chapter 26

The metamorphosis of the movie musical in the Seventies was brought about by two major factors. The first recognized the vital importance of aiming films at young audiences; the second was governed by the sudden awakening of the record industry to the commercial potential of the soundtrack album.

Few film genres had divided the generations as sharply as the musical. The young could hardly sit still through the theatrical and absurdly romanticized posturing of the two-dimensional shows-on-celluloid that had passed for film musicals in the previous decades. Typical examples include film versions of such Rodgers and Hammerstein stage classics as **Oklahoma!** (1955), **Carousel** (1956) and **The King and I** (1956), which represented everything that was middle-aged and middle-class about the movies. Teenagers would rather stay at home and listen to the radio or watch television than accompany their elders to the cinema. And they had a new beat to which to tap their toes: in the very year that Deborah Kerr's governess was teaching Yul Brynner's Siamese monarch to polka, the kiss-curled Bill Haley erupted on to the cinema screens in the crudely made but topical exploitation movie **Rock Around the Clock** (1956). While one generation was sighing wistfully and humming tunes from Broadway, the next was rocking in the aisles to a more urgent beat.

The young audience, abruptly separated from their parents, soon found new idols and new totems that became part and parcel of the rock revolution. Marlon Brando's nihilistic bike boy in **The Wild One** (1954); the sexually suggestive gyrations of Elvis Presley, already denounced by elders and clergy as the Devil's own tool; the violent frustration of James Dean — who never had the slightest connection with the rock movement in movies himself, but who nevertheless became emblematic of the age once he put away his flecked sports jacket, changed into a red windcheater and blue Levis, kicked his motorcycle boot through a family oil painting and went to the bad in **Rebel Without a Cause** (1955).

Right: *"An Aquarian exposition of love and peace" — that's how the half-million young people who gathered on Max Yasgur's New York State dairy farm liked to think of the Woodstock Music and Art Fair. Director Michael Wadleigh was there with 20 cameramen and eight assistants to record the musicians and the audience they played for in* **Woodstock** *(1970), a three-hour-plus documentary that made striking use of split-screen techniques.*

513

A king is born

If the waltzes of the traditional film composers pleased the ear, rock's appeal was more primitively to the loins. The real astonishment was that there were so few bona fide movies celebrating the new music. The teenage audience had fallen away, finding live rock more exciting than the cinema and prepared to hunt it down on radio and television, at theaters and in clubs.

The cinema had yet to discover that young filmgoers were to be of such strategic importance to its commercial future and made only token attempts to woo them. However, the phenomenon of Elvis Presley's success was such that not even a near-comatose musical cinema could ignore him entirely. He was rushed into a Western, **Love Me Tender** (1956), and then given one of the few decent musicals in his fifteen-year movie career, **Loving You** (1957), in which he had to make do with a creaking plot about a young working-class boy who makes good in showbusiness with an unfashionably raucous music. At least this paper-thin plot gave Elvis the chance to be himself which, at that time, was all the fans asked of him on screen. Subsequently Hollywood producers altered, laundered and sanitized him. They did everything *but* what was needed: to let him be. With its traditional fear of new things, Hollywood wasted a golden opportunity: in tampering with the new wine and decanting it into old bottles, they failed to take full advantage of a growing market.

Relieved to see their caution seemingly vindicated by rock's often feeble impact on the box-office, producers turned again to the traditional musical and must have breathed a sigh of genuine and enormous relief when **The Sound of Music** (1965), the most surefire of the Rodgers and Hammerstein confections, combined nuns and children in a sugary mix to create a monster hit. But that film emptied the Rodgers and Hammerstein coffers, so the same star (the newly Oscar-sanctioned Julie Andrews) and the same director, Robert Wise, were pressed into service for **Star!** (1968), a musical biography of Gertrude Lawrence. The sound of its resounding belly flop is one that still echoes in the ears of the middle-aged Fox board who sanctioned it.

Above: *The "phenomenon of innocence" that was Woodstock soon took a nasty knock at the Altamont concert where a spectator died at the hands of Hell's Angels while the Rolling Stones played on. David and Albert Maysles' and Charlotte Zwerin's **Gimme Shelter** (1970) became a chronicle of the times as much as a music documentary.*

Right: In **Woodstock** (1970), ex-Lovin' Spoonful guitarist John Sebastian sang "I Had a Dream", laced his rap with a few trendy obscenities and proved a crowd-pleaser. The group's big hits (1966) had been "Daydream" and "Summer in the City", their only US no. 1.

515

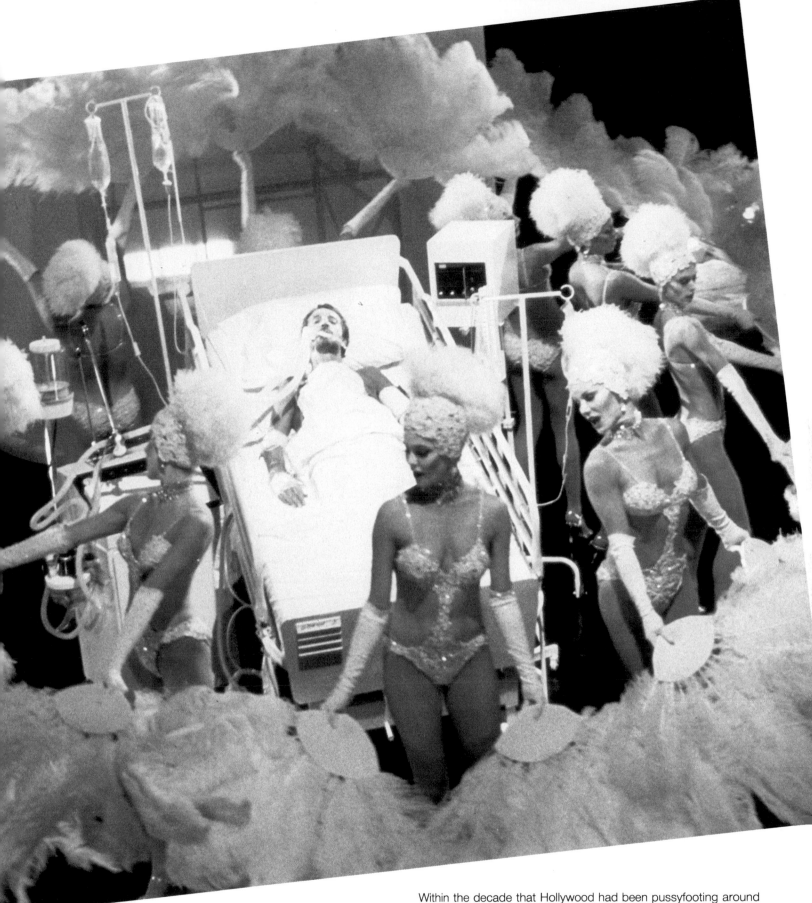

Left and above: *Bob Fosse's partly autobiographical, self-indulgent but occasionally brilliant musical* **All That Jazz** *(1979) had a Fellini-like vision of the life and death of a top choreographer (Roy Scheider). A strange but potent cocktail of whiplash choreography, erotica and open-heart surgery, it concludes with the apposite production number, "Bye, Bye Love(Life)".*

Within the decade that Hollywood had been pussyfooting around the vexed question of the musical, another generation, once newly enfranchised teenagers of the James Dean—Bill Haley—Elvis Presley years, had come to eminence in the film and music industries. They were deft in their assessments and had the confident certainty to act according to their own tastes. While the conventional musical became more sporadic in appearance and more elephantine in budget (**Hello, Dolly!** (1969) and **Camelot** (1967) were the more

successful of these years), younger producers placed their fingers on the cinema's pulse and issued an instant diagnosis: modern music was a certain bait to lure the truant teenage audience back into the movie houses.

The Stones play on

The significant breakthrough film was Michael Wadleigh's **Woodstock** (1970), which became a box-office champion despite being not only a documentary but one which lasted for three hours. It was not the social phenomenon of teenage tribes in peaceful coexistence that brought the young audience back into the cinema: it was the opportunity to see and hear their favorite groups and bands. Building

on that success was **Gimme Shelter** (1970), which recorded the Altamont concert at which the short-lived Woodstock spirit died, along with the music lover stabbed by Hell's Angels as the Rolling Stones played on and the cameras rolled. Concert documentaries proliferated: **Monterey Pop** (1969), **Keep on Rockin'** (1973) and **Wattstax** (1973) were three of the most notable, while a more ambitious documentary, **Let the Good Times Roll** (1973), yoked the musical phenomenon to the wider social one of the youth explosion with a clever and frequently witty use of split-screen photography, sometimes showing contemporary rock stars performing alongside their younger selves.

Now that rock had been embraced by the movie Establishment, the floodgates were open to the tide of modern operas that were enjoying theatrical success. Though most of the output of the prolific Andrew Lloyd Webber has been astutely held back from the cinema,

Left: Director Norman Jewison took the Andrew Lloyd Webber-Tim Rice rock opera **Jesus Christ Superstar** *(1973)* out on to Israeli desert locations, but the film never found a satisfactory style to match up with the driving energy of the music. Ted Neeley played Jesus, and Hawaiian-born Yvonne Elliman (not shown), Eric Clapton's sometime backing vocalist, made an impression as Mary Magdalene with "I Don't Know How to Love Him".

Right: A rock Gospel According to Saint Matthew, David Greene's **Godspell** *(1973)* derived from a successful stage show. David Haskell played a brightly dressed character who was a compression of John the Baptist ("I wanna get washed up," says the clown-garbed Jesus of Victor Garber when Haskell turns up at the fountain in Central Park) and Judas Iscariot.

Above: In his lively film of the Who's rock opera **Tommy** *(1975)*, Ken Russell invented the frantic style of today's video promo. Roger Daltrey played the deaf, dumb and blind messiah and Ann-Margret played his faithless mother.

director Norman Jewison was able to undertake a full-blooded film version of **Jesus Christ Superstar** (1973), set in Israeli desert locations and offering a petulant, flaxen-haired Jesus in Ted Neeley but electrified by the performance of Carl Anderson as Judas Iscariot. The other opera in which religion went pop was **Godspell** (1973), which reached the screen in a version by David Greene that invited almost universal calumny though it seemed a fair, even inventive, account of the stage version. **Catch My Soul** (1974), a modern-dress version of Shakespeare's *Othello* directed by the unpredictable Patrick McGoohan, fared little better and the genre had to look for its salvation to a British director who was now lauded for doing all the very things that had previously brought him into disrepute.

One could say that Ken Russell had been making musicals from the very beginnings of his varied career in television and movies. His biographies of classical composers and artists were marked by fanciful touches, wild extravagances and breaches of taste that often appalled. Where some audiences looked for gentle chamber music, he played the most wayward and experimental of operas — with the volume at full blast. But when he turned his attention to **Tommy** (1975), a rock opera that had been performed on record and in concert by the British band The Who, he suddenly had full license (indeed full need) of all his visual extravagances. Tommy (Roger Daltrey) is a deaf, dumb and blind boy who has been reduced to his near-catatonic condition by the trauma of seeing his father murdered

Left: *In **Tommy** (1975), the "deaf, dumb and blind kid" is tormented by his cousin Kevin (Paul Nicholas). With cousins like that, who needs brothers and sisters?*

Right: *Horribly disfigured, his head caught in a record-pressing machine, the masked hero (William Finley) of Brian De Palma's **Phantom of the Paradise** (1974) lives on, a voiceless mutilation, to haunt the 24-hour rock palace of the title and to supervise the career of a girl singer whom he adores from the touchline.*

Below: *Tim Curry played the "sweet transvestite from transsexual Transylvania" in **The Rocky Horror Picture Show** (1975), a musical that became a camp cult success. Jim Sharman directed, from Richard O'Brien's script.*

by his mother's lover. His liberation, rise and fall as a wizard of the pinball tables and a marketable messiah gave Russell all the scope he could have wished for in striking out at sacred cows. The cinema exposed great yawning gaps in the narrative, cracks which Russell papered over with panache. The film, a true opera with *every* word being sung, was really the forerunner of today's pop video promo.

Gothic rock

The rock musical around which a still extant cult grew was **The Rocky Horror Picture Show** (1975), an unbridled fantasy about an androgynous intergalactic emissary (a role created with impudent brio by Tim Curry) passing the time making creatures for his/her sexual gratification. Into the Gothic castle-den of this "sweet transvestite from transsexual Transylvania" stumble the hapless Brad and Janet (Barry Bostwick and Susan Sarandon) to become entrapped in the nightmare hobbies of Mr Curry. The film clearly has a compulsive "see-again" effect upon sections of its audience, many of whom dress up as the characters and attend midnight screenings at which a duplicate cast arranges itself on the stage and plays out each scene in accompaniment to the celluloid counterparts. This phenomenon emerged in New York, but its documentation in Alan Parker's musical **Fame** (1980) caused imitations in many other countries.

The same air of barely suppressed hysteria attaches to Brian De Palma's **Phantom of the Paradise** (1974), supposedly a rock version of **The Phantom of the Opera** but in fact a satirical fusion of elements of *Faust*, **Frankenstein** and **The Picture of Dorian Gray** as well. Paul Williams, who also wrote the pounding score, plays Swan, the ever-youthful head of Death Records, pledged to contract new souls for his Satanic master. Swan's own earthly instincts are to pirate a new rock cantata written by Winslow Leach (William Finley) and use it to open his 24-hour rock palace, The Paradise. A vengeful Leach gets his head caught in a record-pressing machine and lives on, a voiceless disfiguration, to haunt The Paradise and covertly to supervise the career of an adored girl singer. This part is true to the original, but the climactic orgy of coast-to-coast televised massacre and mayhem as Leach brings a final revenge to purge his soul, are pure De Palma, scenes in which can easily be recognized the excesses of a director who was to make such extreme movies as **Dressed to Kill** (1980), **Scarface** (1983) and **Body Double** (1984).

The traditional musical was barely getting a look in during this period. Elvis Presley had finally admitted the paucity of his own screen material and allowed documentarists to record his electric stage performances in **Elvis, That's the Way It Is** (1970) and **Elvis on Tour** (1972), which were, sadly, to be his last two films. Barbra Streisand asked him to star opposite her in yet another remake of **A Star is Born** (1976), but when Elvis proved unwilling to commit himself, she went ahead with the rock-oriented revision with Kris Kristofferson as the burned-out singer whose career is eclipsed by that of his girlfriend.

Right: *Czech-born director Milos Forman had scored impressively with two American films,* **Taking Off** *(1971) and* **One Flew Over the Cuckoo's Nest** *(1975), before he turned his attention to the musical* **Hair.** *It was rigorously anti-Vietnam, vigorously anti-authority (this is Treat Williams dancing on the dinner table), but still played very much like the Sixties hippie period piece it had already become when it was belatedly made in 1979. Galt MacDermot wrote the music, including the popular "Aquarius".*

Top right: *Alan Parker's celebration of youthful optimism,* **Fame** *(1980), put the New York High School for the Performing Arts on the map, sired a television series and briefly made a star out of the unknown Irene Cara.*

Left and far left: *In the third version (1976) of* **A Star Is Born** *(fourth if you count the 1932* **What Price Hollywood?**) *and the most crass, Barbra Streisand turned the heavy-duty Hollywood story into an egomaniac love feast with herself as the singer on the way up and Kris Kristofferson as the one in decline. One critic called it "A Bore Is Starred": certainly it represented the high-water mark of Streisand's self-absorption.*

Below: *This scene from* **The Wiz** *(1978) would have come as a shock to L. Frank Baum, who published The Wonderful Wizard of Oz in 1900 and followed it with thirteen further Oz books. Even Judy Garland might have had difficulty in recognizing the soporific poppy fields, transformed into Poppy Street, where ladies of easy virtue peddle coke.*

Streisand had remained a potent box-office force in the Seventies, but, although her recording career continued in top gear, she was rarely cast in screen musicals. Neither **Hello, Dolly!** nor **On a Clear Day You Can See Forever** (1970) lived up to the box-office hopes held for them and **Funny Lady** (1975), a belated sequel to her Oscar-winning debut in **Funny Girl** (1968), remained only her second musical of the decade until **A Star is Born**.

Dance fever

The musical emphasis began shifting from song to dance. Health awareness and exercise faddism had driven people in huge numbers to gyms and the new aerobic classes, where a fresh appreciation of dance was gained. Twyla Tharp's choreography for **Hair** (1979), the oddly belated film Milos Forman made of the 1960s stage hit, was one of its strongest selling points. The only Broadway musical that was solidly on Hollywood's books was the dance-centered *A Chorus Line*, which, though seriously considered by such directors as Sidney Lumet and Mike Nichols, did not reach the screen for another decade when Richard Attenborough helmed the project.

The Turning Point (1977) celebrates classical dance, featuring the talented, youthful ballet star Mikhail Baryshnikov, while modern dance is represented by Alan Parker's popular study of young people

Left: *Sidney Lumet's all-black musical,* **The Wiz** *(1978), cast Diana Ross as Dorothy Gale, befriended by Michael Jackson (Scarecrow), Nipsey Russell (Tinman) and Ted Ross (Lion) on the yellow brick road to Oz.*

Bottom far left: **The Turning Point** *(1977) features emigré dancer Mikhail Baryshnikov as a fickle Russian stud and Leslie Browne as the ballerina he toys with.*

Below: *Bob Fosse's* **Cabaret** *(1972) was perhaps the best musical of the Seventies, an intelligent reworking for the cinema (carefully cast and zingingly choreographed) of the Kander and Ebb show, itself derived from Christopher Isherwood's writings about decadent life in pre-war Berlin. Liza Minnelli as the singer Sally Bowles, Joel Grey as the effetely dangerous MC, lighting cameraman Geoffrey Unsworth and director Fosse all richly deserved their Oscars.*

Below: *After small roles in* **The Devil's Rain** *(1975) and* **Carrie** *(1976), John Travolta sprang to stardom in* **Saturday Night Fever** *(1977) as Tony Manero, the disco-dancing young Brooklynite brought to heel by love of a good girl (Karen Lynn Gorney, not shown). It owed its success to more than the expert marketing of its star-studded soundtrack: under John Badham's tight direction it emerged as an engrossing study of the rites of passage of the working-class American male.*

Right: *The ascendant star of John Travolta (right) carried* **Grease** *(1978) into orbit. An inflated Broadway musical about Fifties teenagers, it derived great box-office benefit from the casting of Travolta as Danny Zuko, the greaser with a heart of gold who falls for Sandra Dee clone Olivia Newton-John (not shown).*

at the School for the Performing Arts in New York. **Fame** not only sired a successful television series but ushered in a series of youth-geared musicals that had dance as their theme. **Saturday Night Fever** explained in salty language the tribal rites of the new Saturday night, but also spotlighted tellingly the universal obsession with disco dancing, an art demonstrated brilliantly by John Travolta, who had hitherto been seen only in supporting roles in **The Devil's Rain** (1975) and Brian De Palma's **Carrie** (1976). The teaming of Travolta and Olivia Newton-John was repeated in **Grease**, a nostalgic return to the simplicity of high-school life in the Fifties which was a huge commercial success. But when the couple subsequently went their separate ways, Travolta into the ineffectual **Moment by Moment** (1978) and Newton-John into the dire roller-skating disco musical **Xanadu** (1980), popularity deserted them.

Much of the impact of **Saturday Night Fever** derived from the comparably huge sales achieved by the soundtrack album made by The Bee Gees and other (non-appearing) musicians. The record industry's tardy admission that there was a symbiotic relationship between film and album was of signal importance. Before the Seventies, only a musical with a proven stage pedigree, a **South Pacific** (1958) or a **Carousel**, could expect to notch up significant soundtrack album sales. Furthermore, because of contractual difficulties and the unwillingness of the record business tycoons to simplify or circumvent them, film producers were tied to the commissioning of original music for their scores.

Dennis Hopper and Peter Fonda in **Easy Rider** decided to accompany their images of young people on the road with the very sounds that those hippies listened to, the top chart sounds of the day, not some monotonous score by a studio-retained composer. Although the accompanying soundtrack album was delayed while legal knots were untied (the scale of the film's success was a virtual guarantee of comparable album sales), the exercise pioneered the way for a new approach to music in the movies.

Thereafter films like George Lucas's **American Graffiti** (1973) evoked precise moments in time by the unfettered use of a musical shorthand, and the accompanying albums became more and more an essential part of the film's marketing strategy. The day was not far away when such an album was a prerequisite, sometimes the *raison d'être* of a film, even a non-musical film. This trend reached its nadir in the Eighties.

The Lady is a Champ

Chapter 27

Although a film like Paul Mazursky's **An Unmarried Woman** (1977) reveals its subject and the dynamics of its plot in its very title, the dilemmas faced by Jill Clayburgh – one of Hollywood's most likeable, strongest actresses during the Seventies – are presented in a romantic but fundamentally truthful light. Clayburgh's character, Erica, is unmarried only temporarily in that her successful, wealthy husband of seventeen years has just left her for a girl he met while buying a shirt in Bloomingdale's. The film shows Erica coming to terms with the break-up by revising her opinions of herself, redefining that self in its own right rather than as an extension of somebody else's personality, and finally going out with another man.

The difference between Mazursky's film and romantic comedies from previous decades lies, however, in Erica's refusal to drop everything for Alan Bates' abstract expressionist painter simply out of love for him or because he expects her to. It is not so much loneliness that is her problem, as the problems that men, flitting around this newly "available" woman like moths round a flame, bring to her sense of independence.

Women's rights

The movement in feminism and Women's Liberation was one of the major social issues of the Seventies once the radical image of bra-burning softened and women of every walk of life started to reflect on and to identify with the political thinking which argued that one half of the population had rights equal to the other. In short, that women were people too, that they deserved the same rights and considerations already given to sexual, social, political and ethnic minorities.

Liza Minnelli, in Martin Scorsese's **New York, New York** (1977), chooses her career when a fork in her life suggests a choice has to be made between showbusiness or a brutalizing life with her husband (Robert De Niro). And when Neil Simon uses the self-sacrificing finale of the old-fashionedly romantic **Casablanca** in his droll spoof **The Cheap Detective** (with Louise Fletcher standing in for Ingrid Bergman), Nicol Williamson has the right riposte: "What a brave, beautiful, extremely boring woman," he says.

But, as feminism bubbled under everyday lives that were slow to change, it became difficult for writers to pin down a woman's social role. And because some of the early liberationists were thought to be grim and joyless, confirming the worst fears of those opposed to the movement, a movie on the very subject of equality and independence might have tended to plunge into turgid introspection.

Right: *Jill Clayburgh played the emerging feminist of Paul Mazursky's* **An Unmarried Woman** *(1978) who, abandoned by her husband, discovers a new set of priorities in the relationship she subsequently establishes with a successful painter (Alan Bates).*

531

Women bewailed the fact that they would never see faithful images of themselves reflected on the screen while the Hollywood writing Establishment continued to be male-dominated. Ironically, however, it was a man, Robert Getchell, who penned the breakthrough film, Martin Scorsese's **Alice Doesn't Live Here Anymore** (1974), in which Ellen Burstyn gave an Oscar-winning performance. Alice gave up her dreams of becoming a singer at the age of nineteen for marriage and motherhood. But, abruptly widowed at thirty-two, she picks up the threads, leaves the stifling town of her less-than-perfect marriage and sets off with her son for Monterey, where her abandoned career once looked hopeful. Along the way she suffers the fate of a single woman being exploited by men, before meeting, as happens in Clayburgh's **An Unmarried Woman**, a potential dream lover in Kris Kristofferson. And here too, it is the man who is forced to consider giving up his lifestyle, allowing his new partner to pursue her much sought-after freedom.

Sex change

The star actresses of the Seventies were far from the traditional idea of stereotyped beauty: Streisand and Minnelli in the acting-singing stakes; Burstyn, Fletcher and Clayburgh. The beauties of the previous decades, hour-glass figures with what were presented as second-hand brains, were rejected, possibly by a predominantly female audience. Research shows that more women were attending the cinema at this time than men, and also that it tended to be the woman who chose the movie for the occasional family outing. Clearly they voted out Raquel Welch and Ursula Andress, preferring to watch more realistic versions of womanhood. Another response to this phenomenon was the mushrooming in the early Seventies of the buddy movies, in which male-bonding replaced the traditional boy-girl romance. Mostly these were not even implicitly homosexual in tone, but merely helped to fill the blank which might have been filled by movies tackling the plight of confused women in search of a role.

Once, when asked why there were no good parts being written for women, Shirley MacLaine replied with more than a grain of truth that

Bottom and right: In **New York, New York** (1977), director Martin Scorsese cast Liza Minnelli as the singer whose career eclipses that of her volatile saxophonist husband (Robert De Niro). The theme owes much to **A Star is Born** and, as though in homage to the 1954 version starring Minnelli's mother, Judy Garland, there is a mammoth production number, "Happy Endings", that pays tribute to **Star**'s "Born in a Trunk".

Below: Ellen Burstyn (not shown) was the Oscar-winning Alice of **Alice Doesn't Live Here Anymore** (1975). Part of her liberation and rebirth takes place in the Tucson cafe where she has to conquer the hostility of a prickly fellow waitress (Diane Ladd, right) and also to sort out her own feelings towards the young farmer (Kris Kristofferson, left) who makes a play for Alice herself.

533

there were. It was just that they were all being played by Robert Redford. But gradually the wheel turned and the Paul Newman-Robert Redford partnership, so successful in **Butch Cassidy and the Sundance Kid** that it was repeated in **The Sting** (1973), gave way to a climate in which roles usually reserved for men were often rethought for star actresses. After the Oscar-earning impact of her performance in **One Flew Over the Cuckoo's Nest** (1975), Louise Fletcher won the role of a psychiatrist in John Boorman's **Exorcist II: The Heretic** (1977) from a male contender.

By the mid-Seventies the buddy movies had abated (not before they had seen some admirable teamings: Warren Beatty and Jack Nicholson in **The Fortune** (1975), Clint Eastwood and Jeff Bridges in **Thunderbolt and Lightfoot** (1974), Steve McQueen and Dustin Hoffman in **Papillon** (1973)). A "male" picture had meant action, excitement and adventure with absolutely no restrictions of genre or location; by the same token a "female" picture would be assumed to be set in the home or in a convent. That thinking was grimly satirized in Ira Levin's novel (and Bryan Forbes' film, adapted by William Goldman) **The Stepford Wives** (1975), in which a coven of Ivy League husbands robotize their wives into loyal domestic drudges without a thought in their computerized heads. The Playboy fantasy had become a living nightmare and, in the central role, Katharine Ross earned a quietly satisfying revenge for being the relatively marginal "love interest" in **Butch Cassidy and the Sundance Kid**.

In Michael Ritchie's football comedy, **Semi-Tough**, Jill Clayburgh lives in contented asexuality with team members Burt Reynolds and Kris Kristofferson, to the dismay of her father (Robert Preston), the manager, who thinks the lack of sexual activity within the *ménage à trois* reflects embarrassingly on his players' masculinity: this modern thinking and sexual freedom from stereotypes simply makes the men appear gay. Preston's fears, however, are allayed when Clayburgh

534

Left: *Maybe Alice (Ellen Burstyn), a hashhouse waitress in Tucson in* **Alice Doesn't Live Here Anymore** *(1974), will never get to Monterey to resume her long-gone singing career. Maybe she has found the love of a good man — at least he knocks seven shades of daylight out of her appalling son (a Mott the Hoople fan!), so he can't be all bad. But at least she gets to make the choice — and director Martin Scorsese carries on his love/hate relationship with American male chauvinism (slightly constrained by Robert Getchell's script). Burstyn deservedly won an Oscar.*

Below: *For years Kirk Douglas owned the rights to Ken Kesey's 1962 novel* **One Flew Over the Cuckoo's Nest** *and, when he grew too old to play the rebellious McMurphy, passed the project on to his actor/producer son Michael, who cast Jack Nicholson in the role. Louise Fletcher* **(below far left)** *was outstanding as the loathsome Nurse Ratched who works in the asylum in which McMurphy is incarcerated. Milos Forman directed and they all took Oscars in 1975.*

falls for Kristofferson, surrendering her mental independence as she follows him into a fashionable but bizarre alternative therapy group. The conventional happy ending, complete with wedding ceremony, is fortunately ditched by Ritchie along with Kristofferson, who jilts his bride-to-be at the altar and leaves her to rediscover herself and her happiness in a possibly platonic relationship with the more down-to-earth Reynolds.

Male stereotypes were also the concern of Hal Ashby's **Coming Home** (1978), in which Jane Fonda played an ordinary young Army wife who sees her husband (Bruce Dern) off for a tour of duty in Vietnam and then occupies the time on her hands by working with war veterans in a local hospital. There she meets and falls in love with a young paraplegic (Jon Voight) and finds tender love and sexual satisfaction for the first time in her life. Dern's return from the war, his emotions all the more frozen by months of all-male mess hall camaraderie, brings about the thorough questioning by women of the image of macho virility.

Good girl, bad girl

The question of a woman's unashamed sexual appetite was tackled in **Looking for Mr Goodbar** (1977), which dared to suggest that the madonna and the whore might coexist happily within the same woman, albeit to male irritation and perplexity. Diane Keaton, in her most demanding role away from Woody Allen, played a girl who was a saintly teacher by day and a sexually cruising barfly by night. Having

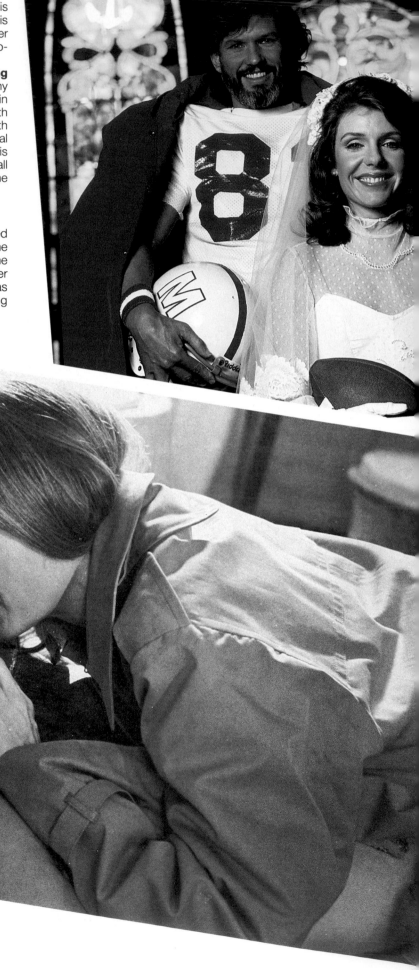

Left: *Michael Ritchie's amusing satire,* **Semi-Tough** *(1977), revolved around a ménage à trois of two footballers (Burt Reynolds, right, and Kris Kristofferson) and their manager's daughter (Jill Clayburgh). A multiple divorcée, she nearly marries Kris Kristofferson, but at the last moment ....*

Bottom far left: **Starting Over** *(1979), Alan J. Pakula's wise, barbed comedy of personal relationships, starred the persistently underrated Burt Reynolds as an attractive middle-aged man who suffers a crisis of confidence when ditched by his ambitious singer wife (Candice Bergen, pictured, who effortlessly stole the picture) until he begins to forge a new relationship with an equally insecure teacher, played by Jill Clayburgh. But when the wife attempts a reconciliation – seduction followed by a truly excruciating song she has composed for him – he realizes where his loyalty lies.*

Below: *One of the best of the "buddy" movies, Michael Cimino's* **Thunderbolt and Lightfoot** *(1974) starred Clint Eastwood as a criminal (initially disguised as a preacher!) in search of loot from an earlier robbery that has gone missing while he was in jail. Jeff Bridges was the young drifter with whom he falls into step. The drag sported by Bridges is worn merely that he might work more distractingly as a decoy in a bullion robbery.*

537

had herself sterilized for fear of transmitting a genetic disability, she no longer cares for the uses and abuses of her own body, and her increasingly risky nocturnal escapades (the danger is a part of the fatal attraction) end in her brutal, undeserved murder at the hands of one of her pick-ups.

The theme of career versus maternity was seldom more handsomely presented than in Herbert Ross' **The Turning Point**, in which Shirley MacLaine plays a woman who gave up her dancing career for marriage and motherhood and Anne Bancroft plays the best friend who pulled down the emotional shutters to become a star, while also being godmother to MacLaine's daughter who is herself at a similar crossroads in her own womanhood.

In Fred Zinnemann's **Julia** (1977), the theme was the laying down in childhood of friendship bonds that will make inexorable demands in adult life. Jane Fonda played the writer Lillian Hellman fulfilled by her own career success and a strong relationship with fellow author Dashiell Hammett (Jason Robards Jnr). Vanessa Redgrave played Julia, a woman whose safety is put at physical risk by her political

commitments. The bonds between them are so strong that Lillian has no option but to help, to halt her career and relationship midflow, when Julia is in danger. The film was notable in showing the intensity of a female friendship while pointing out its platonic nature. When a lout has the gall to suggest that the relationship *must* be sexual to be

Above inset: *In **Looking for Mr Goodbar** (1977), Diane Keaton plays a teacher who cruises the singles bars by night and is murdered by one of her pick-ups. Richard Brooks' film includes an early performance by Richard Gere as one of Keaton's conquests.*

Top: *Which of the characters is **Semi-Tough** in the 1977 comedy? Shake (Kris Kristofferson) is semi-tough enough to stand up Barbara Jane (Jill Clayburgh) at the altar, using his est (here called B.E.A.T.) training — and she, though unmoved by this self-realization therapy, is semi-tough enough to take it and find consolation with another footballer ....*

538

Right: Hal Ashby's **Coming Home** won 1978 Oscars for both Jon Voight as the Vietvet paraplegic and Jane Fonda as the married woman whose love affair with him alters her notions of manliness.

539

Above: *The timeless career-versus-marriage dichotomy was debated in* **The Turning Point**, *a handsome 1977 movie set against a background of classical dance. Anne Bancroft (right) was the ballerina who gave up love and marriage for the stage; Shirley MacLaine (left) the lifelong friend who sacrificed fame for domesticity.*

that close, Lillian rounds on him and knocks him off his chair, a moment that the audience is often moved to cheer.

But, by the end of the decade, the novelty of feminism as a brightly signposted theme was wearing off and gender was altogether less of a factor in casting. As Garbo had said as **Ninotchka** (1939), the Russian envoy sent to Paris to investigate the misdemeanors of the male members of the trade delegation, "Don't make an issue of my womanhood." The movies were finally taking her at her word, though sexist attitudes were still tersely corrected in such films as **Coma** (1978) with Geneviève Bujold as a female doctor battling against a male-dominated medical conspiracy.

Fred Zinnemann's **Julia** (1977) was based on the (more or less) true story of a friendship laid down in girlhood that makes irresistible demands in later years. Jane Fonda played the author Lillian Hellman who finds herself compelled temporarily to jettison her affair with author Dashiell Hammett and her own writing career to help Julia (played by Vanessa Redgrave) when the latter's political activities place her life in danger before World War II.

Bigotry, brutality and the backlash

As women took up key roles in industry and politics, there was a predictable male backlash. It was no longer possible to smile condescendingly at the idea of a woman holding down a job while running the home: millions of women were successfully doing just that and, when the two jobs did prove incompatible, sometimes they left the domestic chores to their husbands. The sexual assertiveness and apparent threat to men's employment opportunities posed by liberated women fed a grass-roots appetite for filmic revenge.

While the end of the decade saw Jane Fonda, Lily Tomlin and Dolly Parton getting their own back on a chauvinist boss (Dabney Coleman) in the black office comedy **Nine to Five** (1980) — with its violent imagery wrapped in sheer farce — the male reaction was less subtle.

Violent and fundamentally sexist thrillers like Brian De Palma's **Dressed to Kill** inspired women to protest and picket cinemas, though it could be argued that this particular example was no more than a hothouse version of Alfred Hitchcock's **Psycho** (1960), which, twenty years earlier, had offered a sacrificial female victim in the cinema's most celebrated murder. But other horror shockers demonstrated an unmistakable misogyny. The terrorizing, humiliation, murder and mutilation of women alone became a recurring theme in such "stalk and slash" movies as **When a Stranger Calls** (1979) and **He Knows You're Alone** (1980).

In each of these films lies the suggestion that the baton of avenging violence is passed from hand to male hand. You have only to accept

Top left: *A superb performance by Jane Fonda (rewarded by an Oscar) lies at the heart of* **Klute** *(1971), a murder mystery that was only the second film as director by former producer Alan J. Pakula. The eponymous private detective is played by Donald Sutherland but the film really scores with the gutsy, modern and brilliantly sustained characterization of the high-class call girl, Bree Daniels, who unwittingly places herself at risk when Klute starts stirring up the muddy waters that are settling over a recent murder case.*

Right: *Jane Fonda and Jason Robards as writers and lovers Lillian Hellman and Dashiell Hammett in Fred Zinnemann's* **Julia** *(1977).*

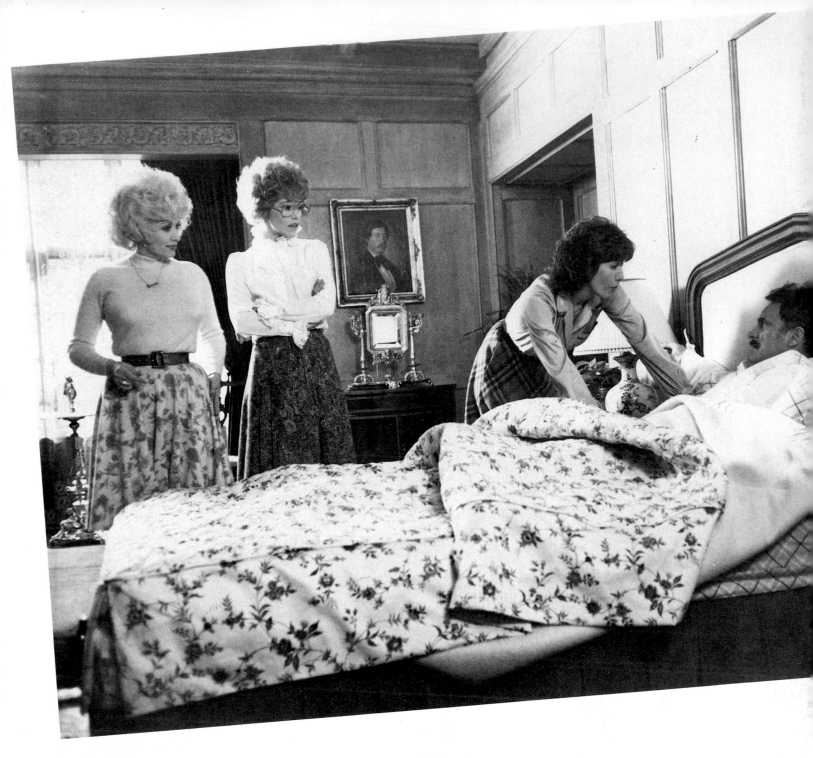

Above : Women's revenge for generations of male domination found a funny side in **Nine to Five** (1980) in which a trio of office workers (Dolly Parton, Jane Fonda and Lily Tomlin) kidnap their chauvinist boss (Dabney Coleman) as a way of getting even.

Right: The reclusive but much admired superstar Robert Redford scooped an Oscar for his first (and thus far only) film as director, **Ordinary People** (1980), about the emotional anticyclones that cause havoc with a repressed middle-class family. Donald Sutherland and Mary Tyler Moore played the parents; Timothy Hutton won a Best Supporting Actor Oscar as the suicidal son.

the basic premise of these films — that the endangering of female life is more exciting, both to the criminal and to certain members of the audience, than the endangering of male life — to pin down the tacit sexual titillation of these pictures. But just as by their efforts radical women all but drove off the screen films that offered rape as a voyeuristic spectacle, so they turned their protesting attentions to this cycle of unlovely "women-in-peril" pictures.

Having made colossal gains through a canny awareness of the way they were portrayed by the media, women were understandably not prepared to give an inch. With the exception of the crudest exploitation movies, many films now viewed them with a fresh understanding and respect.

Top : *Dino De Laurentiis spent a fortune updating (1976) the classic* **King Kong** *(1933) for the Seventies and received no praise from the critics, although the ape effects were superior. Former model Jessica Lange proved herself an attractive light comedienne as the Beauty who tames the Beast.*

Right: *Brian De Palma's* **Dressed to Kill** *(1980) was one of the most extreme of the young director's homages to the works of Alfred Hitchcock. The model here was* **Psycho** *(1960) and De Palma cast his wife, Nancy Allen, as the young hooker whose life is endangered because she accidentally stumbles into an elevator in which the killer, mentally disturbed and sexually confused, has just murdered an adulterous wife and mother (Angie Dickinson) with a straight razor.*

Far right: *An unusual science fiction thriller, Donald Cammell's* **Demon Seed** *(1977) casts Julie Christie as a scientist's wife who is captured, assaulted and impregnated by the household computer which manages to activate normally inanimate objects in the home.*

The Kids with Beards

Chapter 28

Very few people have the sense of balance to observe who is on the ladder behind them. The studio bosses who were reluctantly acknowledging the erosion of their power in the late Sixties could not for the life of them see where the new tycoons would come from. Certainly not from among the ranks of employees of the banks and conglomerates who were taking over the studios. Surely not the directors? Even after the disappointments of **Torn Curtain** (1966) and **Topaz** (1969), Alfred Hitchcock remained the only director whose name alone would sell a mainstream movie. The graduates of the new-fangled film schools couldn't compete with that! What had they ever achieved, the kids with beards who had learnt the theory of film from the blackboard?

Only an opportunistic employer like Roger Corman, then kingpin producer of exploitation movies for American-International Pictures and therefore always on the look-out for cheap young talent, had hired them. And what had he got? A horror film **Dementia 13** (1963) by the then unknown Francis Coppola and a picture about Depression drifters called **Boxcar Bertha** (1972) by one Martin Scorsese. . . .

The other young directors who later became seminal influences in the Hollywood of the Seventies were stirring in their professional prams around this time, some of them making student films. With the exception of Steven Spielberg and Brian De Palma, they were all graduates of the film schools, organizations that were unjustly reviled by movie Establishment figures who believed that cinema was something that simply was or was not in the blood. Previously, the studios themselves had been the film schools. Now this education was provided in more formal surroundings for a generation that had been weaned upon film and had in part, at least, been shaped by the movies they saw. These young Turks sensed where the studios were losing touch with the audience's emotions and expectations, not with a sociologist's overview but simply because they *were* part of that audience at which the movies were imperfectly aimed. They knew what was wrong with the medium; all they needed was the equipment to carry out the repairs. Film school provided it.

St Francis of the film studios

Foremost amongst these newcomers was Francis Coppola, the group's eldest member and the first to break into movies. By the time he made **The Godfather** in 1972 and earned respectability (which in Hollywood equates with box-office returns) for the young graduates,

Right: *George C Scott made sour Oscar history when he declined his Best Actor award for the title role in* **Patton** *(1970). Franklin J Schaffner's complex study of the "red-blooded" American General was cowritten by Francis Coppola and managed at once to be intimate (the opening speech with Scott posed against a gigantic American flag) and epic in the battle sequences.*

he had worked extensively for Corman, written scripts that included **This Property Is Condemned** (1966) and the Oscar-winning **Patton**, directed three films for Warners (**You're a Big Boy Now** (1967), **Finian's Rainbow** (1968) and **The Rain People** (1969)) and seen the shattering of his cinematic Camelot, the idealistic Zoetrope studio system that he had established in San Francisco, and which was later to be resurrected with no more happy an outcome.

Coppola gave George Lucas his first directing chance (**THX 1138** (1971) was the picture that caused the first financial shutdown of Zoetrope) while Lucas went on to become friend, adviser and finally collaborator (on **Raiders of the Lost Ark** (1981)) of Steven Spielberg. Each had and continues to have his own protégés and the names of Zoetrope, Lucasfilm and Amblin' probably mean as much to students of the Seventies as did Paramount, MGM and Universal to earlier film generations.

By the end of the Seventies the three biggest money-spinners in the history of the cinema were all the work of this group. Lucas's **Star Wars** was the leader, closely followed by its 1980 sequel, **The Empire Strikes Back** (actually directed by Irvin Kershner and doing astoundingly well to achieve this position in so short a period of time)

and then by Steven Spielberg's shark saga, **Jaws**. Yet each director retains his integrity and tempers a seeming box-office invulnerability with an occasional appetite for smaller, more personal films that ignore the recipe for surefire hits. For the erratic and unpredictable Coppola it lies in his Zoetrope output; for Lucas the initial commercial disaster of **THX 1138**; for Spielberg it is **The Sugarland Express** and the expensive failure of **1941** (1979). Yet, when they are on form, the names of these directors guarantee box-office success.

Coppola was assigned to **The Godfather** because of his Italian-American background which was supposed to assuage the expressed sensitivity of the Mafia to seeing Mario Puzo's book filmed. In the event it was a handsomely old-fashioned movie, epic in sweep and stature and modern only in the graphic depiction of the violence of organized crime. Coppola's sequel, **The Godfather Part II** (1974), developed the theme of family and the difficulty of one culture assimilating another. To see the two films edited together in the mammoth television version, for which Coppola again shot extra footage, is to appreciate the breadth and complexity of the director's scheme, even though language and violence had been muted for home consumption.

Far left: *Action in North Africa during World War II in* **Patton** *(1970).*

Left: *A canny cocktail of all the myths and legends that excite the appetites of children,* **Star Wars** *(1977) placed writer-director George Lucas among the giants of cinema commerce. Alec Guinness won an Oscar nomination for his performance as Ben [Obi Wan] Kenobi,*

Below: *A self-consciously innovative debut movie by director George Lucas,* **THX 1138** *(1971). Set in the 25th century, it largely features drugged, shaven-headed characters who are dressed in white and photographed against white backgrounds. Robert Duvall and Donald Pleasence (left) are the enemies in this bleak futuristic society.*

Right: *One of Coppola's best films of the Seventies, critically lauded yet not a crowd-pleaser, was* **The Conversation** *(1974) in which Gene Hackman played an electronics surveillance expert drawn into the lives of the people he is bugging, with disastrous results. But the bugger is himself finally bugged, or so he believes – he wrecks his apartment in searching for the elusive device.*

Bottom right and far right: *An irredeemably juvenile sense of humor blocked the success of* **1941** *(1979) and, despite a huge budget and unstinting effects, provided the first real flop for flavor-of-the-month director Steven Spielberg after* **Jaws** *(1975) and* **Close Encounters of the Third Kind** *(1977). A farcical account of one stray Japanese submarine that surfaces off the Californian coast after Pearl Harbor and the chaos engendered in the local community, it remained as mechanically funny as a penny-in-the-slot laughing sailor in an amusement park. Oblivious of war, meanwhile, a soldier (Treat Williams) and a dishwasher (Bobby DiCicco) settle a dispute over the girl played by Dianne Kay.*

In between the twin parts of this massive project came **The Conversation** (1974), a gripping paranoia thriller that captures the mood of Watergate with its depiction of the breakdown of a man (an excellent performance by Gene Hackman) who works in electronic surveillance as a professional eavesdropper. Thereafter Coppola turned his energies to another epic project, **Apocalypse Now** (1979), which he had prepared in the late Sixties and now realized at great personal cost (the near-collapse of his marriage, the mortgaging of his home as the budget whirlwinded to more than 30 million dollars). Homecoming soldiers had reported that the Vietnam War was like a movie; Coppola's film itself became a war, afflicted by everything from the heart attack of one of the principal actors to the destruction of whole sets by a typhoon. Those who endured and survived the combat zone of **Apocalypse Now** spoke of consuming obsession and near-madness in its making, but the picture is its own justification: a great moral work.

Coppola, not only on account of his prodigious talent but also perhaps because he is the spiritual father of the new generation of film-makers, has always been acknowledged by the movie Establishment. Best Picture Oscars went to both **The Godfather** and **The Godfather Part II**, while **The Conversation** won the top award of the Cannes Film Festival. Ironically, the film-making panache and the commercial Titanism of Lucas and Spielberg have yet to be rewarded by Oscar.

Lucas: music and mythology

George Lucas was helped by Coppola in setting up **American Graffiti**, a rites of passage film made almost unbearably nostalgic by the music of the day (1962), as a group of friends spend their last evening together before going their separate ways to college and adult life. This was almost certainly the most influential film of the early Seventies, much imitated and one to which a young audience quickly responded and flocked in droves. But not in the numbers that queued again and again for Lucas's next film, **Star Wars**.

It was no idle stroke of luck that **Star Wars** became the highest grossing movie in the history of the cinema. George Lucas devoted two years to researching the myths that resoundingly appeal to young audiences the world over. He "created" the film in the most cold-blooded, premeditated way possible. Far from making him rich, his previous two films had left him on the brink of poverty; **Star Wars**, he vowed, would make him a millionaire. He acquired the merchandising rights from the studio (an unprecedented request by a film-maker), conceived his story as part of a trilogy (that was itself part of an even larger plan) and worked hard and imaginatively to bring in an expensive-looking film on a modest budget. The result was a special effects fantasy extravaganza that mixes Arthurian legend with

Top far right: *The droids were two of the big attractions of* **Star Wars** *(1977), anticipating the cute E.T. of five years later. The finicky, faintly camp C-3PO (Anthony Daniels, pictured), a worrier of Woody Allen class, was neatly contrasted with the happy-go-lucky Daleklike R2-D2, played by Kenny Baker.*

Right, below right and bottom: ***Apocalypse Now*** *(1979) embroiders on Conrad's original story by having a professional army killer (Martin Sheen) sent to "terminate" Col. Kurtz, who has enlisted local head-hunting tribesmen in an unauthorized sideshow campaign. But the special agent has to assume the persona of his target, now his alter ego, before he can complete the hit.*

frontier mythology, and grafts World War II aerial dogfight choreography on to the clinical fantasy of Kubrick's **2001: A Space Odyssey** (a great favorite of Lucas's). It's a junk-food movie in a designer pack; it is low in nutritional value, but it's fast and fun. That Lucas's genuine understanding of the mechanism that made Saturday matinée serials work was not a flash in the pan was demonstrated when he joined forces with Spielberg for their salute to that all-but-forgotten genre in **Raiders of the Lost Ark**.

Spielberg: brat of brilliance

One could argue that Steven Spielberg had no need of film school in that he was a precocious movie brat from his earliest days. With access to a home movie camera, he was making films before his contemporaries were dating girls. Once, according to legend, on a Universal studio tour, he broke away from the main party and joined the "real" world of the working studio. Months later he had worked his way on to the lot where now stands his own architect-designed suite of offices, a thank-you from the people who banked the checks for **E.T. – The Extra-Terrestrial** (1982).

The made-for-television movie **Duel** brought Spielberg to critical attention: remarkable notices for this tale of a traveling salesman followed and menaced by a seemingly driverless truck resulted in the film's opening on the movie circuit, but **The Sugarland Express** disappointed the studio's high commercial hopes. It was nevertheless an outstandingly accomplished first feature film, the tragi-comic story of a prison break and its consequences. But it was with **Jaws** that Spielberg's earning potential finally matched his prodigious talent.

This nightmare rollercoaster ride, a monster movie torn from real life, probably caused a sharp downturn in the numbers of ocean bathers the world over even in the hot summers of 1975 and 1976. (Swimming pool attendances possibly dipped, too, since Spielberg's

movie was plugged in to primal fears of the water and the idea of people as food.) A difficult film to direct on watery locations, it ran over budget and over schedule, but amply justified the investment of time, trust and money. There was suspense to rival that of Hitchcock and a new mechanical star in Bruce, the killer shark. Or, rather, Spielberg demonstrated the importance of the effect, the film itself, as star rather than the chemistry of actors (good as Roy Scheider, Robert Shaw and Richard Dreyfuss were in their roles).

Even so, Spielberg's understanding of tension and suspense meant that he never retreated into the safe haven of effects for their own sake. This could easily have been the case in a film like **Close Encounters of the Third Kind** (the title being quasi-scientific jargon for contact with extra-terrestrials). By far the largest portion of this long film concerns the telepathic awareness of a group of geographically separated people that something of moment is about to occur at a specific location. The way in which the director delays (and thus increases his audience's desire for) his amazing visual climax is exemplary. Even in the "Special Edition" of the film, a version re-cut by Spielberg and released three years later, the emphasis on effects was hardly accentuated. It was, in any case, a film that appealed to spiritual hungers rather than to genre expectations, one that suggested that God was not only alive and well but even planning a visit. And as the little childlike aliens exchange crew with their human hosts at the film's emotionally draining climax, we get our first glimpse of the ancestors of E.T.

Scorsese: realism and redemption

Unlike Lucas and Spielberg, Martin Scorsese has never claimed the cinema of wonder as his constituency. His films are usually

Left: Steven Spielberg's **Duel** (1971) was a made-for-television movie but admiring critics campaigned for its cinema release. Based on a Richard Matheson story about a traveling salesman (Dennis Weaver) menaced with deadly intent by a huge and seemingly driverless truck, the film became a masterly exercise in suspense. It was on the evidence of this success that Spielberg was entrusted with **Jaws** (1975) and set on the mainstream commercial highway.

Above and top: Close Encounters of the Third Kind (1977) (scientific jargon for actual contact with extra-terrestrials) was a huge success for Steven Spielberg and for the extra-special effects of Douglas Trumbull. Richard Dreyfuss played an electrical repair man whose initial sighting of alien craft leaves him with a telepathic imprint of the site of the imminent landing. When he gatecrashes the reception party being organized for the vast Mother Ship....

passionate, bleak and concerned with redemption, a theme carried over from his religious upbringing (at one point he planned to become a priest). The Italian-American milieu of **Mean Streets** (1973) invited comparison with **The Godfather**, but was more aptly viewed as a preparation for his blisteringly fierce **Taxi Driver**, in which the would-be savior becomes an exterminating angel.

Like the rest of "the kids with beards", Scorsese is a highly cine-literate man who refers to or quotes frequently from the directors he admires and the movies that colored his childhood. Just as **Alice Doesn't Live Here Anymore** opens with the heroine as a child inhabiting the sunset glow of the old Warner Brothers romances of the late Forties and protesting, with anachronistic colorfulness, that she can sing better than 20th Century-Fox's Alice Faye, so **New York, New York**, Scorsese's sober and serious 1977 musical, pounds the same turf as Coppola's **One From the Heart** (1982). Both are highly stylized films and the heightened artificiality of the sets (New York and Las Vegas reconstructed in Los Angeles) pays tribute to the musicals of the years in which the directors were growing up. **New York, New York** has a further dimension in that its plot outline, about a female entertainer's successful rise to fame and the subsequent eclipse of her husband's career, echoes the 1954 version of the classic **A Star Is Born**, in which Judy Garland played the ascendant star. Here her daughter, Liza Minnelli, plays the central role and a big production number, "Happy Endings", mirrors cleverly the classic "Born in a Trunk" production number from the earlier film.

De Palma's nightmare vision

Such quotations could quickly become tedious to a general audience if the films did not add contemporary layers of meaning of their own and entertain even as they imitate (or pay homage). In this regard Scorsese has proved himself a master while another of the young directors, Brian De Palma, has become increasingly introspective. His cinematic obsession with the films of Alfred Hitchcock has lasted from the 1973 **Sisters** to the present day. This was his **Rear Window** (1954) (a murder glimpsed in part from a neighbor's flat); the subsequent **Obsession** (1976) was his **Vertigo** (1958) (a grieving widower comforted and confounded by the seeming double of his dead wife). These same two Hitchcock models are doubled up in his recent **Body Double**, suggesting that inspiration is now running at low ebb, but De Palma's best work in the Seventies was done off his own bat: the vigorous, pounding rock opera **Phantom of the Paradise** and his big commercial breakthrough film, **Carrie**.

Sissy Spacek was outstanding as the shy, tortured teenage daughter of a religious zealot (Piper Laurie), whose burgeoning adolescent sexuality gives her a hellish time at high school, unleashing a frightening telekinetic power through which she wreaks a fearsome revenge on her tormentors. De Palma revived and developed the old split-screen technique of the Sixties to show us cause and effect simultaneously and, in the process, provide us with one of the most powerful and original horror movies of the decade. **Carrie** was taken from the first novel of the prolific Stephen King and, just as De Palma has never since found such stimulating source material, neither has King found a more ideally suited screen interpreter for his bold writing: the two should reunite.

The striking thing about this group (Coppola, Lucas and Spielberg in particular) is the way in which they split and regroup, move from genre to genre and in some instances from studio to studio, but always maintain a selfless love of movies for their own sake. Just as Coppola's protégé George Lucas has already gone on to outgross him with the **Star Wars** cycle, it is conceivable that a Spielberg alumnus like Robert Zemeckis may yet teach his master a thing or two, now that the commercially quiet start of the Beatles-inspired **I Wanna Hold Your Hand** (1978) and the over-the-top comedy **Used Cars** (1980) (projects underwritten by Spielberg) has given way to such blockbusters as **Romancing the Stone** (1984) and **Back to the Future** (1985).

The kids with beards constantly plow back profits and fame, investing in their own futures and that of the industry. The past, as they have learned from the old studio bosses, has taken care of itself.

Index

Picture Credits

Cinema Bookshop 159, 161, 166, 169 bottom, 170-1, 186, 196-7, 198 top, 203, 219:

Joel Finler 121, 125, 129 bottom, 130, 131, 134-5, 137, 138-9, 152, 158-9, 167, 169 top, 171, 174-5, 184, 189, 191, 193 center, 202, 203 right, 204 bottom, 205, 208-9, 218-19, 220 top, 224, 229:

Flashback 122-3, 126-7, 128, 143:

Ronald Grant 124, 126, 127, 129 top, 132-3, 135, 140, 140-1, 142, 144, 145, 146-7, 148-9, 149, 150-1, 151, 153, 155, 156, 172-3, 175, 176, 177, 182, 187, 190, 192, 193, 194, 198 bottom, 199, 200, 201, 204 top, 206, 207, 208, 210, 211, 212, 214, 214-15, 215, 220 bottom, 221, 222, 223, 225, 226, 228, 230, 237, 251, 255, 278 bottom, 293, 302-3 inset, 314, 318, 322, 328-9, 330 top, 332, 333, 339, 341, 355, 377 top, 385 top, 391, 392-3, 395 top, 395 bottom right, 396 bottom, 396-7 inset, 407, 413 bottom, 421, 422-3, 438, 444, 446, 470-1, 481 bottom, 524-5 center, 542:

Kobal Collection 7, 8-9, 10-11, 11, 12 bottom, 12-13, 14, 15, 16, 17, 18-19, 20-1, 21, 22-3, 22 inset, 23, 24-5, 25 top, 26, 26-7, 28, 29, 30, 30-1, 31 inset, 32-3, 32 inset, 33, 34, 34-5, 35, 36-7, 38, 38-9, 39, 40, 40-1, 41, 42-3, 43, 44-5, 45, 46, 46-7, 47, 48, 49, 50, 51, 52-3, 68-9, 70, 70-1, 71, 72, 72-3, 73, 74, 74-5, 75, 76, 77, 78-9, 79, 80, 80-1, 81, 82, 82-3, 83, 84-5, 86, 86-7, 87, 88, 89, 90, 90-1, 91, 92, 92-3, 93, 94-5, 95, 98, 100, 101, 102, 103, 104, 105, 106-7, 107, 108, 108-9, 110-11, 112, 112-13, 113, 114, 115, 116, 116-17, 118, 119, 231, 236-7, 238 bottom, 239-43, 247 bottom, 248-9, 250 top, 253, 254, 256-7, 258, 262 bottom, 263-7, 269-71 bottom, 272 inset, 275-7, 280 bottom, 282, 284-5, 292, 293 right, 294-7, 300-1, 304-5, 306-10, 312 top, 316 top, 320-1, 323 top, 325, 327, 334-8, 340, 342-3, 344-5, 346-7, 348-9, 350-1, 352 top left, 353 top right, 354-5, 356, 357, 358, 358-9 top, 360-1, 362-3, 365, 368, 369 bottom, 370, 371 bottom, 372-3, 375, 376-7, 378-9, 382, 384-5, 388-9, 390, 394, 396-7, 402-3, 405, 406, 408, 410-11, 412, 413 top, 414 bottom, 415, 416 bottom, 417, 418-19, 420 top left inset, 424, 425 bottom, 426-7, 429 right, 430-1, 434-5, 436-7, 440-1, 442-3, 445, 447, 448, 449, 450-5, 457-9, 460 top, 461 top, 462-6, 467 top, 469, 472-3 top center, 473 bottom, 474 top, 476, 477, 478 top, 479, 480, 482-5, 488-9, 491-4, 497, 498 left, 499 top right, 500-1, 503, 504, 505 top, 507 inset, 508 top, 510-11, 514-15, 524 top, 526, 530-1, 532, 532-3, 534-41, 542-3, 546 top left, 548-9, 555 top, 556-7 top, 557 bottom:

Alan McKenzie 272, 273, 274:

National Film Archive 54, 55, 56-7, 57, 58, 59, 59 inset, 60, 60-1, 61 inset, 62, 63, 64, 65, 66, 66-7, 121, 136, 154, 157, 160, 162-3, 163, 164-5, 172, 178, 178-9, 180-1, 181, 182-3, 185, 188, 195, 203 left, 216, 238 top, 244-5, 246 bottom, 250 bottom, 252, 259, 260-1, 262 top, 268, 278 top, 279, 280-1 center, 281 bottom, 283, 287-91, 298-9, 302-3, 311, 312, 313, 315, 316-17, 323 bottom, 324, 326, 432-3, 456-7, 460 bottom, 461 bottom, 467 bottom, 468, 472 bottom, 475, 478-9 bottom center, 481 top, 486-7, 490, 495, 496, 498-9 center, 502, 504-5 bottom center, 508-9, 512-13, 516-17, 525 bottom right, 527, 528-9, 533 top left, 545, 546-7, 552-3, 554, 556 bottom:

David Shipman 96-7, 99, 232-5, 246-7 center, 286, 306 top, 318-19, 330 center, 330 bottom, 331, 352-3, 359 bottom, 362, 363 bottom, 364, 366-7, 368-9, 370-1, 374, 380-1, 383, 386-7, 388 bottom left, 395 bottom left, 398-9, 400-1, 404, 409, 413 left inset, 414 top, 416 top, 420 top right inset, 420, 425 top, 428-9, 439, 442 bottom, 506-7, 544.

Multimedia Books Ltd. have endeavoured to observe the legal requirements with regard to the rights of suppliers of photographic material.